MW01132977

The Peaceful Resolution of Territorial and Maritime Disputes

The Peaceful Resolution of Territorial and Maritime Disputes

EMILIA JUSTYNA POWELL
AND
KRISTA E. WIEGAND

OXFORD
UNIVERSITY PRESS

Oxford University Press is a department of the University of Oxford. It furthers
the University's objective of excellence in research, scholarship, and education
by publishing worldwide. Oxford is a registered trade mark of Oxford University
Press in the UK and certain other countries.

Published in the United States of America by Oxford University Press
198 Madison Avenue, New York, NY 10016, United States of America.

Library of Congress Cataloging-in-Publication Data
Names: Powell, Emilia Justyna, author. | Wiegand, Krista Eileen, 1971– co-author.
Title: The peaceful resolution of territorial and maritime disputes /
Emilia Justyna Powell and Krista E. Wiegand.
Description: First Edition. | New York : Oxford University Press, [2023] |
Includes bibliographil references and index.
Identifiers: LCCN 2022062277 (print) | LCCN 2022062278 (ebook) |
ISBN 9780197675649 (Hardback) | ISBN 9780197675663 (epub) |
ISBN 9780197675656 | ISBN 9780197675670
Subjects: LCSH: Diplomatic negotiations in international disputes—Case studies |
Mediation, International—Case studies. | Inquiry (Theory of knowledge) |
Arbitration (International law)
Classification: LCC JZ6045.P685 2023 (print) | LCC JZ6045 (ebook) |
DDC 327.1/70723—dc23/eng/20230113
LC record available at https://lccn.loc.gov/2022062277
LC ebook record available at https://lccn.loc.gov/2022062278

DOI: 10.1093/oso/9780197675649.001.0001

Printed by Integrated Books International, United States of America

For Scarlett Sophia and Saskia Emilia
For Joseph

Contents

Figures

Tables

Acknowledgments

We have been researching the peaceful resolution of territorial and maritime disputes for many years. We met in 2004, when Emilia interviewed for a position at Georgia Southern University, where Krista had been hired the year before. At Emilia's job talk, Krista took notes, writing down ideas for "potential research with Emilia" if she accepted the position. Given Emilia's research on legal dispute resolution and Krista's research on territorial and maritime disputes, it seemed a natural fit for us to work together. For three years, we worked together across the hall at Georgia Southern, having many conversations and jointly producing several works. Over the years, we have coauthored five journal articles and a book chapter about the peaceful resolution of territorial and maritime disputes. Together, these scholarly pieces serve as a foundation for this book. We are most grateful to many colleagues who supported our joint and individual research over the years, particularly John Vasquez, Paul Huth, Sara McLaughlin Mitchell, Paul Hensel, Gary Goertz, Paul Diehl, Andrew Owsiak, Beth Simmons, Mark Crescenzi, Rich Pacelle, Laurie Nathan, Matt Murray, Renato Cruz de Castro, Jay Batongbacal, and James Kraska. Our book would not be possible without the many experts, international lawyers, scholars, and policymakers who agreed to participate in the many interviews we have conducted over the span of eight years.

We thank Stephen McDowell, who revised our original data collection for the Peaceful Resolution of Territorial Disputes (PRTD) dataset while he was a graduate student at Notre Dame University, and Sojeong Lee, a postdoctoral fellow at University of Tennessee, who helped with the empirical analysis. We also thank our excellent research assistants, Erik Beuck, Quinlin Gray, Aom Boonphatthanasoonthorn, and Rachell Corona at University of Tennessee and Benedikt Graf and Mariko Jurcsak at the University of Notre Dame. Les Harris provided us with invaluable editorial assistance. Several institutions and organizations have supported this project, including the Fulbright Scholar Program, which funded Krista's four months of field research in the Philippines; De La Salle University in the Philippines; the Howard H. Baker Jr. Center for Public Policy, Department of Political Science, and Office of

Research Engagement, all at the University of Tennessee; Kroc Institute for International Peace Studies, Kellogg Institute for International Studies, Nanovic Institute for European Studies, and the Constitutional Studies Program, all at the University of Notre Dame; and the Oxford Centre for Islamic Studies.

Finally, this project would not be possible without the continuous support from our families. We wrote much of this book during the COVID-19 pandemic, while simultaneously homeschooling our children. We are grateful to both of our husbands, Charles W. Powell and Michael Jordan, who helped provide care for our children, as well as immense help with their schooling, while we spent time writing. Krista is particularly grateful to her husband, Michael, who gave up work commitments to take care of their son Joseph while she conducted interviews and field research in Manila for four months in 2017, and her mother, Margaret Neate, who has helped with childcare over the years of research and writing. She also thanks her nine-year-old son, Joseph, for his patience and inspiration. Emilia thanks Charles and their two daughters, Scarlett Sophia and Saskia Emilia, for believing in the value of this research. She is also grateful to her mother, Elżbieta Milan-Szymańska, and father, Jerzy Szymański, whose never-ending passion for her research and life in general inspires her in all endeavors. Dziękuję za wszystko!

1

Introduction

What sort of man is qualified to settle a major boundary contro-
versy? The clever man.

—Whittemore Boggs (1940, 197)

This book is about the peaceful resolution (PR) of territorial and maritime
disputes and states' strategic behavior vis-à-vis methods of peaceful resolution: bilateral negotiations, good offices, inquiry, conciliation, mediation,
arbitration, and adjudication.[1] Though states in these disputes commonly
use armed conflict, fortunately for the stability of the international system,
many states have attempted to resolve them peacefully. Territory is generally considered to be the most salient disputed issue.[2] Frequently stemming
from cultural, ethnic, or purely material interests, territorial disputes occur
when two or more states disagree about legal ownership of a piece of land.[3]
These disputes entail the contesting of sovereignty rights and refusals to cede
claimed territory. More often than not, territorial disputes involve legally
complex baskets of claims over borders, tracts of land, and islands, which

---

[1] In this book we use the terms "PR method," "PR venue," and "PR forum" as follows. A PR
method is a broad category of peaceful settlement offered by international law. PR methods include
negotiations, nonbinding third-party methods—mediation, conciliation, good offices, inquiry—
and binding third-party methods, arbitration and adjudication. We use the terms "PR venue" and
"PR forum" interchangeably. Both of these terms refer to a specific institution or a body—ad hoc or
permanent—that hosts resolution attempts. Examples of PR venues include the International Court
of Justice (ICJ), Permanent Court of Arbitration (PCA), International Tribunal for the Law of the Sea
(ITLOS), specific conciliation commissions, etc.

[2] In a way, a "uniqueness assumption" is associated with these disputes and with the territory itself, as every strip of land arguably possesses inimitable value (Brilmayer and Faure 2014, 213). See,
among others, Gibler 2007; Goertz and Diehl 1992; Hensel 2001; Hensel et al. 2008; Huth 1996; Huth
and Allee 2002; Owsiak 2013; Owsiak and Vasquez 2019; Senese and Vasquez 2008; Tir 2003; Tir and
Vasquez 2012; Vasquez 1993, 2009; Wiegand 2011.

[3] There are several definitions of territorial disputes. For the purpose of this book, we adopt Huth's
(1996, 19) definition: "A territorial dispute involves either a disagreement between states over where
their common homeland or colonial borders should be fixed, or, more fundamentally, the dispute
entails one country contesting the right of another country even to exercise sovereignty over some or
all of its homeland or colonial territory."

The Peaceful Resolution of Territorial and Maritime Disputes. Emilia Justyna Powell and Krista E. Wiegand,
Oxford University Press. © Oxford University Press 2023. DOI: 10.1093/oso/9780197675649.003.0001

often pertain to the delimitation of rivers and maritime boundaries. Ongoing territorial contentions lead to severe consequences, threatening stability and peace not only for states directly involved in the disputes but also for the geographic region and beyond.[4] The recent few years—despite the devastating COVID-19 pandemic—have been no exception. In June 2020, Chinese and Indian forces clashed at the disputed border in the Ladakh-Aksai Chin region, killing at least twenty Indian soldiers.[5] The same year, Armenia and Azerbaijan fought a deadly war over the Ngorno Karabakh region, resulting in mass casualties and the displacement of many Armenians from the disputed territory.[6] In February 2022, Russia invaded Ukraine, starting the most violent territorial dispute in Europe since World War II.[7] Maritime disputes—much like their territorial counterparts—implicate conflicting sovereignty claims.[8] Frequently derivative of territorial disputes, but in some cases a matter of contention in their own right, maritime disputes can also cause severe tensions between states. For example, the South China Sea contention has involved dozens of clashes in the past decade between maritime vessels belonging to China, Malaysia, Vietnam, the Philippines, Taiwan, and Indonesia.[9]

The high stakes associated with settlement of territorial and maritime disputes, the diversity of PR methods employed, and unpredictability of outcomes push states to strategize. Strategic considerations undergird states' choices of the particular PR methods, and states' behavior during

---

[4] These disputes frequently prevent adversarial states from effectively dealing with bilateral or regional issues such as trade, environmental concerns, immigration, border checkpoints, joint security, and economic development, since cooperation is challenged, and in some cases halted altogether. What is more, usually these contentions prevent the parties involved from securely accessing natural resources such as oil, water, minerals, and fishing rights. Because of their inflammatory nature, the costs of monitoring and dealing with repercussions of these contentions is high for the entire international community (refugees, economic crises, arms proliferation, etc.)

[5] James Griffiths, Swati Gupta, Ben Westcott, and Rob Picheta, "Twenty Indian Soldiers Dead after Clash with China along Disputed Border," *CNN*, June 17, 2020.

[6] After three cease-fires failed to end the six-week-long war, the parties agreed to sign a Russia-led peace deal in November 2020. As a result of the agreement, Azerbaijan retained a significant part of the seized territory and acquired additional areas controlled by Armenia. The capital city of Nagorno-Karabakh—Stepanakert—was left under Armenian control. The peace agreement did not end hatred between Armenians and Azeris: in one region that changed hands from Armenia to Azerbaijan—Kelbajar—Armenians set their homes on fire rather than let Azerbaijanis live in them (Andrew E. Kramer, "Armenia and Azerbaijan: What Sparked War and Will Peace Prevail?," *New York Times*, December 1, 2020).

[7] "Live Updates: Russia Attacks Ukraine from Land, Air, and Sea," *New York Times*, February 24, 2022.

[8] As Gamble (1976, 331) wrote, "The sea boundary question . . . lies at the very heart of sovereignty."

[9] These disputes are considered "notable potential future flashpoints" (Schofield 2016, 346) for armed conflict, involving not only the disputants, but also the United States.

the resolution once a particular method, such as negotiations or adjudication, has been initiated. As a mediation expert noted, strategy throughout the resolution process can be likened to chess: "So what they are doing, they are playing chess. They are doing strategic calculation, cost and benefit, expected utility. . . . The costs and benefits are political, economic, and also ideological."[10] Indeed, these strategic calculations are manifested in broad choices—choice of venue strategic selection—regarding selection of a specific PR method.[11] The patterns of resolution during the Bahrain-Qatar contention provide an illustrative example of selecting a PR method.[12] Over the span of many years, the conflict kept developing and resurfacing. Whenever Qatar would bring up its claim over the contested Hawar Islands, Bahrain responded by reaffirming its claim to Zubarah, another disputed territory.[13] During the duration of the dispute, 30 years, each disputant proposed a variety of PR methods. Qatar suggested resolution via nonbinding third-party methods five times, and proposed delegating the dispute to adjudication 11 times. Bahrain attempted bilateral negotiations once, and repeatedly suggested resolution with the involvement of intermediaries (seven attempts at nonbinding third-party venues and eight at binding venues). The dispute was eventually settled at the ICJ, and each state was awarded part of the disputed territory.[14] What factors shaped these states' choices regarding PR methods, and what strategies did these states pursue? Why was the decision-making process in these disputes so convoluted?

Another set of strategic calculations deals with behavior within the context of each chosen PR method—within venue strategic selection—including

[10] Author's interview (EJP) with Laurie Nathan, international mediator, former senior advisor to the UN Mediation Support Unit, January 21, 2022.

[11] When a state's policymakers and legal counsel are homing in on a particular PR method, they often have in mind a particular venue such as the ICJ or a particular conciliation commission. Therefore, to parsimoniously conceptualize a relatively complex process of initial selection, we use the term "choice-of-venue strategic selection" to describe the initial broad choices between the various PR methods and venues. In practice, it is hard, if not impossible, to separate the choice of method from the choice of a specific venue, as benefits/shortcomings of a particular venue factor in to the broad decision of PR methods.

[12] The two states disagreed over five territories: the Hawar Islands, the island of Janan/Hadd Janan, the shoals of Qit'at Jaradah and of Fasht ad Dibal, and Zubarah, a townsite on the northwest coast of Qatar. Maritime Delimitation and Territorial Questions between Qatar and Bahrain, ICJ Rep. 2001, 40, Judgment of March 16, 2001.

[13] For more information, see Schulte (2004, 234–35) and Powell 2020.

[14] Similarly, Eritrea and Yemen attempted a variety of methods in the Red Sea islands dispute. From 1995 until 1998, these two states were involved in an arbitration over the control of three island groups in the Red Sea: Zuqar Island, Great Anish, and Little Anish. While the dispute was ultimately resolved by arbitration, the two states also engaged in negotiation and multiple rounds of mediation during the lifespan of the contention. For further discussion, see Johnson 2000; and Spain 2010.

the selection of legal counsel, arbitrators, or the choice to frame the claim, for example, by relying on a particular map that visualizes the contention to a tribunal. The maritime boundary arbitration between Barbados and the Republic of Trinidad and Tobago provides an excellent illustration of how states strategize within the context of a chosen PR method.[15] This particular example pertains to strategy in visual presentation of claims. Trinidad and Tobago's legal counsel, Professor James Crawford opened his arguments on behalf of his client with the "predatory sea bird" map (Figure 1.1).[16]

Professor Crawford noted, "Actually, it looks to me like a predatory sea bird about to eat the island of Tobago, which makes Barbados' recent overtures to Tobago part of the picture, you might say. After all, they might as well finish the job: having eaten the surrounding environment, there is nothing left but the egg."[17] Obviously, the imagery was cleverly and strategically used by Trinidad and Tobago's counsel to plant the image of a predatory bird in the minds of the arbitrators at the earliest opportunity. Indeed, "once one has the bird lodged in your brain, it is hard to unsee it."[18] In the oral hearings the map was actually first shown to the tribunal by Barbados, which was probably concerned about its potential impact and therefore wanted to discredit it before Trinidad and Tobago had a chance to address the tribunal. Strategically, Barbados's counsel presented a much less dramatic map, "which was clearly shaded to make Barbados' claim look as unaggressive as possible."[19] Barbados ended up not getting any of the 'beak' to the south of the equidistance line. Whether the predatory sea-bird imagery influenced the outcome is impossible to prove. It is however obvious that both disputants, guided by their legal counsel, strategized in preparation for the arbitration proceedings. Why was specific visualization of the legal claims so important in this case? Does such strategizing decrease states' uncertainty about the settlement process?

[15] Barbados v Trinidad and Tobago, PCA (2006) 45 ILM 839, ICGJ 371 (PCA 2006), Arbitral Award of April 11, 2006.
[16] The map was submitted by Trinidad and Tobago in its written countermemorial, but no reference was made to the predatory bird imagery in that document (available at https://pcacases.com/web/sendAttach/1072). Note that the identifier "Figure 6.1" that appears in the key refers to the figure's position in the original source. For clarity of presentation, we obtained the original version of the drawing presented in Figure 1.1 from Martin Pratt (Bordermap Consulting).
[17] Day three of the proceedings, Arbitral tribunal constituted under Annex VII, UNCLOS in the matter of an arbitration between Barbados and the Republic of Trinidad and Tobago, transcription by Harry Counsell & Co Cliffords Inn, Fetter Lane, London EC4A 1LD, available at https://pcacases.com/web/sendAttach/1103.
[18] Author's interview (EJP) with Martin Pratt, Bordermap Consulting, January 27, 2022. Mr. Pratt prepared the brightly shaded map for Trinidad and Tobago's counsel.
[19] Ibid. Map 3 from Barbados's Memorial is available at https://pcacases.com/web/sendAttach/1121.

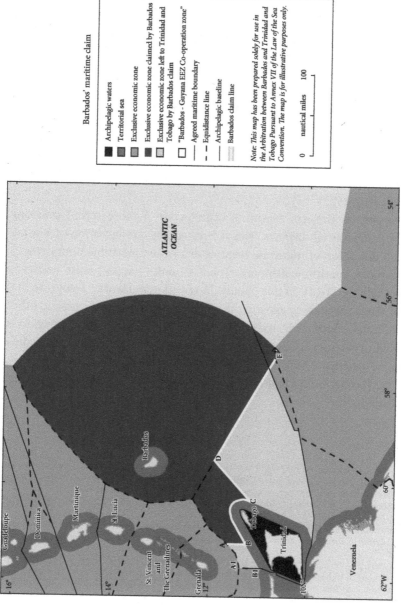

Figure 1.1. The Predatory Sea Bird Map, Barbados v. Trinidad and Tobago, 2006. (Barbados's maritime claims, Dispute between Barbados and the Republic of Trinidad and Tobago Referred to Arbitration in Accordance with Annex VII, UNCLOS by Notification of Barbados, dated February 16, 2004, Annex Maps, Volume 1(2), page 3, available at https://pcacases.com/web/sendAttach/1123.)

Barbados' maritime claim

- Archipelagic waters
- Territorial sea
- Exclusive economic zone
- Exclusive economic zone claimed by Barbados
- Exclusive economic zone left to Trinidad and Tobago by Barbados claim
- "Barbados - Guyana EEZ Co-operation zone"
- Agreed maritime boundary
- Equidistance line
- Archipelagic baseline
- Barbados claim line

Note: This map has been prepared solely for use in the Arbitration between Barbados and Trinidad and Tobago Pursuant to Annex VII of the Law of the Sea Convention. The map is for illustrative purposes only.

0   nautical miles   100

Understanding states' strategies in peaceful resolution of territorial and maritime disputes is absolutely crucial. Territorial disputes tend to last longer than other disputes, and—if not settled peacefully with the full endorsement of all parties—these contentions can fester for centuries. Importantly, territorial disputes pertain to a constitutive element of statehood, one the contestation of which threatens parts or all of the existing state as a unit. Since a state cannot exist without territory, control of territory is "arguably the most rudimentary feature of a state, and state identity is deeply associated with historically occupied land" (Powell and Wiegand 2021, 192). After all, history supplies exceedingly few cases where statehood continued in the absence of territory.[20] Historically, in many ways, the development of international law has been fundamentally linked to the reality that states exercise sovereignty—exclusive authority—over and within a piece of territory.[21]

As a general pattern, maritime disputes are a more recent phenomenon than territorial disputes. This is because the configuration of a coastline and definition of maritime features determine maritime boundaries.[22] Furthermore, maritime disputes evolve as states expand their maritime claims (Lathrop 2014). In this context, it is also important to recognize that coastal states continue to expand the reach of their territorial seas and other jurisdictional zones, reflected in international maritime law conventions (Powell and Wiegand 2021).[23] As a result, new conflicting maritime claims are bound to arise. The United Nations Convention on the Law of the Sea (UNCLOS) constitutes a relatively new framework for the regulation of maritime disputes.[24]

---

[20] To cite one such case, when Poland lost its territory to Nazi Germany, Poland's statehood continued according to international law. According to Shaw (2017, 158), "What matters is the presence of a stable community within a certain area, even though its frontiers may be uncertain."

[21] As Shaw (2017, 361) writes, "Most nations indeed developed through a close relationship with the land they inhabited."

[22] Author's interview (KEW) with Ashley Roach, former judge advocate general, US Navy, and former adviser in the Office of the Legal Adviser, US Department of State, Rhodes, Greece, July 11, 2018.

[23] For example, in January 2021, Greece announced an extension of its territorial sea from six to twelve nautical miles on its western coastline, to be consistent with UNCLOS. This extension occurred just days before Greek-Turkish negotiations started regarding disputed waters off the eastern coast of Greece, signaling Greek compliance with UNCLOS, which Turkey has not signed. "Greek MPs Approve Extension of Territorial Waters in Ionian Sea," Al Jazeera, January 20, 2021, https://www.aljazeera.com/news/2021/1/20/greek-mps-approve-extension-of-territorial-waters-in-ionian-sea.

[24] The United Nations Convention on the Law of the Sea, 1833 UNTS 397, December 10, 1982.

A fundamental principle that governs law of the sea is that "the land dominates the sea" (Shaw 2017, 410). This principle implies that the territorial status quo provides the basis for the demarcation of a coastal state's maritime rights and obligations.[25] Moreover, proper and complete territorial delimitation is the sine qua non for the determination of the maritime rights and entitlements for a coastal state.[26] UNCLOS spells out rules determining the location of baselines, lines that determine maritime boundaries on land formations. Disputes over islands, for instance, involve issues of territorial sovereignty and generated maritime entitlements—territorial seas, contiguous zones, exclusive economic zones (EEZ), and continental shelves. This reality demonstrates deep connections between land and maritime sovereignty. In a way, territorial disputes are more fundamental, and will receive the primary treatment in the book.

A strong international dispute settlement regime solidified in the twentieth century. Article 2(3) of the Charter of the United Nations establishes that states are to "settle their international disputes by peaceful means in such a manner that international peace and security, and justice, are not endangered."[27] As a result, states have many options to propose the peaceful settlement of their territorial and maritime disputes, ranging from bilateral negotiations to adjudication. Since political, economic, and strategic considerations, as well as particulars of legal claims associated with each territorial and maritime dispute, are unique, no single PR method is always most appropriate on each occasion. It is states, guided by their legal counsel, who assess each PR method's suitability. Of course, this suitability may change with time, as a dispute progresses, resulting in the disputants proposing a wide variety of PR methods over the lifespan of a dispute.

---

[25] It is important to add that in contrast to international law regulating territorial sovereignty—which has developed mainly through international custom and the jurisprudence of international courts—contemporary law of the sea is predominantly based on treaty law, such as UNCLOS. Yet, the jurisprudence of the ICJ continues to contribute to the conceptualization and interpretation of law of the sea. By way of illustration, the ICJ's judgment in the Territorial and Maritime Dispute, Nicaragua v. Colombia (ICJ Rep. 2012, 624, Judgment of November 19, 2012), presented innovative techniques for maritime boundary delimitation.

[26] ITLOS Judge Rüdiger Wolfrum (2018c) recalls a statement made by state counsel: "only the final determination of maritime boundaries and the possibility to exploit the marine living or non-living resources result in completing the sovereignty of that state." International Tribunal for the Law of the Sea, https://www.itlos.org/.

[27] UN Charter, Article 2(3).

A Theory of Strategic Selection

As practice shows, states' actions are largely shaped by political considerations—both domestic and international—as well as the nature, character, and value of the disputed territory and the relationship of the disputing states. While recognizing the importance of all these streams of influence, our theory homes in on how proposer states—those states making the proposal to resolve the dispute—make strategic choices about selecting a PR method and venue, and both disputants strategize throughout the duration of the settlement process.[28] These strategic choices are necessitated by states' desire to minimize uncertainty and maximize their likelihood of winning a contention. We ask: Why do some states propose means to resolve their disputes using bilateral negotiations, while others are willing to take their case to the ICJ or an arbitration tribunal? Do states have a priori preferences about settlement mechanisms or—in contrast—are all of these methods deemed to be equally attractive as long as they yield a preferred outcome? More generally, what factors shape proposer states' choices regarding PR methods, and what strategies do disputants pursue during an ongoing resolution process? How do disputants frame the particulars of territorial and maritime claims? How do they select their legal counsel and legal procedures? The entire dispute resolution process—the choice of PR method and states' behavior during the resolution—is strategic.

The process of selecting an optimal venue—a venue that is most likely to yield the preferred outcome—entails uncertainty. Each disputant's goal is to reduce this uncertainty, avoid losing, and, most preferably, win, irrespective of the merits of their legal claims. As in any bargaining context, states involved in territorial and maritime disputes cannot fully predict the outcome of the resolution (Bilder 1981). Levels of uncertainty are highest when a contention is delegated to an intermediary, in particular to an international court or an arbitration panel. Indeed, as states move away from bilateral negotiations, and consider the more formal PR methods, international law—rather than political interests or power—becomes the basis for settlement. Yet, states can reduce this uncertainty in a number of ways, thereby increasing the amount of control they have over the resolution process. States that propose settlement initially can reduce uncertainty through the careful

---

[28] We examine the strategies of proposer and nonproposer states instead of challenger and target states since both groups of states can be proposers and nonproposers.

selection of a PR method and venue, and both disputants can reduce uncertainty by making strategic decisions throughout the settlement process.

The reduction of uncertainty entails strategic use of specific PR methods and adapting certain tactics in the context of a chosen venue. Intense gathering of information about PR methods and specific venues lies at the core of this strategizing before and during the resolution process. Armed with such information, disputants hope to achieve some degree of control over the resolution outcome, effectively reducing uncertainty and uneasiness associated with a certain resolution process. Uncertainty about the outcome drives states to pursue what we call *strategic selection*. The process of strategic selection occurs at two interrelated stages: the initial pursuit of a particular PR method, and decision-making once a PR method has been identified. We divide these separate though deeply interrelated stages into *choice-of-venue strategic selection* and *within-venue strategic selection*.[29] The goal of the choice-of-venue strategic selection stage is for proposer states to pursue a PR method that will provide the best outcome for the proposing state, which usually involves securing all or the majority of territorial/maritime concessions. The within-venue strategic selection stage refers to choices made by both disputants about how to frame their claims and design rules and procedures of the settlement process, if possible. The driving force behind strategizing in these two settlement stages is the hope of reducing uncertainty and of increasing the chances of winning. Importantly, as the disputants progress through the settlement process, states reconsider and refine their strategies.

For each stage of strategic selection, we identify several mechanisms that influence states' strategies. In the context of choice-of-venue strategic selection, we examine the influence of past experience of proposer states with PR methods: positive past experiences (winning) and negative past experiences (losing). The outcome of previous interactions with different PR methods conveys important information to states about expectations for future settlement attempts. By examining their own and other states'—in particular states within the same geographic region—past experiences in territorial and maritime disputes, proposer states can obtain clues that inform their future strategies of dispute resolution.

We also believe that there is a close connection between the legal nature of international disputes—as well as their resolution—and domestic law.

---

[29] For a detailed description of both stages of strategic selection, as well as our causal mechanisms, see Chapters 3 and 4.

Thus, the interaction between the two legal systems, domestic and international, is crucial to understanding how proposer states strategize in territorial and maritime dispute resolution. After all, to some extent, all disputants evaluate international law through the lens of their domestic legal system. There are three aspects of the domestic law/international law relationship that we believe act as mechanisms influencing states' behavior in the process of peaceful settlement: (1) international law's position in the domestic legal system, (2) the extent of a state's commitment to rule of law, and (3) type of domestic legal tradition. These three characteristics fundamentally shape the dynamic of choice-of-venue strategic selection.

In the context of within-venue strategic selection, we theorize about specific mechanisms that states employ to reduce uncertainty with an ongoing settlement process. Once a particular PR method is determined, both disputing states remain uncertain about the outcome, and they therefore pursue strategies to increase their likelihood of winning. If states select arbitration or adjudication, international law being subject to interpretation, a multiplicity of factors complicate the disputants' ability to foresee how an intermediary—a tribunal or court—will decide. In light of this reality, both disputants attempt to frame their claims in the most beneficial, one-sided manner, selecting claims, arguments, and maps that are advantageous, and avoiding those that are weaker. Legal advisors and state counsel assess strengths and limitations of both sides' claims and hypothesize what configuration of claims is most likely to yield a favorable outcome for their clients. The disputants can also try to fully take advantage of a venue's design by shaping the venue's rules and procedures, as well as by selecting actors involved in the proceedings. After all, every contention is inherently dynamic and multilayered. By seeking to shape and configure settlement proceedings and by framing their claims, states expect to further reduce uncertainty associated with the resolution process.

Broader Significance of the Project

The successful settlement of territorial and maritime disputes has a multitude of benefits that go far beyond the termination of the hostile relationship in the dyad (Vasquez and Henehan 2011; Huth 1996; Kocs 1995; Vasquez and Henehan 2001). On the global level, long periods of universalist peace tend to be associated with the existence of fewer territorial disputes (Wallensteen

1984). Other benefits include democratic regimes being more likely to emerge in the aftermath of the positive resolution of territorial contentions (Gibler 2007), and increased levels of bilateral trade between the former adversaries (Simmons 2005). Understanding how states strategize to settle these disputes therefore helps to further the promotion of positive peace with multiple benefits of peaceful resolution.

There are very few studies that provide a comprehensive overview and empirical test of theories about the entire peaceful resolution process in the context of territorial and maritime contentions.[30] Most such studies speak directly to specific factors or conditions that have a bearing on states' choice of resolution methods. These factors include the role of regime type and democratization (Ellis, Mitchell, and Prins 2010; Gibler 2012; Mitchell and Hensel 2007; Mitchell, Kadera, and Crescenzi 2009), alliances (Frazier 2006), salience or value of disputed territory or maritime areas (Hensel 2001; Hensel and Mitchell 2005; Huth 1996), a history of past conflict (Hensel et al. 2008), and membership in international organizations (Hansen, Mitchell, and Nemeth 2008; Nemeth et al. 2014; Shannon 2009).[31] Building on insights gleaned from this literature, we provide a comprehensive examination of peaceful dispute resolution that is steeped in the quantitative and qualitative methods of scientific inquiry.

The scholarship also provides much insight into the importance of relative strength of disputants' legal claims (Brilmayer and Faure 2014; Huth, Croco, and Appel 2011), considers the issue of forum shopping (Black, Nolan, and Connolly 2009; Koskenniemi 2007; Koskenniemi and Leino 2002; Mondre 2015; Scott 2014; Shannon 2009; Shany 2003; Wiegand and Powell 2011a), and highlights the significance of institutional design (Cockerham 2007; Guzman 2005; Koremenos 2016; Koremenos et al. 2001). Much of the international law scholarship on these topics has been mainly descriptive, providing insights into the law and practice of international settlement methods.[32] A relatively considerable portion of the traditional scholarship has focused mainly on whether dispute settlement should be voluntary or compulsory (De Brabandere 2018, 459). In-depth case studies devoted to specific PR methods or specific territorial and maritime disputes are

[30] In this context, we wish to highlight a study by Mondre (2015), which argues that a combination of state interests and institutional design of legal dispute resolution venues helps explain the choice of venue.

[31] We review this literature in great detail in Chapter 5.

[32] Additionally, as De Brabandere (2018, 549) writes, "The area of international dispute settlement is relatively new in the international legal discipline as an academic enterprise."

common. Quite a bit has also been written about individual international adjudicators—in particular the ICJ, ITLOS, and PCIJ (Aljaghoub 2006; Brown 20077; Collier and Lowe 2000; Klein 2014; Merrills 2017; Schulte 2004; Spiermann 2005). This scholarship highlights the structure, procedure, practice, and compliance with decisions of these institutions. While the international law literature has generated insights that are deeply interesting and rich in detail, it has not historically engaged in much empirical, systematic analysis.[33] In fact, many contributions in this area have been written by legal practitioners and policymakers involved in specific cases, and thus address practical problems. As a result, more often than not, questions of why and how—the reasons standing behind states' preferences and strategies—are seen as lying outside of the scope of law-focused inquiry.

Peaceful resolution of territorial and maritime disputes entails multilayered, dynamic, and continuously evolving interaction between many streams of influence, some of a political and some of a legal nature. As a consequence, and with the normative perspective dominating international law academic conversations, a lacuna has emerged between the scholarly writings about peaceful dispute resolution and observable state behavior. The dynamics of contemporary territorial and maritime disputes prompt many questions concerning the interactions of law—domestic and international—politics, and strategy. The more we understand and acknowledge the commingling of these influences, the better we are able to comprehend the reality and dynamics of these disputes.

To our knowledge, this is the first study that conceptualizes the peaceful resolution process as consisting of two separate—though deeply interconnected—phases. This two-stage disaggregation has a profound effect on how we view the dynamics unfolding during territorial and maritime disputes from beginning to end. The process starts with a disputant attempting settlement via a specific method—negotiations, mediation, arbitration, adjudication, etc.—and a specific venue, for instance the ICJ, PCA, or ITLOS (the choice-of-venue strategic selection). The process continues with states designing strategies of behavior in relation to a particular venue (the within-venue strategic selection). Though several studies have examined

---

[33] Granted, some academically oriented research has been done since the late 1990s—largely owing to the increased importance, relevance, and use of many international settlement methods. Since then, questions of a theoretical, conceptual, and empirical character have gained more traction in the international law scholarship. For an excellent review of the scholarly developments in the field of international dispute settlement, see De Brabandere 2018 and Schultz 2015.

states' motivations in venue selection, no other international relations study has delved into the within-venue stage of dispute resolution—an absolutely key part of settlement dynamics.

Recognizing that it is the intermingling of politics and law that shapes states' strategic behavior and their continuously evolving preferences, our theory is embedded in the political science and the international law scholarship. Indeed, settling disputes is fundamentally practical as well as legal in nature, regardless of PR method. From a rational choice perspective, we portray states' behavior as strategic, based on simple cost-benefit analysis targeted at maximizing any concessions. This cost-benefit analysis necessitates intense gathering of detailed information about potential claims, intermediaries, pertinent international law, method and venue structure, procedure, all potential outcomes, and preferences of the opponent. Though obtaining complete information in the context of any PR method is not feasible, states hire a host of legal advisors and legal counsel to guide them in the quest to secure maximum concessions. As in any bargaining context, by increasing their access to relevant information—through examining past dispute resolution outcomes and the relationship between domestic and international law—states reduce their uncertainty and feel more confident in their pursuit of certain PR methods. From a normative perspective, the structure and procedures of each PR method, and more specifically, each venue—including the de jure set up and de facto practice—constrain the execution of states' rational choices. International law looms over the entire resolution process. In this context, the character of states' domestic legal systems—domestic levels of rule of law and the relationship between domestic and international law—factors into how states strategize. Thus, it is the interaction of states' rationally designed strategies with specific venue designs that shapes outcomes of the international settlement process.

The book embraces a multimethod approach to examining territorial and maritime contentions.[34] While recognizing shortcomings of each methodological approach, we believe that taken together, statistical analyses and in-depth qualitative interviews contribute to accumulating scholarly and practical knowledge of peaceful dispute resolution. There are important restrictions to insights that quantitative data are able to offer, since statistical analyses do not explain causation.[35] To understand the casual mechanism

---

[34] Though useful, most studies devoted to territorial and maritime disputes rely either on quantitative analyses of large datasets or individual case studies.

[35] See Chapter 5 for discussion of this issue.

of strategic selection in dispute resolution, and to confirm regularities and patterns detected in our quantitative data (Goertz 2017; Gerring 2017), we draw insights from numerous interlocutors directly involved in strategizing about settlement decisions: states' legal counsel, judges, arbitrators, public international law scholars, government officials, journalists, and other experts from multiple countries. Along with insights from other instances of peaceful resolution, we devote much attention to the 2013–2016 Philippines v. China arbitration case. These conversations allow us to carefully parse out specific mechanisms at play during the two stages of strategic selection. Though our main focus is on general patterns of dispute settlement, we cannot overlook mechanisms at play mainly in the context of the within-venue strategic selection, some of which are inherently hard to operationalize in a quantitative manner. Our book demonstrates that it is many human experiences—an amalgamation of a multiplicity of individual-level decisions—that combine to generate states' strategic choices of specific PR methods and decisions about claims and procedures.

Our comprehensive approach helps, both theoretically and methodologically, to shed light on the ongoing interaction between the mechanisms of both stages of strategic selection in the context of all PR methods ranging from bilateral negotiations to adjudication. This book contributes to the empirical study of international law by understanding how international law works in specific contexts, situations, and in relation to specific states.[36] To the extent possible, states tailor PR methods to their own specific needs. Many PR methods constitute quite flexible frameworks that enable states and their legal counsel to tweak, adjust, and cherry-pick between the numerous potential strategies. Thus, states pursue their own specific goals without altering PR methods' rudimentary structures.[37]

This book does not purport to provide a conclusive account of all the dynamics that characterize territorial and maritime dispute settlement. Even though we capture important details of states' strategic behavior, there are always other aspects associated with peaceful resolution that are beyond the scope of this study. For instance, this study is not an attempt to explain why states pursue peaceful resolution to begin with. Indeed, instead of peaceful settlement, states may prefer to maintain the status quo and, thus, take no action at all. Such strategy is typical in many contentions. In some

---

[36] For discussion of the empirical study of international law, see Shaffer and Ginsburg 2012.
[37] Powell (2020) provides a discussion of this phenomenon in the context of Islamic law states.

circumstances, states choose to threaten the opponent or to use force in an attempt to acquire disputed territory or maritime areas. Although understanding why states decide to peacefully settle rather than pursue military action is important, this topic has already received much scholarly attention (Hensel 2001; Hensel et al. 2008; Huth 1996; Huth and Allee 2002; Vasquez and Henehan 2001). Our intention is not to directly challenge this literature, but to build on it by acknowledging that states' choices of peaceful versus military solutions are interrelated, with some degree of selection effect. We seek to answer the question of *how*—via what means—proposer states pursue peaceful settlement. We assume that once a government selects the peaceful route, the choice of PR method and decisions about procedure are as important as the initial decision to pursue settlement, not only for the proposing states, but also the state that agrees to attempt resolution.[38]

Organization of the Book

In Chapter 2, we comprehensively review rules, institutional features, efficiency, and relevance of the various PR methods: bilateral negotiations, nonbinding third-party methods (inquiry, good offices, mediation, and conciliation), and binding third-party methods (arbitration and adjudication). This chapter is largely descriptive and provides a foundation for the rest of the book. We devote considerable attention to real-world, mostly contemporary territorial and maritime disputes. Mapping the specific features of each PR method provides a detailed picture of the normative environment in which states pursue their strategies. We acknowledge that law, international rules and norms, and the prospects of adjudication loom over all territorial and maritime contentions, including those that do not fall squarely under the jurisdiction of any international adjudicator. In explaining the fundamental dynamics associated with the functioning of each method, we draw on insights from international law and international relations scholarship.

In Chapter 3, we develop the theoretical argument. Our theory of strategic selection explains the underlying reasons for states' commitment to strategy during the entire process of peaceful settlement: uncertainty associated with the resolution process and the preference to win. The second part of this chapter focuses on the first stage of strategic selection: the choice of

---

[38] For discussion about the initial stage of decision-making, see Chapter 2.

venue. We delve into discussion of the mechanisms that reduce uncertainty for proposer states during the process of choosing PR methods: past experience in peaceful resolution and the relationship between domestic and international law. We present a set of testable hypotheses regarding each mechanism of choice-of-venue strategic selection. Chapter 4 is devoted to the second stage of strategic selection, within-venue. In this stage of peaceful resolution, patterns of states' behavior are quite distinct in that regardless of external factors, all disputing states strategize to optimize their experience within a particular PR method and a specific venue. Consequently, disputants involved in active resolution attempts maximize their efforts to shape the procedures and frame their claims in an optimal way in the pursuit of victory. Both of our theoretical chapters are deeply entrenched in qualitative examples of states' strategic behavior in contemporary and past territorial and maritime contentions. Insights from in-depth interviews with interlocutors personally involved in peaceful resolution shed light on the specifics of our theory's causal mechanism.

Chapter 5 is devoted to our research design. Our multimethod approach combines quantitative analysis of an original dataset of attempts at peaceful resolution in territorial disputes (1945–2015), primary documents, and a series of qualitative interviews, with a particular focus on the 2013–2016 Philippines v. China arbitration. Our quantitative data, the Peaceful Resolution of Territorial Disputes (PRTD) dataset (Wiegand, Powell, and McDowell 2020), provides us with observations of proposer state-level behavior, and allows us to gauge preferences of challenger and target states.[39] Importantly, the dataset allows us to analyze proposer states' preferences—as expressed by attempts or proposals of specific PR methods—in cross-sectional time series analyses. Chapter 5 also devotes considerable attention to patterns of territorial dispute resolution since 1945, and discusses trends and frequencies of resolution attempts via specific PR methods across the geographic regions of the world: Europe, the Americas, Africa, the Middle East, and Asia/Oceania.

[39] The terms "challenger" and "target" are commonly used in much of the literature on territorial disputes. In the PRTD data, it is usually the proposer state—the challenger—who is challenging the status quo. But the target state may respond to the proposal by agreeing or refusing to participate in a particular resolution method, and as a result, the target becomes the proposer. Moreover, as the dispute continues, the nonproposer state may put forth a proposal for an alternative dispute settlement method, thus becoming a proposer state. For a much more detailed discussion of our empirical design, see Chapter 5.

Chapter 6 focuses on the empirical analysis of the choice-of-venue strategic selection stage, which involves proposer states' choices of the various PR methods during territorial disputes. This chapter provides solid evidence, qualitative and quantitative, for our supposition that proposer states engage in strategic behavior when selecting PR methods. While attempting to settle their territorial or maritime contentions, proposer states make carefully preplanned, rational choices to seek optimal resolution outcomes. A variety of factors—mechanisms of strategic selection—influence the choice-of-venue stage of the resolution process. Controlling for a multitude of confounding factors, our analyses suggest that proposer states' past experience with resolution methods and international law's position in the domestic legal system matter as these states strategically choose between available PR methods.

Chapter 7 focuses on the application of the within-venue strategic selection stage, not only for the proposer state, but also for the target state that has agreed to a resolution process. Our discussion in this chapter further expounds and illustrates the causal mechanisms at the core of our theory in the context of strategic selection's second stage. We rely exclusively on qualitative data, primarily interviews, with a heavy focus on the Philippines v. China arbitration case. The main takeaway from all our conversations with a variety of experts and those involved in dispute resolution is that states are indeed strategic when planning the details of settlement as they filter a dispute through a particular PR method. Since no disputant is able to predict the settlement outcome with certainty—especially in arbitration and adjudication—the careful framing of claims and shaping of the resolution procedures are critical.

We conclude the book with an overview of the theory, the main arguments, and empirical results, stressing the applicability and timeliness of our inquiry. We also position this research in the wider context of international law and international relations literatures, considering the deep implications for policymakers and practitioners of international law. We argue that in order to fully understand the dynamics of peaceful settlement in territorial and maritime disputes, we must appreciate and account for the complicated and multistage character of the settlement process. To be sure, the convoluted and inherently legal nature of disputes over sovereignty, coupled with the intricate framework of most PR methods—especially arbitration and adjudication—results in a fertile environment for strategic behavior. This book demonstrates that the deep-rooted, complex diversity of the international peaceful settlement regime should give rise to many empirically grounded studies about how strategic, political, and legal considerations shape states' preferences.

To a large extent, each PR method, including bilateral negotiations—which take place in the shadow of the law—reflects the efficacy and value of international law as it operates within challenging realities of power politics. Focusing on international law's inherent flexibility allows us to appreciate the commingling of states' self-motivated, rationally preplanned strategies with the structures and procedures of the various PR methods. Thus, this book demonstrates that even institutionalized international law—in our case, PR methods—is in many cases remarkably malleable and allows states to tailor their specific frameworks to their specific needs and wants. Simply put, states can fulfill their divergent preferences by designing and carrying out unique strategies in the context of each PR method. We can fully appreciate and study this reality only by combining insights from international law—with its normative, descriptive bent—and from international relations—with its empirical as well as theoretical advantages. We also need to recognize the fundamental reality that international dispute settlement constitutes a human-led enterprise whereby strategies and actions are carried out by international law practitioners, legal counsel, and decision makers on the domestic side. Consequently, research devoted to dispute resolution should not be based merely on analyses of large-N data sets nor purely normative examinations. While these are indeed illuminating, a full appreciation of general patterns requires that we draw on insights from both fields, emphasizing the human involvement in the settlement process.

2

Peaceful Settlement of Disputes
in International Law

In this chapter, we lay the groundwork for our theory of strategic selection in the peaceful resolution of territorial and maritime disputes by describing the different peaceful resolution (PR) methods available in international law.[1] While we highlight the efficacy of each PR method, our discussion here is largely descriptive and provides a solid foundation for the rest of the book. Though we are engaging much of the political science—in particular, international relations—literature, a considerable part of the chapter refers to international law itself and international law scholarship. Because our goal is to meticulously describe the characteristics of PR methods, we must address these methods' rules, institutional features, and procedures.

This chapter begins with a discussion of the possible initial strategies that states involved in territorial and maritime disputes can undertake: no action, use of force, and peaceful settlement. We then provide a detailed account of institutional and procedural features of each PR method: bilateral negotiations; nonbinding third-party methods—inquiry, good offices, mediation, and conciliation; and binding third-party methods—arbitration and adjudication. In the context of each method, we offer examples from territorial and maritime disputes, mostly after 1945, highlighting the dynamics of resolution attempts.

Territorial and Maritime Dispute Strategies

States can pursue several PR methods with regard to their territorial and maritime claims. However, instead of peaceful settlement, a state may choose to maintain the status quo for some time, and thus take no action all. In these cases, the dispute continues with no attempts at settlement. Such a strategy

---

[1] For a definition of PR methods and PR venues or forums, see Chapter 1.

The Peaceful Resolution of Territorial and Maritime Disputes. Emilia Justyna Powell and Krista E. Wiegand, Oxford University Press. © Oxford University Press 2023. DOI: 10.1093/oso/9780197675649.003.0002

is quite typical. Usually, the long periods of no action occur in the dispute's beginning phases. In many contentions, challenger states—the states that seek to challenge the legal status quo—make merely rhetorical claims and take no costly actions to gain control over the disputed area. When a contention pertains to an area with low value or salience, and thus when the cost of maintaining the claim is low, and the benefit of resolution is minimal, there can be little incentive to take action on a legal claim.

In particular, target states have limited motivation to seek peaceful resolution, since they already maintain the status quo control of the disputed area. Typically, target states hold a firm belief that they indeed possess the legal right of sovereign control. It may also be the case that the target's costs of maintaining the status quo are minuscule or nonexistent. Again: such circumstances discourage the target from using force or seeking any type of peaceful solution. Of course, when the challenger state is actively inciting discord, the target's costs of maintaining the status quo dramatically increase. Both states can accept, explicitly or implicitly, that the maintenance of their contention is not detrimental, and thus poses minor or no obstacles to their bilateral relations and the relations in the region. At times, states engaged in a territorial or a maritime contention are simultaneously able to enjoy continued bilateral cooperation, jointly exploit natural resources, and pursue scientific explorations (Wiegand and Powell 2011b). Maintaining the dispute without engaging in conflict or peaceful settlement attempts is considered to be a form of "negative peace" (Goertz, Diehl, and Balas 2016; Klein, Goertz, and Diehl 2008).[2] It is within this spectrum of negative peace that most interstate dyadic relationships reside.

When the costs of continuing a dispute's status quo are no longer tenable, states may choose to pursue peaceful settlement, or alternatively threaten the opponent, or use force. Using force to resolve a dispute entails attempts to seize territory or deny the opposing state access to claimed maritime areas. While nonviolence is less costly and less risky than any type of military resolution, not every state is willing to attempt peaceful settlement, especially in situations when the costs of maintaining the dispute—continuing the status quo—are relatively low. In comparison with other disputes, territorial

---

[2] Goertz, Diehl, and Balas (2016, 24) describe negative peace as constituting "the middle, transition point of the peace scale. Relationships are neither hot nor cold. In these relationships, there is evidence for neither positive peace nor rivalry. It is, however, peaceful in the absence-of-war sense, as negative peace is a zone typically with no actual militarized exchanges, and hence virtually no battle deaths."

contentions are more frequently associated with the use of force, and are also more likely to escalate to a full-scale war (Senese and Vasquez 2003, 2008; Vasquez and Henehan 2001). Issues of territorial sovereignty are also essential in Vasquez's "steps to war" model (Senese and Vasquez 2008), and other theoretical as well as empirical accounts of war (Tir and Vasquez 2012). According to Goertz, Diehl, and Balas (2016, 89), "territory has consistently constituted the issue over which states have most frequently gone to war, and this is true by a wide margin. In all time periods, territory was the most common war issue, with more than 80 percent of the cases having a territorial component."

Wars fought to overturn the territorial status quo include the Arab-Israel wars (1948, 1967, and 1973) between Israel and Egypt, Syria, and Jordan; wars between India and Pakistan (1947, 1965, and 1971); the Korean War (1950–1953); the Football War between El Salvador and Honduras (1969); the Iran-Iraq War (1980–1988); the Gulf War between Iraq and Kuwait (1991); the Ethiopian-Eritrean War (1998–2000); the Azerbaijan-Armenian War (2020); and most recently the Russian invasion of Ukraine (2022). The use of force can also manifest itself via midlevel armed conflict such as the Russian annexation of the Crimea region from Ukraine in 2014, or relatively minor clashes of troops, such as the deadly 2020 confrontation between India and China. Of course, according to international law, since 1945 the use of force to take control of sovereign territory is unacceptable.[3] Nevertheless, history provides multiple examples of conflicts where a piece of territory is taken by force and the target eventually cedes its territorial control to the challenger. By way of illustration, in December 1961, Indian Armed Forces seized and annexed the island of Goa, thereby ending the 451-years-long Portuguese rule of the island. In 1974, after the overthrow of Portugal's authoritarian Estado Novo regime, the Portuguese government recognized India's sovereignty over Goa. In 2020, Azerbaijan effectively seized the disputed Nagorno Karabakh region from Armenia, leading to the displacement of thousands of people. However, there are other cases, such as Morocco's 1975 seizure of the Western Sahara, Israel's 1967 occupation of the Gaza Strip and West Bank,

---

[3] Article 2(4) of the UN Charter stipulates that "all members shall refrain in their international relations from the threat or use of force against the territorial integrity or political independence of any state, or in any other manner inconsistent with the purposes of the United Nations." It is also crucial to recognize that this provision constitutes a principle of customary international law and is therefore "binding upon all states in the world community" (Shaw 2017, 854).

and Russia's 2014 annexation of Crimea from Ukraine, all of which constitute clear violations of international law.

Although in comparison with territorial disputes, maritime disputes involve armed conflict less frequently, these contentions are nevertheless still likely to involve some use of force (Hensel et al. 2008). Of the 270 maritime disputes that took place between 1900 and 2010, 33 percent experienced some degree of militarization (Mitchell 2020). Thus, similar to their territorial counterparts, maritime contentions with a previous history of militarized conflict or those concerning highly salient areas are prone to militarization.[4]

In general, though both territorial and maritime disputes are indeed quite prone to escalate into military confrontations and even full-scale war, the majority of these contentions experience prolonged periods when both parties make repeated attempts at peaceful settlement (Hensel 2001).[5] Additionally, the incidence of territory-related wars has declined substantially since the mid-twentieth century. Instead of force, most disputants engaged in these contentions prefer either to maintain the status quo or to actively seek peaceful solutions. It seems that with time, the peaceful settlement of these contentions—and not the use of force—has become the norm for interstate relations. Because issues of territorial sovereignty in particular are inherently convoluted and frequently indivisible, an overwhelming portion of these contentions experience multiple attempts at peaceful resolution.

Attempting to peacefully resolve a dispute constitutes generally an attempt at "positive peace" (Klein, Goertz, and Diehl 2008), whereby the disputants agree to end adversarial relations previously generated by conflicting claims. A genuine attempt at settlement goes beyond mere negotiations. Instead, such an attempt must deal with actual terms of sovereignty and/or maritime rights, and entail offers of some territorial or maritime concessions, whether minor or major. Usually, the resolution of a territorial or a maritime contention involves detailed procedures and prolonged discussions and decision-making about sovereignty.[6] It is also feasible—though fairly rare—that

---

[4] Mitchell (2020) shows that in the 1900–2010 time period, maritime disputes were more likely to occur if they dealt with more salient maritime areas (presence of oil, natural gas, migratory fish stocks, etc.). Not surprisingly, the presence of additional, maritime-unrelated issues in these disputes—such as territorial sovereignty—increases the likelihood of violent conflict. Interestingly, Mitchell also shows that states have been more likely to militarize their disputes since UNCLOS came into effect.

[5] As Huth and Allee (2002) demonstrate, in the time frame between 1919 and 1995, challenger states threatened or used force in merely 6 percent of their territorial disputes dataset's observations.

[6] In this context it is worth noting that change in ownership of particular territory or a maritime area simultaneously entails modification in sovereignty, legally justified control, and authority over

a challenger drops its claims or, alternatively, a target peacefully cedes the disputed area to the challenger without force or negotiations. By dropping its claims, the challenger is officially accepting the status quo: the target's legal ownership—sovereignty—of the formerly disputed areas. Of course, in an overwhelming portion of these contentions, challengers do not drop their claims and targets refuse to willingly give up control over the disputed area. In such circumstances, the most common option is to engage in peaceful settlement.

The idea that states should resolve their disputes in a peaceful manner is critical to international security. Article 2(3) of the UN Charter requires that states "settle their international disputes by peaceful means in such a manner that international peace and security, and justice, are not endangered."[7] Chapter 6 of the UN Charter, which is specifically devoted to peaceful dispute settlement, lists these methods in Article 33: "The parties to any dispute, the continuance of which is likely to endanger the maintenance of international peace and security, shall, first of all, seek a solution by negotiation, enquiry, mediation, conciliation, arbitration, judicial settlement, resort to regional agencies or arrangements, or other peaceful means of their own choice."[8] Most of the Charter's discussion about peaceful settlement centers on the Security Council.[9] No PR method can be forced on the feuding states. Thus, most attempts at resolution must be preceded by both parties' consent. The jurisprudence of the International Court of Justice (ICJ) provides guidance on the meaning of the term "consent," and we elaborate on this important point in Chapter 3, noting that consent is inherently dynamic and must be sustained throughout the resolution process.

Throughout the lifespan of a dispute, states frequently resort to more than one or two PR methods. In fact, there are specific patterns of resolution that hold for different stages of a dispute. More often than not, the less formalized PR methods, such as negotiations and mediation—if unsuccessful—are followed by the more law-based methods, for instance, adjudication. Naturally, the lack of a genuine compulsory jurisdiction means that a contention may never end up at an international court. In this regard, dynamics

---

the area. As Shaw (2017, 363) writes, "This means that the nationality of the inhabitants is altered, as is the legal system under which they live, work and conduct their relations."

[7] UN Charter, Art. 2 (3).

[8] UN Charter, Art. 33.

[9] Chapter VI includes articles 33–38, each of which focuses on the Security Council's role in settling disputes through peaceful means.

of territorial and maritime disputes tend to be similar to those of other international disputes. As a general rule, states try to push back against pressures to move the dispute to adjudication.[10] Most states prefer not to give up their decision-making power to a third-party forum. Even so, one should not think of international law as having an impact only through the most formal resolution venues, arbitration and adjudication. Quite the opposite is true. Law, international rules and norms, strength of the parties' legal claims, and the prospect of adjudication loom over all territorial and maritime disputes, including disputes that do not squarely fall under the jurisdiction of international courts.[11]

Bilateral Negotiations

In many territorial and maritime contentions, bilateral negotiations are attempted first as an antecedent to the more formal settlement venues.[12] It is often quite useful to avoid unnecessary formalities associated with any third-party method, whether binding or nonbinding. Negotiations are flexible and simple and incur low costs. Intuitively, it would seem reasonable to expect that only if negotiations fail to provide a solution will states subsequently use nonbinding third-party PR methods. Using the same logic, one might expect that states would be most likely to resort to binding third-party methods only if nonbinding methods do not bring about a settlement.

At times states may avoid negotiations altogether even at the beginning of the settlement process. The jurisprudence of the ICJ provides important insight in this regard. The Court has declared that "Neither in the Charter or otherwise in international law is any general rule to be found to the effect that the exhaustion of diplomatic negotiations constitutes a precondition

---

[10] Literature on this topic is extensive. See, among others, Ratner 2006, 821; Goertz, Diehl, and Balas 2016. The scholarship has been prolific in trying to explain why and under what conditions states use legal mechanisms. See Allee and Huth 2006; Davis 2012; Gent and Shannon 2010; Helfer and Slaughter 1997; Huth, Croco, and Appel 2013; Mitchell and Powell 2011; Posner and Yoo 2005; Powell and Wiegand 2014. Koremenos (2016) describes why countries use specific dispute resolution provisions in their agreements. We return to this issue in Chapter 3 in the context of our theoretical framework.

[11] We discuss the definition of a legal dispute in Chapter 3. Also see Bilder (1998) for a discussion of out-of-court effects.

[12] The ICJ has addressed the timing of negotiations in the Mavrommatis Palestine Concessions case, PCIJ, Series A, No. 2, 1924, 15. The Court stated that before a dispute becomes "the subject of an action at law, its subject matter should have been clearly defined by diplomatic negotiations."

for a matter to be referred to the Court."[13] In many situations the parties are bound via previous commitments to attempt negotiations as a first method of settlement. By way of illustration, the 1982 UN Convention on the Law of the Sea requires state parties to "proceed expeditiously to an exchange of views" with hopes of settling their dispute "by negotiation or other peaceful means."[14] Similarly, Article 8(2) of the 1959 Antarctic Treaty stipulates that "the Contracting Parties concerned in any case of dispute with regard to the exercise of jurisdiction in Antarctica shall immediately consult together with a view to reaching a mutually acceptable solution."[15] However, in the context of many disputes, states are not legally bound to first negotiate. Instead, states may decide to employ any settlement mechanisms at any point during a dispute. In fact, even when states choose a PR method and specific PR venue, there is nothing stopping the disputants from changing venue after the settlement procedures have commenced (Martin 2018). Moreover, disputants may attempt two settlement methods simultaneously, hoping one of them will yield a preferred outcome.[16]

Bilateral negotiations are not based on a fixed set of procedures. As Bercovitch and Jackson (2009, 8) note, "negotiation is essentially an approach to conflict that is symmetric, equal, and voluntary." Negotiations entail discussions between the parties with the hope of reaching an agreement. Many territorial and maritime disputes are resolved via simple, though at times protracted, two-party dialogue. This PR method is the most frequently employed option, and often the best option for effective settlement, especially if the solution truly fits interests of both sides. Several of our interlocutors emphasized this point. Hans Corell noted, "it is the best thing if you can negotiate and come to a solution where both sides can say that 'well, we solved the issue and we are pleased with the result.' "[17] When the parties perceive

---

[13] Land and Maritime Boundary between Cameroon and Nigeria, Preliminary Objections, ICJ Rep. 1998, 275, 303, December 18, 1985.

[14] Article 283(1) of the United Nations Convention on the Law of the Sea, December 10, 1982, 1833 UNTS 397, entered into force on November 1, 1994. The article refers to a situation when a dispute arises between state parties that deals with the application or interpretation of the Convention. The ICJ has also explained in its jurisprudence that negotiations must be conducted in good faith (Legality of the Threat or Use of Nuclear Weapons, Advisory Opinion, ICJ Rep. 1996, 226, 263–264, July 8, 1996. Negotiations must also go beyond "mere formalities" and "must be genuine" (German External Debt case, ILR 418, 454).

[15] The Antarctic Treaty, 402 UNTS 71, entered into force June 23, 1961.

[16] However, when several methods are used at the same time to resolve a dispute, all these methods remain distinct and are executed by distinct intermediaries or organs (see Collier 2009, 366).

[17] Author's interview (EJP) with Hans Corell, former Under-Secretary-General for Legal Affairs and the Legal Counsel of the United Nations, January 13, 2021.

their territorial or maritime claims as divisible, negotiations can prove very effective. By way of illustration, the 2016 Meuse River negotiations between Belgium and the Netherlands solved a protracted contention between the two countries. The disputants, who had formalized their border in the 1843 Treaty of Maastricht, negotiated a peaceful exchange of swaths of land each state had, which were located "on the wrong bank of the river."[18] There are many benefits to negotiations, and usually the disputants are eager to attempt negotiations even in circumstances where objectively the probability of negotiated agreement is slim. Thus, there are multiple attempts at negotiations, and "most disputes between states get resolved nonviolently at the bilateral level."[19] It is, therefore, not surprising that negotiations—more specifically, their importance to international peace—have been repeatedly acknowledged in the jurisprudence of international courts. For instance, in the 1969 North Sea Continental Shelf case, the ICJ referred to negotiations by stating that "there is no need to insist upon the fundamental character of this method of settlement."[20]

Though negotiations may seem uninteresting because of the lack of a third-party involvement, as Merrills (2017, 3) writes, "in one form or another, negotiation has a vital part in international disputes." If one conceptualizes the lifespan of a dispute as a sequence of proposals issued by the proposer, either challenger or target, it is obvious that negotiations constitute an inherent segment of a wider bargaining environment between the disputants.[21] The parties' preference to control the resolution process as much as possible plays a crucial role in negotiations' popularity: "the desire to reduce uncertainty in the process is one of the reasons why states stick with negotiations for as long as they can in most cases."[22] According to one of our interlocutors, "When you're negotiating resolution of a dispute, you have complete control of the process. You can't be forced to do something you don't want to do and you

[18] "Belgium and the Netherlands Swap Land, and Remain Friends," *New York Times*, November 28, 2016.

[19] Author's interview (EJP) with Laurie Nathan, former Senior Advisor to the UN Mediation Support Unit, January 21, 2022.

[20] North Sea Continental Shelf, Federal Republic of Germany v. Denmark; Federal Republic of Germany v. Netherlands, 1969 ICJ Rep. 3, 48, Judgment of February 20, 1969.

[21] Huth, Croco, and Appel (2013, 92) define dispute resolution as a process "consisting of a series of proposals and counterproposals as leaders try to limit concessions while holding out for better terms."

[22] Author's interview (EJP) with Martin Pratt, Bordermap Consulting, January 27, 2022.

can dictate to some degree the pace and the nature of the interaction with the other State."[23]

As a key part of the broader step-by-step issuing of resolution attempts, the proposer's attempts at negotiations provide the parties with an opportunity to gain information about the other side's preferences. Additionally—and specifically in the context of territorial and maritime contentions—attempts at negotiations allow the parties to assess the salience of the contested issue to the opponent, the opponent's commitment to their own bargaining strategies, as well as the opponent's capability and willingness to mobilize resources to fulfill its preferences (Slantchev 2003; Sticher 2021). Simply put, attempts at negotiations allow parties to learn. Conceptualization of negotiations as embedded in the larger over-time relationship between the disputants has firm support in the scholarship that focuses on the interdependence of conflict-management attempts (Diehl 2006; Diehl and Regan 2015), and on the importance of negotiation in international politics (Bueno de Mesquita 2004; Zartman 1974). Negotiations are far from being merely a residual category of the peaceful dispute resolution process, and many territorial disputes have been either successfully resolved or heavily influenced by negotiations. For instance, before and after the 1969 border conflict between China and the Soviet Union, negotiations played a crucial role in ending the long-standing protracted dispute.[24] The Iran-Iraq war—initiated as a result of both states' claim for the Shatt-al-Arab waterway along the border—was also resolved through bilateral negotiations in 1990.

Negotiations are also used before resort to violence—with the hopes of boosting a disputant's capacity to engage in a military confrontation (Urlacher 2015)—to end violence, as well as in the interval between, and in the aftermath of, other PR methods.[25] Merrills (2017, 17) writes that the connection between negotiations and adjudication is particularly important since frequently "states choose to make the exhaustion of attempts to settle

[23] Author's interview (EJP) with Sean D. Murphy, professor of international law, George Washington University, January 28, 2022. Murphy has represented several countries in international courts and tribunals, has served as an arbitrator in inter-state and investor–State arbitrations, and has been an ad hoc judge on ITLOS.

[24] The 1991 Agreement on the Eastern Section of the Boundary between the Union of Soviet Socialist Republics and the People's Republic of China (the Sino-Soviet Border Agreement) provided a detailed border demarcation and established a boundary demarcation committee. The Agreement effectively resolved multiple, though not all, aspects of the disagreement between China and the Soviet Union.

[25] Merrills (2017, 3) notes that "on the occasions when another method is used, negotiation is not displaced, but directed towards instrumental issues, for example, the terms of reference for an inquiry or conciliation commission or the arrangements for implementing an arbitral decision."

a dispute by negotiation a condition of an adjudicator's jurisdiction." Thus, negotiations are frequently a de facto prerequisite to adjudication. An international court can be called upon only if a contention at hand is of a legal nature. Often, it is during negotiations that the parties can isolate a specific issue of a legal nature that lies at the heart of their contention. Alternatively, during negotiations the parties may conclude that their dispute is merely of a political nature and therefore does not fall under the jurisdiction of an international adjudicator (Wolfrum 2018a). Importantly, however, as stated by the ICJ, the absence of negotiations does not per se preclude an international court from exercising jurisdiction over a dispute at hand.[26] This is the case when one disputant makes it explicitly clear that it is not willing to attempt resolution via negotiations.[27]

Negotiations may be indispensable in finalizing the settlement even if an international court has issued a judgment. For instance, in the North Sea Continental Shelf cases, the parties—West Germany, Denmark, and the Netherlands—requested that the Court merely specify rules of international law that would constitute an appropriate basis for the resolution of the dispute.[28] After the decision, the parties settled their dispute via negotiations. A similar situation obtained in the context of the Jan Mayen dispute over delimitation of the continental shelf and fishery zones between Jan Mayen and Greenland.[29] After the 2003 ICJ judgment, Denmark and Norway agreed to marginally alter the Court's decision. Similarly, in the Sovereignty Over Certain Frontier Land case between the Netherlands and Belgium, after the ICJ found that sovereignty over both areas belonged to Belgium, the disputants took it upon themselves to delimit areas not discussed in the judgment.[30]

---

[26] This general norm may not hold if a treaty or a convention obliges the disputants to negotiate, exchange views, etc., before a more formal method is employed. Such is the case in the UN Convention on the Law of the Sea. According to Article 283(1), if a dispute over interpretation or application of the Convention arises, the parties "shall proceed expeditiously to an exchange of views regarding its settlement by negotiation or some other peaceful means." However, in its jurisprudence, ITLOS has repeatedly interpreted this requirement in a relatively loose way. Also, if a dispute over land, or any other issue, arises out of a particular treaty, states may be bound to negotiate in good faith by the general norms of international law (see Merrills 2017, 19 and 24).

[27] See, for instance United States Diplomatic and Consular Staff in Tehran, United States of America v. Iran, ICJ Rep. 3, Judgment of May 24, 1980.

[28] North Sea Continental Shelf, Federal Republic of Germany v. Denmark; Federal Republic of Germany v. Netherlands, ICJ Rep., Judgment of February 20, 1969.

[29] Maritime Delimitation in the Area between Greenland and Jan Mayen, Denmark v. Norway, ICJ Rep., Judgment of June 14, 1993.

[30] Sovereignty over Certain Frontier Land, Belgium v. Netherlands, ICJ Rep., Judgment of June 20, 1959. Also see Boisson de Chazournes and Angelini 2013.

Interpretation, analysis, and evolution of particular international law norms are often brought up in the context of negotiations. This is specifically the case for territorial and maritime disputes since claims of such nature deal with sovereignty rights and interpretation of historic treaties. For example, the many attempts at peaceful settlement during the Bahrain-Qatar contention over the Hawar Islands and maritime rights dealt with interpretation of agreements (Schulte 2004). More specifically, Qatar disagreed with an interpretation of a 1939 British ruling that awarded Hawar to Bahrain (Wiegand 2012). Likewise, talks between Afghanistan and Pakistan over their disputed border revolved around interpretation of international principles and rules, specifically the validity of the 1893 Durand Treaty that demarcated the border between the two states. Afghanistan claimed that the treaty was signed under duress, and was thus invalid (Kaura 2017). The central point is that policymakers' actions in negotiations are to a large extent constrained by what international law puts forth on an issue, as well as on what international courts and arbitration tribunals have ruled in the past.

At times, domestic audiences can cause problems for their governments during the process of bilateral negotiations (Putnam 1988). In fact, domestic concerns have the potential to stall any compromises or concessions on the international level, because state leaders want to avoid domestic punishment (Fearon 1994). Importantly, throughout the duration of a contention, domestic audiences can remain sensitive about a piece of land or even a rock in a nearby sea. Such heightened domestic sensitivities may further encourage state leaders to submit their disputes to an intermediary. As Sean D. Murphy notes:

> Sometimes there is an interesting phenomenon of a domestic constituency that is fervently pushing for a particular outcome and so the government does want to pursue an action to try to achieve that outcome, but the government may have doubts that it is going to win. Nevertheless, if the government uses a very authoritative dispute settlement body, such as the ICJ, and it then loses, the government can then turn around and say to that domestic constituency "we pushed it as hard as we could, we hired the best lawyers, and we made the best arguments available, but unfortunately we lost." So that's a loss in terms of what the court decided, but it's a "win" of sorts for a government that is trying to deal with internal pressures and trying to move on in a bilateral relationship.[31]

---

[31] Author's interview (EJP) with Sean D. Murphy, January 28, 2022.

In a way, policymakers can seek domestic cover and avoid having to make unpopular decisions about the disputed area (Huth and Allee 2002; Malintoppi 2015).[32] Merrills (2017, 311) directly addresses this situation: "Referring a dispute to a court which is demonstrably impartial can be very useful when a government is anxious to settle a dispute, but is under pressure not to make concessions. As the decision is not the government's responsibility, then, provided it has been arrived at fairly, a strong case can be made out for accepting it even if it is unfavorable." To sum up, negotiations constitute a settlement method that is rife with commitment credibility problems and uncertainty about resolve and accurate information. Though states, to some extent, are in control of the settlement process, there are many challenges making the path of the settlement unpredictable.[33]

At times, the dynamics of a particular dispute may prompt states to formalize negotiations, thereby solidifying their future cooperation. For instance, negotiators may institute permanent commissions to address any ongoing or anticipated issues. An illustrative example is the contention between Nigeria and Cameroon over the Bakassi Peninsula. The countries set up the Nigeria-Cameroon Joint Boundary Commission and held a number of peaceful negotiations throughout the 1970s, which culminated in the Kano Agreement. This agreement reaffirmed previous agreements that had put the Bakassi Peninsula under Cameroonian territorial authority (Essien Umoh 2015). After a coup in 1975, Nigeria repudiated the Kano Agreement. Armed clashes broke out in 1994, and consequently Cameroon took the case to the ICJ. On October 10, 2002, the ICJ awarded sovereignty over the peninsula to Cameroon.[34] To facilitate the implementation of the judgment, the two states set up the Cameroon-Nigeria Mixed Commission (CNMC).[35]

---

[32] For instance, once a court issues a judgment, the leader can emphasize the decision's binding nature to the public.

[33] Frequently, states engaged in territorial and maritime disputes are unwilling to negotiate. By way of illustration, Japan has not pursued bilateral negotiations or mediation with China during the Senkaku/Diaoyu islands dispute in the East China Sea. Instead, Japan proposed adjudication at the ICJ as its first attempt at peaceful settlement. Depending on the type, strength, salience, and degree of territorial or maritime claim, states—such as the Philippines or Japan—may feel as though arbitration or adjudication will grant them higher levels of control over a dispute.

[34] Land and Maritime Boundary Between Cameroon and Nigeria, Cameroon v. Nigeria, ICJ Rep 2002, 103, Judgment of October 10, 2002.

[35] Cameroon-Nigeria Mixed Commission (CNMC). United Nations Office for West Africa and the Sahel. Information available at https://unowas.unmissions.org/cameroon-nigeria-mixed-com mission. Another interesting example is the 1991 United States–Canada Air Quality Agreement. In this treaty, the parties agreed to establish the Air Quality Committee, charged with several tasks, including the progress and implementation review, as well as preparation and submission of a progress report to the parties (Collier and Lowe 2000, 22).

Notwithstanding their benefits and low costs, negotiations may become ineffective. As Bercovitch and Jackson (2009, 8) write, "parties in negotiation may use stalling techniques to produce deadlocks and disillusionment, often requiring the addition of a third-party as a mediator to assist the parties to get out of an impasse." Additionally, serious disputes may cause disputants to strain or sever their diplomatic relations. Such developments rule out bilateral talks, or render them ineffective. This was the case in the dispute between the United States and Iran following the 1979 seizure and detention of US diplomats and consular staff in Tehran. Similarly, in the ongoing dispute over access to the Pacific Ocean between Bolivia and Chile (and Peru), Bolivia broke all diplomatic relations with Chile in 1964 when the Chilean government planned to divert the riverbed of the Lauca River. Relations between the two states stabilized in 1975 after two years of secret negotiations, but after further refusals of the Chilean government to alter their actions, Bolivia again broke all diplomatic relations with Chile in 1978 (Brunet-Jailly 2015, 63). In such circumstances, disputants are likely to request help from an intermediary with the hope of "reconciling the opposing claims and appeasing the feelings of resentment which may have arisen between the States at variance," as the 1899 Hague Convention stipulates.[36]

Nonbinding Third-Party Methods

Article 33 of the UN Charter lists the most frequently used methods of nonbinding third-party methods, such as inquiry, conciliation, and mediation. Importantly, however, states have the option to "resort to regional agencies or arrangements, or other peaceful means of their own choice."[37] In other words, disputants can be creative in constructing a novel or a hybrid venue for peaceful resolution. Such hybrid procedures may also appear in international treaties. For instance, the Conference on Security and Cooperation in Europe (CSCE) offers a dispute settlement mechanism that is an amalgamation of conciliation and mediation.[38] Known as the Valletta Procedure, it structures dispute resolution in two separate stages, and during each stage the disputants may agree to alter or amend the procedure for the

---

[36] The Hague Convention for the Pacific Settlement of International Disputes, July 29, 1899.
[37] UN Charter, Art. 33.
[38] Website of CSCE: https://www.csce.gov/about-commission-security-and-cooperation-europe.

betterment of the resolution process (Merrills 2017, 80–81). It is also possible that states may willingly allow one PR method to evolve into another one. This is often the case with mediation and conciliation, good offices, and inquiry. There are several instances when a commission of inquiry, initially charged with a fact-finding task, has evolved into a quasi-arbitral panel whose job was to decipher matters not only of fact, but also of law.[39] All methods that entail participation of third parties require the parties' consent, and entail rules, procedures, and decisions about the settlement. We elaborate on the characteristics of each method below.

Inquiry

When the contention centers on a specific question of law or of fact, inquiry can prove useful. A neutral intermediary is brought in to provide an objective evaluation of the situation and to inquire into facts and pertinent law. Inquiry can be undertaken by one person, or by a commission. Agreement on the facts is especially important in the context of territorial and maritime contentions, since the disputants often disagree about the legal status quo of an area. Discrepancy in how the parties perceive facts is often the reason that "negotiations are bogged down" (Koh 2011, 59). At times, inquiry may evolve into quasi-judicial proceedings. As one would expect, this transformation might occur when jurists are asked to serve as intermediaries. In such circumstances, a commission's findings may actually put forward legal rulings, de facto turning inquiry into arbitration (Merrills 2017, 55). Yet, as a general rule, the objective of an inquiry commission is not to direct the process of reconciliation or agreement, but instead to focus on informing the parties of facts and laws.

Since World War II, states have rarely resorted to inquiry as a method for settlement of territorial and maritime disputes. At the same time, however, inquiry appears in many international treaties such as the UN Watercourses Convention.[40] The commentary to the Convention stipulates that "inquiry and fact-finding are procedures specifically designed to produce an impartial

---

[39] See, for instance the Red Crusader inquiry and the Letelier and Moffitt case, as discussed by Merrills (2017, 51–56).

[40] Convention on the Law of the Non-Navigational Uses of International Watercourses, May 21, 1997.

finding of disputed facts by engaging a third-party."[41] In the framework of this Convention, Pakistan requested inquiry in its dispute with India, after India proposed to erect the Baglihar Dam on the Chenab River. Pakistan was not in favor of the dam and claimed that it would violate the 1960 Pakistan-India Water Treaty. In 2005, Pakistan requested that the World Bank appoint an unbiased investigation to look into the facts of the disagreement. In 2007, the expert issued a decision, which was subsequently accepted by both sides. The dispute was eventually submitted to arbitration. In 2013, the PCA in the Indus Water Kishengaga Arbitration (Pakistan v. India) issued its award settling the contention.[42]

Arguably, one of the reasons for the lack of state interest in inquiry is the increased use of adjudication. Indeed, there are several permanent international courts with an established body of jurisprudence, and part of any court's mandate is to investigate facts and appropriate law. These standing courts, such as the ICJ and the International Tribunal for the Law of the Sea (ITLOS), have developed expertise in disputes dealing with issues of territorial and maritime sovereignty. Thus, disputing states frequently prefer to submit their disputes to such institutions, especially if the existing jurisprudence on a particular topic offers hope of a favorable outcome.

Good Offices

Good offices are not explicitly regulated in the UN Charter. Yet, this relatively informal method has repeatedly proved to be a useful means to settle a dispute. A good officer's task is straightforward: to motivate the disputants to begin communicating and maintain dialogue throughout the process of settlement. In contrast with mediation and conciliation, a good officer does not actively participate in the construction of settlement terms (Collier and Lowe 2000, 27). Frequently, a regional organization provides its members with a forum for communication. This was the case in the dispute over the status of Cyprus between Greece, Turkey, and the United Kingdom. In 1964, the UN Secretary General established good offices to ensure that the parties

---

[41] Convention on the Law of the Non-Navigational Uses of International Watercourses, Part VI, Miscellaneous Provisions, Article 33.1.7 Fact-finding and inquiry, May 21, 1997. See https://www. unwatercoursesconvention.org/the-convention/part-vi-miscellaneous-provisions/article-33-set tlement-of-disputes/33-1-7-fact-finding-and-inquiry/.

[42] Indus Water Kishengaga Arbitration, Pakistan v. India, PCA Case No. 2011-01, December 20, 2013.

continued to exchange their views, in spite of high tensions and repeated use of force.[43] In a similar way, the Organization of African Unity (OAU) provided good offices for Algeria and Morocco during the dispute over their shared border.[44] In fact, OAU instituted an ad hoc commission that was quite successful in resolving the dispute by encouraging the reinstatement of diplomatic relations and resolving several pressing issues such as the withdrawal of armed forces (Merrills 2017, 283). Not only international organizations, but individuals too can prove to be effective good officers. For instance, in the contention over the Falkland Islands between Argentina and the United Kingdom in the 1980s, after attempts at mediation by US Secretary of State Alexander Haig, UN Secretary General Javier Pérez de Cuéllar, proposed his good offices. While there are substantive and procedural differences between good offices and other nonbinding third-party methods, in practice, good offices frequently evolve into mediation (Shaw 2017).

Conciliation

The procedure and rules of conciliation have been codified in the 1928 General Act on the Pacific Settlement of International Disputes.[45] Conciliation entails an intermediary producing a proposal or a series of proposals that set out the terms of the settlement. In a way, conciliation has some aspects of mediation and inquiry, and historically "the process of conciliation emerged from treaties providing for permanent inquiry commissions" (Shaw 2017, 773). However, conciliation constitutes a relatively fluid framework, within which the disputants can pursue several options. As a result, a conciliation commission can be charged with a variety of responsibilities and tasks. In general terms, the aim of conciliation is to provide an informal framework of settlement for conflicts where facts and law are at the heart of the contention. Some

---

[43] United Nations Peacekeeping Forces in Cyprus, "About the Good Offices," https://unficyp.unmissions.org/about-good-offices.

[44] For more information see, for instance, Wild 1966.

[45] General Act for the Pacific Settlement of International Disputes, September 26, 1928, 93 LNTS 343. The 1928 Act underwent revisions in 1949. Conciliation is also defined in the 1961 Resolution of the Institut de Droit International as "a method for the settlement of international disputes of any nature according to which a commission set up by the parties either on a permanent basis or on an ad hoc basis to deal with a dispute, proceeds to the impartial examination of the dispute and attempts to define the terms of a settlement susceptible of being accepted by them, or of affording the parties, with a view to its settlement, such aid as they may have requested" (Justitia et Pace Institut de Droit International, Session of Salzburg—1961, International Conciliation, available at http://www.idi-iil.org/app/uploads/2017/06/1961_salz_02_en.pdf).

view conciliation as a step up from negotiations, whereby the intermediaries introduce more structure to bilateral talks. Others see conciliation as a PR method that partially resembles arbitration in that the intermediaries are to base their proposed solution on norms of international law.

Conciliation commissions can draw expertise from a variety of specialists and technical experts, depending on the specifics of the dispute at hand and on the exact mandate placed on the commission by the disputants. Territorial and maritime contentions frequently require expertise from geographers, geologists, geophysicists, and lawyers who specialize in a particular region, land, or maritime area.[46] There is no final binding decision, and thus the parties do not have to accept results or proposals offered by the conciliator. However, these proposals may play a crucial role in bringing a dispute to an end. One of the main features of conciliation that distinguish it from mediation is that a conciliator usually offers proposals officially, and these proposals are based on independent investigation. In contrast, a mediator typically suggests settlement informally and on the basis of material provided by the parties (Merrills 2017, 26).

Overall, conciliation is more formal in its procedure than mediation, although both methods retain a nonlitigious character, as the parties are under no obligation to accept the intermediary's recommendations. Subsequently, in both methods disputants maintain partial control over the contention and participate in the crafting of settlement terms. Conciliation—in an informal form—remains very popular in the Middle East, especially under the auspices of the Arab League and the Organization of Islamic Cooperation (OIC).[47] The Islamic legal tradition promotes a specific approach to dispute resolution that is based on a unique logic of social interaction. This sharia-led social interaction is firmly planted in the nonconfrontational dispute settlement and inclusion of Islamic principles in the resolution process. While the prevailing preference in the West is to use formal approaches to conflict resolution, traditional Islamic law uses reconciliation and constructive dialogue between the disputing parties. As Powell (2020, 11) writes, "Islamic jurisprudence teaches that amicable informal settlement without resort to

---

[46] For instance, the Jan Mayen conciliation (Conciliation Commission on the Continental Shelf area between Iceland and Jan Mayen: Report and Recommendations to the Governments of Iceland and Norway), decision of June 1981, available at http://legal.un.org/riaa/cases/vol_XXVII/1-34.pdf. Also see Shaw (2017, 774).

[47] Revised Charter of the Organisation of Islamic Cooperation, Article 27, March 14, 2008, 914 UNTS 111. The Organisation of Islamic Conference changed its name to the Organisation of Islamic Cooperation in 2011.

formal venues such as courts constitutes a righteous and morally superior method of seeking justice."[48] The Islamic philosophy of conflict management encourages states of the Middle East and other states representing the Islamic legal tradition to use conciliation along with other nonformal methods in settling their international contentions.

Mediation

The 1899 and 1907 Hague Conventions regulate procedures and rules of mediation.[49] The UN Secretary General, regional leaders, regional organizations, the Pope, heads of state, and diplomats frequently serve as mediators in many international contentions. Thus, a multiplicity of political forums such as the UN Security Council, UN General Assembly, the EU Commission, the North Atlantic Treaty Organization, African Union, the Association of Southeast Asian Nations, and so on play a crucial role in the resolution of these disputes. The UN Security Council plays a particular role as a mediator based on its charge to maintain international peace and security.[50] While the UN Security Council has some adjudicative ability, it acts as a mediator when handling dispute settlement (Mondre 2015). Unlike other mediation efforts, decision outcomes of mediation by the UN Security Council are binding, though compliance is not very high. The UN Security Council was actively involved in the 1967 dispute between Egypt and Israel, the 1976 dispute between Argentina and the United Kingdom, and the peace negotiations after the Gulf War between Iraq and Kuwait. Despite these and other territorial and maritime disputes being mediated by the UN Security Council, there are limitations that might influence states to not seek mediation by the Council. As Mondre (2015, 35) notes, "the process of alerting the Security Council is fraught with uncertainty. At the very start, it is not even guaranteed that the Council will deal with the dispute put before it. . . . Moreover, if a meeting

[48] See also Othman 2007.
[49] The First Hague Peace Conference of 1899 was convened with the goal of revising the declaration concerning the laws and customs of war elaborated in 1874 by the Conference of Brussels. The 1899 Hague Conference resulted in adopting a Convention on land warfare to which Regulations are annexed. Later, in 1907, the Convention and the Regulations were revised during the Second International Peace Conference in 1907 (Hague Convention [IV] Respecting the Laws and Customs of War on Land and Its Annex: Regulations Concerning the Laws and Customs of War on Land [1907]).
[50] UN Charter, Article 24, para. 1.

takes place, the result of the debate is hard to predict for a party involved in the dispute."

There are many forums and institutions that offer mediation. In most circumstances, there is "an oversupply of mediation offers."[51] There are a variety of political forums and regional organizations that may try to help, including the UN Security Council and other UN organs. For instance, "in Africa you may have both the sub-regional body like SADC, ECOWAS or IGAD and the African Union. You may have a former colonial power, the UK or France, attempting to mediate. You may have religious bodies attempting to mediate. And then . . . if we are looking at state mediators . . . Switzerland, Germany, Norway, Sweden all position their foreign policy around mediation to a greater or lesser extent."[52] Thus, to some extent, recourse to mediation "probably also has to do with the regional dynamics and whether there's a strong regional organization in place. If you start having a fractious relationship between neighboring states in Africa, you're going to see the African Union start to get involved and ask questions and that's the type of thing that often may lead to a mediator getting involved. Maybe you could see ASEAN doing the same thing. But if you're not in a situation that has that sort of outsider offering, proposing, and suggesting mediation, I think it would be less likely for two states to on their own accord elect to go out and get a mediator."[53]

Performing the duties of a mediator enables an official or an organization to access and guide the particulars of the dispute's settlement. Thus, states with a vested interest in a specific resolution outcome frequently offer their services. For instance, in early stages of the Kashmir dispute between India and Pakistan, mediation by the Soviet Union was crucial in promoting a ceasefire. The Soviet Union had strategic interests in the dispute, and its involvement in the peace process enabled the Soviets to enlarge their area of influence in the region at that time. In the context of the Kashmir dispute, Wanis St. John (1997, 2) writes that "a powerful mediator is useful to gradually shift the state rivals away from their competitive national security perceptions towards a cooperative and interdependent security arrangement." Similarly, Saudi Arabia has repeatedly offered its services as a mediator in several regional disputes. For example, during the Bahrain-Qatar

---

[51] Author's interview (EJP) with Laurie Nathan, January 21, 2022.
[52] Ibid.
[53] Author's interview (EJP) with an anonymous arbitration practitioner, February 7, 2022.

territorial and maritime dispute,[54] Saudi Arabia's goal was for the two disputants to involve the Saudi monarchy in the resolution process: "As the big sister to which the other Gulf states defer to various extents, Saudi Arabia does not want to see itself defending its borders at the ICJ, and would rather reach solutions by mutual consent through direct and candid negotiations."[55]

Territorial and maritime disputes are particularly appealing to third-party mediators (Wilkenfeld et al. 2003). More often than not, mediations in these disputes occur when the contention has previously involved militarized conflict. In these instances, or when the likelihood of violence is high, "parties don't look for mediation in those situations, they have mediation thrust on them."[56] For instance, during the Ethiopia-Eritrea war (1998–2000), several actors tried to mediate, including the Organization of African Unity, the predecessor of the African Union, and the World Council of Churches, as well as the United Nations.[57] Higher levels of intensity of such disputes make them similar to enduring rivalries—which inherently involve high levels of distrust. These characteristics dampen the likelihood of peaceful resolution through bilateral negotiations and increase the need for third-party intervention (Greig 2001). Third-party mediators or conciliators can help the disputing states reduce asymmetries of information (Kydd 2003; Regan and Aydin 2006; Savun 2008; Regan et al. 2009). What is more, when compared with arbitration and adjudication, these methods are much less costly (Regan et al. 2009).

Mediation can prove a useful means to resolve a dispute in the event that a decision of a binding method is found unacceptable to one or both parties. This was the case in the Beagle Channel dispute between Argentina and Chile. The contention dealt with sovereignty over three islands and the maritime boundary in the Beagle Channel. In 1977, an arbitration tribunal issued an award that was for the most part rejected by Argentina. Several years later, in 1984, Pope John Paul II mediated the dispute, trying to preserve neighborly relations between the two Catholic states (Collier and Lowe 2000). Similarly, there is a preference for nonbinding resolution in the border

[54] The disagreement was over five territories: the Hawar Islands, the island of Janan/Hadd Janan, the shoals of Qit'at Jaradah and Fasht ad Dibal, and Zubarah, a townsite on the northwest coast of Qatar. The dispute was eventually settled at the ICJ (Maritime Delimitation and Territorial Questions between Qatar and Bahrain, Qatar v. Bahrain, Judgment, ICJ Rep. 2001, 40, Judgment of March 16, 2001).

[55] Statement made in the context of the Bahrain v. Qatar dispute. Mideast Mirror 2000. Also cited in Powell (2020, 165).

[56] Author's interview (EJP) with Laurie Nathan, January 21, 2022.

[57] Ibid.

dispute between Sudan and Ethiopia owing to the tribal nature of the border region and historic ties between the states in the region. Mustafa Osman Ismail Elamin, former Minister of Foreign Affairs of Sudan, explains that "You cannot settle it by force, you cannot settle it using international law . . . because at the border there are tribal links. . . . I will tell you how it should be settled, how I think it should be settled: through the Intergovernmental Developmental Organization. Sudan is part of it and Sudan is one of the founders [with] Ethiopia, Eritrea, Somalia, Djibouti, Kenya, Uganda. . . . We will make a comprehensive settlement and this is the only way for us to settle the conflict in that region because it is interconnected."[58]

Arbitration and Adjudication

Via arbitration and adjudication, the two binding third-party mechanisms, disputes are settled according to international law. Decisions of arbitral panels and international courts are binding. In the process of adjudication, a dispute is submitted to a permanent adjudicative body, usually with a largely fixed composition. In arbitration, the disputants play an active role in selecting arbitrators.[59] As Merrills (2017, 88) writes, arbitration "requires the parties themselves to set up the machinery to handle a dispute, or series of disputes, between them." The development of arbitration as a method of dispute settlement preceded the development of adjudication. In many ways, arbitration spurred the emergence of permanent adjudicators. Arbitration— as offered via the framework of the Permanent Court of Arbitration (PCA)— was popular in the first thirty years of the twentieth century. With time, states have increasingly moved away from this PR method. In general states willing to use a binding method usually prefer adjudication over arbitration. Yet, in recent years the PCA specifically "has started to play an increasingly important role, so much that an element of 'institutionalisation' of arbitration has been detected by some writers" (Shaw 2017, 796).

While both arbitration and adjudication entail formal procedures, the rules of arbitration are more flexible than those of adjudication. As mentioned above, states have a high degree of flexibility in the composition

---

[58] Author's interview (EJP) with Mustafa Osman Ismail Elamin, former Minister of Foreign Affairs of Sudan, Oxford, UK, May 26, 2022.

[59] Merrills (2017, 88) writes, arbitration "requires the parties themselves to set up the machinery to handle a dispute, or series of disputes, between them."

of an arbitral tribunal. There can be a single arbitrator—usually a person highly qualified to issue a decision on the basis of international law. However, the most common form of an arbitral tribunal in modern state practice is a collegiate body consisting of either three or five arbitrators. Maritime and territorial disputes follow these general patterns. The three-member tribunal was used, for instance, in the Maritime Delimitation dispute between Guinea-Bissau and Senegal, as well as between Guinea and Guinea-Bissau.[60] A five-member tribunal issued a decision in the Eritrea-Yemen arbitration dealing with sovereignty over a group of islands in the Red Sea and the location of a maritime boundary.[61] Similarly, a five-member arbitral tribunal was asked to consider the contention between Egypt and Israel over Taba, a disputed Sinai desert beachfront.[62] One important characteristic of arbitration is that the disputants play a key role in laying out the arbitration procedure and framing the issues that the arbitrators are asked to consider.[63] Prior to the proceedings, the parties stipulate how the tribunal is to acquire evidence, and whether arbitrators can issue separate opinions. Moreover, the parties' ability to restrict the publication of the final award distinguishes arbitration from adjudication. Decisions of the main judicial organ of the UN—the ICJ—are always published.

Another respect in which arbitration and adjudication differ is the relative speed of proceedings. Unlike adjudication, which can last as long as five or ten years, arbitration proceedings may be conducted over a much shorter time. In fact, some arbitration cases have taken as little as two years to wrap up. The fast pace of arbitration matters especially in highly salient territorial or maritime disputes that involve military threats or hostilities. For instance, the key reason for the urgency in the Eritrea v. Ethiopia arbitration was the fact that from May 1998 to June 2000, the two states had fought a war over the disputed boundary, necessitating a peaceful resolution. It took only six months for arbitration to begin. In December 2000, a boundary commission

---

[60] Guinea-Bissau v. Senegal Maritime Delimitation Case, ICJ Rep. 1995, 423, Judgment of November 8, 1995; Guinea—Guinea-Bissau Maritime Delimitation Case (1985) 77 ILR 636, Arbitral Award of February 14, 1985.

[61] Sovereignty and Maritime Delimitation in the Red Sea, Eritrea v. Yemen, PCA, phase I (1998), phase II (1999), 2001, 40 ILM 900 and 983, Awards of October 9, 1998 and December 17, 1999.

[62] Dispute concerning Certain Boundary Pillars between the Arab Republic of Egypt and the State of Israel, 80 ILR 224, Arbitral Award of September 29, 1988.

[63] Interestingly, during the Eritrea-Yemen arbitration, the disputants could not come to an agreement with regard to which islands fell within the range of arbitration. Therefore, the disputants asked the arbitration tribunal to decide on this issue, taking into consideration the diverging opinions of the parties.

was created and charged with delimitation and demarcation of the border. The Eritrea-Ethiopia Boundary Commission's arbitral award came quickly—in April 2002, after merely sixteen months—and it ended not only the tensions that provoked the war, but also the territorial dispute.[64] The potentially extended duration of adjudication is frequently a key consideration for states. For instance, in 2008, Belizean government officials were skeptical of pursuing adjudication against Guatemala partly because of "the cost of an ICJ suit, the binding and final quality of an ICJ decision, and the amount of time a decision would take" (Willard 2009).

Despite the differences, arbitration and adjudication share many common features. Most importantly—and as stated above—both methods are largely based on precepts of international law. Speaking about arbitration, Collier and Lowe (2000, 33) write, "It is, in the broadest terms, an attempt to bring the Rule of Law into international relations and to replace the use of force with the routine litigation." The procedures involved in international adjudication and arbitration are relatively complicated. Both methods usually involve formal stepwise progression through different stages of proceedings. Comprehensive statutes and rules of procedure regulate the functioning of the various international courts and arbitration tribunals.[65] At times, arbitration tribunals are asked to use the ICJ's rules of procedure, as was the case in the maritime delimitation dispute between Guinea and Guinea-Bissau.[66]

Adjudication is the most legalized method of dispute resolution. Territorial and maritime disputes occasionally end up on dockets of the ICJ under the Court's contentious jurisdiction, or, if they have a maritime component, such as sovereignty over an island and related maritime boundaries, ITLOS. The ICJ adjudicates interstate disputes and issues advisory opinions on legal questions that may be referred to the Court by several authorized UN organs and specialized agencies.[67] The Court has jurisdiction only with respect to states that have expressly agreed to its jurisdiction. States may file declarations recognizing the ICJ's compulsory jurisdiction through

[64] The Decision on delimitation of the border between Eritrea and Ethiopia was delivered by the Commission on April 13, 2002.

[65] See, for instance, the Statute and Rules of the ICJ (ICJ website at www.icj-cij.org). Procedure in the PCA is meticulously regulated (see the PCA website at www.pca-cpa.org), and differs for proceedings in disputes between states and disputes where only one side is a state. ITLOS's rules and procedures are spelled out in great detail in its Statute, as well as its Rules of the Tribunal (see ITLOS website, www.itlos.org/).

[66] See Guinea—Guinea-Bissau Maritime Delimitation Case (1985) 77 ILR 636, Arbitral Award of February 14, 1985.

[67] ICJ website: http://www.icj-cij.org/homepage/index.php.

acceptance of the Optional Clause in Article 36(2) of the ICJ Statute for all or some legal disputes.[68] For states that file such declaration, the Court has compulsory jurisdiction only with respect to other states that have also filed such declaration. Thus, the designation "compulsory jurisdiction" is somewhat of a misnomer in the context of the ICJ. Alternatively, states can accept the ICJ's jurisdiction in bilateral and multilateral treaties. These compromissory jurisdiction clauses appear in international agreements pertaining to a variety of issue areas, such as the environment, maritime cooperation, fisheries, and organized crime.

The ICJ is composed of fifteen judges elected to nine-year terms of office by the UN General Assembly and the Security Council. To be elected, a candidate has to receive an absolute majority of the votes in both of these organs. It is important to note that the nomination and election processes are frequently politicized and subject to different influences at the national level (Mackenzie and Sands 2003). The composition of judges is supposed to reflect geographic representation and diverse legal traditions of the world.[69] A disputant that does not have a judge of its nationality on the bench presiding in a particular case may designate an ad hoc judge. Interestingly, an ad hoc judge does not have to be of the nationality of the designating state. The composition of the ICJ can, therefore, vary from one case to another. Nevertheless, once the Court has been constituted for a given phase of a case, that is, from the opening of the oral proceedings until the delivery of judgment, the Court's composition does not change. States frequently attempt to use the institution of an ad hoc judge to influence the outcome of the proceedings. However, ad hoc judges may vote against the claims of the appointing state.[70]

---

[68] Nearly all countries have customized their ICJ commitments via reservations in declarations under the Optional Clause in Article 36(2). These restrictions may pertain to specific states (*reservations ratione personae*), time periods (*ratione temporis*), and specific areas of international law (*ratione materiae*). For a detailed discussion of reservations, see Alexandrov 1995.

[69] Article 9 of the ICJ Statute states: "At every election, the electors shall bear in mind not only that the persons to be elected should individually possess the qualifications required, but also that in the body as a whole the representation of the main forms of civilization and of the principal legal systems of the world should be assured." Interviews conducted by Mackenzie et al. (2010, 35) indicate that "representation on the courts remains an important political concern for many states."

[70] The most recent example is in the ICJ decision in a nonterritorial dispute, Alleged Violations of the 1955 Treaty of Amity, Economic Relations, and Consular Rights, Islamic Republic of Iran v. United States of America, Summary of the Order of October 3, 2018 (https://www.icj-cij.org/en/case/175/summaries). The ICJ's unanimous decision obliged the United States not to hinder the flow of money between Iran and its trading partners for a list of products such as medical devices, agricultural commodities, and equipment necessary for the maintenance of Iran's civil aviation.

ITLOS and UNCLOS Annexes

It is important to point out that despite the significant overlap between territorial and maritime disputes, there are some legal aspects that differentiate the peaceful resolution in the two categories. States can pursue peaceful resolution in both types of contentions through all the PR methods discussed above, but there are additional means of dispute resolution available to states involved in maritime disputes. The UN Convention on the Law of the Sea (UNCLOS) provides a supplementary, highly institutionalized and comprehensive framework for these contentions.

One can argue that the introduction of UNCLOS has substantially increased consistency in the jurisprudence and methodology of international courts dealing with maritime disputes.[71] Prior to 1994, if states wanted to pursue a binding third-party method in the context of a maritime dispute or a dispute with a maritime component, these contentions were delegated either to the ICJ or to arbitration. Article 279 of UNCLOS stipulates that parties shall settle maritime disputes through peaceful means. Substantively, for the purpose of delimitation, the Convention embraces the principle of equidistance as a line between the nearest points of states' respective baselines. UNCLOS also promotes the equity principle by assessing whether the equidistance line is equitable (Anderson 2008). Arguably, states' hesitance to submit their maritime disputes to the ICJ can be partially explained by the relative lack of precision in defining some concepts and terms crucial to these contentions. For instance, according to former ITLOS president Judge Rüdiger Wolfrum, "a court deciding maritime boundaries is problematic because terms like 'equitable' are not clear. This is a shortcoming of legal adjudication, that it can take into account law only" (Wolfrum 2018c). UNCLOS—the main treaty regime for maritime law—promotes the use of ITLOS, a tribunal that is designed specifically to deal with maritime disputes. ITLOS is considered a specialized court with much technical knowledge and tailored jurisdiction for maritime issues and not territorial sovereignty.

Maritime disputes frequently follow unique patterns of peaceful settlement. According to Part XV, Article 279 of UNCLOS, states are obligated to use peaceful means to resolve their maritime disputes. Although ITLOS is the promoted settlement mechanism, states must first attempt negotiations or other peaceful means such as conciliation. Article 284 stipulates that

---

[71] United Nations Convention on the Law of the Sea, December 10, 1982, 1833 UNTS 397.

a disputing state can pursue conciliation by inviting the other disputant to submit to an Annex V conciliation or another conciliation procedure.[72] If either party fails to agree to the terms of conciliation, proceedings shall be terminated. Similar to conciliation in territorial disputes, conciliation in maritime disputes is designed to help the parties reach an amicable settlement. The first case of compulsory conciliation based on UNCLOS Annex V is the 2016 Timor Leste Conciliation with Australia.[73] In a May 2018 report, the commission settled the maritime boundary between the two states, affecting their exclusive economic zones (EEZ), continental shelves, and, therefore, access to oil and gas fields.

If nonbinding PR methods are not effective—"where no settlement has been reached" (Article 286)—Article 287 of UNCLOS lays out several further choices of legally binding procedures. Upon signature, ratification, or accession, states agree to one or several resolution forums in case a dispute dealing with interpretation or application of the Convention arises: ITLOS, ICJ, an Annex VII arbitration panel, or a special arbitral tribunal for nonmaritime boundary issues, Annex VIII. However, on the basis of Article 298, state parties can exempt themselves from the mandatory dispute settlement in cases dealing with delimitation of maritime boundaries of territorial sea, contiguous zone, the EEZ, and continental shelf; the interpretation of historic bays; disputes concerning military activities; and disputes that are on the agenda of the UN Security Council. The courts or tribunals have jurisdiction over all other maritime issues mentioned in UNCLOS. ITLOS is composed of twenty-one judges: legal experts with specialty in law of the sea. Geographical representation is supposed to be ensured, and each state party may nominate up to two judges to the Tribunal. Judges serve a term of nine years and may be re-elected. The Tribunal may form special chambers with three or four judges as deemed necessary in the context of certain cases. Both state parties must agree to the Tribunal jurisdiction, and the Tribunal's decisions are final and binding.

Annex VII arbitration can occur even if one of the disputants refuses to participate. This was the case, for instance, in the Philippines v. China case about the South China Sea. The Philippines brought its case to an Annex VII Tribunal, and though China refused to participate, the Tribunal was still able

---

[72] Annex V describes conciliation procedures, including functions of the commission, lists of conciliators, the method of constituting the commission, and other related issues.

[73] Maritime Boundary Between Timor-Leste and Australia (The Timor Sea Conciliation), PCA Case No. 2016-10, Arbitral Award of May 9, 2018.

to hear the merits of the case as long as it did not consider issues exempted by China.[74] Annex VII arbitration does not require that the members of the tribunal possess any specific legal qualification. In contrast, under Annex VIII arbitration, a list of experts is drawn up in several specific areas such as fisheries, navigation, and marine scientific research. At least four of the five members of a tribunal must be selected from this expert list.

As in territorial contentions, in the context of maritime disputes, states may attempt a variety of PR methods. For example, in the Bangladesh v. Myanmar dispute over maritime boundaries, Bangladesh initiated Annex VII arbitration proceedings, because Myanmar initially refused to participate in the case.[75] Yet, upon Myanmar's consent, the contention was delegated to ITLOS. A similar situation occurred with the Ghana v. Ivory Coast dispute over maritime boundaries.[76] The contention was initially delegated to Annex VII arbitration, but subsequently moved to a five-member Special Chamber of ITLOS.

Whether a maritime dispute goes to a more general adjudicator (the ICJ) or a more specialized judicial body (ITLOS), the parties choose a method that entails a detailed procedure as well as adherence to the rule of international law. The ICJ and ITLOS share several institutional design features. In the spirit of the civil legal tradition, both adjudicators embrace the doctrine of good faith, and formally reject the doctrine of precedent, *stare decisis*.[77] Additionally, both courts operate as highly formal institutions that regulate in detail the conduct of judges and the disputing parties. Shared commitment to these principles is evident in the courts' statutes and their jurisprudence. Despite these similarities, ITLOS's procedures have been designed to increase the Court's effectiveness, user-friendliness, and practicality (Merrills 2017, 200–201; Powell and Mitchell 2022). These features include the setting of a fixed date for the opening of oral proceedings, the ability of judges to exchange views concerning the conduct of the case and written pleadings,

---

[74] South China Sea Arbitration, Philippines v. China, PCA Case No. 2013-19, Arbitral Award of July 12, 2016.

[75] Dispute Concerning Delimitation of the Maritime Boundary between Bangladesh and Myanmar in the Bay of Bengal, Bangladesh v. Myanmar, Judgment, ITLOS Case No. 16, 52014XC0830(01), ICGJ 448 (ITLOS 2012), March 14, 2012, International Tribunal for the Law of the Sea [ITLOS].

[76] Case Concerning Delimitation of the Maritime Boundary Between Ghana and Côte d'Ivoire in the Atlantic Ocean, Ghana/Côte d'Ivoire, Case No. 23, Judgment of September 23, 2017.

[77] *Bona fides*, or good faith principle, has three constitutive moral elements: honesty, fairness, and reason (see Mitchell and Powell 2011). For the lack of official doctrine of the precedent, see Articles 33 and 124 of the Rules of UNCLOS, and Article 59 of the ICJ Statute. These provisions limit the court judgment's binding force to the disputants and to the case in question.

the Seabed Disputes Chamber, and the use of electronic means of communication.[78] These characteristics reflect the need for more flexibility in the resolution of maritime disputes. Though neither court is obliged to follow precedents in its jurisprudence, in practice, all international tribunals and courts frequently refer to each other's decisions.[79] Such dialogue between the various courts and tribunals solidifies the body of established international jurisprudence. As Shaw (2017, 850) notes, "increasing co-operation between the International Court and other judicial bodies is taking place and all the relevant courts and tribunals are well aware of each other's work."

Conculsions

All territorial and maritime disputes, though frequently highly politicized, constitute inherently legal disputes that deal with legal considerations. According to Hans Corell, "First of all, there has to be a legal regime everywhere. And when you come to a territory, the legal regime is the regime of the country/the state, which 'owns' this territory. If there are disputes, then there are competing regimes: the legal regime of one state versus the legal regime of another state. But there is an international rule that applies, of course, always."[80] As this chapter shows, international law offers states a plurality of methods for dispute settlement, with negotiations and adjudication constituting the polar opposites. The nonbinding third-party methods sit in between these two extremities. Each PR method offers disputants an alternate legal design of dispute resolution. Though, on average, as we move toward the legally binding methods, there is increased presence of law, legal argumentation, formality, and structure in the settlement process, each PR method is unique, and can adapt to the needs and wishes of the disputants. In other words, there is considerable flexibility in how each PR method is employed in practice, and how formal or legalistic the proceedings are. Though legally nonbinding, bilateral negotiations, especially those that took place in nineteenth-century Europe, were quite formal: admission to the talks was based on the formal status and authority criteria, and the end result was a legally binding agreement. Likewise, while some mediators may

---

[78] For more discussion, see Rao (2002, 217).
[79] For more discussion, see Mitchell and Powell 2011; and Powell 2020.
[80] Author's interview (EJP) with Hans Corell, January 13, 2021.

invoke international law and legal arguments, some may not. This practical variation may explain why certain instances of third-party settlement may be viewed as coached.[81] Despite the fluid formality of most PR methods, Merrills (2017, 17) portrays negotiations and adjudication as two very different approaches: "Negotiation is a process which allows the parties to retain the maximum amount of control over their dispute; adjudication, in contrast, takes the dispute entirely out of their hands, at least as regards the court's decision."

Peaceful resolution of territorial and maritime disputes is fundamental to international peace. These disputes are burdensome not only for the disputants involved in a particular contention and the region affected, but also for international security. International law offers states a variety of PR methods to effectively settle their grievances. These methods range from bilateral negotiations to adjudication. However, though all methods of peaceful settlement constitute separate legal regimes, it is important to recognize the intricate relationship between all of them. In the words of ICJ judge Bernardo Sepúlveda Amor (2013, 8), "more often than not, diplomatic negotiation and third-party adjudication are mutually supportive, and tend to reinforce and complement each other rather than prevail over or contradict one another in the attainment of their fundamental goal, namely the peaceful settlement of disputes. In international practice, diplomatic and judicial means are often inextricably intertwined, interacting in a variety of ways, as part of the dispute settlement." In practice, during a lifespan of a dispute, states may resort to a multiplicity of PR methods. What is more, states do not always start with bilateral negotiations and subsequently move forward to adjudication. Additionally, the same PR method can be attempted several times. What this chapter demonstrates is that though each method operates within a framework set out by international law, there is enough flexibility within each to offer states considerable maneuvering room to fulfill their preferences. To a certain extent, each PR method's scaffolding is relatively fluid, and as the following theoretical and empirical chapters make clear, states explore this fluidity in search of their preferred outcomes. In the process of strategizing, states carefully analyze legal structures and their own past experiences with

---

[81] In a way, and only to a certain extent, the degree of PR methods' formality depends on the actors involved in the settlement. It would be useful to develop a formality measure for each territorial/maritime dispute. Research on hard and soft law, legalization, credible commitments, and monitoring can provide good insights (Abbott and Snidal 1998, 2000; Vabulas and Snidal 2013, 2020).

each method. The goal is to "win" the dispute resolution attempt in light of a state's preferences, which can range from ensuring the opposing state's claim is ruled illegal to securing full sovereignty over a disputed piece of land or a maritime area. The dynamic of strategy in the context of peaceful resolution of territorial and maritime disputes is the main topic of our next chapter.

3

A Theory of Strategic Selection

Choice-of-Venue

What drives proposer states to seek different peaceful resolution (PR) methods? In the previous chapter, we described the different methods of dispute resolution that states can pursue: negotiations, inquiry, good offices, mediation, conciliation, arbitration, and adjudication.[1] Although a multiplicity of factors influence the timing and selection of a PR method (salience or value of territory, strength of legal claims, regime type, and domestic audience costs, among others), our theory of strategic selection, presented in this chapter, addresses how proposers—states that issue a call for a particular settlement venue—strategically select a PR method.[2] The objective of strategic selection is the reduction of uncertainty with the hopes of attaining the highest possible advantage over the opponent, and an overwhelming drive to win the territorial or maritime contention. Strategic selection is a nuanced and protracted process by which states are strategic in their choices to pursue certain PR methods, and the process of selecting and honing strategies as states move within the framework of a chosen method. Therefore, strategic selection is a carefully thought-out plan that is deemed best to maximize control over the contention and fulfill preferences of a disputant in the process of peaceful settlement. During the course of attempting the settlement, states make rational choices to seek the optimal resolution outcome.

All states seeking resolution want to choose the method and design the pathway toward settlement. To capture these dynamics, our theoretical

---

[1] For our definition of PR method and PR venue/forum, see Chapter 1.

[2] For the importance of territory's salience, see Gent and Shannon 2011; Hensel 2001; McDowell 2018; and Mitchell, Kadera, and Crescenzi 2009. For discussion of how strength of legal claims shapes the timing and selection of settlement forums see Hensel and Tures 1997; and Huth, Croco, and Appel 2013. The scholarship has extensively investigated the link between regime type, domestic audience costs, and states' preferences toward dispute settlement mechanisms (Allee and Huth 2006; Gent and Shannon 2011; Huth and Allee 2002; Huth, Croco, and Appel 2011; Mitchell 2002; Hensel and Mitchell 2005; Mitchell, Kadera, and Crescenzi 2009; Raymond 1994; Shannon 2009; Simmons 2002). Koremenos (2016) discusses why states include specific dispute resolution provisions in their agreements.

The Peaceful Resolution of Territorial and Maritime Disputes. Emilia Justyna Powell and Krista E. Wiegand,
Oxford University Press. © Oxford University Press 2023. DOI: 10.1093/oso/9780197675649.003.0003

framework focuses on two stages of strategic selection: the choice-of-venue strategic selection and the within-venue strategic selection (see Figure 3.1). This distinction is fundamental to our argument, because it recognizes that strategic considerations are paramount throughout the entire resolution process, from beginning to end.[3] Though there is no one unified, unchanging pattern according to which all disputes are settled, several specific mechanisms affect states' preferences at each stage. At the choice-of-venue stage, a proposer considers the disputants' past experience in peaceful resolution as well as the relationship between domestic and international law. Past experience in peaceful resolution refers specifically to the win-loss record in the various PR methods. We focus on the win-loss record of the disputants and that of other states in the same geographic region. The relationship between domestic and international law comprises three distinct factors: international law's position in the domestic legal system, the state's domestic commitment to rule of law, and the type of domestic legal tradition. At the within-venue stage—the focus of Chapter 4—the ability to frame the claim and shape the procedures provides disputants with more control over the process. These mechanisms help states reduce uncertainty of dispute resolution, increasing the likelihood of winning. Thus, proposer states engaged in territorial and maritime contentions strategically express their preferences throughout the duration of the settlement process, long after a PR method is chosen.

While recognizing that strategic back-and-forth dyadic interaction is at the core of peaceful dispute resolution, our theory and empirical analyses adapt a monadic level of analysis, and focus specifically on the proposer state's preferences/decision-making vis-à-vis PR methods. A proposer issues a resolution attempt and the nonproposer either rejects or accepts the resolution process. Usually one side prefers settling the dispute more than the other: "There are cases where both sides want binding settlement, but more often than not, it's one side and not the other because one party or the other is happier with the status quo."[4] If the nonproposer rejects the attempt, that state can then propose its own method, thus becoming itself a proposer. Precisely because we home in on the proposer's own preferences toward resolution, we treat these cases no differently from cases where a nonproposer agrees to the

---

[3] Though the scholarship recognizes that states' choices between PR methods are strategic, we contend that states reformulate their strategies repeatedly throughout the lifespan of the settlement process.

[4] Author's interview (EJP) with anonymous arbitration practitioner, February 7, 2022.

PR method. Thus, our conceptualization allows us to account for strategic selection as a dynamic process that moves forward with each side of the dispute putting forward subsequent settlement proposals. Importantly, we examine each state's preferences when they are acting as proposer states, and not the response of the other side. Our theory is anchored in qualitative examples of states' strategic behavior in contemporary and past territorial and maritime contentions. These real-world examples illustrate how concerns for strategy and control guide states' behavior throughout the entire duration of a dispute.

Winning the Dispute

One of the first questions that states ask themselves when determining which PR method to pursue is what is the probability of winning, or at least improving the status quo. However, the concept of winning can have different meanings to different disputants. Though objectively, a settlement may seem to yield a clear winner and a clear loser, it is the parties' perceptions of the outcome that matters.[5] Winning denotes gaining legally sanctioned control over disputed territory or maritime areas, securing some territorial or maritime concessions, or achieving other goals such as a ruling against the opponent's claims, punishing the adversary, or acquiring concessions on related issues.[6] States can shape how their own constituencies perceive the settlement outcome: "But then, you [the disputant] got the deal, you have to work out how you are going to sell this deal. You may want to obviously minimize the compromises and concessions, you want to proclaim this as a victory."[7] States "definitely care about winning. They care, I think, most about being able to say that they won and convince their own population that they won. Because somebody's head is going to roll, you know, if they didn't win and sometimes that might even be literal, but it's at least figurative, political heads. So, there's a lot on the line to winning. So, yes, states

---

[5] Empirically, it would be ideal to consider subjective perceptions of each state in the context of 166 territorial disputes considered in our quantitative analysis. As we discuss in Chapter 5, our quantitative analysis relies on a universal, or rather, objective, measure of winning that operationalizes the concepts of winning and losing in the most generalizable and parsimonious way.

[6] For example, Fravel (2008) shows that China was willing to agree to territorial concessions with several bordering states in negotiations in exchange for assistance from those neighboring states regarding internal security threats from minorities.

[7] Author's interview (EJP) with Laurie Nathan, international mediator, former Senior Advisor to the UN Mediation Support Unit, January 21, 2022.

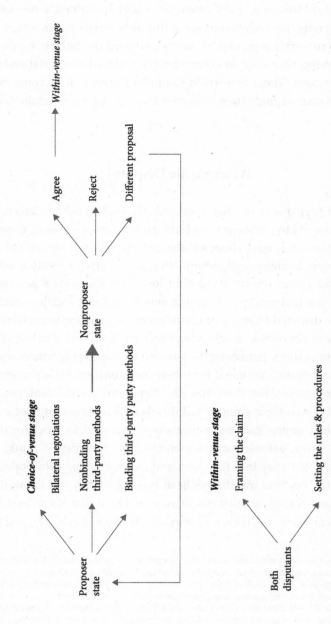

Figure 3.1. Decision tree for choice-of-venue and within-venue strategic selection.

care about winning."[8] There are also situations where the policymakers "have considered the range of possible outcomes and are entirely comfortable with any of them. Then you want to go through the process, you want to show that you've made a good effort in standing up for your position, particularly if it's in public. But, you're not actually trying to strategically get every bit of advantage that you can potentially get out of it."[9] Therefore, policymakers have to be careful in how they frame the settlement. Indeed, any proclamation of settlement as a one-sided victory can hurt the image of the other disputant. Thus, "a mediator would encourage you [the parties] to claim victory in a way that doesn't undermine your opponent. . . . This is a victory for you [the parties], collectively."[10]

At times, via settlement, states may simply want to score some diplomatic or political points.[11] It may also be the case that states seek dispute resolution for the sake of reaching a settlement and consider such an outcome a win. In all contentions, expectations of certain alternative results—beyond securing territorial or maritime concessions—play a powerful role in shaping both parties' perceptions of the settlement outcome. In fact, these party-specific perceptions determine compliance with the settlement decision, regardless of how the outcome is perceived by other actors. Thus, if a state considers dispute resolution for the sake of resolution itself as a win, the outcome constitutes in fact a win for that disputant.[12] For example, in the Philippines v. China arbitration case, one of the main objectives of the Philippines was for the Tribunal to rule that China's nine-dash line was illegal based on maritime law, and that therefore China could no longer justify its legal claims. The Philippines considered the outcome a win owing to this ruling, in addition to several other similar rulings included in the arbitral award.

Disputes among otherwise cordial states may experience unique patterns of resolution. One of our interlocutors noted: "Although not common, I think there are some situations where a government may not be sure if it

---

[8] Author's interview (EJP) with Coalter G. Lathrop, Sovereign Geographics, International Boundary Consultancy, March 14, 2022.

[9] Author's interview (EJP) with an anonymous arbitration practitioner, February 7, 2022.

[10] Author's interview (EJP) with Laurie Nathan, January 21, 2022.

[11] Negotiators are always looking over their shoulders to decipher the response of domestic audiences. We discuss the "domestic political cover" argument (Allee and Huth 2006; Huth and Allee 2002) in the context of alternative explanations in Chapter 5.

[12] Our objective is to explain states' strategies about how to successfully and positively achieve dispute resolution. Thus, disputant-specific perceptions constitute an important point in our coding decisions, as explained in Chapter 5. For instance, we code the 50-50 splits of territory as wins in an effort to directly capture each disputant's perceptions.

is going to win, in the sense of successfully securing the specific objective it publicly seeks, but nevertheless values resolving the dispute definitively, so that it can move on in its relationship with the other country."[13] Disputants with a long-standing good relationship are more likely to move forward with solutions that may objectively seem suboptimal: "With the friendly neighbor, there may well be an acceptance that 'we'll take a loss on this, but in the long term, the relationship is more important.' That willingness to compromise may well change completely for disputes with other, less-friendly countries."[14] According to Coalter G. Lathrop, "If two states go together with a special agreement there's an inherent understanding that, by resolving the dispute, in whatever way it gets resolved, that alone is a win. Under that scenario, the purpose of bringing this case together as brothers is to resolve the dispute, and then no matter how the thing turns out, you can go back and say 'we no longer have this centuries-long problem with our neighbor.'"[15] Friendly states will likely keep talking until they reach an amicable solution, especially if the disputed issue is not too damaging to the states' dyadic relations: "If you have two states that are basically on good terms with each other and get along, but have a particular point on which they disagree, but it's not jeopardizing the overall relationship as neighbors, I think in most cases they'll just keep talking."[16] Of course, "if at some point it [the dispute] gets to the point where they just need an answer, that might be one of those cases that you see get referred by agreement to binding dispute settlement."[17] Yet, as explained above, such moves are likely to be associated with the parties' increased willingness to accept win-win, nondichotomous solutions.

A good example of a dispute that ended in a neighborly compromise is a disagreement between Guinea and Sierra Leone over the location of the Makonnen riverbank. The bank formed a section of the boundary between the two states. The conflict escalated when Guinean soldiers occupied both sides of the bank: "And this local tension had gone on for quite a few years and the two negotiating teams were stuck and again it was the head-of-state-level meeting where it seemingly, in a matter of a few hours, the heads of state said 'look we need to end this, let's reach an agreement and move on.' . . . There was a sense [that] the formal negotiation process was failing and whether

[13] Author's interview (EJP) with Sean D. Murphy, professor of international law, George Washington University, January 28, 2022.
[14] Ibid.
[15] Author's (EJP) interview with Coalter G. Lathrop, March 14, 2022.
[16] Author's (EJP) interview with an arbitrator practitioner, February 7, 2022.
[17] Ibid.

or not the agreement of the two heads of state was ideal for both sides, it was more important to move on. They [the policymakers] understood that at the political level, but perhaps the lawyers and the surveyors who struggle with these things on a day-to-day basis lose sight of."[18] The Gulf of Maine dispute between Canada and the United States is also informative in this context.[19] The dispute concerned the Gulf of Maine—full of rich fishing grounds—which is located between the Canadian provinces of Nova Scotia and New Brunswick, and two US states, Maine and Massachusetts. The disputants engaged in a series of resolution efforts, mainly via negotiations, but finally resorted to the International Court of Justice (ICJ). The key motivation in the decision to adjudicate was to put the issue to rest in the most efficient manner. Both states felt that there was a risk that the conflict would escalate into a war over fishing rights, and wanted to avoid criticism from domestic constituencies (McDorman 2009). The Court's decision—a split of the contested area—was not perceived as optimal by either party. The United States was granted roughly two-thirds of the Gulf of Maine and three-fourths of Georges Bank, whereas Canada acquired the remaining parts: fishing areas on Georges Bank, also known as the Northeast Peak and the Northern Edge. Yet, the driving force for moving forward with compliance was to end the disagreement once and for all. Thus, in a way, though the United States' claims were not fully satisfied, because the country arguably lost a great deal of maritime areas, the United States could, at the same time, claim a win in the Gulf of Maine case.

The Canada-France dispute over fishing and oil exploration rights near two small islands in the Gulf of St. Lawrence, Saint-Pierre and Miquelon, provides another good example here. In 1989 both parties agreed to submit the dispute to an ad hoc arbitration panel, and two years later they reached an agreement with regard to specifics of arbitration. As McDorman (1990, 359) explains, Canada not only was worried about the French overfishing the area but also "had confidence of a favourable outcome."

The Tribunal was asked to "to draw a single line that would serve for all purposes, including rights to the floor of the continental shelf, fishing rights, and exclusive economic zone rights" (Blakeslee 1991, 361). According to the Tribunal's 1992 decision, France received a much smaller exclusive economic

---

[18] Author's (EJP) interview with Martin Pratt, Bordermap Consulting, January 27, 2022.
[19] Delimitation of the Maritime Boundary in the Gulf of Maine Area, Canada v. United States, ICJ Rep. 1984, 246 Judgment of October 12, 1984.

zone than the country claimed, thus providing access to less fish. In general, though arguably the ruling was mostly in favor of Canada, the boundary established in the ruling was "a compromise between the rights and interests of both parties" (de La Fayette 1993, 102). Though prior to the hearing, both sides accused each other of " 'imperialism' and 'ludicrous claims' of sovereignty," the dispute was dormant for many years after the ruling was issued.[20] As the above discussion highlights, winning is a convoluted concept. Wider geopolitical context as well as parties' perceptions contribute substantially to the way a dispute settlement outcome is framed. Of course, it is the legal counsel's role to realistically estimate their client's probability of winning, and thus shape the client's perceptions of what it means to secure victory in the context of a particular contention. According to Coalter G. Lathrop, "As a first step, a good Ministry of Foreign Affairs is going to ask for an expert opinion: 'Where is this likely to end up?' So that's a good starting point because inside their echo chamber everybody's—a phrase of an old mentor of mine—everybody's 'drunk on their own wine.' That is, they've convinced themselves that their position is a winner. . . . With an outside expert opinion, maybe they read it and throw it in the trash because they're outraged, or maybe they read it and they think about it."[21]

Uncertainty: The Underlying Reason for Strategic Selection

The primary goal of states involved in territorial and maritime disputes is to shape the outcome of the settlement process in whatever form it may occur— a negotiated settlement, conciliation, mediation, an arbitral award, or a judgment—in a manner that secures maximum concessions, while reducing uncertainty with the settlement process. We assume that states are rational actors whose preferences are to maximize their own subjectively perceived gains. States engage in both stages of strategic selection—choice-of-venue and within-venue strategic selection—because of uncertainty associated with peaceful settlement (Powell 2020; Powell and Wiegand 2014; Wiegand and Powell 2011a). Uncertainty is present in every PR method and each specific venue, such as the ICJ, a conciliation commission, an arbitration panel, and

---

[20] William Claiborne, "France and Canada Dispute Fishing Rights," *Washington Post*, August 4, 1991, accessed January 19, 2022.
[21] Author's interview (EJP) with Coalter G. Lathrop, March 14, 2022.

so on. If it were not, the losing party would never consent to any proposed PR method. In the words of one of our interlocutors, "[states] can't possibly be certain about the outcome in advance. Whether it's mediation, arbitration, or adjudication . . . , uncertainty comes with the territory."[22] In general, the level of uncertainty associated with interpretation of international law is much higher than with that of domestic law. Numerous factors, such as lack of information about the other state's resolve, uncertainty concerning the strength of legal claims, and lack of well-developed jurisprudence on an issue, complicate states' ability to forecast the outcome of a dispute resolution. To remedy the situation, proposer states engage in forum shopping with hopes of increasing control over the settlement process. By carefully thinking through the costs and benefits of each PR method and subsequently by selecting the most favorable method, states feel as though they can influence the progress of the settlement.

By definition, resolution of territorial and maritime disputes—both of which are legal in nature—involves interpretation of ownership rights and obligations and deciphering of convoluted sovereignty claims. In this context, it is important to briefly mention the differences between political and legal disputes, because, arguably, uncertainty is higher in legal disputes. The mere possibility of legal interpretation leads to loss of control over the outcome. Article 36(2) of the ICJ Statute stipulates that all disputes brought before the Court should be of a legal and not a political character. In its jurisprudence, the ICJ and its predecessor, the Permanent Court of International Justice (PCIJ), addressed the nature of a legal dispute, juxtaposing such a contention with one of a political nature. By way of illustration, the PCIJ in the Mavrommatis Palestine Concessions (Jurisdiction) case declared that a legal dispute should be understood as "a disagreement over a point of law or fact, a conflict of legal views or of interests before two persons."[23] Naturally, most legal disputes are entangled with disagreements of a political nature and politics often determines how each disputant proceeds with a legal dispute (Scott 2014).

In contrast to bilateral negotiations, if the disputants' preferences converge on an external intermediary, generally speaking, uncertainty is high.

---

[22] Author's interview (EJP) with Laurie Nathan, January 21, 2022.

[23] PCIJ, Series A, No. 2, 1924, 11. In its jurisprudence, the ICJ has also established that for a disagreement to constitute a legal dispute, "it is sufficient for the respondent to an application before the Court merely to deny the allegations made even if the jurisdiction of the Court is challenged" (Shaw 2017, 811).

While negotiations entail exchange of views between only the parties, additional concerns come into play with the involvement of an intermediary (Bilder 1981; Kohen 2013). In the context of arbitration and adjudication, the ambiguity of international norms becomes a serious challenge to both disputants and their legal counsel. In both these methods, the settlement necessarily involves the interpretation of international law, which creates a degree of uncertainty and impedes the parties' ability to control the settlement process. While the nonbinding third-party methods leave considerable control to the parties, arbitration and adjudication entail channeling the contention into a formal, detached arbitral or judicial apparatus.[24] Indeed, even in situations where applicable legal norms and facts may appear sufficiently clear, it is up to the arbitral panel or the court to choose between different legal justifications favoring one over the other.[25]

When choosing between alternative "legal regimes," any settlement venue will hark back to what it "understands as its mission, its structural bias" (Koskenniemi 2007, 6). Additionally, to a significant extent, every contention and every dyadic relationship is unique. Territorial and maritime disputes deal with idiosyncratic issues pertaining to the delimitation of land or maritime areas, and in the case of islands, both of these issues. As a result, the disputants may find it challenging to form general expectations about the applicable all-encompassing legal regime. Lauterpacht (2011), a renowned scholar and practitioner of international law, actually recommended avoidance of international adjudication if possible. Arbitration—though a more flexible method than adjudication—is still associated with high levels of uncertainty for the disputants. Resorting to a third-party binding method necessitates that the disputants give up some control. Judicial independence necessitates an apolitical and unbiased application of legal norms to a particular contention. To states, this reality generates unforeseen risks. Thus, states try to manipulate as many aspects of the proceedings as they can. As Chapter 4 explains, in the context of within-venue strategic selection, if the parties are satisfied with the way their settlement proceeds—that is, if the parties are able to put forth claims in a desired form—they are more likely to trust the arbitral tribunal or the court. The parties' success in influencing

---

[24] For more information, see Chinkin and Sadurska 1991. As we note in Chapter 2, arbitration allows the parties to keep partial control over the contention (selection of arbitrators, choice of procedure, etc.).

[25] As Mondre (2015, 42) writes, a ruling can be "predictable to the extent that procedural rules and the body of law are known to the disputing parties in advance."

the composition of a judicial bench or a tribunal has immense repercussions. Sustained levels of trust in the intermediary are crucial for the parties' continued consent to the process of settlement.

In some circumstances—in particular when the disagreement centers on issues of law—parties may perceive arbitration or adjudication as optimal PR methods. Thus, "how legally complex the issue is, how specialized it is" matters in determining the suitability of the binding methods.[26] To avoid an unfavorable outcome in a binding venue, within-venue strategic selection allows the disputants to regain a fraction of control over the procedural and substantive aspects of the settlement process.

In maritime disputes and territorial disputes involving maritime rights— for instance, sovereignty over islands—states can use International Tribunal for the Law of the Sea (ITLOS), which favors equitable solutions that provide disputants with more confidence about potential outcomes, thereby reducing uncertainty. By way of illustration, because of the equitable solution norm, in their dispute over the maritime boundary in the Bay of Bengal, Bangladesh and Myanmar turned to ITLOS despite the uncertainty associated with international adjudication: "since any ruling was likely to leave the country with some of the area believed to hold gas deposits, both were able to accept the risk of submitting to a neutral arbiter" (Watson 2015). Therefore, in comparison with territorial disputes, states seeking to settle maritime boundaries face less uncertainty with regard to the outcome. As Anderson (2008, 6) writes, "Together all these consistent decisions have tended to complement the guiding principle of the 'equitable solution' in the Convention." Yet, though it might seem most logical for maritime contentions to end up at ITLOS, many states, including Indonesia, Malaysia, Singapore, Colombia, and Nicaragua, have used the ICJ to determine the status of maritime rights and boundaries. This suggests that states take multiple factors into account when selecting a PR method to reduce uncertainty.

States face uncertainty with nonbinding methods as well, though to a lesser degree. Chinkin and Sadurska (1991, 543) note that the nonbinding third-party methods "are fluid processes which depend upon tasks entrusted to the third-party, that third-party's implementation of them and the disputants' willingness to accept that implementation. These processes can be adapted to the needs of the particular participants in the context of the specific dispute." While the disputants may reject decisions or suggestions of a nonbinding

---

[26] Author's interview (EJP) with Laurie Nathan, January 21, 2022.

forum, the resolution process itself still entails some uncertainty. Among the nonbinding third-party methods, good offices—as a means of influencing the disputants to start negotiations—entail the least amount of uncertainty. Indeed, providing the parties with concrete settlement terms is not the duty of a good officer. In contrast, mediation, conciliation, and inquiry may cause the opposing sides to feel uncertain about the anticipated solutions as well as the entire resolution process. Mediation and conciliation, in particular, rely on active participation of the intermediary. Furthermore, in many instances the settlement terms may be heavily influenced by the intermediary's own proposals, and not so much by the preferences of the parties. However, since a conciliator's responsibilities are more formalized and institutionalized than those of a mediator, conciliation probably gives rise to higher levels of uncertainty. In the words of one of our interlocutors, "Approaches to dispute resolution that lie between negotiation and binding dispute settlement— conciliation in particular, but maybe even mediation—presents greater uncertainty, because the State doesn't know quite where it's going and where it will get to, and the outcome doesn't necessarily resolve the dispute."[27] Inquiry, as a method employed in instances when the disputed issue deals with facts rather than law or policy, also entails uncertainty. As Merrills (2017, 61) writes, the disputants must account for the possibility that "their version of events may be shown to be wrong."

Managing levels of uncertainty is the main driver behind strategy: choice-of-venue and within-venue strategic selection. By reducing uneasiness and uncertainty associated with the resolution process, strategizing about the settlement and their own legal claims, each disputant hopes for the optimal settlement outcome: solidifying territorial or maritime control, or at least gaining the highest amount of concessions. This reality provides a fertile environment for both types of strategic selection. Below, we discuss choice-of-venue strategic selection and the mechanisms that influence proposer states' selection of PR methods. The next chapter focuses on within-venue strategic selection and the mechanisms that shape proposer states' behavior while operating in the context of a chosen PR venue.

[27] Author's interview (EJP) with Sean D. Murphy, January 28, 2022.

Choice-of-Venue Strategic Selection

States involved in territorial and maritime disputes select PR methods via strategic choices. When borders, territory, or islands are at stake, both disputants cannot simultaneously gain sovereignty over the contested areas. The proposer is aware that strategy is key in securing a victory. The choice-of-venue strategic selection is partially analogous to litigants' behavior in domestic jurisdictions. When allowed, individuals choose settlement methods—courts or alternative dispute resolution (ADR) forums—to maximize their chances of securing the most favorable outcome. This process is known as forum shopping. In the domestic realm, forum shopping has been defined as a litigant's attempt "to have his action tried in a particular court or jurisdiction where he feels he will receive the most favorable judgment or verdict" (Black, Nolan, and Connolly 2009).[28]

Forum shopping is at the core of choice-of-venue strategic selection. Proposer states' strategic quest for the best PR method and the best venue— the gist of international forum shopping—is idiosyncratic since decisions to use binding, nonbinding, or bilateral resolution entail broad choices between types of conflict management techniques. In an important way, such choices differ from selection between judges or jurisdictions, which characterizes forum shopping in the domestic context.[29] In many aspects, forum shopping in domestic jurisdictions relies on a substantially different mechanism from that of forum shopping entertained by states on the international level.[30] Wiegand and Powell (2011a, 51) show that "States return to the same PR methods, but not necessarily to the same third parties after previous victories." For instance, if a proposer state has had a positive experience with

---

[28] Also see Koskenniemi and Leino 2002; Shany 2003; Sykes 2008; Whytock 2011.

[29] In some domestic jurisdictions, transnational litigation constitutes an important part of forum shopping (Whytock 2011). While domestic forum shopping entails choices between courts within one state's domestic legal system, transnational forum shopping necessitates choices between adjudicators within domestic legal systems of multiple states (Sykes 2008). See Chapter 4 for an in-depth discussion of the selection of actors in the context of within-venue strategic selection.

[30] The factor of institutional design itself is nothing new in legal studies in particular. Studies on forum shopping recognize that states will compare venues according to rules, procedures, known biases or reputations of judges, the projected duration of proceedings, and other similar institutional design factors (Ferrari 2002, 689–90; Juenger 1989, 573; Sykes 2008, 342; Weintraub 2002, 463).

mediation in the past, it is more likely to revert to mediation in the future, even though a different international organization or a different individual may be asked to perform the duties of a mediator. It is the overall favorable experience with the normative framework of a particular PR method that encourages states to entertain this type of resolution.[31]

The reason why plaintiffs—whether individuals on the domestic level or states on the international level—engage in forum shopping is to win the dispute. In both types of forum shopping, a disputant attempts to identify the forum that maximizes anticipated gains. Naturally, the freedom of forum selection—and thus, forum shopping—is far greater in the international realm. Indeed, proposers have full freedom to select a PR method and a specific venue, while nonproposers have a choice to consent to or reject the PR method selected by the proposer. Under international law, states have no obligation to resolve their differences, and this rule "applies in the case of serious legal conflicts as well as peripheral political disagreements" (Shaw 2017, 765). In short, all methods of dispute settlement can be used only when states in question give consent.[32] The ICJ has on several occasions elaborated on the meaning of the term "consent." In the Tunisia v. Libya Case, for instance, the Court declared that "the consent of state parties to a dispute, is the basis of the Court's jurisdiction in contentious cases" and that this rule constitutes "a fundamental principle."[33] The Court also spoke about consent in the context of the doctrine of *forum prorogatum*. This doctrine stipulates that if a state has not recognized the Court's jurisdiction before the initiation of proceedings, such state may subsequently do so.[34] To ensure that there is no undue expansion of the term "consent," the Court has clarified that such consent must be "voluntary and indisputable."[35] The fact that the ICJ may only exercise its adjudicative prerogatives upon receiving a state's consent also implies that the Court may not decide on rights and obligations of nondisputing states.

---

[31] As Mondre (2015, 19) points out, the "lesson learned from legal scholarship on forum shopping is to pay close attention to the procedural nuts and bolts of specific dispute resolution methods."

[32] For a discussion of the consensual nature of third-party settlement of international disputes, see Crawford 2012.

[33] Application for Revision and Interpretation of the Judgment of February 24, 1982, in the Case concerning the Continental Shelf, Tunisia/Libyan Arab Jamahiriya, Tunisia v. Libyan Arab Jamahiriya, December 10, 1985.

[34] Basis of the Court's Jurisdiction, available at https://www.icj-cij.org/en.

[35] Corfu Channel, United Kingdom of Great Britain and Northern Ireland v. Albania, Preliminary Objection, ICJ Rep. 1948, 27.

In practice, consent to participate in a PR method must continue throughout the resolution process. Bringing this statement to the monadic level of analysis, at each stage of the resolution process, the proposer updates and adjusts its preferences, and consequently issues specific resolution proposals. Then, the nonproposer has an option to reject these proposals, accept them, or propose a different resolution venue.[36] For instance, while certain features of arbitration—parties' ability to shape the procedure and select arbitrators—may encourage the initial consent to arbitration proceedings, it may prove difficult for the parties to uphold their commitment throughout the settlement process. On the monadic level, an initial consent may be transformed into a rejection. As Smit Duijzentkunst and Dawkins (2015, 140) write, "without the consent of parties, the proceedings are doomed. The challenge is that consent is dynamic; once granted, consent can wax and wane, it can be delivered under duress and it can be withdrawn as fast as it is given."

Though to a degree, international PR methods resemble their domestic equivalents, the former are unique and perform different functions, tailored to the realities of interstate interactions. These differences can be partially traced to the lack of unified government in the international sphere, and the availability of many PR methods and specific venues with overlapping jurisdictions. Moreover, while compliance with judgments of domestic courts is usually ensured by a strict enforcement system, the same is not true in the international realm. Though the mere existence of international third-party binding methods—arbitration and adjudication—has preventive effects with regard to conflict, there is no international police force to force states into compliance with third-party decisions.[37] As the main judicial organ of the UN, the ICJ does not have an obligation to ensure that states fully embrace the Court's judgments. The ICJ has directly reaffirmed its lack of competence in this regard by stating that "once the Court has found that a state has entered into a commitment concerning its future conduct it is not the Court's function to contemplate that it will not comply with it."[38]

---

[36] As we explain in Chapter 1, the last option indicates that a nonproposer becomes a proposer.
[37] See Shaw (2017, 794 and 840).
[38] The Nuclear Tests case, Australia v. France, ICJ Rep., 1974, 477, December 20, 1974.

The lack of a unified and all-embracing hierarchy of international PR methods and the requirement of state consent for deployment of any method provide a fertile environment for unfettered forum shopping (Koch 2003; Maloy 2005; Mondre 2015; Petrossian 2007; Petsche 2011). Expectations with regard to the other state's preferences can largely be inferred from that state's past behavior (Lake and Powell 1999). In essence, the intricate inter-action between monadic-level strategies of both disputants is a function of mutually accessible information about previous conduct. Empirically speaking, in territorial and maritime disputes, these mutually constitutive, step-by-step dynamics are best captured by focusing on the proposer's own preferences toward PR methods throughout the lifespan of a dispute. Of course, the proposer's preferences and thus, subsequent proposals of reso-lution are influenced by the nonproposer's experiences and characteristics as well.[39]

There is much debate about whether forum shopping on the international level is ethical, given that any rule-of-law system should eliminate concerns about uncertainty (Mondre 2015, 18). Arguably, in a rule-of-law system—domestic or international—decisions made by any resolution forum in the context of a specific dispute should be substantively similar, regardless of forum type. In other words, the gist of any settlement decision should not be different if the decision emerged as the result of arbitration proceedings (an award), adjudication (judgment), or even nonbinding PR methods. Otherwise, a normative system may become, to some extent, disjointed.[40] However, as practice shows, states' choice of PR venues not only influences states' levels of uncertainty, but can also influence the outcome. Put differ-ently, mediation, arbitration, and adjudication frequently yield partially—and at times substantially—distinct results. The outcome: who wins, who loses, and the specifics of territorial or maritime delimitation may be shaped as much by the choice of PR method or specific forum as by the merits of each side's arguments.[41] Scholars frequently refer to this reality as the main reason

[39] See Chapter 5 about how we capture this reality empirically.

[40] For discussion of fragmentation of international law, see Koskenniemi and Leino 2002; and Koskenniemi 2007. For discussion of how procedural concerns of particular domestic jurisdictions shape international forum shopping, see Petsche 2011.

[41] Mondre (2015, 18) notes that technicalities of a venue's institutional design "can be decisive in winning a case. It is the same perspective that defends forum shopping as a good legal practice—after all, lawyers are supposed to maximize their clients' chances of success." See also Huth, Croco, and Appel (2011) for arguments about legal strength of claims.

why forum shopping on the international level is harmful to the global order (Petrossian 2007). As Spelliscy (2001, 156) notes, "Such diversity may be seen as contributing to the disintegration of international law because each organ is committed to applying its own views and resolving disputes within its own formally isolated system, thereby thwarting the tendency towards homogeneity and increasing the uncertainty of the standards of behavior to which states are supposed to conform." Simply put, the scholarly consensus is that any international dispute should be resolved according to its substantive content and the merits of each party's claims, and not hinge on the specific institutional features of a particular PR forum. For the sake of consistency and cohesiveness of international law, this argument proposes that it is best if a venue's institutional design does not influence the dispute outcome.

States forum shop with much care. The monadic-level decision to forum shop emerges as the result of strategically weighing all PR methods, considering all the material as well as nonmaterial, image-shaping repercussions. For instance, proposing adjudication must be done very carefully, as such an act is usually perceived by the opponent as a hostile step. As Crawford (2012, 732) notes, "hauling another state before the Court is often regarded as unfriendly." Thus, by pursuing a specific method, proposers explicitly express their preference for a particular technique—a set of rules and procedures—that is applied to decipher the particulars of a contention.

The selection between broad categories of PR methods is guided by certain mechanisms that affect the proposer's decisions. The mechanisms of choice-of-venue strategic selection include (1) past experience in peaceful resolutions and (2) the relationship between domestic and international law. There has been a good amount of research done on institutional design of international dispute resolution forums and how this institutional design—a relatively static feature—shapes states' decisions. However, institutional design by itself cannot account for all the variation in states' choices of different venues during the duration of a dispute. Owing to the uncertainty inherent to dispute resolution, each proposer indeed analyzes and re-analyzes structure and procedure of all available forums before making any move. Such analysis allows the proposer to gather and update information about the resolution process. We assume that states' policymakers and legal counsel strive to obtain the best outcome in the dispute: gaining as much of the concessions as possible.

Past Experience in Peaceful Resolution

> Surely, you are not going to waste time and money by going to the
> Court if you don't want to or expect to win.
> —Anonymous ICJ state advocate and international arbitrator[42]

Win-Loss Record

Past experience with dispute resolution—the record of past losses and
wins—influences the proposer's choices of PR methods, and thus as a mechanism plays a key role in choice-of-venue strategic selection. States use
their own as well as other states' past experiences with the various venues
to gather information about particular PR methods they are considering in
an ongoing dispute. In this section, we discuss how proposers (states that
issue a call for a particular settlement venue) consider their own and the nonproposer's past experiences in winning and losing past territorial and maritime disputes. As we discuss in detail in Chapter 5, we use a batting average
of past wins and losses from 1945 to the year before the dispute resolution
attempt to examine the effect of past experience on PR method selection.
We also examine how proposer states take into consideration past experience of other states, especially states within the same geographic region. As a
mechanism of choice-of-venue strategic selection, a proposer's own win-loss
record affects its behavior in a straightforward manner. We argue that states'
a priori experiences with different PR methods determine their a posteriori
perceptions of these methods. Winning encourages repeated use of a method
in subsequent disputes. Losing dampens a state's interest in a method.[43] In the
words of one of our interlocutors, "success begets success and failure begets
failure. So, negative response generates negativity."[44] For example, Malaysia's
experience in its case against Indonesia over Pulau Ligitan and Pulau Sipadan
influenced its subsequent case with Singapore. Malaysian officials noted that
the Pedra Branca issue "has taught us a lesson on territorial claims."[45]

---

[42] Author's interview (EJP), United Kingdom, October 2013.

[43] States that have avoided using the ICJ, for example, often cite a fear of losing a case as the reason
for not using the Court (Mondre 2015, 42; Romano 2002, 551). In the context of third-party methods,
Simmons (1999, 7) argues that "prior [positive] experience with quasi-judicial procedures can often
lead to their repeated use in settling border disputes."

[44] Author's interview (EJP) with Laurie Nathan, January 21, 2022.

[45] Ibrahim Zuraidah, "Pedra Branca Ruling a Good Start But . . . : The Historical Baggage between
the Two Countries Will Require More Than Brief Spurts of Discipline to Unload," *The Strait Times*,

In the context of bargaining strategies, decision makers understand unsuccessful outcomes—such as losses in international PR venues—as policy failures (Jervis 1976; Mansbach and Vasquez 1981). These unsuccessful results can have dire domestic consequences. As a result, decision makers react by switching to an alternative bargaining strategy. Similarly, a successful past bargaining outcome—such as a win in a PR method—is likely to reassure the policymakers in their venue choices. As a consequence, this effective bargaining strategy is probably going to be used again in subsequent disputes. For example, if an arbitral award is favorable to a particular disputant, this disputant is more likely to use arbitration in its ensuing disputes. This holds for future disputes over different issues, other territories or maritime areas, and disputes with other opponents. Thus, it should not be surprising that in the context of third-party methods, "prior [positive] experience with quasi-judicial procedures can often lead to their repeated use in settling border disputes" (Simmons 1999, 7).

As rational actors, proposer states must anticipate responses of nonproposers. Therefore, of great interest to each proposer state is the win-loss record of the nonproposer state. The strategy of juxtaposing their own win-loss record with that of an opponent provides proposer states with clues about the optimal way to attempt settlement. For example, the agents who represented the United States in the Gulf of Maine case explained that they had to examine Canada's record in international disputes when preparing for their case: "Having watched Canadian efforts in various forums, we knew on the U.S. side that we faced a formidable opponent that would spare nothing in the preparation and presentation of its case" (Robinson, Colson, and Rashkow 1985, 586). For a proposer, the best possible forum would be a method that has not only previously yielded a good win-loss record for them, but has also not proved to be too favorable to the nonproposer state.[46]

Previous scholarship has examined how the nature of a dyad's past relationship influences the dyad's future interactions.[47] In some studies, a history of failed attempts at peaceful settlement as well as a history of recent

May 25, 2008, https://www.asiaone.com/News/The%2BStraits%2BTimes/Story/A1Story20080525-66883.html.

[46] The nonproposer state, analogous to the defendant in a domestic legal system, may respond to the proposer state's PR attempt by accepting the proposal, requesting a different method, or rejecting the settlement attempt overall. There are numerous ways through which a nonproposer state can defy the proposer's choice of a PR method. The nonproposer may simply refuse to participate in bilateral negotiations, question the challenger's choice of a third-party, or challenge the jurisdiction of an international adjudicative body.

[47] For extended discussion of this topic, see Powell and Wiegand 2021.

militarized conflict over the same issue have been shown to increase pressure to undertake further action to resolve the particular territorial contention. The disputants become more open to binding PR methods once negotiations do not deliver a result satisfactory to both sides. Hensel (1999) finds that a history of failed settlement attempts in a particular dispute increases the probability of subsequent third-party assistance, while a history of successful settlement attempts increases the probability of bilateral negotiations. Similarly, several studies confirm that third-party methods such as mediation or arbitration are more likely to be employed by adversaries with a history of failed agreements (Hensel 2001; Hensel et al. 2008; Lefler 2015; McDowell 2018). Yet, Allee and Huth (2006) and Hensel (2001) find that past failed negotiations do not have a systematic impact on the choice to turn to legal PR methods. Likewise, Gent and Shannon (2011) show that the likelihood of states pursuing binding methods actually decreases as the number of failed settlement attempts increases.

Though informative, the above-mentioned studies focus only on past experience with peaceful settlement in a particular dispute. Past experience with different methods in other or prior territorial or maritime disputes has not been examined. Building on our own previous work, we argue that proposer states learn from all of their past interactions with each PR method (Powell and Wiegand 2014; Wiegand and Powell 2011a) and from the past experiences of nonproposers and other states in their region. Thus, outcomes of resolution attempts in other territorial contentions play a vital role in states' subsequent choices of settlement methods. This is particularly true with regard to the legally binding methods, arbitration and adjudication, but can also be the case with nonbinding third-party methods. For instance, research on mediation shows that "the previous experiences with mediation that may directly affect the expectations of both the parties and the mediators of how a current mediation should be carried out or how effective it will be" are quite important (Bercovitch and Houston 2000, 172).

Mediation, conciliation, and other nonbinding third-party methods frequently soften the winner/loser dichotomy: "Instead of declaring conflicts to be completely intractable they are [to] be dealt with in procedures that do not end in a binding decision likely to establish a winner/loser result but to make use of the conciliation procedure" (Wolfrum 2018d, 174). One way to avoid the winner/loser outcome is by using feedback from previous mediation efforts, including "information, experience, learning and understanding gained by the mediator and the parties," all of which can be used by mediators to "gain control of potentially volatile situations" and help resolve a dispute (Bercovitch and Houston 2000, 183). Nonbinding methods establish an active dialogue between the disputants and the intermediary, and the "mediator's job is to broker an agreement that both of you [states] can live with."[48]

An intermediary's proposal can be rejected if deemed unacceptable by the parties. More often than not, both sides are content with at least part of the proposed terms of settlement. However, despite their consensus-based nature, nonbinding third-party methods may still foster positive or negative perceptions when the interests of one side are favored. The frontier dispute between France and Siam (now Thailand) that intensified after World War II provides a good illustration. Siam argued that its border with Indo-China, a French colonial territory, should be changed because of economic, ethnic, and geographic considerations. France, of course, disagreed with Siam's claims. The disputants agreed to resort to conciliation. After lengthy deliberations, in its report, the Franco-Siamese Conciliation Commission suggested minor adjustments of the border. The final decision of the Commission was supportive of the French position, as "the Commission's Report was effectively a rejection of the Siamese claim" (Merrills 2017, 66).

Winning or losing in an international court or an arbitral tribunal has stronger effects on a state's behavior in its subsequent contentions. Importantly, it is a state's perception of the outcome that matters. For instance, at times, the object of the settlement—specifically in the case of nonbinding methods, such as negotiations or mediation—is not always about the concessions. Rather it may be, simply, about reaching a settlement. Either way, more often than not, winners and losers in prior contentions delegated to binding PR methods can usually be easily identified. In all ICJ, PCIJ, and ITLOS cases, parties' initial claims can be juxtaposed against the court's judgment. Naturally, there are cases where both sides are awarded relatively equal territorial concessions. In such instances, it can be argued that a settlement outcome constitutes a form of compromise, or a collective win.[49] In other cases, though each party gains some concessions, both may be discontent. However, generally, the outcome of a legal dispute resolution will leave one party dissatisfied; there is a "winner-loser situation," which is "not helpful for future relations" (Wolfrum 2018a).

Some international intermediaries strive to avoid clear-cut "winner takes all" decisions by embracing consent-based mechanisms of recommendations

[48] Author's interview (EJP) with Laurie Nathan, January 21, 2022.
[49] We discuss such situations and how they affect our coding decisions in Chapter 5.

in place of formal judgments or awards.[50] Yet, states frequently persist in holding on to the winner/loser dichotomy (Alvarez 2005). In maritime disputes or territorial disputes with a maritime component, states can turn to ITLOS, which generally seeks an equitable solution for the disputing parties, instead of a zero-sum outcome, as we discussed earlier. The statute of ITLOS reads that "In the Tribunal . . . equitable geographical distribution shall be assured," but litigation is adversarial by nature, and decisions may still be interpreted quite frequently as producing winners and losers (Roach 2018).[51]

In the context of two ICJ cases, the *Diplomatic Staff in Teheran* and the *Nicaragua* cases, Merrills (2005, 176) argues that winning constituted an important part of the postadjudicative scene as "a state which takes its case to the Court and wins, gains vindication for its position from an authoritative and disinterested source."[52] Often, in such situations, the third party is likely to be criticized by the losing side for acting in a coercive manner instead of simply resolving the dispute (Shapiro 1981, 19). US relations with the ICJ constitute a vivid illustration of this mechanism. As one of the supporters of the creation of the ICJ, the United States accepted the Court's compulsory jurisdiction in 1946. Threatened by the prospect of a disadvantageous decision in the *Nicaragua* case, in 1985 the United States withdrew its declaration of compulsory jurisdiction to the ICJ, stating that "our experience with compulsory jurisdiction has been deeply disappointing" (US Department of State Bulletin 1985). Similarly, after Chile lost its maritime dispute case to Peru at the ICJ in 2014, and expecting a similar maritime claim from Bolivia, the Chilean Foreign Minister considered withdrawing Chile from the Pact of Bogota in order to avoid jurisdiction of the ICJ in future cases.[53]

More than other disputes, the settlement of territorial contentions usually entails creating sharp winner/loser perceptions. Compromise is quite onerous to fashion or may be beyond the bounds of possibility. Even when both disputants gain some amount of territory as a result of settlement, one side's preferences are typically satisfied to a greater degree than the other's. Cases such as Libya v. Chad, Botswana v. Namibia, and Indonesia v. Malaysia

---

[50] By way of illustration, several human rights bodies composed of politicians and experts issue "views" in place of binding judgments (Alvarez 2005, 530).

[51] ITLOS Statute, Article 2.

[52] United States Diplomatic and Consular Staff in Tehran, United States of America v. Iran, Order, 12 V 81, ICJ Rep. 1981, 45, Judgment of May 12, 1981; Case Concerning Military and Paramilitary Activities in and Against Nicaragua, Nicaragua v. United States of America, ICJ Rep. 1986, 14, Judgment of June 27, 1986.

[53] "Heraldo Muñoz se abre a debatir retiro de Chile de Pacto de Bogotá: 'Es una discusión legítima,'" *La Segunda*, January 28, 2014, https://perma.cc/2UG3-XAVM. See Gates (2017) for more discussion about domestic backlash resulting from losing maritime dispute cases.

that ended up at the ICJ "entailed relatively simple interpretation of treaties, resulting in a complete victory for one side" (Ratner 2006, 816).[54] Looking at general patterns in our data described in Chapter 5, of all the territorial disputes settled between 1945 and 2015, 41 percent have involved some division of territory, while the remaining 59 percent involved the challenger or target receiving all or most of the disputed territory. Brilmayer and Faure (2014, 195) note, "The world has only a fixed amount of territory, unlike most other assets. Territorial disputes can be perceived as zero-sum in a very fundamental way: what one state wins comes necessarily from what another state loses. And once lost, territory will most likely not be replaceable. Ordinarily, states would not be expected to trade their territorial claims for advantages of other sorts." This is particularly the case when territory is perceived to have intangible salience such as ethnic ties to territory (Hensel and Mitchell 2005). This is not necessarily the case with maritime disputes, which often represent tangible salience and more abstract conceptions of ownership compared to territory. According to Coalter G. Lathrop, "The area of maritime boundaries is often less fraught than land boundaries because no one lives there, there's not much of a history, there's not much of a fact pattern. . . . So, maritime boundary disputes are much less about national identity, much less about where people have lived and farmed, and done their thing, and they are much more about reaching some sort of solution that allows for the exploitation of the resource."[55]

Some remedies employed by binding third-party methods frequently reinforce the winner/loser dichotomy. For example, in the El Salvador v. Nicaragua case, the Central American Court of Justice awarded restitution by holding that Nicaragua was obliged to re-establish and maintain the legal status of the border that was in place prior to the Bryan-Chamorro Treaty, thereby awarding most of the territory in contention to El Salvador.[56] Similarly, in the Temple of Preah Vihear case between Cambodia and Thailand, the ICJ not only demarcated the border between the two states in favor of Cambodia, but also instructed Thailand to give back to Cambodia several objects previously removed from the temple by Thai authorities

---

[54] Territorial Dispute, Libyan Arab Jamahiriya v. Chad, ICJ Rep. 1994, 6, Judgment of February 3, 1994; Kasikili/Sedudu Island, Botswana/Namibia, ICJ Rep. 1999, 1045, Judgment of December 13, 1999; Sovereignty over Palau Ligitan and Palau Sipadan, Indonesia/Malaysia, Application for Permission to Intervene, ICJ Rep. 2001, 575, Judgment of December 17, 2002.

[55] Author's interview (EJP) with Coalter G. Lathrop, March 14, 2022.

[56] El Salvador v. Nicaragua, Central American Court of Justice (CACJ), Judgment of March 9, 1917, 11 Am. J. Int'l L. 674 (1917).

(Brown 2007, 196).[57] These types of decisions and remedies, along with mandatory orders, compensation, and so on, make clear which side has taken a larger loss as result of a judgment or an award. Though not all decisions lead to a "winner-takes-all" outcome, most do generate a "winner-takes-most" solution.

Similar to adjudication, arbitration is likely to produce clear winners and losers because arbitral awards usually yield a starkly asymmetric award (Baratta 1989; Urpelainen 2009).[58] An illustrative example of the dichotomous nature of an award is the Eritrea-Yemen Arbitration (1998–1999), one of the most significant international arbitrations of the twentieth century.[59] In its final decision, the tribunal determined that most of the disputed archipelago belonged to Yemen, while Eritrea kept the fishing rights in the waters around all disputed islands. Eritrea also retained sovereignty over the Mohabbakhs, the Haycocks, and the South West Rocks because of their proximity to the country's coast. Nevertheless, as a result of the award, Yemen emerged as a clear winner. Immediately after the decision, in November 1998, just hours after Eritrean troops withdrew from the area, the Yemeni government raised Yemen's flag over Greater Hanish, and the Yemeni military took up their posts on the island.[60]

Winning

Winning disputes encourages states to return to the same PR methods. An early example of the effect of winning is the dispute between the United Kingdom and Spain over Gibraltar. In 1966, the United Kingdom proposed ICJ litigation to settle the contention. As Merrills (2017, 23) writes, the United Kingdom was reluctant "to place the issue of sovereignty on the agenda of its discussions with Spain." Negotiating a critical issue—that of legal title over Gibraltar—was not a viable option for the United Kingdom. The ICJ litigation proposal came 13 years after the United Kingdom successfully settled

---

[57] Temple of Preah Vihear, Cambodia v Thailand, ICJ Rep. 1962, 6, Judgment of June 15, 1962.

[58] Documenting 451 cases of interstate arbitration in the time frame of 1789 and 1990, Stuyt (1990) demonstrates that in 225 of these cases, a winner could be identified, and only 30 arbitration cases constituted a compromise.

[59] Sovereignty and Maritime Delimitation in the Red Sea, Eritrea v. Yemen, PCA, phase I (1998), phase II (1999), 2001, 40 ILM 900 and 983, Awards of October 9, 1998 and December 17, 1999.

[60] "Yemeni FM Thanks Assad for His Support in Dispute with Eritrea," *Agence France Presse—English*, November 2, 1998, https://advance-lexis-com.proxy.lib.utk.edu/api/document?collection=news&id=urn:contentItem:3V12-H2K0-00GS-K4MT-00000-00&context=1516831.

its ICJ dispute with France over Minquiers and Ecrehos, suggesting that the positive experience with the ICJ could have been influential in the United Kingdom's proposal to return to the ICJ in a different dispute.[61]

The Libya v. Chad contention over the Aouzou Strip, a barren strip of territory located alongside the border between these countries, provides another good illustration.[62] In the 1980s, Libya was involved in several territorial and maritime disputes, including the Gulf of Sidra contention with the United States, and the disputes with Tunisia, and then Malta, over its continental shelf. The favorable outcomes of these contentions, particularly the ICJ cases with Tunisia in 1982 and Malta in 1985—both of which dealt with maritime delimitation—shaped Libya's strategy in its subsequent dispute with Chad over the Aouzou Strip. Despite Libyan support for Chad's leader Idriss Deby, Chad announced that it would continue the ICJ case against Libya. The case was initiated in September 1990 by Chad's previous leader Hissein Habré on the basis of an agreement stipulating that in the absence of a political settlement, the two states would submit the dispute to the Court. The Court was asked to establish a clear line of demarcation between Chad and Libya. Rather than rebuff Deby, Libyan leader Muammar al-Gaddafi agreed to continue the case at the ICJ. Gaddafi did so partially because according to him and his legal counsel, Libya's legal claim against Chad was relatively strong. Arguably, Libya's policymakers were encouraged by its positive experiences with the past two ICJ cases against Tunisia and Malta (Ciarli and McLachlan 1996; Paulson 2004).[63] In both these cases, the outcome was "comparatively favorable to Libya" (Paulson 2004, 440). This relative success caused Libya to perceive its interactions with international adjudication as positive. During the trial, Libya "realized it wasn't going to win that case. . . . But it was an easier out than them backing off."[64]

Likewise, following its success in the ICJ against the United States in 1986, Nicaragua quickly filed cases against its neighbors—Costa Rica and Honduras—also at the ICJ (Mondre 2015, 130).[65] In fact, Nicaragua brought

---

[61] Minquiers and Ecrehos, France/United Kingdom, ICJ Rep. 1953, 47, Judgment of November 17, 1953.

[62] Territorial Dispute, Libyan Arab Jamahiriya v. Chad, ICJ Rep. 1994, 6, Judgment of February 3, 1994.

[63] Case Concerning the Continental Shelf, Tunisia v. Libyan Arab Jamahiriya, ICJ Rep. 1982, 18, Judgment of February 24, 1982; Case Concerning the Continental Shelf, Libyan Arab Jamahiriya v. Malta, ICJ Rep. 1985, 13, Judgment of June 3, 1985.

[64] Author's interview (EJP) with Martin Pratt, January 27, 2022.

[65] Case Concerning the Military and Paramilitary Activities in and Against Nicaragua, Nicaragua v. United States of America, ICJ Rep. 1986, 14, Judgment of June 27, 1986.

both these disputes to the Court just one month later after its victory against the United States.[66] Another example is Honduras. The country has had repeated engagements with the ICJ owing to its success rate in the Court. In 1960, Honduras won its case against Nicaragua, then in 1986, decided to submit its dispute against El Salvador to the Court. Upon winning the latter in 1992, Honduras initiated ICJ proceedings against El Salvador yet again in 2002. A more recent example of how winning affects strategic selection is Malaysia's choice of settlement method in its dispute with Singapore over Pedra Branca, Pulau Batu Puteh, Middle Rocks, and South Ledge.[67] Arguably, the chief motivating factor behind Malaysia's decision to resort to adjudication against Singapore was its recent victory in the ICJ case against Indonesia.[68] The very next day after the Court issued the judgment in the Indonesia v. Malaysia case on December 17, 2002, the Malaysian deputy prime minister announced publicly that winning the case against Indonesia had encouraged Malaysia to submit its dispute with Singapore to the ICJ: "Pulau Batu Puteh will be next . . . following the positive outcome of arbitration by the International Court of Justice (ICJ) on the dispute between Malaysia and Indonesia over Sipadan and Ligitan."[69] Malaysia "believed that it had a sound case and had at least 50 percent probability of regaining control over Batu Puteh, Middle Rocks and South Ledge via the international legal process" (Kadir 2015). According to observers of the Malaysia v. Singapore case, between 1998 and 2002, "there was no movement towards ICJ resolution. However, Malaysia's victory in its Sipadan dispute with Indonesia last December [2002] reignited its media's interest in Pedra Branca," prompting Malaysia to agree to ICJ resolution of its dispute with Singapore on February 6, 2003, only six weeks after Malaysia won its case against Indonesia.[70]

---

[66] Nicaragua's cases against Costa Rica and Honduras were eventually discontinued.
[67] Sovereignty over Pedra Branca/Pulau Batu Puteh, Middle Rocks and South Ledge, Malaysia v Singapore, ICJ Rep. 2008, 9, Judgment of May 23, 2008.
[68] Sovereignty over Pulau Ligitan and Pulau Sipadan, Indonesia/Malaysia, Application for permission to Intervene, ICJ Rep. 2001, 575, Judgment of October 23, 2001.
[69] "Malaysia to Focus on Island Dispute with Singapore, Says Deputy Premier," Bernama News Agency, Kuala Lumpur, December 18, 2002.
[70] Lydia Lim, "Pedra Branca: Key Step Forward Today; Singapore and Malaysia Will Sign an Accord in KL to Refer the Dispute over the Island to International Court of Justice," The Straits Times, February 6, 2003.

Losing

Naturally, it is difficult for states to suffer the loss of territory or maritime features and rights. As a consequence, losing states usually perceive arbitral awards and court judgments as detrimental to their international and domestic image. In the context of territorial disputes, a loss is palpable, since land may change hands. Thus, the quarreling states approach the disputed issue with much fervor.[71] Moreover, the losing side typically perceives the settlement outcome as biased and illegitimate.[72] Domestically, parting with a piece of land is sometimes highly unpopular and can even be humiliating: "The decision makers don't want to bear the blame for losing the crown jewels, in whatever way those might be defined. Maybe it's an island, maybe it's a particular location at sea."[73] For example, the 1975 Iran-Iraq dispute, which involved Iraq ceding much of the Shatt al-Arab waterway to Iran, "was a source of deep humiliation to Iraq" (Swearingen 1988, 408).[74] When Saddam Hussein assumed the office of Iraq's President in 1978, he immediately vowed to rectify "the boundary situation" through war to reinstitute "national pride" (Swearingen 1988, 408). Although the loss of territory for Iraq was fairly small, the psychological repercussions were immense. By losing the Shatt al-Arab waterway, Iraq felt as though it had lost its status as a major power in the Persian Gulf.

Losing dampens states' enthusiasm toward a particular PR method. Speaking of international adjudication, Gamble and Fischer (1976, 21) write that "states are reluctant to submit important disputes to judicial settlement because of the risk of losing. On the other hand, where no great national interests are involved, the risk of losing may be offset by the chance of winning as well as interest in having the matter authoritatively settled." For example, following India's loss of the 1968 Kutch-Sind arbitration award to Pakistan, "The process of the Kutch-Sind settlement had left the Indian government apparently unwilling to repeat this experience" (Untawale 1974, 838). Pakistan, "on the other hand, had deemed it [winning through

---

[71] Former UN Secretary General Boutros Boutros-Ghali has stated in the context of dispute resolution offered by the UN that "the parties to a dispute are extremely sensitive and this makes it important that they should have confidence in the impartiality or the objectivity of the United Nations and its Secretary-General" (SG/SM/3525, 4, 5 [1992], also quoted in Franck [1995, 175]).

[72] For the description of equivalent dynamics in domestic jurisdictions, see Shapiro 1981.

[73] Author's interview (EJP) with Coalter G. Lathrop, March 14, 2022.

[74] In exchange for Iran's promise to stop supporting a Kurdish revolt against Iraqi government control, Iraq ceded a large section of the vital Shatt al-Arab waterway to Iran in the 1975 treaty (Swearingen 1988, 408).

arbitration] as a precedent for resolving other Indo-Pakistani disputes and problems (as they had existed then, particularly in the eastern region) including the intractable Kashmir issue" (Untawale 1974, 838). In another case, in 1975, Nigeria and Cameroon agreed to the Marouna Declaration, which delineated their disputed maritime boundary in favor of Cameroon. As the losing party, the Nigerian government repudiated the agreement shortly after signing it, while Cameroon, as the winning party, claimed it as binding and valid (Evans and Merrills 1997).

More recently, in 2005, the ICJ ruled primarily in favor of Niger in a case against Benin.[75] The two states had asked the Court to adjudicate in a four-decade dispute between them. The judgment established that Niger had sovereignty over the largest of disputed islands, Lete, and fifteen other smaller islands. Benin was, of course, deeply dissatisfied. At the time, Benin was involved in another territorial dispute with Burkina Faso over their shared border near the village of Koalou. In 2006 and 2007, Benin's policymakers agreed to mediation by the Economic Community of West African States (ECOWAS) (Central Intelligence Agency 2018). In 2008, the two states held talks and decided to set up a neutral zone where neither country would be allowed to make any changes to their sovereignty. Later, in 2009, Benin and Burkina Faso agreed to submit the contention to the ICJ, and also agreed that the territory be governed by a joint committee composed of fourteen members from both states until a judgment was reached.[76] However, until now, no formal application to the Court has been made and the dispute remains dormant.

The dissatisfaction of Nigeria with the 2002 ICJ ruling in the Nigeria v. Cameroon case also illustrates how losing affects other disputes.[77] The border dispute dealt with the oil-rich Bakassi Peninsula. The judgment was mostly in favor of Cameroon, but it also provided Nigeria with what the Court believed was a fair amount of territorial concessions. Yet, within a week of the September 2002 ruling, Nigeria, the self-perceived loser, submitted a position paper to the ICJ, complaining that "the judgment did not consider 'fundamental facts' about the Nigerian inhabitants of the territory, whose 'ancestral homes' the Court adjudged to be in Cameroonian

---

[75] Frontier Dispute, Benin v. Niger, ICJ Rep. 2005, 90, Judgment of July 12, 2005.

[76] "Différend frontalier Burkina-Bénin: Kourou/Koalou déclarée zone neutre," *Lefaso.net*, May 22, 2009, https://lefaso.net/spip.php?article31781.

[77] Land and Maritime Boundary between Cameroon and Nigeria, Cameroon v. Nigeria: Equatorial Guinea intervening, ICJ Rep. 1998, 275, Judgment of October 10, 2002.

territory."[78] In its official statement, Nigeria would accept only favorable parts of the ICJ's decision and criticized parts that it found unsatisfactory.[79] As a result of Nigeria's dismissal of the Court's findings, UN Secretary General Kofi Annan agreed in November 2002 to further attempt resolution of the dispute through mediation. More than four years later, in June 2006, Nigeria and Cameroon signed the Greentree Agreement, in which Nigeria agreed to abide by the 2002 ICJ judgment. This decision was largely caused by the fact that mediation by the UN Secretary General's office had helped the two states agree to additional nonterritorial concessions for Nigeria.[80]

Losing in a venue encourages states to quickly pursue alternative settlement options. For instance, Guinea-Bissau was dissatisfied with a 1989 arbitration ruling concerning the country's maritime boundary dispute with Senegal. After the arbitration award was issued, Guinea-Bissau turned to the ICJ to reject the legality of the arbitration award. With the ICJ proceedings underway, Guinea-Bissau brought a second case to the ICJ regarding the maritime delimitation in the Gulf of Guinea region.[81] Ruling on the first case, the Court found that the arbitral award was valid, but acknowledged that the dispute had not been resolved. The Court also stated that it is "highly desirable that the elements of the dispute that were not settled by the arbitration award . . . be resolved as soon as possible, as both Parties desire."[82] The two states subsequently engaged in negotiations and agreed to discontinue the proceedings of the second case.[83] Negotiations effectively ended the dispute. It was obvious that its dissatisfaction with the arbitration award provoked Guinea-Bissau to pursue other PR methods.

Even though international courts and tribunals are not required to follow precedent, the increasing volume of case law in the successful resolution of

---

[78] "UN-Chaired Commission on Cameroon-Nigeria Border Dispute Holds Fourth Meeting," *UN News*, June 13, 2003, https://news.un.org/en/story/2003/06/71262-un-chaired-commission-camer oon-nigeria-border-dispute-holds-fourth-meeting.

[79] For more discussion, see Paulson 2004.

[80] The Greentree Agreement provided further guarantees for the treatment of Nigerians living in the territory to be transferred to Cameroon, established a follow-up committee to deal with any difficulty in implementation of the transfer of territory, and arranged for Nigerian police and local administration to remain in the territory to be transferred for a two-year transitional period (UN Secretary General 2006).

[81] While the first case was underway (regarding the validity of the arbitral award), Guinea-Bissau submitted the second one regarding the maritime delimitation, but the parties then agreed to discontinue the proceedings after the first judgment was delivered.

[82] Land and Maritime Boundary between Cameroon and Nigeria, Cameroon v. Nigeria: Equatorial Guinea intervening, ICJ Rep. 1998, 275, Judgment of October 10, 2002.

[83] For a more detailed analysis of the border dispute between Guinea-Bissau and Senegal, see Okafor-Yarwood 2015.

territorial and maritime disputes provides a significant amount of information that states can use in selecting a venue.[84] In-depth analysis of the existing jurisprudence reveals which strategies seem to work.[85] From previous judgments states also learn about judges' preferences. Such information helps states choose PR methods and specific venues.

Regional Win-Loss Record

In addition to examining their own past experiences with the various PR methods, proposer states consider the past win-loss record of other states in the region. For example, the Philippine legal team, which also represented Mauritius in the Chagos maritime dispute against the United Kingdom, applied lessons learned from the Chagos case to their own legal strategy in the Philippines v. China case.[86] According to one of the Chagos case arbitrators, ITLOS Judge Rüdiger Wolfrum, the Philippine legal team had learned from its past experience in the Chagos case. In the Chagos case, the legal team realized they could not address sovereignty claims because ITLOS and an Annex VII tribunal would not have jurisdiction over territorial boundary delimitation (Wolfrum 2018a). The same legal strategy of avoiding issues of sovereignty in maritime delimitation was subsequently used in the Philippine v. China case just a couple of years later.

States can—and certainly do—examine the win-loss records of states worldwide, based primarily on similarity of dispute. In particular, the jurisprudence of arbitral tribunals and courts provides a vast amount of publicly available information regarding the submission of claims, the strategies used by legal teams, the types of evidence used in the claims, jurisdictional arguments and rulings, rules and procedures used in a case, and the specific

---

[84] In this context, it is crucial to recall that—as we explain in Chapter 2—the ICJ does not follow the doctrine of *stare decisis*, or judicial precedent. Thus, all Court's judgments are binding only between the parties. Nevertheless, the ICJ has been relatively consistent in its jurisprudence and—for the most part—does not depart from previously established interpretations (Mitchell and Powell 2011).

[85] As an illustration, many states were interested in the results of the first ICJ case that dealt with delimitation of a continental shelf, the North Sea Continental Shelf cases in 1969, involving Germany, Denmark, and the Netherlands (Oude Elferink 2018). States that had ongoing continental shelf claims paid close attention to the proceedings and the subsequent ruling in the North Sea Continental Shelf case to consider strategies in their own ongoing contentions (North Sea Continental Shelf Judgment, Federal Republic of Germany v. Denmark and Federal Republic of Germany v. The Netherlands, ICJ Rep. 1969, 3, Judgment of February 20, 1969).

[86] Chagos Marine Protected Area Arbitration, Mauritius v. United Kingdom, PCA Case No. 2011-03, March 20, 2015.

preferences of judges. These materials constitute helpful guidance on what worked and what did not work for substantively similar cases. However, states in the same geographical region in particular will be more likely to pay close attention to each other's past experiences with PR methods. Observing the Philippine victory against China in the South China Sea arbitration case prompted Japanese Diet legislators to consider a similar strategy in the Japanese dispute with South Korea over Dokdo/Takeshima island between Japan and South Korea. Because the Annex VII arbitration proceedings did not require the consent of the other party, unlike general ICJ litigation, a Diet legislator asked if the Dokdo issue could follow the same course.[87] Later, the Diet member requested that the minister of foreign affairs take the Dokdo case to UNCLOS arbitration.[88] As we discuss in Chapter 5, there are important patterns of shared dispute resolution norms and histories in distinct geographic regions. States also care whether their regional customs are considered in international PR methods. According to one of our interlocutors, "looking at whether regional culture or legal traditions are given any weight in previous cases may be a factor. . . . There have been times when the ICJ was accused of being a neocolonialist institution and ignoring the traditions and perceptions of people in the region."[89]

Several studies discuss the importance of geographic region and shared, regional experiences (Buzan and Waever 2003; Chi and Flint 2013; Murphy 2002; Väyrynen 1984).[90] For instance, Chi and Flint (2013, 556) find strong support for their argument that explaining territorial dispute behavior requires a regional level of analysis. These authors highlight the reality that "countries in the same region are more likely to have similar political-territorial circumstances, such as similar colonial experiences, or the formation of new countries." These common characteristics—further solidified via regional organizations that imbibe shared norms and values—provide states with a neighborhood-like identity. There is also a substantial body of scholarship that focuses on regional social influence in a broader sense. Indeed, there are powerful regional effects in how states participate and conceptualize the global order across many issue-areas, including ratification of

---

[87] DMSS, March 10, 2015, https://kokkai.ndl.go.jp/txt/118905268X00120150310/25. Cited in Kwon 2022.

[88] DMSS, February 25, 216, https://kokkai.ndl.go.jp/txt/119005268X00120160225/321.

[89] Author's interview (EJP) with Martin Pratt, January 27, 2022.

[90] It is also interesting to note that in the context of research on deterrence, Huth (1988) and Huth, Gelpi, and Bennett (1992, 1993) find that states' perceptions of reputation for resolve are tied to whether states are located within the same geographic region.

treaties on human rights and rights of children and women (Beckfield 2010; Simmons 2009; Wotipka and Ramirez 2008). Rational convergence in behavior suggests strong regional acculturation (Goodman and Jinks 2013). In many ways, states learn about the best ways to participate in international dispute settlement by observing localized, regional practices. More often than not, these regional practices become regional standards.

Examining regional-level experiences provides states with clues about their own future choices in dispute resolution. For example, in the Mediterranean region, in 1981 Malta attempted to intervene in the Tunisia v. Libya ICJ case regarding its claims to the continental shelf protruding from the North African coast toward Malta.[91] Malta was concerned that "its own continental shelf rights might be affected by the decision of the Court" (McGinley 1985, 671). Although the Court rejected Malta's intervention request, Malta strategically awaited the ICJ's judgment in the Tunisia v. Libya case. The judgment turned out to be fairly equitable and awarded comparable gains to both disputants.[92] Because Malta was satisfied with the judgment, a few years later, Malta and Libya agreed to take their continental shelf claims to the Court.[93]

As discussed further in Chapter 5, in Latin America, many states signed and ratified the 1948 American Treaty of Pacific Settlement, or Bogota Pact, in which they agreed to resolve their disputes through peaceful means and confer jurisdiction to the ICJ.[94] Not only has this peaceful settlement norm influenced common histories of peaceful dispute resolution but also it has led to increased use of arbitration and adjudication. ICJ jurisprudence provides Latin American states with a wealth of information that is useful in the process of strategizing. For example, in the Peru v. Chile maritime dispute that was submitted to the ICJ in 2008, Peru "pursued the very same legal strategy that other Latin American countries had followed when they invoked the powers of The Hague" (Sotomayor 2015, 56). Peru was able to

---

[91] Continental Shelf, Tunisia v. Libyan Arab Jamahiriya, Merits, 1982 ICJ Rep. 18, Judgment of February 24, 1982.

[92] The Court was asked to identify rules and principles of international law that were applicable for the delimitation of the continental shelf between Libya and Tunisia. The Court also considered relevant circumstances that should be considered in achieving an equitable delimitation between the two countries. The decision stipulated that the application of the equidistance method could not generate an equitable result.

[93] Continental Shelf, Libya v. Malta, ICJ Rep. 1985, 13, Judgment of June 3, 1985.

[94] Signatories and Ratifications to the Pact of Bogotá, Department of International Law, Organization of American States, Washington, DC, http://www.oas.org/juridico/english/sigs/a-42.html.

learn from the experiences of several regional states—Bogota Pact member states—all of which had used the ICJ to resolve their own territorial and maritime disputes: Nicaragua, El Salvador, Costa Rica, and Honduras.

There are also strong common patterns of dispute resolution in states located in the Middle East. As we explain later in the book, regionally embedded norms of the Islamic legal tradition draw this region in particular to nonbinding third-party methods (Powell 2015, 2016, 2020). In Southeast Asia, several states carefully observed the strategies and experience of the Philippines in its arbitration case against China. For instance, on March 30, 2020, Vietnam issued a note verbale to the Secretary General of the United Nations, in which the country not only protested recent submissions by Malaysia and China to the Committee on the Limits of the Continental Shelf (CLCS), but most importantly, made claims similar to those of the Philippines in the arbitration case against China. In the note verbale, the Vietnamese government specifically cited UNCLOS Article 121(3), which defines maritime features that cannot be considered islands: "[T]he baselines of the groups of islands in the East Sea, including the Hoang Sa Islands and Truong Sa Islands, cannot be drawn by joining the outermost points of their respective outermost features; low-tide elevations or submerged features are not capable of appropriation and do not, in and of themselves, generate entitlements to any maritime zones."[95] This argument, pursued by Vietnam to deny China the right to claim maritime entitlements based on the reality that an island generates rights to exclusive economic zones (EEZs) and continental shelves, is nearly identical to the legal strategy used by the Philippines in its arbitration case against China. Echoing the Philippine strategy, Vietnam claims that the Spratly and Paracel Islands are not actually islands. This argument suggests that much of the South China Sea is to be considered as the high seas. Most importantly, high seas are not able to generate EEZs and continental shelves for coastal states, including Vietnam. In the midst of the CLCS submissions, Vietnam has also been considering initiation of an arbitration case against China with regard to disputes over islands and maritime rights in the South China Sea. This potential strategy is likely strongly influenced by the positive experience of the Philippines in its 2016 decision

---

[95] Note Verbale from Permanent Mission of the Socialist Republic of Viet Nam to the United Nations to the Secretary-General of the United Nation, No. 22/HC-2020, https://www.un.org/Depts/los/clcs_new/submissions_files/mys_12_12_2019/VN20200330_ENG.pdf.

by an ITLOS Annex VII arbitration panel, which awarded about 90 percent of the Philippines' claims to the Philippines.[96]

Past outcomes provide "a repository of legal experience to which it is convenient to adhere; because they embody what the Court has considered in the past to be good law; because respect for decisions given in the past makes for certainty and stability" (Lauterpacht 1958, 14). States use previous rulings, arbitral awards, expert opinions, and writings about rulings involving regional states to help proposer states identify the most strategic PR method for their current disputes. This is particularly the case if the outcome may affect their own sovereign rights to territory or maritime entitlements.

Based on our theory, we propose the following hypotheses:

Hypothesis 1: A proposer state with a positive win-loss record in a PR method is more likely to use this method again than if the state did not have a positive record.

Hypothesis 2: A proposer state in the same geographic region as other states with positive win-loss records in a PR method is more likely to use this method again than if the regional win-loss record is not positive.

The Relationship between Domestic and International law

There are some states that don't like to be subject to third-party examination or scrutiny and there are some states that don't mind. England doesn't mind. Australia doesn't mind. But each of these countries has reservations, limitations upon its acceptance, which those limitations are determined by their consideration of their national interests. But otherwise, most states which are law abiding are happy to go to the Court or to some other system of settlement—to arbitration, and as you know, there are many different types of arbitration available now. And so, it's just a matter of what your attitude is to the law. If you see advantage in obeying the law or having the

---

[96] David Hutt, "Vietnam May Soon Sue China on South China Sea," *Asia Times*, May 7, 2020, https://asiatimes.com/2020/05/vietnam-may-soon-sue-china-on-south-china-sea/; The South China Sea Arbitration, The Republic of Philippines v. The People's Republic of China, PCA Case No. 2013-19.

law obeyed in the relations of other states with you, you are willing
to go to the Court.
         —Anonymous ICJ state advocate and international arbitrator[97]

We now turn to the relationship between domestic and international law, the
second mechanism that influences states' choice-of-venue strategic selection. As noted earlier, all PR methods constitute fundamentally a legal under-
taking via which the disputants' legal rights and obligations are determined
through legal processes. This is especially true for the binding third-party
methods, but legal aspects are present in other PR methods as well. More
often than not, even the settlement of disputes through bilateral negotiations
involves legal treaties or agreements signed by the disputants about the legal
status of boundaries, territorial control, or maritime rights. States' claims and
rights regarding a particular piece of land, institutionalized rules of conflict
management, and interstate agreements have indispensable legal aspects. In
a way, international conflict management takes place within the framework
of international law, as laid down in the UN Charter and other international
conventions.

The peaceful resolution of territorial and maritime disputes involves
"supranational legal or quasi-legal processes" (Simmons 2002, 831). Thus,
states' use of PR methods—especially third-party venues—differs from
relationships that states develop with any other international organizations or institutions. There is an intricate connection between the legal
nature of international disputes and their resolution, on one hand, and domestic law on the other. In a broad sense, the two legal systems—domestic
and international—interact in the process of dispute resolution and this
intermingling is crucial in how states strategize. Disputants involved in territorial contentions see, assess, and evaluate international law via the lens of
their domestic law. They juxtapose their own domestic laws against those of
international law in order to discriminate between the available PR methods.
Thus, at the heart of states' preferences toward international PR methods is
the interaction between domestic legal systems and international law. Our
theory places this interaction at the forefront.

There are three aspects of the domestic law/international law relationship that we believe act as mechanisms that influence states' behavior in
the process of peaceful settlement: (1) international law's position in the

---

[97] Author's interview (EJP), United Kingdom, October 2013.

domestic legal system, (2) rule of law, and (3) type of domestic legal tradition. These three characteristics fundamentally shape the dynamic of the choice-of-venue strategic selection. Both disputants—the proposer and the nonproposer—pursue or agree to venues that are similar to norms and legal values embedded in their own domestic legal systems. Shared values, beliefs about rule of law, and the role of legal solutions constitute a powerful force linking the domestic and international realms. Domestically, each society embraces unique views about conflict management, justice, and law in general. Usually, with time, these societal beliefs become institutionalized via a domestic legal system. In other words, more often than not, there is a strong link between societal morality, societal values, and so on, and the law. Thus, the structure of a state's domestic legal system provides a credible signal of the state's underlying identity and its attitude toward conflict management.[98] More generally, the three characteristics of a domestic legal system—international law's position in the domestic legal system, rule of law, and type of domestic legal tradition—collectively signal a state's approach to international law, and thus dispute resolution.

Typically, the domestic legal system provides a formal structure within which a state's policies are fashioned. More often than not, legal norms, mechanisms, and principles—as expressed in constitutions, codes, legislation, and so on—constitute a state's credible commitment to function in a predetermined manner. Hence, a state's domestic legal system prearranges that state's relation to international law and its institutions. It lays out the rules of the game when it comes to a state's strategic choices of a particular PR method. All else equal, certain states might be a priori predisposed to view specific international dispute settlement venues as superior.[99] Merrills (2017, 306) talks about the "social element," or the nonmaterial aspect of international disputes. According to him, this aspect is important "because the traditions, interests and attitudes of states are very different, as also is the power which each can bring to bear in a particular situation." Granted, to some extent, states adopt practices and patterns of behavior widely practiced by other states.[100] By way of illustration, for many years, arbitration has been

---

[98] For a detailed discussion of the relationship between a domestic legal system and a state's preferences with respect to international conflict settlement venues, see Powell (2020, 125–28).

[99] In addition to rules of official domestic legal systems, local rules and unwritten practices frequently shape the nature of social interactions, including dispute settlement, in domestic jurisdictions (see Powell 2020).

[100] For an excellent analysis of acculturation, see Goodman and Jinks 2013. According to these authors, acculturation is "a general process by which actors adopt the beliefs and behavioral patterns of the surrounding culture" (4).

relatively unpopular as a settlement method for territorial and maritime disputes. However, nowadays more and more states seem to acknowledge arbitration's value. Though surely many other factors are at play—including the speed and flexibility of arbitral proceedings—it seems as though some states, simply put, mimic other states' use of arbitration. As a consequence, arbitration is becoming a strong contender to adjudication.[101] However, the relationship between domestic and international law determines how receptive or resistant a state is to the powers of acculturation (Goodman and Jinks 2013). In the subsections below, we explain how three specific aspects of a domestic legal system exert influence on the process of choice-of-venue strategic selection.

International Law's Position in the Domestic Legal System

We believe that the position international law occupies within a domestic legal system has a large bearing on how states navigate through the choice-of-venue strategic selection. Before we delve into the details of this relationship, it is necessary to briefly consider the two broad ways in which a domestic legal system may structure the interaction between domestic law and international law. In states whose domestic legal system embraces monism, international law does not need to be translated into corresponding provisions of domestic law. Monist theories of international law claim that domestic and international law are based on one common principle, such as that of social unity and solidarity, or *pacta sunt servanda*, the principle that all agreements must be fulfilled (Shaw 2017). In other words, monism conceptualizes domestic law and international law as two constitutive parts of one legal system, where domestic law acquires its authority from the international legal system (Damrosch, Fisler, and Murphy 2019). Some theorists justify the monist approach by appealing to the overarching duty to uphold human rights.[102] Others argue that the unity between domestic and international law can be maintained on the basis of legal logic.[103]

In states that embrace monism, the act of treaty ratification ipso facto incorporates a treaty into domestic law. Consequently, the treaty is applicable

---

[101] We discuss these over-time patterns in detail in Chapter 5. For an interesting discussion of socialization or mimicking in the context of international adjudication, see Powell, Graefrath, and Graf 2022.

[102] See, for instance, Lauterpacht 1950.

[103] For an excellent explanation of this argument, see, among others, Kelsen 1952.

within the domestic sphere and its provisions can be directly enforced in do-mestic courts.[104] There is no need of implementing legislation. In such do-mestic jurisdictions, courts can give direct effect to international treaties. Put differently, this mechanism—known as direct effect—enables courts to base their decisions on concrete rules of international law.[105] This privileged formal position of international law in a domestic legal system signals, in a credible way, a state's general respect for its international commitments. If the power of international law is sanctioned via domestic courts, international law does not merely provide aspirational goals for the domestic legal system. Instead, international law is allowed to thrive in such domestic jurisdictions.

In contrast to monism, dualism proposes that international law and do-mestic law exist separately. According to the dualist theory, neither the in-ternational nor the domestic legal system can be assumed to be superior to the other. In domestic jurisdictions that lean toward dualism, most interna-tional law is not directly and automatically applicable in the domestic sphere. Instead, domestic legislation that implements international law is neces-sary for domestic courts to enforce a state's international commitments.[106] Thus, international law must be formally transformed and translated into the language of domestic law. Only then can precepts of international law be enforced by domestic courts (Verdier and Versteeg 2015). The domestic procedures that govern the "translation" of international law into domestic law differ across states. In some states, these procedures are quite strenuous and lengthy, and in others, enacting such legislation entails less formalized processes.

The monist and dualist theories portray the relationship between do-mestic law and international law in quite different ways. In fact, one can view these two theories as lying on opposite ends of a spectrum. In reality, however, international law's position in a domestic jurisdiction is regulated in a much more nuanced manner, going beyond the dichotomous distinc-tion between monism and dualism. Indeed, municipal laws of most states

---

[104] This statement must, of course, be qualified because monist states differ in how the treaty incor-poration into domestic law takes place. In some states, direct incorporation into domestic law occurs only for self-executing international agreements. In other monist states, the act of ratification is the sole requirement for a treaty's automatic incorporation into domestic laws.
[105] According to Verdier and Versteeg (2015), in 55 percent of states, treaties have direct effect. Also see Lupu, Verdier, and Versteeg 2019.
[106] For more detailed discussion of the dualist legal systems, see Damrosch, Fisler, and Murphy 2019.

embrace something of an intermediate position between the two extremes. In the words of Shaw (2017, 99), in most states "the rules of international law are seen as part of a distinct system, but capable of being applied internally depending on circumstance, while domestic courts are increasingly being obliged to interpret rules of international law." Put differently, the realities of the relationship between the two legal systems—domestic and international—do not neatly reflect the monist/dualist divide. Looking at actual states' policies, it seems that "national systems do not adopt a monolithic approach to international law; most of them combine aspects of the monist and dualist approaches" (Verdier and Versteeg 2015, 516). But more generally—despite the many differences among countries in how they regulate coordination between domestic and international law—substantial hurdles in translating international law into domestic law signal a more cautious attitude toward the international normative system. By contrast, states where many international rules apply directly, or where there are few barriers to their implementation, can be viewed as friendlier toward international law. This argument dovetails nicely with that of Simmons (2009, 69), who in the context of international human rights argues that "the higher ratification hurdle, the less likely a government will be to ratify an international human rights agreement, even if sympathetic to its contents."

Our argument goes beyond ratification costs and deals with a more general attitude toward international law, as expressed by specific mechanisms embedded in a domestic legal system. More often than not, willingness to resort to the binding PR methods, arbitration and adjudication, signals greater trust in the overarching framework of international law. Indeed, these two methods entail intense reliance on formal rules and procedures of international law. It is reasonable to expect that states with few domestic barriers to international law will be friendlier to arbitration and adjudication than states with more of these barriers. We hypothesize that:

Hypothesis 3: Proposer states whose domestic legal systems incorporate more features of the monist approach are more likely to use binding PR methods in comparison with other states.

In the above hypothesis, we anticipate that the effect will be strongest when states in the dyad share the monist approach to international law. The reason for this expectation is that the dyadic-level shared monist approach accelerates the state-level effects. If both states in a dyad share the monist approach, the proposer has more information about the preferences of the nonproposer, and thus can make an appropriate attempt at resolution.

Rule of Law

We acknowledge that there exist several definitions of rule of law. Whereas some definitions merely identify key features of a rule-of-law system, some are more comprehensive, and focus instead on the underlying philosophy, general mechanisms, and normative values. Dicey (1889) wrote that rule of law has the following basic constituent parts: the categorical supremacy of law in contrast to arbitrary execution of power, equality before law for all citizens as well as the government, and the authority of the judicial process. This definition, then, requires that law is to be applicable to everyone in a like manner, irrespective of political or legal system and culture.[107] Consequently, no state organ can exercise its powers arbitrarily, or outside the overarching framework of the law. Laws should be accessible, transparent, and easily understandable.[108]

Keeping in mind the overarching message conveyed by the various definitions of rule of law, it seems quite reasonable to expect that there is an intricate link between domestic respect for the principle of rule of law and proposer states' choices of PR methods. Indeed, any attempt at legalization of international conflict management is based on the supposition that law is in some way impartial and thus likely to advance the functioning of the international community. Granted, the well-being of the international rule of law is regularly challenged by considerations of power. As Koskenniemi (1990, 5) writes, "The fight for an international Rule of Law is a fight against politics, understood as a matter of furthering subjective desires and leading into an international anarchy."[109] Yet, arguably, international binding PR methods—courts and arbitration tribunals—in a most direct manner embody the international rule of

---

[107] It is important to recognize that rule of law and democracy are separate concepts that are capable of existing independently of the other. See for instance Gutmann and Voigt (2018, 346). For this reason, in addition to rule of law, we account for democracy in our statistical analyses as discussed in Chapter 5.

[108] See Chesterman (2008) for an analysis of the concept of rule of law. See Hurd (2017) for an interesting analysis of the rule of law in the domestic and international realms. It must be noted that the concept of rule of law is understood differently across the various domestic legal traditions. See Powell (2020, 120–23) for an analysis of rule of law in Islamic law states.

[109] Also see Ratner 2015.

law.[110] Despite the tension between power politics and global justice in the modern era, international courts and, more generally, legalized conflict management venues "are the backbone of the international system" (Powell 2020, 32).

Considering the nature of the binding PR methods, the literature has long pondered the relationship between the quality of domestic law and states' support for international courts, and international law more generally. Some democratic peace scholars argue that because binding third-party conflict management is based on the principle of rule of law, democracies that embrace an analogical principle domestically must naturally be supportive of international arbitration and adjudication (Dixon 1993; Raymond 1994). In contrast, some maintain that states where strong respect for rule of law is not engrained in democratic domestic governance are not automatically attracted to international legal institutions (Gent and Shannon 2011; Mitchell, Kadera, and Crescenzi 2009; Shannon 2009). This argument rests on the similarity logic: in countries with strong rule of law, the population regards law to be a necessary framework for relations between individuals and collectivities, such as states. In these countries, people are accustomed to delegating disputes to courts and alternative dispute resolution (ADR) mechanisms. This respect for—or this acclimation to—formal domestic dispute resolution translates into like preferences for international binding PR methods. Thus, a population that is comfortable with a strong role for domestic courts will be more likely to perceive rulings of international courts and arbitration tribunals as legitimate (Huth, Croco, and Appel 2011).

It seems reasonable to expect that a country's low levels of domestic rule of law will influence the citizenry's expectations about their policymakers' behavior in the international arena. Indeed, where domestic levels of rule of law are low, citizens may be unlikely to assume that the instinctive reaction of their policymakers is to abide by international law. Additionally, more often than not, the judiciary in these societies lacks independence, and many judicial decisions are likely to reflect unwarranted political influences. Thus, it is possible that the absence of robust domestic rule of law may dampen enthusiasm for arbitration and adjudication. Additionally, as Kelley (2007, 578) writes, "States with a low rule-of-law should also be in a better position to silence domestic criticism, because they can use methods outside the law."

---

[110] For a discussion of the link between domestic levels of rule of law and states' support for the International Criminal Court (ICC) and the ICJ, see Powell 2013.

Put differently, coercive domestic governance typically constitutes an impediment to state support for international legalized conflict-management methods.[111]

As a general rule, the international community does not anticipate that a low rule-of-law state will prefer binding PR methods to resolve its territorial contentions. Indeed, when a low rule-of-law state attempts such methods, other states usually express skepticism and astonishment. Moreover, the international community routinely assumes that in the aftermath of an unfavorable arbitral award or a court judgment, low rule-of-law states will likely refuse compliance. In other words, though the obligation of compliance with binding PR methods pertains to all states, in reality, the expectation of compliance seems to decline for low rule-of-law countries. By way of illustration, Colombia—where domestic levels of rule of law are relatively low—lost in a maritime boundary case against Nicaragua at the ICJ in November 2012.[112] Shortly after the judgment was rendered, Colombia openly rejected the ruling. Colombian president Juan Manuel Santos publicly criticized the ICJ judgment. Santos declared that "the decision is 'seriously wrong' and replete with 'omissions, errors, excesses and inconsistencies that we cannot accept' " (Rogers 2012).[113]

Pakistan, another low rule-of-law state, has repeatedly projected a relatively ambivalent attitude toward international third-party binding PR methods. In 1968 Pakistan was successful in maintaining the territorial status quo in its dispute over the Rann of Kutch region with India. The Rann of Kutch arbitration has been called "one of the major instances of international arbitration in the post-war period" (Wetter 1971, 346). Despite such a prominent victory, Pakistan has not attempted arbitration or adjudication to resolve its other territorial contention with India: the dispute over Kashmir and Jammu. Both countries claim the entire Kashmir region, but each controls only parts of the territory. These parts are recognized as Pakistan-administered Kashmir and Indian-administered Kashmir. For many years, Indian-administered Kashmir has been given a special position, associated with a degree of autonomy within India. Yet, in 2019, Indian-Pakistani bilateral relations significantly worsened and Kashmir continues to be one of

---

[111] For more discussion, see Simmons 2009.

[112] Territorial and Maritime Dispute, Nicaragua v. Colombia, ICJ Rep. 2012, 624, Judgment of November 19, 2012.

[113] President Santos not only criticized the Court but also ordered Colombian naval warships to deploy to the newly appointed Nicaraguan waters (Rogers 2012).

the most conflict-prone and militarized territories in the world, with frequent armed actions and hostile rhetoric between the two states. Pakistan's Prime Minister Imran Khan criticized India's political decision—splitting Indian-administered Kashmir into two separate territories, Kashmir and Jammu—and declared "If . . . the developed world does not uphold its own laws, then things will go to a place that we will not be responsible for."[114] Though Pakistan emerged as a clear winner in the arbitration proceedings against India in the Rann of Kutch dispute, there have been no attempts at any binding PR method in the dispute over Kashmir and Jammu. Instead, policymakers on both sides have only contemplated nonbinding methods such as negotiations and mediation. Therefore, even with a positive experience with binding PR methods, Pakistan with its low rule-of-law level has not pursued binding methods for the dispute over Kashmir and Jammu.

Interestingly, the scholarship has produced mixed findings on the relationship between regime type, rule of law, and states' support for specific international PR methods. While there is some corroborating evidence that democratic commitment to rule of law draws democracies to the binding dispute settlement (Allee and Huth 2006; Mitchell 2002; Raymond 1994), more recent empirical studies have questioned the nature of this relationship (Gent and Shannon 2011; Mitchell, Kadera, and Crescenzi 2009; Powell 2020; Powell and Wiegand 2014; Shannon 2009). [115]The reality seems to be that low rule-of-law states attempt binding PR methods just as frequently as high rule-of-law states. As we have shown in our previous work, domestic levels of rule of law are not squarely the driving force in states' choices of settlement (Powell and Wiegand 2010, 2014; Wiegand and Powell 2011a). Indeed, many territorial and maritime disputes in Europe since the early 1950s have been resolved via bilateral negotiations and the nonbinding methods, despite the reality that European democracies enjoy high levels of domestic rule of law. Also, several low rule-of-law states, including Argentina, Burkina Faso, Eritrea, Libya, and Yemen, have effectively settled their territorial and maritime disputes via adjudication and arbitration. These patterns fall in line with arguments put forth by Goldsmith and Posner (2005), who assert that democratic states are less open to any type of cosmopolitan engagement.

---

[114] "Kashmir: Why India and Pakistan Fight over It," *BBC News*, August 8, 2019, https://www.bbc.com/news/10537286, accessed April 6, 2020.

[115] Mitchell, Kadera, and Crescenzi (2009) demonstrate that democratic dyads are not more likely to select third-party methods. Moreover, most of their empirical models of third-party settlement attempts show that joint democracy decreases the likelihood of using a third-party for dispute resolution.

Extending support for international courts and delegating disputes to these forums definitely constitute such cosmopolitan engagement.

Based on the above discussion, we propose two competing hypotheses:

Hypothesis 4a: Proposer states with high levels of domestic rule of law are more likely to attempt binding PR methods in comparison to states with low domestic levels of rule of law.

Hypothesis 4b: Levels of domestic rule of law do not influence proposer states' decisions to attempt binding PR methods.

As with our expectation dealing with the monist approach, we anticipate that the effect of domestic levels of rule of law will be accelerated on the dyadic level. For instance, proposer states in a high rule-of-law dyad are more likely to attempt binding PR methods in comparison with dyads in which states have diverse levels of rule of law.

Domestic Legal Traditions

Domestic legal traditions—our last mechanism—play an indispensable role in the choice-of-venue strategic selection.[116] To reduce uncertainty concerning the interpretation of international norms and the process of settlement, states seek out PR methods that resemble their own domestic legal tradition. Reaching into domestic legal traditions may be necessary when the dispute deals with substantive areas of international law that contain loopholes. If this is the case, a court or an arbitral panel must engage in creative, and at times discriminatory, norm interpretation, by advancing a particular meaning of international law.[117] As the scholarship in comparative international law demonstrates, different states—influenced by their own

[116] For more discussion of how domestic legal traditions factor into states' choices of conflict management venues see Powell 2015 and 2020; Mitchell and Powell 2011; Powell and Mitchell 2022; Powell and Wiegand 2014.

[117] For more discussion, see Alter 2014. In reality, some PR venues may be disregarding or modifying norm interpretation advanced by other tribunals, courts, etc. By way of illustration, in the area of maritime disputes, the divergence of interpretation has been visible in the context of delimitation of the continental shelf between opposing or adjacent states. The principle of equidistance establishes that the boundary must be determined "from the nearest points of the baselines from which the breadth of the territorial sea of each State is measured" (Convention on the Continental Shelf of 1958, Article 6).

domestic legal traditions, customs, and cultures—see international law differently.[118] International law is taught and talked about distinctly in the various domestic jurisdictions.

Rules and procedures of all international PR venues contain elements that draw from particular domestic legal traditions: civil, common, and Islamic. In the comparative law literature, there are several ways of categorizing countries with remarkably similar domestic laws. For instance, David (1985) wrote about families of law. With time, the notion of legal traditions—a concept that focuses on the societal conceptualization of legal systems—was brought into use by Glenn (2014).[119] In contemporary times, civil, common, and Islamic legal traditions are the three major legal traditions. Each of them has unique characteristics, substantial and procedural. Most importantly for our argument, each legal tradition espouses a specific philosophy of justice and dispute resolution that can influence the choice-of-venue strategic selection.

Most countries represent the civil legal tradition, which is rooted in the laws of the Roman Empire. In this legal tradition, the written letter of law—codes—constitutes the chief source of legal rules and principles. Of all legal traditions, civil law most heavily regulates dispute resolution: procedure, rights, and obligations of the disputing parties, as well as the conduct of the intermediaries, judges, and arbitrators (Mitchell and Powell 2011; Siems 2014). The parties' behavior, judicial powers, remedies, time limitations, and other modalities are meticulously regulated in codes of procedure: civil procedure, criminal procedure, administrative procedure, etc. Going beyond dispute resolution, of all legal traditions, civil law is the most formal, detail oriented and places the heaviest emphasis on all-encompassing and thorough legal regulation.[120] Though nowadays countries representing all domestic legal traditions—civil, common, Islamic, and mixed—have codes, the philosophy of codification is unique in civil law. As Siems (2014, 44) writes, "The main codes of civil law countries follow the idea of the Enlightenment to provide a clear, coherent, systematic, self-contained and complete treatment of particular branches of law." This is not always the case in common law and Islamic law jurisdictions.

---

[118] For in-depth discussion of comparative international law, see Roberts et al. 2015, 2018; Powell 2021; and Roberts 2017.

[119] There is extensive literature devoted to categorizations of domestic legal systems. For instance, see Mattei 1997; and Merry 2010.

[120] Comparative law scholarship on the various domestic legal traditions is abundant. For more detailed description of the civil legal tradition, see Merryman 1985; and David 1985.

Historically, civil law has rejected the doctrine of precedent, *stare decisis*. As a general rule, in the process of adjudicating, civil law judges rely on codes and not on previous judicial decisions. Thus, court decisions lack binding force beyond parties to the dispute. In most civil law jurisdictions, the legislature has the power to make law. Comparatively speaking, the role of judges operating within this legal tradition is fairly passive. Their foremost obligation is to apply norms that are included in codes. In the spirit of the civil legal tradition, the high degree of formality promotes transparency of a domestic legal framework. Additionally, it reinforces a sharp distinction between the law and non-law spheres (Jouannet 2006). Civil law, therefore, embodies a relatively strict and formal interpretation of rules. Judges interpret the law, but they do so according to formal and relatively inflexible rules set by a pre-existing normative framework.

The common legal tradition, originating in the British Isles, is fundamentally based on the *stare decisis* doctrine, according to which judges are bound primarily by precedents established by previous judgments.[121] The principle of *stare decisis* has "the benefit of ensuring consistency and predictability, in the absence of comprehensive codifications. At the same time, the reasoning from case to case can ensure that the law is adaptable to changing circumstances" (Siems 2014, 57). Most scholars regard common law as much more flexible than civil law. Less formalism is required in the judicial procedure, and a traditional common law trial places a great deal of importance on orality.[122] Judges operating within this legal tradition have historically been creative in applying law to real cases, and are known for including arguments from social sciences such as economics in their legal argumentation and reasoning (Bell 2006). The strong position of common law judges as lawmakers fosters judicial independence, which arguably guards against overarching by the executive. Thus, in comparison with civil law, common law is based on a much more spontaneous, independent, and dynamic interpretation of law. In an important way, this legal tradition fosters the development of law from the bottom up. Law across its various substantive areas evolves in a gradual manner. Writing about the differences between the civil and common law traditions, Jouannet (2006, 309) notes that "Americans [common law] see

---

[121] For more detailed discussion of *stare decisis*, see Glenn 2014; Opolot 1980; Powell and Mitchell 2007; Siems 2014.
[122] The institution of the jury has historically fostered common law's emphasis on orality. For more discussion, see Glenn 2014.

law as an all-encompassing sociological and political phenomenon, while the French [civil law] see it exclusively as a body of rules and principles."

The Islamic legal tradition arose with the birth of Islam in the seventh century CE and is based primarily on religious principles of human conduct. Islamic law is intricately connected to Islamic faith. *Shari'a* is conceptualized as the flawless expression of God's will for people.[123] Islamic law has two primary textual sources, the Quran and the sunna. The remaining two sources—judicial consensus and analogical reasoning—are non-textual and are perhaps best understood as "analytical, methodological tools for determining the law" (Powell 2020, 103).[124] In comparison with common law and civil law, Islamic law regulates dispute resolution in a very unique way, emphasizing apology, reconciliation, coming together of the parties, forgiveness, and restoration of balance in the community. In fact, communal repercussions are frequently given more weight than individual wins and losses (Abou El Fadl 2003). The parties may help the judge search for the truth and the applicable God-revealed law. Consequently, the role of advocates and legal representatives is much smaller than in other legal traditions. There is little procedural law. In general, traditional *shari'a*-based court proceedings take place as a rudimentary, commonsense mechanism, without much written documentation, formal procedure, or strict rules of evidence (Rosen 2000).

Reconciliation between the parties, guided by informal help from an intermediary, is given precedence over a formal judgment of a court. *Sulh*, a settlement between the disputants, was the Prophet Muhammad's preferred method of dispute resolution: "An old Islamic maxim teaches *al-Sulh seyed al-ahkam*, mediation/reconciliation is the superior rule" (Powell 2020, 143). In civil and common law, an intermediary to a dispute—a judge, an arbitrator, or a mediator—is to be formally trained, neutral, and unbiased. In contrast, according to Islamic legal tradition, an optimal third party engaged in resolving a dispute has deep connections with the community and understands the wider context of the contention. In other words, Islam embraces "collective embeddedness of the third party" (Powell 2020, 146). Naturally, since

---

[123] For definitions of *shari'a*, see Abou El Fadl 2012; An-Na'im 2008; Bassiouni 2014; Powell 2020.
[124] According to the Muslim faith, the Quran contains God's divine revelation, and it is perfect in substance and form. See also Mallat 2007; and Weiss 2006. The sunna comprises traditions, words, actions, and silences of the Prophet Muhammad (see Hallaq 2005). Judicial consensus, *ijma*, is common religious conviction of Islamic legal scholars that expresses the importance of collective agreement (see Vikør 2005). Analogical reasoning, *qijas*, is a juristic technique by which a rule found in Islam's textual source can be applied to a novel problem or another legal issue (see Powell 2020).

shariʿa is believed to provide a superior set of laws for humanity, it is best to settle all disputes within the framework of the Islamic legal tradition.

The scholarship in comparative international law notes that domestic actors, governments, and policymakers perceive international law through their own legal culture (Roberts et al. 2015, 2018; Roberts 2017; Zartner 2014). Civil-law-trained actors—who often determine what PR methods their government will pursue—apply civil law principles in the process of understanding how international law works. The same holds for common-law-trained actors. Finally, many Islamic law states feel excluded from Western-influenced international law. With regard to several substantive areas of international law—areas that are deemed incompatible with the principles of *shariʿa*—these states seem to follow their own partially distinct preferences (Powell 2022). In the spirit of informal reconciliation promoted by the Islamic legal tradition and culture, Islamic law states mold the broad framework of dispute settlement on international structures and norms to fulfill their own expectations.[125] Following this line of argument, proposer states rationally and strategically select PR methods that in their own estimation—based partially on their domestic legal tradition—will be most predictable and most understandable. Of course, proposer states also take into consideration domestic legal tradition of non-proposers. Similarity between domestic and international legal principles not only lowers uncertainty, but also increases states' trust in the resolution procedures, and a proposer state can easily monitor the subsequent stages of dispute resolution with better understanding.

The underlying rules of all PR methods contain elements that resemble particular domestic legal traditions. Many of these characteristics were embedded in the various PR methods and venues at their conception. Other rules, especially procedural rules, developed with time as specific international conflict-management institutions accumulated cases and jurisprudence. In most instances, international adjudication, especially at the ICJ, is structurally and procedurally similar to civil law. Among all legal traditions, we expect civil law states to prefer the binding PR methods, since civil law embraces a high degree of formalism, legalism, and strict interpretation

---

[125] According to Powell (2020, 1), an Islamic law state is "a state with an identifiable substantial segment of its legal system that is charged with obligatory implementation of Islamic law in personal, civil, commercial, or criminal law, and where Muslims constitute at least 50 percent of the population." Importantly, the Islamic law category comprises not only Middle Eastern states, but also states located in Africa and Asia/Oceania.

of rules. In particular, these states will more likely gravitate to international adjudication in their attempts to settle contentions. More than states representing other legal traditions, civil law states feel comfortable—and thus less uncertain—when dealing with relatively formal international courts. Moreover, civil law states' attraction to international courts is based on the reality that more often than not, international courts make their decisions within a well-defined framework of written international law. The practices of the ICJ and, to some extent, ITLOS are similar to those employed in domestic courts operating in civil law jurisdictions (Mitchell and Powell 2011; Powell and Mitchell 2007 and 2022).[126] For instance, though in practice past judgments carry much authoritative weight, officially, statutes of both courts reject the doctrine of precedent.[127] Though less formal than adjudication, arbitration is also attractive to civil law states with its emphasis on international law in the decision-making process. Indeed, arbitration panels operating within the framework of the Permanent Court of Arbitration (PCA) offer states sought-after formality.

In contrast, common law states are likely to prefer less legalized methods of conflict management since, comparatively speaking, interpretation of norms in common law entails a more free and dynamic process. These states should especially prefer negotiations because of their inherently flexible nature. In addition, common law embraces a more horizontal ideal of administering justice "with judges and juries as the protagonists of such decentralised system" (Siems 2014, 50). In a way, decentralization of decision-making lies at the core of bilateral negotiations. More broadly, negotiations are most reflective of common law's adversarial system of proceedings where parties and their legal representation are intensely involved in horizontal exchanges of views and arguments. As explained above, most international adjudicators are constructed largely to reflect the spirit of the civil legal tradition. It is reasonable to expect that this reality makes common law states less enthusiastic about international adjudication and arbitration.

We expect Islamic law states to be more likely to resort to nonbinding third-party PR methods since the Islamic legal tradition favors simple reconciliation between the disputants guided by an insider. Indeed, "Islamic

---

[126] There are many important similarities between ICJ and ITLOS. However, ITLOS constitutes a much more flexible adjudicative forum that partially embeds common law's commitment to dynamic and speedy conflict resolution (Powell and Mitchell 2022).

[127] Statute of the International Court of Justice, https://www.icj-cij.org/en/statute.

norms of dispute resolution match international nonbinding third-party methods: mediation and conciliation. The resemblance manifests itself in logic, procedure, and goals of settlement" (Powell 2020, 148). Intermediaries involved in conciliation and mediation have the freedom to pivot when the realities of a contention demand flexibility. Reconciliation may take place outside the strict, legalistic framework of international law. Though Islamic law does not prohibit it, adjudication is considered inferior to nonconfrontational dispute resolution. This is important because the various schools of Islamic jurisprudence agree that many aspects of Islamic law pertain to international relations: relations among Muslim collectivities, and relations between Muslim and non-Muslim collectivities. In an important way, Islam's preference for *sulh*, the informal compromise, extends to domestic and international realms. Mediation and conciliation resemble proceedings in front of a *qadi*—Islamic law judge—who in the process of decision-making takes into consideration not only law, but also ethics and communal well-being. Of course, there are several ways through which Islamic law states can mitigate their uncertainty with international dispute settlement. Frequently, these states hire legal counsel educated in Western institutions that operate with ease in international PR methods. This reality notwithstanding, the fact of the matter is that Islamic law states "simply prefer to settle their disputes in a nonconfrontational manner owing to intrinsic cultural norms of dispute resolution" (Powell 2020, 138).

Based on our theory, we propose the following hypotheses:

Hypothesis 5: Common law proposer states are more likely to seek bilateral negotiations than other PR methods.

Hypothesis 6: Civil law states are more likely to seek binding third-party PR methods than other PR methods.

Hypothesis 7: Islamic law states are more likely to seek nonbinding third-party PR methods than other PR methods.

In the context of the above hypotheses, we anticipate that the effect of legal traditions will be strongest in shared domestic legal tradition dyads. In other words, we expect that proposers from a specific legal tradition will seek the preferred PR method when dealing with a nonproposer sharing the same legal tradition.

Conclusions

Our theory distinguishes between two separate, though deeply interrelated, stages of strategic selection for the proposer state: choice-of-venue and within-venue strategic selection. This chapter presents the first part of our theoretical framework that focuses on proposer states' choices of resolution methods and venues. Uncertainty associated with the resolution process and the desire to win a contention cause states to behave strategically. While we recognize that there is a multiplicity of ways in which states understand winning, it is the drive to increase the probability of victory—however conceptualized—that guides policymakers and state counsel in selecting optimal strategies throughout the resolution process. Our discussion parses out different mechanisms that reduce uncertainty during the process of choosing methods and forums: past experience in peaceful resolution and the relationship between domestic and international law. The relationship between domestic and international law comprises three distinct factors: international law's position in the domestic legal system, the state's domestic commitment to rule of law, and the type of domestic legal tradition.

Our monadic-level framework provides important insights into choices regarding dispute resolution, and constitutes a parsimonious way to capture the proposer states' decision-making process. Our theory and empirical model account for the reality that the proposer takes into consideration characteristics and past experiences of the nonproposer state. In other words, proposer states do not issue proposals for the various PR methods in a vacuum. Instead, they anticipate potential responses by the nonproposer state.[128] There is a need for more scholarship that embraces the game-theoretic approach specifically in the context of territorial and maritime contentions. In particular, informal game theory has great potential to increase our understanding of the strategic interaction between states involved in dispute resolution (Carter 2010; Caselli, Morelli, and Rohner 2015; Maas 2022; Schultz and Goemans 2019). The research presented in this book provides a stepping stone for future research promoting the more game-theoretic approach.

Our theory, like any social science theory, is based on simplified patterns, and does not directly address all of the complicated reality of territorial and maritime disputes. Indeed, it is impossible to account for every factor that

---

[128] See Chapter 5 for a detailed discussion of our independent variables for shared proposer and nonproposer experiences and characteristics.

matters for the resolution of these contentions. Our goal is to represent a specific mechanism—strategic selection—and parse out how this mechanism operates. Certainly, a multiplicity of factors influences the proposer's selection of PR methods. To a large extent, each territorial and maritime dispute is unique as far as its historical, geographical, and political context is concerned. Additionally, since all decision-making associated with peaceful dispute resolution is in the hands of individual leaders, state counsel, lawyers, and other actors, not all actions are always fully rational. There is some idiosyncrasy, confusion and, perhaps even cynicism in why, when, and how states enter into dispute resolution. As with any other social science phenomena, attempting to explain peaceful resolution of territorial/maritime disputes is not immune to these unforeseeable factors.[129] As Laurie Nathan noted, "it is the idiosyncratic element. . . . And it adds this extra flavor. At the end of the day, who decides which is the right [method] for resolving our dispute? It is not the state."[130] These sentiments are confirmed by another of our interviewees who pointed out, "There has to be some decision-making or some movement made by high-level leadership in a direction towards resolution. So, what prompts that decision? It could be anyone, or a combination of factors."[131]

[129] We elaborate on this issue in Chapter 5.
[130] Author's interview (EJP) with Laurie Nathan, January 21, 2022.
[131] Author's interview (EJP) with Coalter G. Lathrop, March 14, 2022.

4

A Theory of Strategic Selection

Within-Venue

> A State is not just deciding to allow the train leave the station, but is also analyzing what would be the best route for it to get where the State wants it to go, and whether there are risks that the train gets diverted or derailed.
>
> —Sean D. Murphy[1]

When the nonproposer accepts the proposer's proposal, disputants' preferences converge on a particular settlement method and venue. This marks the beginning of the within-venue strategic selection stage. States pursue an elaborate planning scheme—a strategy—with hopes of reducing uncertainty and maximizing their gains: avoiding losing and increasing chances of victory. While the theoretical argument and empirics for the choice-of-venue strategic selection stage focus only on the proposer state, in this part of our theory, our approach considers the strategy of both disputants since they are equally invested and involved in the chosen method and venue. Strategizing within a venue entails navigating the myriad rules and mechanisms associated with the venue. This chapter demonstrates that within-venue strategic selection constitutes an incredibly intricate process, replete with a multiplicity of carefully planned, strategic decisions for both disputants.[2] In what follows, we discuss two mechanisms of within-venue strategic selection: framing the claim and shaping procedures. Strategic framing of claims can involve the following: calculated designing of legal

[1] Author's interview (EJP) with Sean D. Murphy, professor of international law, George Washington University, January 28, 2022.

[2] As with choice-of-venue strategic selection—which does not focus on the strategic interaction of the disputants—our conceptualization of the within-venue strategic selection stage does not address strategic interaction. Instead, our analysis of the within-venue stage accounts for anticipatory actions by each disputant in the context of framing their claims and shaping the procedures.

The Peaceful Resolution of Territorial and Maritime Disputes. Emilia Justyna Powell and Krista E. Wiegand, Oxford University Press. © Oxford University Press 2023. DOI: 10.1093/oso/9780197675649.003.0004

arguments, rephrasing of sovereignty claims within the framework of the chosen settlement method/venue, focusing on certain aspects of the dispute, and leaving out other aspects that could lead to an unfavorable outcome. States also try to fully take advantage of a venue's flexible design by shaping the venue's rules and procedures and selecting the actors involved in the proceedings. Patterns of state behavior in the context of within-venue strategic selection are quite distinct in that, regardless of external factors, all states strategize to optimize their experience at a chosen venue: all states maximize their efforts to shape the procedures and frame their claims to the greatest extent possible.

Before we turn to the discussion of the two mechanisms, we should like to emphasize that the two stages of strategic selection—choice-of-venue and within-venue—are intricately interconnected. By selecting and limiting issues considered by a venue (within-venue strategic selection), states can simultaneously or subsequently make use of different peaceful resolution (PR) methods to resolve different aspects of the dispute (choice-of-venue strategic selection). These decisions deal with a variety of issues associated with the settlement: decisions with regard to framing the claim and shaping the procedures.

Framing the Claim

The way you frame the case certainly may lead you to a win or a loss,
so that's going to be extremely important.

—Sean D. Murphy[3]

When disputants agree on a certain PR method and a particular venue, it is up to each side to identify their legal territorial or maritime claims and fashion the specifics of their own contentious issues. To a large degree, "the material element in a dispute is not a fixed quantity but depends on the parties' perceptions" (Merrills 2017, 307). These perceptions are malleable and can be strategically projected onto the opponent and the intermediary. In this context, it is useful to think of each territorial or maritime contention as a basket of multilayered competing claims. Legal advisors and state counsel assess strengths and limitations of both sides' claims and hypothesize what

---

[3] Author's interview (EJP) with Sean D. Murphy, January 28, 2022.

configuration of claims is most likely to yield a favorable outcome for their clients. As Coalter G. Lathrop notes, when he has advised clients in territorial and maritime cases,

> a state might reach out and say: "we want to have you [the expert] in to tell us about our case." I can usually assess "here's what I think is going to happen, here's where I think you're weak, here's where I think you're strong, here's the approach I think you should take. . . . Typically, when I provide an expert opinion, I will give them [a state] a range. I don't provide a mathematical probability, but instead, these are the kinds of things that you're likely to see from a third-party decision, you are not going to see this and you are not going to see this . . . it's going to be somewhere in between. . . . If they accept that opinion and want to move forward, the next step is thinking about framing the case: what are the precedents we are going to rely on, what's the story we're going to tell about the law and the facts?[4]

Many factors are taken into consideration: legal principles, pertinent international jurisprudence, and the broader geopolitical background. In essence, states guided by their legal counsel discriminate between potential claims that may be advanced in a dispute, and choose claims that are likely to hold up against arguments of the other side. Thus, all these strategic choices are not made exclusively by policymakers themselves.

Though territorial disputes in particular are frequently emotionally charged, certain claims are—simply put—unlikely to withstand the settlement process. On its face, it may seem appealing to put forth the widest possible sovereignty claims, but strategically refined, limited claims may yield better results. Granted, disputes over narrow, technical issues or over specific treaty obligations are less likely to lend themselves to strategic manipulation. In contrast, territorial disputes more often than not involve complicated sovereignty claims that can be divided or combined, and framed in a multiplicity of ways. In fact, while in some other disputes the parties may view the resolution of a contention as more important than the result, this is rarely the case in territorial disputes. Territory is one of the constitutive elements of statehood, and states frequently care about every inch of land. This reality,

---

[4] Author's interview (EJP) with Coalter G. Lathrop, Sovereign Geographics, International Boundary Consultancy, March 14, 2022.

coupled with profound emotional aspects of territorial contentions, makes the actual result of these disputes very important.

The levels of uncertainty are a bit lower in the context of maritime disputes. The main reason for this reality is the equity principle embedded in the UN Convention on the Law of the Sea (UNCLOS).[5] However, the reliance on the principle of equity does not automatically mean that states are certain about the potential outcome of an International Tribunal for the Law of the Sea (ITLOS) or Annex VII tribunal ruling. As in other areas of international law, maritime law is subject to a wide variety of interpretations. There are also several inconsistencies in maritime law (Mitchell 2020). For example, there is varied and changing interpretation of the necessary conditions that must be met for a maritime feature to be defined as an island. Specifically, in the 2016 arbitration ruling in Philippines v. China, arbitrators introduced a more elaborate definition of an island. The ruling stipulated that in addition to human sustainability, there also must be economic development on a consistent basis and a permanent and significantly sized population.[6] Arguably, uncertainty may reach higher levels if maritime disputes are brought to the International Court of Justice (ICJ). In contrast to ITLOS, the ICJ in its jurisprudence can go beyond UNCLOS and instead take into consideration international custom and general principles of international law.[7] This is especially the case for maritime disputes with a territorial component.

There are many approaches to viewing, interpreting, and dissecting the issue at stake; the disputants may choose the way in which they characterize their differences. Calculated framing of the claim gives states the perception of increased levels of control over a resolution method, reducing uncertainty. Naturally, stronger legal claims—claims perceived as advantageous—increase a disputant's confidence in the likelihood of winning. Weaker legal claims increase uncertainty. Framing also causes states to be more confident in the PR method and a specific venue, particularly with regard to binding third-party venues. While strength of legal claims—evaluated objectively—can certainly play a role in dispute settlement patterns (Huth, Croco, and Appel 2011), our argument is based on a unique logic, which highlights states' aptitude to manipulate and select certain legal claims. Indeed, the

---

[5] See Chapter 2 about the principle of equity in UNCLOS.

[6] The South China Sea Arbitration, The Republic of Philippines v. The People's Republic of China, PCA Case No. 2013-19, Arbitral Award of July 12, 2016.

[7] The ICJ was the only adjudication option prior to the set-up of ITLOS. The first maritime delimitation case that was brought to ITLOS was Bangladesh v. Myanmar in 2009.

main job of states' legal advisors is to officially put forth only the claims that seem stronger, while leaving out weaker claims.[8] Therefore, the path of settlement is determined not necessarily by the overall strength of legal claims, but by how states frame their claims.

Framing claims in a particular manner by one disputant affects the response of the other disputant. As one of our interlocutors noted:

> You don't want to lose and you also want to put your best foot forward with a court or tribunal, so I think it's inevitable that you try to avoid addressing the less attractive parts of a dispute and aim instead for the more attractive parts. Of course, the other side, in thinking about how to present its defense, will be focusing on whether to bring a counterclaim or to bring a separate case that parallels the first case. The respondent may well be thinking "they aren't raising these issues that are important because it shows them in a bad light, so I want to raise them, and I'm going to do that by means of a counterclaim or a parallel case."[9]

Of course, states' perceptions play a crucial role with regard to strength of territorial and maritime claims. These perceptions allow both disputants to converge on a PR method, because both—guided by their state counsel—have selected claims that each perceives as advantageous. The hope is that a tribunal or court can rule in a positive way for both states to some degree.[10] The strategy of framing the claim also affects how the dispute is handled via negotiations or any third-party method. A state can choose to pursue merely part of a specific claim if doing so is perceived as advantageous. To be sure, in some instances pursuing a narrow fraction of a claim may yield greater benefits by leading to a positive solution. Alternatively, a state may put forth a relatively broad claim, but rely on a particular legal justification to substantiate its sovereignty claims. A disputant may also modify its claims during an ongoing dispute to help secure a favorable decision. It is within this set of legally acceptable arguments that the parties try to strategically present the most advantageous version of the facts. Granted, interpretation

---

[8] Huth et al. (2011) establish that domestic audience costs as well as strength of legal claims cumulatively affect dispute settlement patterns. We argue that it is in the power of the disputants to frame their claims as strong.

[9] Author's interview (EJP) with Sean D. Murphy, January 28, 2022.

[10] Indeed, there are several ICJ, ITLOS, and Permanent Court of Arbitration (PCA) cases that have ended in a relatively equal distribution of territorial and maritime concessions, so that both sides perceive themselves as winning.

of international law advanced by each side is more often than not channeled through its strategic interests (Powell and Wiegand 2010, 134).

The looming possibility of arbitration or adjudication—and thus the possibility that a case will be deciphered by legal means—delimits states' behavior during bilateral negotiations, mediation, and so on. In a crucial way, the mere chance of legalized settlement can shape strategizing in earlier stages of a dispute.[11] Though states strategize in the normative framework of every PR method, not every method lends itself equally to successful territorial or maritime claims. In bilateral negotiations, although there is more direct control of the process, states can still have uncertainty about their legal claims. For example, a state may have more confidence in some aspects of a boundary dispute where there are clearer historical documents to support it, while other aspects are less certain owing to a lack of historical evidence. Similarly, one state may bring certain claims to the table, while the other side refuses to acknowledge that those claims even exist.

To strengthen a state's bargaining position in bilateral negotiations, states' representatives resort to their own interpretation of facts, rules regulating the status of territorial borders, and general principles of international law. Thus, though political rhetoric and a host of nonlegal factors such as strategic considerations or power balance play an important role in negotiations, law is just as crucial in how disputants frame their claims. As Baxter (1980, 565) notes, international norms of behavior establish "new standards of relevance for the negotiations between the parties. Certain arguments will be ruled out." Put differently, rules of international law compel the disputing states to present their views in a certain space of argumentation. International law outlines the borders of this space. Law contours claims, assertions, and demands that can credibly be put on the bargaining table.[12]

The ability to carefully narrow disputed issues is not always feasible in negotiations. Frequently, negotiations may frustrate disputants' ability to control the contention. Though the parties set goals for the talks, both sides can refuse to participate in discussions and use this potential as a threat to settlement. Thus, achieving a definitive outcome through negotiations may be difficult. The informal and flexible nature of negotiations can potentially lead to procedural disagreements between the states, interfering with the actual

[11] For more discussion, see Charney 1998.
[12] As Ratner (2006, 821) put it, standards and norms of international behavior "represent a sort of fact on the ground that neither party can ignore."

subject of a dispute. Both disputants may bring a variety of issues to the table, including issues that the other side may not want to discuss (Mondre 2015).

Strategic framing of a claim is particularly crucial when a contention is submitted to an intermediary. In all third-party methods, framing of a dispute directly affects how an intermediary—a mediator, a conciliation commission, an arbitral panel, or a court—views each party's assertions. Design of third-party methods, both nonbinding and binding, allows for considerable structural flexibility. In mediation or conciliation, frequently, the disputants are able to instruct the mediator about the legal claims on which they wish the mediator to decide. Arbitration and adjudication enable strategizing by endowing the parties to define the scope of issues and legal claims. In a way, therefore, "by defining the issue narrowly, they [states] can prevent an investigation of wider questions," which "might cause more problems that it would resolve" (Merrills 2014, 4). In their efforts to frame their client's legal claims in an optimal manner, the legal counsel tries to obtain information with regard to the arbitrators' or judges' preferences: "you might put in the long shot claim, the one that you don't really think you're going to win on but maybe there's strategic reasons to advance that. For instance, you know that there's somebody on the tribunal who's really interested in a particular issue and if you frame the claim that way, maybe it will bite for that particular judge or arbitrator."[13]

Carefully choosing and designing maps constitutes a crucial part of within-venue strategy. As Martin Pratt told us, "maps are very powerful in terms of depicting international boundaries. . . . The visuals can be very powerful and choice of color and choice of what you include and leave out of any illustrative map can have a significant impact."[14] Maps can stifle or buttress a claim. However, the parties must be careful not to be accused of "refashioning geography, where you try something too fancy," thus "using maps in a way that is distorting what we should be looking at."[15]

Usually, there are several ways to view the dispute's patterns. Most aspects of any dispute—its historical background, the sides' perspectives, legal arguments, and so on—can strategically be brought to the forefront or made insignificant. For instance, when a dispute is submitted to the ICJ, while it is for the disputants to present their respective views and claims to the Court, it

---

[13] Author's interview (EJP) with an anonymous arbitration practitioner, February 7, 2022.
[14] Author's interview (EJP) with Martin Pratt, Bordermap Consulting, January 27, 2022.
[15] Ibid.

is the Court's prerogative "to isolate the real issue in the case and to identify the object of the claim."[16] However, during the process of identifying the object of the contention, the Court consults the application, the written and oral pleadings of the disputing sides. Specifically, when isolating the real issue, the ICJ "takes account of the facts that the applicant identifies as the basis for its claim" (Shaw 2017, 812). At the time of submitting the contention to adjudication, each party must identify "as far as possible the legal grounds upon which the jurisdiction of the Court is said to be based; it shall also specify the precise nature of the claim, together with a succinct statement of the facts and grounds on which the claim is based."[17] Furthermore, each disputant's memorial "shall contain a statement of the relevant facts, a statement of law, and the submissions."[18] Therefore, the particular framing of each disputant's claim, the strategic description of facts, and the contention's legal grounds are immensely important for how the ICJ outlines the real matter at hand. In a way, those aspects of a dispute that make it to the Court's docket usually constitute a judiciously constructed skeleton of the all-inclusive dyadic relationship.[19]

Framing the claim to address uncertainty was evident in the context of the Bangladesh v. India and Bangladesh v. Myanmar arbitration cases. Both conflicts mostly dealt with delimitation of the territorial sea. Each state held irreconcilable views of their respective maritime boundaries. In 2009, Bangladesh filed two arbitration cases with ITLOS regarding its maritime boundaries: one against India, and one against Myanmar. Interestingly, prior to 2009, ITLOS had not yet been asked to judge on a maritime boundary dispute. In its judgment, ITLOS specified the boundary to lie almost exactly in between lines originally proposed by Myanmar and Bangladesh.[20] However, ITLOS's rejection of Bangladesh's full claim encouraged the state's policymakers and legal counsel to redesign its subsequent case against India. In particular, Bangladesh strategically came up with a different maritime line and alternative arguments in its contention with India (Burke 2014). As some

---

[16] The Nuclear Tests case, Australia v. France, ICJ Rep, 1974, 253, 262, December 20, 1974 (also cited in Shaw 2017, 812).

[17] Article 38(2) of Rules of the Court, adopted on April 14, 1978 and entered into force on July 1, 1978.

[18] Article 49(1) of the Rules of the Court.

[19] As Collier (2009, 370) writes, "There is always the possibility that the parties 'dress up' the case to make it appear that they are putting a dispute before the Court."

[20] Dispute Concerning Delimitation of the Maritime Boundary between Bangladesh and Myanmar in the Bay of Bengal, Bangladesh v. Myanmar, ITLOS Case No. 16, 52014XC0830(01), ICGJ 448, Judgment of March 14, 2012.

have noted, "The decision in the Bangladesh v. India case was a logical follow-on to a March 2012 judgment delineating the adjacent Myanmar-Bangladesh maritime boundary, which made it possible for the PCA to quickly demarcate the adjacent boundary between Bangladesh and India" (Rosen and Jackson 2017, 1). Bangladesh's legal counsel and representatives were well aware that putting forth the widest possible sovereignty claims against India was not strategic. While it is often the case that without careful strategizing, states may want to argue for the entirety of their sovereignty claims, such arguments are less likely to succeed in binding third-party methods. As a result of strategic framing, Bangladesh was able to secure significant gains, as was Myanmar.

There are, of course limits to framing the case that states are aware of. Guided by their legal counsel, states usually proceed with caution while presenting one-sided versions of a story. As Martin Pratt noted:

> But there will also be a degree of caution. Pretending that a document that doesn't support your case doesn't exist is unlikely to get you through an entire case because almost all of the time there are very clever people working on the other side who will be doing in-depth research and this kind of material will come to light and being super selective about what you show will often, I think, potentially backfire because you'll be accused of "why are you not presenting this information, what else have you got to hide?" . . . Sometimes it's better to put all the cards on the table and then make your positive case as much as possible, try and diminish the impact of the material that doesn't support your case without outright pretending it doesn't exist. It is a delicate balancing act.[21]

Shaping the Procedures

In addition to framing the claims, to reduce uncertainty and increase their likelihood of winning, states strive to shape the chosen PR venue's procedures. The degree to which states are able to do so depends on a venue's inherent flexibility. In general, states can attempt to shape procedures in two ways: through influencing specific rules and procedures, and through the selection of mediators, legal counsel, arbitrators, and judges. Although the

[21] Author's interview (EJP) with Martin Pratt, January 27, 2022.

different PR methods and specific venues have differing degrees of formality, states are able to influence both rules and procedures as well as selection of actors involved in dispute resolution at all levels of PR venues.

Rules and Procedures

As we established in Chapter 3, the presence of intermediaries increases uncertainty and decreases the parties' control over the dispute resolution process. However, states engaging in bilateral negotiations still have a degree of uncertainty since they cannot control every single aspect of the resolution. Such uncertainty is due to the dyadic nature of all negotiations, the lack of information about the opponent's willingness to compromise and to provide or accept concessions, and ever-present credible commitment problems (Fearon 1995; Walter 2002; Hartzell and Hoddie 2003). States attempting bilateral negotiations will work vigorously to shape procedures directly in several ways: by determining the rules, the setting, the number of people involved in the negotiations and who represents the government, whether the negotiations are open or secret, the degree of formality, and what is placed on the agenda (Bercovitch and Jackson 2001).

In nonbinding methods, states have a higher level of uncertainty and lower level of control because it is the third party that makes a recommendation concerning the outcome of a dispute. Shaping the procedures starts at the outset of mediation. The disputants meet with the mediator to lay out their contentions, as well as the expected procedures. More often than not, mediators do not engage in independent investigations, as they do in the case of conciliation (Merrills 2011). Therefore, in a way, an intermediary comes to understand the contention after it has been presented by the parties via their own strategic lens. It is the actors themselves who, with the assistance of the mediator, determine the parameters, expectations, and context of the mediation (Bercovitch and Houston 2000). In reality, the entire process of mediation can be conceptualized as a continuous interaction between the three actors' strategies: "[the disputants] are strategizing, they are working on their tactics, and they are working on how they can manipulate the mediator. So the mediator is trying to work out how to manipulate the parties, and the parties are doing the same thing with respect to the mediator."[22]

---

[22] Author's interview (EJP) with Laurie Nathan, January 21, 2022.

Of course, in the context of nonbinding third-party methods, the parties may or may not choose to treat the intermediary's decision as binding. As we explained in Chapter 2, all these methods, though institutionalized through international law, constitute relatively fluid frameworks, much more so than arbitration and adjudication. As a result, intermediaries can be charged with a spectrum of responsibilities and duties. More generally, though all the nonbinding third-party methods introduce some structure to the resolution process, it is largely up to the parties to shape the specifics of the procedure. For instance, though conciliation may practically resemble arbitration and the solutions offered by a conciliator or a conciliation commission are frequently based on international law, conciliation may—at the parties' discretion—take on a much more flexible nature. Though the Model Rules approved by the UN General Assembly contain a code of rules regulating conciliation, these Model Rules have no binding force.[23] Instead, disputants may choose to adopt these rules or modify them as they see fit for the particular contention.

Within-venue strategic selection via shaping rules and procedures is particularly important in binding methods, where there is more uncertainty associated with a legally binding decision. Among the various venues for binding dispute resolution, states are able to shape rules and procedures in a more limited manner at the ICJ and ITLOS. Because of its inherent flexibility, arbitration at the PCA, ITLOS Annex VII arbitration, and independently named arbitration tribunals provide states with greater ability to engage in this aspect of within-venue strategic selection. Parties to arbitration proceedings have considerable control over the procedure regarding: time limits, the number of oral and written pleadings, obtaining the evidence, choice of languages used in the proceedings, the role of expert witnesses, allowance of separate opinions, publication of the award, and so on. Additionally, states have the ability to select some of the arbitrators.[24] Such ability to shape the arbitration proceedings allows the disputants to determine questions considered by the panel. Moreover, the parties may parse out the issues so that the panel deals with different issues at different stages of the proceedings.[25] In some

---

[23] UN General Assembly Res. A/50/50 (1996). Also see Merrills (2017, 79–80).

[24] This prerogative helped Bangladesh in its maritime boundary dispute with Myanmar and subsequently with India, since three members of the tribunals were the same in both cases (Burke 2014).

[25] Because of the ad hoc nature of arbitration tribunals, disputing states are responsible for setting up the tribunals and deciding on the procedures. This can be a time-consuming and costly process. Arguably, for states seeking timely and cheaper means to resolve a dispute, ad hoc arbitration panels are not the best forum. Adjudication at the ICJ can be cheaper than arbitration, since the Court, the

circumstances, it is more logical and effective to break down the disputed sovereignty issues. For instance, territorial issues may be discussed in the first stage of arbitration, and maritime issues in the second stage. By splitting issues into multiple stages, disputants are able to strategically shape their behavior in stage-by-stage manner, based on how the proceedings progressed. In other words, the panel's initial decision determines whether—and if so, how—the parties will split other issues in follow-up stages (Malintoppi 2015).

The ability to engage in within-venue strategic selection makes arbitration particularly attractive for some states.[26] As Wang (2014, 434) writes, "states generally have more confidence and willingness to go for arbitration," because there is more control over rules and procedures.[27] In the context of territorial disputes, it is also up to the disputants to instruct the arbitral tribunal whether to delineate the boundary on a map, or merely to identify the general principles pertinent to demarcation of the borders. If maritime claims are under consideration, the arbitral tribunal must be instructed whether, and if so, how, to deal with the various zones of coastal waters. Finally, it is up to the parties to specify the basis of the decision: international law, a particular subset of international rules, a domestic legal system, international practice, or equity.[28] In all of these ways, states can attempt to shape the rules and procedures to reduce uncertainty. For instance, in the Eritrea-Ethiopia border dispute, the parties charged the arbitration commission with reaching a decision on the basis of particular colonial treaties. At the same time, the commission was instructed not to use principles of equity (Merrills 2017, 100). In this way, both states sought to shape the procedures of the arbitration by requesting dependence on colonial treaties as well as a preference to not consider equity.

Practice has shown that parties frequently ask the tribunal to take equity into consideration—another way that states attempt to shape rules and procedures. This was the case in the Rann of Kutch dispute between India and Pakistan. The chairman of the Indo-Pakistan Western Boundary Case Tribunal stated that "it would be inequitable to recognize these inlets

---

settlement infrastructure, and the procedures are already in place. Moreover, the judges are paid by the Court and not the disputants.

[26] Trust is critical for states to perceive that they have partial control over a dispute. As Merrills (2014, 5) notes, trust in arbitrators is "a factor of fundamental importance in international litigation."
[27] In the context of maritime disputes, using an Annex VII arbitral tribunal is "an increasingly popular forum to settle disputes" (Kingdon 2015, 142).
[28] For more discussion, see Merrills (2017, 95–106).

as foreign country. It would be conducive to friction and conflict. The paramount consideration of promoting peace and stability in the region compels the recognition and confirmation that this territory, which is wholly surrounded by Pakistan territory, also be regarded as such."[29] Arbitration within the framework of UNCLOS for maritime disputes about the exclusive economic zones (EEZ) and the continental shelves of states also uses the principle of equitable solutions, based on Articles 74 and 83 in UNCLOS.

A further means by which states try to shape rules and procedures of arbitration is through setting certain fixed time limits in the case. The malleable framework of arbitration allows disputants to set shortened fixed time limits for the written pleadings, memorials, counter-memorials, and replies. For instance, in the Eritrea v. Yemen arbitration, it was very important that a fairly quick resolution occur given the civil conflicts occurring in both states.[30] The disputants were able to shape the procedure, calling for very short time limits at all stages of proceedings, and as a result, the proceedings lasted a total of only sixteen months.[31]

In arbitration, to a large extent, the parties can increase or decrease the level of formality during proceedings. Before the actual dispute is considered by a tribunal, the disputants sign a compromise—a document that outlines the location of the proceedings and the procedural details, as well as the question to be considered by the deciding body. The compromise covers whether the tribunal can resort to experts, whether tribunal members can issue separate opinions, whether the final decision will be published, and how the tribunal can acquire evidence. However, rarely do states negotiate each of these details separately. Instead, standard provisions, procedures, and established other standing tribunals constitute the benchmark for arbitral proceedings.

The willingness and ability of any international adjudicator to depart from its procedural rules varies from institution to institution as well as over time. Although in the past, the ICJ has—albeit rarely—consented to slightly modify its procedures at the request of the disputants, the increase in its caseload has compelled the Court to adhere to its standard procedural rules.[32]

---

[29] Case Concerning the Indo-Pakistan Western Boundary (Rann of Kutch), India v. Pakistan, Arbitral Award, February 19, 1968, 571. Available at https://legal.un.org/riaa/vol_17.shtml.

[30] Territorial Sovereignty and Maritime Delimitation in Scope of the Red Sea Dispute, Eritrea v. Yemen, PCA, phase I (1998), phase II (1999), 2001, 40 ILM 900 and 983, Arbitral Awards of October 9, 1998, and December 17, 1999.

[31] The oral proceedings in the case took only three months after the final written submissions, and an award was provided within only three months from the oral proceedings (Malintoppi 2015).

[32] Overall, disputes between states are usually more flexible and drawn out than disputes adjudicated by a domestic court. In the words of Rosenne (2003, 91), "The litigants are sovereign

Selection of Actors

Decision makers can attempt to influence a third-party venue's proceedings through the selection of actors involved in the settlement: conciliators, mediators, arbitrators, judges, legal advisors, and lawyers. These choices are fundamental to the outcome of the resolution process. For instance, states can make assessments about their likelihood of winning based on the makeup of a court as well as the record of individual judges. The same is true for arbitration and the nonbinding third-party methods. Particularly vital for any state involved in a territorial or a maritime dispute is the choice of counsel who guide policymakers and represent the state in the settlement process. Throughout the settlement proceedings, an experienced lawyer is indispensable for successful navigation of the myriad rules and procedures of international law. According to William Thomas QC, "running major inter-State dispute resolution effectively is very much a team effort. Usually, it isn't just a question of getting in one or two brilliant lawyers who, by themselves, are going to win your dispute for you. Inter-State disputes generally require much more than that because they are often large in scale and may well need multidisciplinary input that extends beyond just legal expertise."[33] With time, hiring professional legal counsel became the norm. Whereas "in the early days of boundary cases, it was almost entirely professors of international law who were recruited by governments, . . . there has been a move over the last 20 years to involve commercial law firms as well who can offer logistical support as much as anything else in terms of case management because often these cases are far more than one or two academic professors can handle it in terms of managing the scale of the evidence that is collected now and coordinating an international team."[34]

States which do not easily accept outside interference in how they conduct their affairs. Speed in the conduct of the proceedings is not always appropriate and the saying 'justice delayed is justice denied' not always pertinent, since proceedings can be significantly affected by diplomatic developments outside the control of the Court, or even of the parties themselves, and diplomacy can have its own time-table."

[33] Author's interview (EJP) with William Thomas QC, March 9, 2022. William is a Partner and Global Head of Public International Law at Freshfields Bruckhaus Deringer LLP. He has acted as counsel and advocate for states and state entities in numerous institutional and ad hoc arbitral proceedings, including under ICC, LCIA, ICSID, and UNCITRAL rules. He has also represented state parties before both the International Court of Justice and the Iran-US Claims Tribunal, as well as advising clients before the European Court of Human Rights.

[34] Author's interview (EJP) with Martin Pratt, January 27, 2022.

A good legal counsel is well-versed in the intricate procedural framework of the chosen venue. For instance, lawyers who are consulted or hired as state representatives in arbitration or adjudication proceedings have knowledge of substantive international law, and they are acquainted with the procedures of international courts and tribunals. There are also state counsel who specialize in specific PR method or venue. In general, it is safe to say that it is not diplomats but lawyers who are typically driving the international legal settlement process.[35] Acquiring a reliable legal counsel can significantly mitigate states' uncertainty associated with the resolution process. Setting any other issues aside, the services of an excellent legal counsel may give states a perception that they themselves have increased control over the settlement.

Interestingly, legal counsel is usually sought from Western lawyers and Western law firms with extensive international experience and a proven record of winning. This is true for Western and non-Western states, such as Islamic law states (see Powell 2020). While Islamic law states prefer, other things being equal, to settle their disputes via the nonbinding third-party methods, when using international courts or arbitration tribunals, these states hire Western legal counsel to improve their chances of winning. In some venues, states have the prerogative to designate the intermediary. This is largely the case for nonbinding third-party methods: mediation, conciliation, good offices, and inquiry. Interestingly, with the exception of adjudication, the disputants may choose the intermediaries from among a broad assortment of technical experts and specialists, depending on the particulars of the ongoing dispute. Naturally, all these choices are guided by the parties' strategic considerations. In mediation, states are able to select mediators who are knowledgeable about the disputants (Regan et al. 2009; Svensson and Lundgren 2013; Wiegand, Keels, and Rowland 2021), as well as mediators who are perceived to be impartial or unbiased (Beber 2012; Favretto 2009; Melin 2011). Selecting mediators who understand the disputants' preferences increases chances of successful settlement. The selection of a particular mediator can also determine the specifics of the settlement in terms of concessions. A mediator's personal characteristics—trustworthiness, the ability to speak authoritatively and convincingly, a proven record of past success in delivering mediation—all matter to the disputing states. It is not

---

[35] This is especially the case in the context of territorial disputes. Disputes over territory, perhaps more than other disputes, resemble domestic litigation because they require a plethora of evidence, maps, and technical expertise. For more discussion, see Ratner 2006.

always necessary that a mediator's relationship to each side is of a similar nature. Indeed, when a mediator is closer to one party, the opposing side may anticipate a better solution. After all, it is likely that a friend may keep all channels of communication open (Zartman and Touval 1985).

In arbitration, states are able to decide who sits on an arbitration panel. The PCA does not operate as a proper court and, unlike the ICJ, does not have a permanent number of judges. Instead, the PCA retains a list of potential arbitrators who can be nominated by the disputants for a particular contention. At present, there are more than 120 persons listed on the PCA's website "of known competency in questions of international law, of the highest moral reputation and disposed to accept the duties of an arbitrator."[36] Once the disputants' preferences converge on arbitration as a PR method, states can choose members of the arbitral tribunal from the list.

In contrast, in adjudication, states have a very limited ability to select judges. For example, when disputants do not have a judge of their nationality on the bench, an ad hoc judge may be appointed. The prerogative to select a judge came about in 1972 when the ICJ revised its Rules in an effort to increase use of the Court. The change in Rules encourages disputants to use ad hoc chambers and allows them to shape the bench's size and makeup. The parties may also request that their case be heard by a smaller chamber, generally consisting of five judges, instead of the full bench of fifteen judges. Explaining the dearth of disputes reviewed by the ICJ in the 1960s and 1970s, Miyoshi (1996, 49) notes that the ICJ "was not kept very busy for some time because States hesitated to go there. That was why an attempt was made to invigorate the Court by devising easier access to a chamber as provided for in Article 26, paragraph 2, of its Statute. This was done by "facilitat[ing] recourse to Chambers of the Court and conced[ing] to the parties some influence in the composition of ad hoc Chambers." These revisions were first put into practice in the Gulf of Maine case between Canada and the United States.[37] Although it seems that both parties preferred arbitration, "they found it easier to submit their dispute to a Chamber of the Court since they were assured under the new Rules of Court that they could have substantial influence on its composition" (Miyoshi 1996, 50).

---

[36] Website of the Permanent Court of Arbitration, available at https://pca-cpa.org/en/about/struct ure/members-of-the-court/.

[37] Delimitation of the Maritime Boundary in the Gulf of Maine Area, Canada v. United States, 1984 ICJ Rep. 246, Judgment of October 12, 1984.

Selection of international judges and arbitrators is important since they are usually trained in diverse legal traditions, as discussed earlier. This reality further complicates the disputants' ability to foresee a court's or a tribunal's legal reasoning. Arguably, judges' and arbitrators' practical knowledge of a particular domestic legal tradition may partially impact the manner in which a judgment or an arbitral award is crafted and justified. Indeed, each domestic legal tradition "produces a unique domestic community of international law academics, with different legal training, professional skills, and experiences" (Powell 2020, 135). It is to be expected that international lawyers draw partially on their own domestic legal training to understand norms of international law. Thus, in some instances, proposer states are unable to anticipate if and how a domestic legal tradition will factor into the process of interpreting general principles of international laws (Powell 2013; Powell and Wiegand 2014; and Wiegand and Powell 2011a).

In the process of preparing for in-court proceedings, legal counsel examine positions that specific judges have taken in past legal rulings. Judges may be known for political inclinations and their judicial writings can also suggest the way they may rule in specific cases.[38] This information is especially important in cases that involve particular interpretations of international law. Such background research helps legal teams in framing their client's claims, thus reducing uncertainty of potential outcomes. Examining the intermediary's past record is even more critical in the context of arbitral proceedings. Both parties can select their most preferred arbitrators on the basis of this information.

Conclusions

We have in this chapter focused on the second stage of strategic selection, within-venue, that occurs when the disputants agree to settle their contention via a particular PR method and venue. As a crucial step in the dispute resolution process, selection of a method/venue thrusts the parties into a victory-focused, intricate scheme of strategic choices vis-à-vis the opponent and vis-à-vis the venue itself. There is a multiplicity of choices that can bring

---

[38] For more information, see Scott 2014. More broadly, see Mackenzie et al. (2010, 52). According to these authors, although there is no "ideal international judge" for every disputant, states examine the widely varied experiences and backgrounds of judges.

the parties closer to their most preferred outcome, victory. We conceptualize these choices into two broad mechanisms of within-venue strategic selection: framing the claim and shaping procedures. The degree of inherent flexibility associated with the various PR methods and venues can either propel or constrain parties' strategizing. For instance, the parties' ability to select judges in the context of ICJ proceedings is limited to ad hoc judges. Yet, in arbitration, the disputants may select the arbitrators.

It is also crucial to add that to some extent, the nature of the contention determines the parties' ability to engage in some aspects of within-venue strategic selection. For instance, the degree to which the disputants may frame their claims is largely dictated by the realities of a territorial or a maritime contention. Simply put, the geography on the ground may allow for more latitude in some cases, but constrain the parties in other cases. As this chapter shows, there is a deep connection between the two stages of strategic selection, choice-of-venue and within-venue. Policymakers link their decisions about what method and venue to choose with their perceptions of subsequent success in manipulating the venue. The point is that there are many approaches to interpreting, dissecting legal arguments, and—more generally—the issue at the heart of any territorial or maritime contention. States, guided by their legal counsel, take advantage of this reality to further their own preferences.

As a final thought, we wish to highlight that while engaging in the process of strategic selection, states—guided by their legal counsel—make choices that are deeply influenced by several audiences. As one of our interviewees noted, "there's a couple of different audiences at play and they don't necessarily lead in the same direction . . . the audience of the tribunal you're pleading in front of, but there's also the audience of your minister, of public opinion back home. . . . And those audiences could potentially push in different directions."[39] All these streams of influence shape policymakers' and the legal counsel's decisions. These factors determine whether, and if so, how, sovereignty claims are rephrased, whether certain aspects of the dispute are emphasized or downplayed, and so on. In sum, all states strategize with hopes of optimizing their experience at a selected PR method and venue. But the strategizing may be limited or propelled by the realities of each deeply idiosyncratic contention.

---

[39] Author's interview (EJP) with an anonymous arbitration practitioner, February 7, 2022.

5

Research Design and Trends in
Territorial and Maritime Disputes

In this chapter, we discuss the data and research design that guide our mixed-methods approach. First, we present the Peaceful Resolution of Territorial Disputes (PRTD) dataset, which covers territorial disputes worldwide from 1945 to 2015 (Wiegand, Powell, and McDowell 2020) used in our quantitative analysis. We provide an overview of trends in territorial dispute resolution across all geographic regions of the world. Second, we discuss the qualitative data used in this book, covering the same time period. Our mixed-method, or multimethod, approach to studying territorial and maritime disputes is optimal. According to Goertz (2017, 1), "Multimethod can mean many things," such as "combining case studies with statistics, qualitative comparative analysis (QCA), experiments, or game theory models." In this book, we combine statistical analyses, insights from in-depth qualitative interviews, and primary documents/materials to accumulate scholarly and practical knowledge of peaceful dispute resolution. Together, these methodologies allow us to gather knowledge of mechanisms that explain central political phenomena—in our case, states' strategic behavior in dispute resolution. Indeed, as King, Keohane, and Verba (1994, 43) write, "social science research should be both general and specific: it should tell us something about classes of events as well as about specific events at particular places."

In Chapter 6 we test the hypotheses that we derive from our theory by applying statistical techniques to the PRTD dataset, while controlling for a variety of confounding influences.[1] Quantitative analysis is widely used in the international conflict management literature, and in the context of our study it helps greatly in examining relationships between variables and the likelihood of certain outcomes. But it is important to recognize that

---

[1] Models, whether theoretical, statistical, or game-theoretic, "are always simplifications, ignoring much of what is going on in the target" (Ashworth, Berry, and Bueno de Mesquita 2021, 13). Yet, simplifying reality through a model has numerous intellectual payoffs, even if all the details of a phenomenon are not captured.

The Peaceful Resolution of Territorial and Maritime Disputes. Emilia Justyna Powell and Krista E. Wiegand, Oxford University Press. © Oxford University Press 2023. DOI: 10.1093/oso/9780197675649.003.0005

quantitative analysis suffers from lack of context and an inability to demonstrate causality. Indeed, "statistical analyses do not provide explanations" (Goertz 2017, 4), and thus statistical models should be best used as "devices for testing explanations" (Clarke and Primo 2012, 154). Though our goal is to identify general patterns of dispute settlement, we do not wish to ignore unique mechanisms that our data cannot measure—mainly, the within-venue strategic selection. Thus, our incorporation of qualitative data helps to confirm regularities and patterns demonstrated in the statistical analyses (Gerring 2017).

Our choice to base our empirics on comprehensive statistical data and in-depth qualitative interviews makes our book unique. Though each source of our data and each type of method has advantages and disadvantages, they largely complement each other to provide a vivid picture of strategizing in international dispute resolution. The multimethod approach aids us in our efforts "to explain social phenomena in terms of mechanisms" (Ashworth, Berry, and Bueno de Mesquita 2021, 45). While they can be deeply informative, most empirical studies of territorial and maritime disputes rely mainly on statistical analyses of large datasets or individual case studies. Rarely are direct interviews with decision makers involved in peaceful settlement used to elucidate the dynamics of these contentions. Such qualitative research enables us to understand practices and decision-making processes that bring about states' strategic choices of settlement venues. Collectively, these practices and decision-making processes produce patterns and regularities reflected in our statistical results. It is the togetherness of human experience and many individual-level decisions that combine to generate states' choices of specific settlement peaceful resolution (PR) methods and venues. Our comprehensive approach aids us in shedding light on the ongoing interaction between mechanisms of strategic selection—past experience and the relationship between international law and domestic law—and within-venue mechanisms of uncertainty about the process and legal claims.

Our quantitative analyses introduce over-time dynamics into the measurement of patterns in dispute resolution—the exchange of settlement proposals between the challenger and the target. As mentioned in Chapter 1, we use the terms "proposer state" and "nonproposer state," instead of "challenger" and "target state." Either the challenger or target can be a proposer state. The proposer state is the equivalent of a claimant in domestic jurisdictions. It is the disputant who initiates the dispute PR attempt, that is, proposes that a particular method—negotiations, mediation, arbitration, etc.—is attempted. The nonproposer state is the addressee of the proposer state's attempt at dispute resolution. Thus, the nonproposer state—similar to a respondent in domestic jurisdictions—is the disputant who engages in the dyadic dispute resolution attempt following the proposer state's proposal.[2]

The proposer state is more often the challenger state, whose goal is to gain some concessions, whether territorial or maritime. Sometimes it is the target state that makes a settlement proposal in order to solidify the legal status quo. The nonproposer may respond to the proposal by agreeing or refusing to participate in a particular PR method. Moreover, as the dispute continues, the nonproposer state may put forth a proposal for an alternative PR method, thus becoming a proposer state. As we explain below, we measure the status changes, from proposer to nonproposer and vice versa, on a yearly basis. In some disputes it is indeed the case that the two sides switch their places as proposers and nonproposers, since most disputes involve a prolonged interaction with exchanges of proposals forthcoming from both sides.

In an overwhelming number of cases, each side issues multiple calls for settlement that are met with the opponent's disapproval. A recent example of such dynamics is the one-sided attempt by Slovenia in July 2018 to obtain adjudication at the Court of Justice of the European Union (CJEU) against Croatia regarding its disputed land and sea border at Piran Bay on the Adriatic Sea.[3] Earlier, in 2017, the Permanent Court of Arbitration (PCA) had ruled on the matter. Yet, according to Slovenia, Croatia failed to implement the ruling. Since both disputants are part of the European Union, Slovenia's goal was to seek justice under EU law. In December 2018, Croatia refused to participate in the CJEU proceedings, citing jurisdiction issues (Hristova 2020). In the end, in January 2020, the Court declared that it lacked jurisdiction on the matter.

In our analysis of the choice-of-venue stage, our focus is primarily on the proposer state's strategies since it is the proposer state that seeks to resolve the contention. Dispute resolution constitutes an inherently dyadic and strategic interaction that rests on both sides' continuous and repeatedly given consent. While we recognize that strategic interaction occurs in international disputes, our theory and analyses take a monadic approach. However,

[2] Granted, in domestic jurisdictions, in an overwhelming majority of cases, a respondent does not have a choice whether to engage in a particular dispute resolution method. This is especially the case in the context of adjudication.
[3] The website of the Court of Justice of the European Union is accessible at https://europa.eu/europ ean-union/about-eu/institutions-bodies/court-justice_en.

our statistical analyses take into consideration some characteristics of the non-proposer states coded as independent variables. We believe that this approach best reflects our concentration on the proposer state's strategies. There are, indeed, many cases in which a proposer state issues a resolution attempt and the nonproposer state rejects it either implicitly or explicitly. Precisely because we home in on the proposer's own (monadic) preferences toward resolution, we treat these cases no differently than cases where a nonproposer agrees to the PR forum or proposes an alternative resolution venue, thus becoming itself a proposer state. To fully capture the dyadic interaction between the proposer and nonproposer in each year of an ongoing dispute is beyond the scope of this book. Our approach is not unique in this regard, as most studies of territorial and maritime disputes, whether dealing with armed conflict or peaceful resolutions, focus on the challenger state's strategies.

In the context of the within-venue stage, our qualitative analysis examines the strategies of both the proposer and nonproposer states, because at this stage, both actors are actively seeking to reduce their uncertainty. In the process of an ongoing resolution process, both disputants need to work tirelessly to reduce uncertainty and increase the likelihood of victory. This means that both states engage in strategic behavior. As with the choice-of-venue stage, we do not examine their strategic interaction, only their individual preferences and strategies.

The Peaceful Resolution of Territorial Disputes (PRTD) Data

The main source for testing our choice-of-venue hypotheses is a dataset on peaceful resolution attempts in territorial disputes. This dataset includes disputes focusing on territory exclusively, including land, boundaries, and islands, as well as disputes that include both territorial and maritime components. The dataset does not cover disputes that deal exclusively with maritime features. The PRTD dataset provides researchers with panel level dispute-year data that include all proposals for peaceful settlement in territorial disputes (Wiegand, Powell, and McDowell 2020). The core list of territorial disputes used for creation of these data is taken from the Issue Correlates of War (ICOW) project's provisional dataset (Frederick, Hensel, and Macaulay 2017, v. 1.01). The data cover 200 territorial disputes from all regions of the world, and include all years that disputes are ongoing between 1945 and 2015. We define a territorial dispute as a disagreement between two or more states over title to territory (Hensel et al. 2008).[4] The term "title" refers to the factual and legal conditions that authorize the exercise of territorial sovereignty.[5] The unit of analysis is the dispute-year. Thus, each observation represents one year in which a state is involved in a territorial dispute, regardless of whether settlement attempts were made or not.

We define a peaceful settlement proposal as any observable indication by formally authorized representatives of a state that the state prefers a particular peaceful settlement method in a particular year (Wiegand and Powell 2011a). As discussed above, dispute settlement is a dynamic process whereby both disputants continue to issue peaceful settlement proposals throughout the duration of a contention. To capture this reality, our data pay close attention to the ongoing dialogue between states and their unique preferences. Importantly, we code when a state continues to participate in a peaceful settlement process initiated in a previous year, and years when a peaceful process settles a dispute. There are also types of observable behavior that do not constitute peaceful settlement proposals: when a state does nothing to settle an ongoing dispute, when a state only uses coercive measures (e.g., militarized interstate disputes [MIDs], war, occupation) to settle a dispute, or when a state merely reiterates its claim to a disputed territory but proposes no method for arriving at a settlement. Finally, not all talks between disputants classify as peaceful settlement proposals. For instance, opponents may agree to negotiations regarding issues in the disputed region, but the talks do not involve the question of sovereignty.

Altogether, there are 9,610 proposer-year observations in our data. In 2,983 observations, a proposer state attempted a PR method. Territorial disputes enter our dataset in the first year that a state challenges sovereignty rights, or in 1945 if such claims existed prior to that year. Disputes exit the dataset when the dispute is resolved through armed conflict, peaceful settlement, a dropped claim, or a turnover of sovereign territory to an adversary. Disputes also exit the dataset in 2015, the end of our observation period. To be included in the data, an attempt could be unilateral or pursued by both states. In the latter case, two separate observations enter our dataset. Our

---

[4] We do not include maritime disputes in the PRTD dataset. See the ICOW Maritime Claims dataset for details about the peaceful settlement of maritime disputes.

[5] For more discussion, see Shaw (2017, 363–67).

dataset goes beyond merely capturing only settled disputes. Rather, our data include observable indications that a particular state preferred one peaceful settlement method to other methods, regardless of the preferences or actions of opponents. Importantly, the specific proposed settlement method did not have to actually ensue. In other words, the data include many observations in which states proposed a settlement method, but the opposing state rejected the proposal. To summarize, what matters is whether a state *attempted* to peacefully resolve a territorial dispute, not whether that resolution attempt was successful, though in many cases a resolution process did occur (Wiegand, Powell, and McDowell 2020).

Sources of the Data

To compile the PRTD dataset, we used several sources. We started first with data on bilateral negotiations pursued by challenger states in the Huth and Allee (2002) dataset on territorial disputes (1945–1995), verifying these data.[6] We then recorded all these bilateral negotiation attempts made by target states (1945–2015), and all attempts made by challenger states between 1995 and 2015 using three main types of sources.[7] First, we examined all International Court of Justice (ICJ) judgments, arbitral awards, and related legal documents and coded all attempts at settlement. We also examined secondary sources. These sources had to meet two criteria of reliability: they had to be specific with regard to the timing and types of peaceful settlement proposals, and they had to cite specific and accessible primary sources as direct evidence of peaceful settlement proposals. We used several encyclopedia-type sources about disputed territory, including Allcock (1992), the Central Intelligence Agency (CIA) World Factbook (2018), Day (1987), Downing (1980), and International Boundary Research Unit (IBRU) briefings and news stories about territorial disputes (IBRU 2018). Finally, we searched for newspaper stories about settlement proposals using the Nexis-Uni database.[8] Importantly, all these sources had to cite proposals by policymakers on behalf of a state and could not include media or analyst

---

[6] The Huth and Allee (2002) dataset covers all territorial disputes from 1919 to 1995, but for our purposes, we only included those attempts made from 1945 on.

[7] These sources were used for all other settlement types as well.

[8] We verified the cases using the ICOW dataset (Hensel et al. 2008) for disputes up to 2001, the last year in that dataset publicly available.

speculations about whether a peaceful settlement proposal might or should occur. To be included in the data, an attempt at peaceful settlement had to be in the form of a call for negotiations, nonbinding third-party assistance, arbitration, or a submission of the dispute to an international court. To qualify, the settlement attempt had to comprise discussions regarding recognition of sovereignty, potential territorial concessions, or changes in ownership. In other words, discussions planning future talks or other related issues do not count as a peaceful settlement proposal. Thus, only substantive attempts at settlement, as opposed to functional or procedural attempts, are included in the data. There are many examples of negotiations that were not meant to deal with questions of territorial sovereignty. For example, several negotiations between Argentina and the United Kingdom during the Falklands/Malvinas Islands dispute in the 2000s have dealt with hydrocarbon exploitation, joint exercises of troops in sea rescue operations in the South Atlantic, and shared attempts to halt poaching by Asian fishing vessels without licenses. None of these proposals are included in our data.

Dependent Variable

For each observation, we code whether the challenger state or the target state attempted peaceful settlement, as well as the specific type of PR method. Importantly, our data code information on states' preferences for peaceful settlement and not militarized conflicts. While considering peaceful settlement, states may engage in militarized activities or issue threats of such actions. There are several extensive datasets devoted to militarized conflicts in territorial disputes including the ICOW project and the Huth and Allee (2002) dataset. We have designed our dataset for easy merging with these and other datasets, including the Militarized Interstate Disputes (MID) dataset (Palmer et al. 2020).

Settlement Proposal Type, our primary dependent variable, is a nominal variable that comprises the different PR methods. The *Settlement Proposal Type* variable ranges from 0 to 3: no action taken (0), bilateral negotiations (1), nonbinding third-party methods (2), and third-party binding methods (3). Of the observations in which a proposer state attempted a PR method, 71.7 percent are bilateral negotiations, 14.4 percent are nonbinding third-party attempts, and 13.9 percent are binding PR methods (4.1 percent arbitration and 9.8 percent adjudication). Because there are fewer instances of attempts at arbitration and adjudication, we combine the two methods into one category, binding methods.

Any nonzero coding represents a preference for a particular settlement method. A preference may be expressed by proposing a PR method or suggesting a particular venue such as the ICJ or PCA.[9] If both the challenger and the target are coded as proposers in the same year (two different observations), our dataset includes information on which side proposed a settlement method (the proposer state) and which side merely agreed to the proposal (the nonproposer state). *Settlement Proposal Type* is coded 0 if, for an entire year, no state issued a proposal for settlement. There are many instances when intermittent negotiations spanned a period of several years, with breaks lasting less than a year. If a state attempted different settlement methods over a period of several years, the coding reflects these changes from year to year. If there are multiple attempts made within one year, we code the most legalized method attempted. The design of the data enables us to examine how mechanisms of strategic selection—past experience as well as the relationship between international law and domestic law—influence preferences of individual disputants.

Past Experience Variables

To test our hypotheses about how states' past experiences influence their selection of settlement methods, we generated variables for the proposer state and the nonproposer state, and their past win-loss record in each dispute PR method. We expect that these experiences with the various PR methods will affect the proposer states' preferences in ongoing territorial disputes. In particular, as Hypothesis 1 states, we anticipate that a proposer state with a positive win-loss record in a particular resolution method—in dispute with a nonproposer with a less favorable win-loss record in that same method—is more likely to use this method again. In Hypothesis 2, we extend our general expectation about past experience by predicting that a proposer state in the same geographic region as other states with positive win-loss records in a PR method is more likely to use this method again. As noted in Chapter 3, it would be ideal to test for the influence of past experiences of all states worldwide in different venues. Yet, it is likely the case that states pay

---

[9] For our conceptualization of how PR venues relate to PR methods, see footnote 12 in Chapter 1.

closest attention to cases that are similar to their own ongoing or ensuing contentions.

In the construction of the past experience variables, we code each observation as 1 if the proposer state won or lost in the past using bilateral negotiations, nonbinding third-party methods, or third-party binding methods. Similarly, we code whether the nonproposer state won or lost using each method in the past. This measure operationalizes the concept of winning in the most parsimonious, generalizable, and widely accepted manner: winning more than 50 percent of territorial concessions.[10] To determine the past win-loss record for the proposer and nonproposer state, we generated a variable originally used in Wiegand and Powell (2011a). First, we gathered information on states' victories and losses in each PR method for the period 1945–2003, then we updated the data to 2015 for this study. To do so, we relied on the same source materials used for the dependent variable, focusing on the final settlement outcome of each territorial dispute between 1945 and 2015. In other words, we coded the final outcomes of each resolution method, and counted the total number of past wins and losses that had occurred since 1945, the start of our dataset. By way of illustration, when a state attempts peaceful settlement—for instance mediation—in 1999, this state's past win-loss record is measured for the 1945–1998 period, provided that the state has been a state according to international law during that time frame.

Keeping in mind our definition of winning discussed in Chapter 3, coding for a victory—a win that emerges as a result of a settlement—may not appear clear-cut, since both disputants may have received substantial territorial concessions in the final agreement, award, or judgment. In such cases, more often than not, both sides claim victory and perceive themselves as winners. If territorial concessions were roughly equal, we coded both the proposer and the nonproposer state as winners. To be clear, while we do not require evidence that states themselves perceive the concessions to be equal, in an overwhelming number of cases, the political rhetoric indicates that both disputants perceive the outcome as equitable. This coding decision is based on the logic that a "50-50" outcome does not produce a clear loser, and this outcome could still encourage both proposer and nonproposer states

---

[10] This operationalization does not take into consideration states' subjective perceptions of resolution outcomes. As discussed in our theoretical chapter, it is not possible to code 166 states' subjective perceptions of winning. Future research could focus on states' subjective impressions of winning.

to return to a particular method in the future. For example, in the territorial dispute over the Hawar Islands between Qatar and Bahrain, both states perceived the 2001 ICJ judgment as favorable.[11] The ruling awarded both disputants part of the territory. Bahrain kept the Hawar Islands and Qit'at Jaradah, and the Court decided that Qatar had sovereignty over Janan/Hadd Janan, Zubarah, and the Fasht ad Dibal.[12] Bahrain and Qatar openly agreed to comply with the judgment soon after it was issued. This increased cooperation allowed for joint economic development, including joint oil exploration ventures (Powell 2020; Wiegand 2012). Many settlements lack a clear division of territory that would enable us to assign exact percentage values to concessions gained by each disputant. Thus, in all types of settlement, we consider a state a winner of a territorial dispute settlement if the state achieved territorial concessions of more than 50 percent of the disputed territory.[13] The opposing side is therefore coded as the loser. Thus, our coding decisions are based on relative gains and losses of both sides in the context of each settlement outcome.

The next step in coding was to combine the information about winning and losing into one measure per PR method for both proposer and nonproposer states. To do this, we divided the sum of wins by the sum of wins and losses, resulting in a batting average for proposer and nonproposer states using each different settlement method in any given year. The resulting batting average is a scale that goes from 0 to .5 to 1. The lowest score, 0, indicates a totally negative experience of only losing in a particular forum, and 1 indicates a perfectly positive experience of only winning in the past. If a state won and lost an equal number of disputes using the same method, they have a score of .5. Similarly, for states that had no experiences with dispute settlement in the past because they were not involved in any other territorial disputes, or they had no experience with a particular resolution method, we assigned a value of .5 to represent indifference toward a specific method.[14] The resulting variables used to test Hypothesis 1 are: *Proposer Win-Loss Negotiations, Proposer Win-Loss Third-Party Nonbinding, Proposer Win-Loss*

---

[11] Maritime Delimitation and Territorial Questions between Qatar and Bahrain, Qatar v. Bahrain, ICJ Rep. 2001, 40, Judgment of March 16, 2001. See Schulte 2004.

[12] In November 2017, Bahrain's official news agency published a press release suggesting that Bahrain has "every right to claim what was cut off forcibly from its land and to dispute the legitimacy of the Qatari rule" ("Sovereignty and Legitimate Rights: Historical Facts," *Bahrain News Agency,* November 4, 2017).

[13] In most cases, the settlement makes it clear which side won and which side lost the dispute.

[14] Otherwise, for all states with no wins and no losses, the value indicating their Win-Loss Record would be missing (the denominator would be 0).

Third-Party Binding. Our data has equivalent variables for the nonproposer states: *Nonproposer Win-Loss Negotiations, Nonproposer Win-Loss Third-Party Nonbinding, Nonproposer Win-Loss Third-Party Binding.*

Between 1945 and 2015, states have peacefully resolved 122 territorial disputes. In 41 percent of these settled disputes, both states involved received relatively equal territorial concessions. This group consists of cases where both sides agreed to accept or trade territorial sovereignty in relatively equal parts as a result of bilateral negotiations or mediation. Also in this group are cases where an arbitral tribunal or court awarded each state approximately 50 percent of the contested territorial claims. Indeed, while adjudicating a dispute, the ICJ is aware of how winning and losing matter to states. Thus, when legal considerations justify such an outcome, the Court is likely to divide the concessions in a 50-50 manner. As one of our interviewees noted, "The Court is always conscious of the delicacy of the situation. But its decisions would be by reference to legal considerations."[15] Our data reveal that peaceful settlement yielded a clear victory to challenger states—the challenger won the entirety of the contested territory—in 16 percent of cases. In 6 percent of peacefully settled disputes, the challengers were awarded the majority of the contested land. Patterns are different for targets. In 29 percent of settled disputes target states maintained sovereign control by winning all the disputed territory. These states kept the majority of their territorial sovereignty in an additional 8 percent of dispute settlements.

Table 5.1 shows the number of settled disputes by type of PR method. One interesting observation is that 62 percent of bilateral negotiations result in a relatively equal division of territorial sovereignty. Cases when either the challenger or the target gains all the disputed territory account for merely 6 and 17 percent of the disputes, respectively. These patterns suggest that in almost two-thirds of disputes settled bilaterally by the parties, bargaining leads to compromises and mutual gains. In contrast, 63 percent of settlements via nonbinding third-party methods result in the target state keeping the majority of the territory already under its control.[16] These patterns suggest that intermediaries involved in nonbinding third-party methods support the existing territorial status quo.

---

[15] Author's interview (EJP) with an anonymous ICJ state advocate and international arbitrator, United Kingdom, October 2013.
[16] No target state achieved all territorial concessions through mediation.

Table 5.1 Percentage of territorial dispute wins for challenger and target states by PR method, 1945–2015

	Both Challenger and Target Win 50%	Challenger Wins All	Challenger Wins Majority	Target Wins All	Target Wins Majority
Bilateral Negotiations	62%	6%	9%	17%	6%
Nonbinding Third-Party	13%	25%	0%	63%	0%
Arbitration	55%	9%	0%	9%	27%
Adjudication	28%	17%	6%	33%	16%

Our descriptive data reveal interesting patterns with regard to arbitration. Just over half of arbitral awards resulted in a 50-50 split of territorial sovereignty between the contestants. Indeed, there are much fewer situations in which the challenger or the target won all or the majority of the disputed territory. In only one arbitration case—the 1994 arbitration between Argentina and Chile—did the challenger win all or the majority of claimed territory. In 36 percent of the cases, target states using arbitration won all or the majority of territorial concessions. Finally, in adjudication, victories of target states (49 percent) are much more frequent than those of challenger states (23 percent).

Regional Patterns

In order to evaluate the overall success levels of different PR methods in a particular region, we generated variables that measure the win-loss record for all proposer states in each geographic region of the world (Europe, the Americas, the Middle East, Africa, and Asia/Oceania).[17] Recall that Hypothesis 2 expresses our expectation that proposer states examine not only their own and their opponents' win-loss records, but also the win-loss record of other states in the region. After coding each proposer state's geographic

---

[17] We only include past experience of proposer states for Hypothesis 2 because the nonproposer experience is almost parallel to the proposer state, but reversed. Including the record of the nonproposer in the region does not add any new information to examine.

region, we then combined the batting average of all proposer states in each PR method in the same region to create these variables: *Proposer Win-Loss Negotiations*Region, Proposer Win-Loss Third-Party Nonbinding*Region,* and *Proposer Win-Loss Third-Party Binding*Region.* Most territorial disputes occur in dyads in the same geographic region, but there are a few exceptions such as the Falklands/Malvinas Islands dispute between Argentina and the United Kingdom. In such cases, we code the geographic region based on the location of the disputed territory.

When we examine geographic regions, we find interesting patterns. Asia and Oceania together have the highest percentage of all dispute years (33 percent). This is followed by two regions—the Americas and Africa—with 21 percent each, and then the Middle East and Europe with 12 percent each. Figure 5.1 shows that during the postwar years, Europe, Asia and Oceania, and the Americas were experiencing relatively high numbers of territorial disputes. Over time, this number increased, especially in Asia and Oceania, with a peak of sixty-three disputes in 1998. During the time span of our data, the Middle East has also experienced its share of territorial disputes. However, most of these contentions have been resolved, with only four remaining in 2015—a comparatively low number. In contrast,

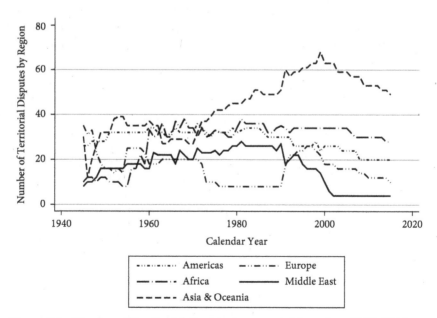

Figure 5.1. Number of territorial disputes by geographic region, 1945–2015.

Asia and Oceania had forty-nine ongoing disputes as of 2015. Most of these contentions are in East Asia and several involve China. As of 2015, Africa had twenty-eight and Europe had ten ongoing disputes. If we only look at years in which a PR proposal occurred, the numbers are similar: Asia and Oceania account for 36 percent of proposals, followed by the Americas (21 percent), Africa (18 percent), Europe (14 percent), and the Middle East (11 percent). When we examine types of PR proposals by region, we find that dispute settlement preferences vary substantially, particularly when it comes to third-party dispute resolution. Though negotiations constitute the most frequently pursued PR method used, relative frequency of bilateral talks varies by region. For example, negotiations are the most frequent PR method in Asia and Oceania. Mediation is quite common in the Middle East and the Americas. Interestingly, states in Africa and the Americas are the most frequent users of the ICJ for territorial dispute resolution.

Americas

In the Americas, negotiations were the most popular settlement method until around 2005, though the decline began about 1980. A modest rise in the popularity of the nonbinding third-party methods during this time is accompanied by a considerable increase of proposals for adjudication, but not arbitration. In this region, over the time span of our data, mediation was attempted in 21 percent of disputant-years, the highest percentage in all regions. With time, states in the Americas have increasingly turned to adjudication (16 percent) and arbitration (7 percent) in efforts to resolve intractable boundary disputes. This trend has been noticed by one of our interviewees, ICJ judge Al-Khasawneh:

> Latin America has generated more cases than any other part of the world, and that is indicative of a strong propensity to seek the resolution of certain disputes before the Court. It's part of an old tradition going back to the Spaniards and also the Catholic concept of international law, with the emphasis on natural law and so on and so forth. And it has proven to be a very wise decision. Look at Nicaragua. Most of its borders now have been settled by judicial decisions.[18]

[18] Author's interview (EJP) with Judge Awn Shawkat Al-Khasawneh, former Vice-President, ICJ, and former Prime Minister of Jordan, Amman, Jordan, February 18, 2015.

With the exception of the 2018 case between Guyana and Venezuela, all of the ICJ territorial dispute cases have been in Central America and not in South America or North America (Sotomayor 2015). The ongoing Belize v. Guatemala case is unique in that it was the first time both disputants held referenda requesting public approval of submission of the territorial dispute to the ICJ.[19] Originally planned for 2013, the referenda eventually took place in April 2018 in Guatemala and in May 2019 in Belize.[20]

It is also crucial to note that upon gaining independence in the early nineteenth century, former colonies in the Americas accepted previous colonial boundaries as the new state boundaries. This legal doctrine—*uti possidetis de jure*—helps to explain the relatively small number of territorial disputes in the region in the nineteenth and twentieth centuries. This norm became legalized in the twentieth century in the 1948 Charter of the Organization of American States (OAS), Article 21: "The territory of a State is inviolable; it may not be the object, even temporarily, of military occupation or of other measures of force taken by another State, directly or indirectly, on any grounds whatever."[21] Several scholars have argued that the territorial integrity norm, together with peaceful resolution provisions of the OAS Charter, and many treaties signed in the nineteenth and twentieth centuries, have reduced territorial conflict in Latin America (Castellino and Allen 2003; Kacowicz 2005; Zacher 2001). Another influential factor is that most Latin American states have signed the Pact of Bogota, legally known as the American Treaty of Pacific Settlement. Article 21 allows for submission to the ICJ without any special agreements, which means that one state can submit to the ICJ without the consent of the opposing state.[22] This is a key reason why there

---

[19] In this context it is crucial to note that both states are constitutionally obligated to use referenda to resolve such disputes ("Guatemala v Belice acuerdan resolver diferendo en La Haya," *Prensa Libre*, December 8, 2008).

[20] The vast majority of Guatemalans (96 percent) agreed to submit the dispute to the ICJ (Economist Intelligence Unit ViewsWire, "Belize/Guatemala Politics: Quick View—Guatemalans Vote to Submit Border Dispute with Belize to ICJ," April 16, 2018, http://viewswire.eiu.com/index.asp?layout=VWArticleVW3&article_id=216623805&region_id=&country_id=1300000330&channel_id=210004021&category_id=&refm=vwCh&page_title=Channel+Latest), and 55 percent of Belizeans agreed to do so (Jose Sanchez, "Belizeans Vote to Ask U.N. Court to Settle Guatemala Border Dispute," *Reuters*, May 9, 2019, https://www.reuters.com/article/us-belize-referendum-guatemala-border/belizeans-vote-to-ask-u-n-court-to-settle-guatemala-border-dispute-idUSKCN1SF1QT).

[21] Organization of American States Charter, 1948. Available at http://www.oas.org/en/sla/dil/inter_american_treaties_A-41_charter_OAS.asp. For more discussion, see Hensel, Allison, and Khanani 2009.

[22] "Signatories and Ratifications to the Pact of Bogotá," Department of International Law, Organization of American States, Washington, DC, http://www.oas.org/juridico/english/sigs/a-42.html.

are so many more Latin American cases at the ICJ compared to other regions (Wolfrum 2018a). Finally, it could be that since many Latin American states were military regimes in the latter twentieth century, using legalized dispute resolution for territorial disputes helped to depoliticize and demilitarize these disputes. Additionally, resorting to the ICJ aided in diverting the focus of the military away from these disputes (Sotomayor 2015).

Europe

In Europe, 80 percent of all dyad-years consist of bilateral negotiations. Mediation was attempted in only 7 percent of observed years: by the UN between Spain and the United Kingdom in their dispute over Gibraltar (1963–1965), by the United States in the border dispute between Italy and the former Yugoslavia (1953–1954), and mediation between Cyprus and Turkey in 1964 and 1974. The only arbitration case of a territorial dispute in Europe dealt with the border between Slovenia and Croatia, resolved in 2006 (a total of 2 percent of dyad-years). Adjudication accounts for 10 percent of the observed years, and only four cases—three of which involved the United Kingdom (against France, Chile, and Argentina).[23] It is important to note that all these cases took place in the 1950s, the first decade of the ICJ's existence, and no additional cases about territorial contentions have been pursued since then.[24] At the same time, bilateral negotiations experienced a steep downward trend around the turn of the twenty-first century. Increased acceptance of the territorial status quo in Europe, the positive influence of the European Union (EU), and strong respect for international law are all likely the main reasons for these patterns. For example, the EU has taken a strong stand in response to Russian invasions in Georgia and Ukraine in 2008, 2014, and 2022. Of course, there are still a few ongoing territorial disputes, including the 2022 full-scale war in Ukraine based on territorial claims of Donetsk and Luhansk and the 2021 war between Azerbaijan and Armenia over the Nagorno-Karabakh region, as well as disputes in Gibraltar, Cyprus, and Kosovo.[25]

---

[23] See the ICJ website at https://www.icj-cij.org/en/cases for full citations and further details.

[24] In 2004, Romania and Ukraine submitted a maritime dispute case to the ICJ. See Maritime Delimitation in the Black Sea, Romania v. Ukraine, ICJ Rep. 2009, 61, Judgment of February 3, 2009.

[25] For more information on European territorial disputes, see Scalera and Wiegand 2018.

Africa

Patterns of dispute settlement in Africa are fairly similar to those of the Americas. In both regions, the postcolonial acceptance of former colonial boundaries largely shaped the trajectory and nature of territorial contentions. In Africa, the legal doctrine of *uti possidetis de jure* has been incorporated into the Charter of Organization of African Union (OAU), now the African Union. Article 2 of the Charter obliges every member state to share "Respect for the sovereignty and territorial integrity of each State and for its inalienable right to independent existence."[26] Additionally, the Charter explicitly highlights the importance of peaceful dispute settlement via "negotiation, mediation, conciliation or arbitration."[27] The attitude of African countries toward the various resolution forums has fluctuated over time (Etekpe 2013). These states became wary of international adjudication when the ICJ decided to dismiss the case against South Africa initiated by Liberia and Ethiopia in 1960. At the time, many criticized the Court for its perceived unwillingness to speak against racial discrimination in South Africa.[28] However, the 1986 Nicaragua case—though it did not in a direct way pertain to the African continent—improved the region's perception of the Court's legitimacy.[29] Many non-Western states interpreted Nicaragua's victory as furthering interests of less powerful states.[30] By settling a long-standing territorial dispute between the two rivaling states Burkina Faso and Mali in 1986, the ICJ further strengthened its position in Africa. With time, proposals for adjudication and nonbinding third-party methods became more frequent. There have been six ICJ cases in Africa, involving ten states, accounting for 13 percent of dyad-years.[31] Only one of these cases involved a state in North Africa—Libya (v. Chad)—and only one other case involved states in southern Africa. Attempts at arbitration account for 9 percent of dyad-years. As in other regions, bilateral negotiations account for the majority of settlement attempts (63 percent). This frequency is similar to that in the Americas. Yet, bilateral negotiations have been used less in Africa than

[26] Organization of African Union Charter, Article 3.
[27] Ibid.
[28] For more discussion of this topic, see Falk 1967.
[29] Case Concerning Military and Paramilitary Activities in and against Nicaragua, Nicaragua v. United States of America, ICJ Rep. 1986, 14, Judgment of June 27, 1986.
[30] Frontier Dispute (Burkina Faso v. Republic of Mali), Judgment, 1986 ICJ (December 22).
[31] See ICJ website at https://www.icj-cij.org/en/cases for full citations and further details.

in Europe and Asia/Oceania. African states have attempted mediation in 14 percent of the dyad-years in our data.

Middle East

To a large extent, patterns of dispute resolution in the Middle East are unique to this region. Although 72 percent of the dyad-years consist of bilateral negotiations, mediations account for 18 percent. With a few exceptions, almost all of the mediation attempts made by Middle Eastern states involve intermediaries from the region, including the Arab League, Organization of Islamic Cooperation, Gulf Cooperation Council, the king of Saudi Arabia, the king of Jordan, the president of Egypt, and the king of Morocco.[32] The logic of justice in the Islamic legal tradition explains these patterns. In contrast to the Western, relatively stringent and legalized nature of conflict management, the Islamic legal tradition embraces reconciliation and dialogue between the feuding parties. *Fiqh*, Islamic jurisprudence, promotes informal settlement with the help of an insider. *Sulh*—amicable settlement, a true compromise of action—was the Prophet Mohammad's favored method of settlement (Othman 2007). Furthermore, the Quran—the primary source of Islamic law—explicitly highlights the importance of reconciliation (Powell 2020). For instance, in sura 94, verse 128, the Quran states, "There is no blame on them if they arrange an amicable settlement between themselves, and such settlement is best."

Thus, informal dispute resolution has traditionally been embraced by Islamic society on all levels: interpersonal, social, and international. The goal of Islamic law, stemming from its divine nature, is to bring the Muslim community to the highest levels of perfection, and that includes peaceful coexistence. To that end, international nonbinding PR methods, especially mediation, seem to prevail in the Middle East. In fact, as Powell (2020, 169–70) demonstrates, in the context of post–World War II territorial disputes, Islamic law states have embraced the nonbinding third-party methods to a larger degree than other states.[33] Not surprisingly, both groups of states—Islamic law and non-Islamic law states—share a strong preference for bilateral negotiations. Granted, not all Islamic law states use mediation. The

---

[32] The Organisation of Islamic Conference changed its name to the Organisation of Islamic Cooperation in 2011.

[33] For the definition of the category of Islamic law states, see Chapter 3.

Middle Eastern states—connected by their Arab ethnic roots—are more committed to nonbinding third-party methods than Islamic law states from other regions such as Africa and Asia/Oceania (Powell 2020). Interestingly, there have been only two cases of arbitration in the Middle East. The first arbitration occurred in the context of the border dispute between Egypt and Israel that took place from 1982 to 1988.[34] The second arbitration was the Eritrea v. Yemen arbitration (1996–1998) that ended the dispute between the two countries over ownership of the Hanish Islands.[35] There is only one case of adjudication in the Middle East, between Qatar and Bahrain (1992–2001).[36]

Asia and Oceania

In Asia and Oceania, the proportion of settlement attempts via bilateral negotiations is unprecedentedly high (92 percent), much higher than any other region in the world. In contrast, mediation and other nonbinding third-party methods, as well as the binding methods, are proposed quite rarely in this region (a total of 8 percent). Among all third-party methods, attempts at mediation occur most rarely. Even though regional mediation is "preferable to international involvement," for Southeast Asian states, it "is not always viable due to fears that regional actors may have vested interests in certain cases. Moreover, ASEAN's current stance on intervention in regional disputes renders a greater regional role in the resolution of territorial disputes unlikely in the impending future" (Strachan 2009, 5). ASEAN member states, when ratifying the treaty, agreed to "endeavour to resolve peacefully all disputes in a timely manner through dialogue, consultation and negotiation" (ASEAN Charter 2008, Chap. 8, 23). Additionally, ASEAN member states find the dispute settlement mechanism of mediation "highly impractical" (Askandar and Sukim 2016, 72), and therefore are unlikely to turn to the regional organization for mediation. The only

[34] Location of Boundary Pillars between Egypt and Israel, 80 ILR 224, Arbitral Award of September 29, 1988.
[35] Sovereignty and Maritime Delimitation in the Red Sea, Eritrea v. Yemen, PCA, phase I (1998), phase II (1999), 2001, 40 ILM 900 and 983, Awards of October 9, 1998, and December 17, 1999.
[36] Libya also participated in a case at the ICJ against Chad, but this is considered an African dispute. Territorial Dispute, Libyan Arab Jamahiriya v. Chad, ICJ Rep. 1994, 6, Judgment of February 3, 1994.

arbitration attempt in the region is the 1968 Rann of Kutch case between Pakistan and India.[37]

States located in Asia/Oceania have submitted more than a few cases to the ICJ, even though there exist several regional forums that offer conflict management.[38] All five of the ICJ cases in the region involve Southeast Asian states, and four pertain to the same dyads. Moreover, all but one case—the Cambodia v. Thailand case—made it to the Court's docket after 1997.[39] Interestingly, none of the major powers in Asia have pursued adjudication. China has consistently avoided the ICJ during all of its numerous territorial disputes. Instead, all of China's territorial disputes have been resolved via bilateral negotiations.[40] Also, for several decades, Japan has not actively engaged in dispute resolution in its contentions with China, Russia, and South Korea. South Korea, in addition to its dispute with Japan, upholds its claims for reunification with North Korea, but to no avail. In a similar way, India has been involved in several disputes with neighbors, most notably Pakistan and China. None of these states have seriously considered adjudication in the context of these disputes.

Despite the fact that a few territorial disputes originating in Asia/Oceania have ended up at the ICJ, there is a lack of widespread acquiescence to international adjudication in the region. Arbitration and adjudication are fairly uncommon in states of the region "because of their traditional legal culture" (Wang 2014, 435). It is also crucial to recognize that Asian states "have maintained different legal concepts and mindset based on their respective traditional values and lifestyle" (Lee 2013, 77). China seems to prefer to follow its own rules, and the country consistently avoids legalized dispute settlement. Indeed, considerations of power and strategy may overshadow any regional or international norms of settlement. Additionally, as in any geographic region, the pressure to initiate formal litigation mitigates the effectiveness of any local norms of conflict management. However, though long-standing customs in Asia/Oceania embrace nonconfrontational conflict management, these states may at times use the ICJ. Because of the region's huge reach, it is also crucial to recognize Asia/Oceania's diversified and multifaceted legal cultures. Many of these states' legal systems have been

---

[37] Indo-Pakistan Western Boundary (Rann of Kutch), Between India and Pakistan Award, February 19, 1968.

[38] See ICJ website at https://www.icj-cij.org/en/cases for full citations and further details.

[39] Temple of Preah Vihear (Cambodia v. Thailand), Judgment, 1961 ICJ (May 26).

[40] See Fravel 2008 for further information about China's territorial dispute settlements.

influenced by customary law and Confucian legal thought, as well as the Western legal traditions, civil law and common law.[41]

Domestic and International Law Variables

The independent variables pertaining to the relationship between domestic and international law are designed to capture our expectations about how these characteristics influence proposer states' choices of different PR methods. We specifically focus on three features of a domestic legal system: (1) international law's position in the system, (2) rule of law, and (3) type of legal tradition, anticipating that these factors collectively signal a state's approach to international law. Expecting that proposer states take into account characteristics of the domestic legal system of the nonproposer as well, our models include both proposer's and nonproposer's characteristics in a dyadic manner.

International Law's Position in the Domestic Legal System

To gauge international law's position in the domestic legal system, we use two variables from the dataset generated by Lupu, Verdier, and Versteeg (2019), to measure whether both proposer and nonproposer states both have indicators of direct effect and canon of interpretation.[42] These variables—*Direct Effect Dyad* and *Canon of Interpretation Dyad*—capture the main mechanisms that enable the domestic judiciary in each disputant state to apply international treaties in a direct manner. If treaties are granted direct effect within a domestic jurisdiction, then a domestic court is able to base its decision on specific treaty provisions. In these jurisdictions, the courts "may also invalidate statutes inconsistent with the treaty" (510).[43] The *Direct Effect Dyad* variable is dichotomous and coded 1 if both states "apply treaties directly and designate them as having higher status than domestic legislation *or* if they have incorporated an international human rights agreement directly into their

---

[41] For more in-depth discussion of this topic, see Bundy 2014.
[42] The details of the dataset are included at http://yonatanlupu.com/Strength%20of%20Weak%20Review%20Supplementary%20Information.pdf.
[43] For a comprehensive study of direct effects, see Nollkaemper 2011 and 2014; and Sloss 2009.

constitution" (515).[44] The *Canon of Interpretation Dyad* variable measures whether domestic laws—including legislation, statutes, regulations, and others—are to be interpreted by both states according to their obligations under international treaties. Thus, in contrast to the direct effect mechanism, which implies a treaty's direct incorporation into a domestic legal system, the canon of interpretation mechanism provides domestic courts with a way to apply domestic law in light of a state's international treaty obligations. The variable is coded 1 if the answer to the following question is yes for both disputing states: "Is there a rule or presumption that domestic statutes (and/or other law) should be interpreted in conformity with obligations under ratified treaties?" (515).

Each variable is designed to measure international law's position in domestic jurisdictions and go beyond the rough dichotomous distinction between monist and dualist legal systems. These two mechanisms may jointly or separately appear in states' domestic legal systems.[45] Dualist states rarely allow for direct effect. Consequently, though a state has signed and ratified an international treaty, domestic courts may not enforce such a treaty short of implementing domestic laws. Interestingly, however, several states that have traditionally leaned toward dualism, such as Australia and Israel, have made the canon of interpretation mechanism available to their domestic judiciary. Importantly, canon of interpretation does not provide domestic courts with equivalent powers to those of the direct effect mechanism. Yet, under the canon of interpretation doctrine, international law may still enjoy a privileged position in a domestic jurisdiction. By way of illustration, courts in New Zealand—a country that traditionally follows the dualist approach to international law—have been basing their reviews of administrative decisions on human rights conventions.[46]

There are several domestic jurisdictions, such as South Africa, that do not fall neatly into the monist/dualist distinction, but instead incorporate elements of both. Similarly, there is a great deal of variation in how monism

---

[44] Answers to the following three questions were combined to create a single binary variable *Direct Effect*: "1) Do ratified treaties automatically become part of domestic law without implementing legislation? 2) If the answer to (1) is yes, what is the relationship of treaties to ordinary statutes (superior, equal, or inferior)? 3) Does the constitution expressly refer to international human rights treaties (e.g., the ICCPR or the European Convention on Human Rights)? If so, which ones, and are they formally incorporated into domestic law?" (Lupu, Verdier, and Versteeg 2019, 515).

[45] The doctrine of direct effect is usually enshrined in constitutions. In contrast, the canon of interpretation mechanism is more often than not introduced in the subconstitutional legal system (Nollkaemper 2011 and 2014; Shelton 2011)

[46] For further discussion, see Butler and Butler 1999.

and dualism are practiced across the different countries over time. Moreover, international law is rarely treated in the same manner across the various aspects of state governance. For example, a legislature may approach international law in ways that courts do not. It is also possible that a domestic jurisdiction may officially authorize the direct integration of international customary law, but demand that international treaties be implemented into the legal system via domestic legislation. Our reliance on the *Direct Effect* and *Canon of Interpretation* variables for both proposer and nonproposer states allows us to introduce more nuance into the relationship between domestic law and international law, and go beyond the monist/dualist dichotomy. In our data, 47 percent of proposer states and 46 percent of nonproposer states are coded as having direct effect, but only 6.5 percent of dyads are coded as sharing direct effect. Similarly, 57 percent of proposer states and 58 percent of nonproposer states are coded as having canon of interpretation, while only 7.3 percent of dyads share the status of having canon of interpretation.

Rule of Law

We use several measures from the Varieties of Democracy (V-Dem) dataset to gauge the quality of domestic legal systems (Coppedge et al. 2020).[47] It is important to keep in mind that our indicators not only capture domestic levels of rule of law but also measure other aspects of state governance, in particular the relationship between a state's high court and the executive. To capture the effect of rule of law, we use four variables that measure whether both disputing states have high levels of rule of law—*Compliance with High Court Dyad, High Court Independence Dyad, Judicial Constraints on the Executive Dyad*, and the *Rule of Law Index Dyad. Compliance with High Court Dyad* is a dummy variable that is coded as 1 if the governments of both disputing states have high compliance with adverse rulings from the state's high court. This variable is based on an interval variable from V-Dem that asks how often the government complies with important decisions of the high court with which it disagrees—never (0), seldom (1), about half of the time (2), usually (3), and always (4). In our data, the breakdown is as follows: proposer states never comply with the high court 6.5 percent, seldom 24 percent, almost half 10.5 percent, usually 47 percent, and always 12 percent. The percentages

---

[47] We use version 10 of the V-Dem project state-year dataset.

for nonproposers is very similar. We code compliance with the high court as high if the interval measures for both disputing states is above 2. In our data, 41.3 percent of dyads are coded as usually or always complying with the high court.

The *High Court Independence Dyad* variable is a dummy variable that considers the answer to the following question for both states as used by V-Dem: "When the high court in the judicial system is ruling in cases that are salient to the government, how often would you say that it makes decisions that merely reflect government wishes regardless of its sincere view of the legal record?" (Coppedge et al. 2020, 156). The categories of the interval measure include: always (0), usually (1), about half of the time (2), seldom (3), and never (4). Thus, a score of 0 indicates a high court that lacks judicial independence, while 4 notes a highly independent court. In our data, the dyadic variable is coded as 1 if both disputing states have a score above 2. Proposer states with high courts that merely reflect the government seldom is 31 percent and never 8 percent. Therefore, proposer states have independent judicial decisions 39 percent of the time. The percentages for nonproposer states are similar. For dyads in our data, 47 percent are coded as having high levels of judicial independence.

The third measure, *Judicial Constraints on the Executive Dyad*, is a dummy variable that measures whether both states have high levels of judicial constraints on the executive branch. The variable is generated by examining a V-Dem index that ranges from 0 to 1, with 1 representing the highest amount of judicial constraints on the executive. The mean value for proposer states and nonproposer states with judicial constraints is .52. Our variable is coded as 1 if both disputing states have a measure above .5 in the V-Dem index. Dyads that are above .5 total 31 percent of all observations in the data.

Conceptually, these variables each gauge the strength of the judiciary's position in relation to the executive. In general, the relationship between the judiciary and the executive, de jure and de facto, is a fundamental aspect of rule of law.[48] Apart from these three variables, we also use a variable, *Rule of Law Index Dyad*, which measures the V-Dem question "To what extent are laws transparently, independently, predictably, impartially, and equally enforced, and to what extent do the actions of government officials comply with the law?" (Coppedge et al. 2020, 269), for both disputing states. The

[48] As a concept, judicial independence is difficult to measure. For more discussion, see Linzer and Staton 2015 and Staton et al. 2019.

V-Dem Rule of Law Index is a composite of several V-Dem measures, and it is constructed via Bayesian factor analysis.[49] The resulting index is scaled from 0 to 1, with 1 indicating the highest level of rule of law, and 0 indicating the lowest level of rule of law. Our variable, *Rule of Law Index Dyad*, is coded as 1 if the scale for both disputing states is above .5. The mean value for both proposer and nonproposer states in our dataset is .53. In our data, 24.6 percent of observations are coded as a dyad that has a higher level of rule of law based on this index.

Legal Tradition Variables

To measure domestic legal traditions of proposer and nonproposer states, we employ four dichotomous variables that code whether the two disputing states shared the same domestic legal tradition: *Civil Law Dyad*, *Common Law Dyad*, *Islamic Law Dyad*, and *Mixed Law Dyad*. These dyadic-level variables enable us to see whether disputants who share domestic legal traditions have distinct patterns of preferences toward different PR methods. In our dataset, 41 percent of states in a dyad shared the same type of domestic legal tradition. We use the Powell and Mitchell (2007) dataset and the Powell (2020) dataset on Islamic law states. This classification was constructed using the CIA World Factbook (2018), which describes major characteristics of legal traditions of each state in the international system, and other subsidiary legal sources: Nexis Uni; JSTOR; Otto (2010); Glendon, Gordon, and Osakwe (1994); Opolot (1980); Kritzer (2002); NYU GlobaLex; the Asian Legal Information Institute; and JuriGlobe.[50] Other scholars propose different classifications of legal traditions. For instance, a frequently used typology is a "legal origin" variable, which has the following categories: English, Socialist, French, German, and Scandinavian legal origin. For the purpose of our empirical analysis, splitting the civil law family into French and German

---

[49] Specific indicators used for the construction of the *Rule of Law Index* include compliance with high court, compliance with judiciary, high court independence, lower court independence, executive respect of the constitution, rigorous and impartial public administration, transparent laws with predictable enforcement, access to justice for men, access to justice for women, judicial accountability, judicial corruption decisions, public sector corrupt exchanges, public sector theft, executive bribery and corrupt exchanges, and executive embezzlement and theft (See V-Dem codebook available at https://www.v-dem.net/en/data/data-version-10/).

[50] The website of JuriGlobe is available at http://www.juriglobe.ca/eng/; see NYU GlobaLex at https://www.nyulawglobal.org/globalex/; see Asian Legal Information Institute at http://www.asianlii.org/.

yields an unnecessary subcategorization, since both of these legal families are based on highly similar procedural and substantive concepts. La Porta et al. (1997, 1131) refer to this reality: "French, German, and Scandinavian laws, in contrast, are part of the scholar and legislator made civil law tradition, which dates back to Roman Law." Importantly, the La Porta et al. (1997) dataset on domestic legal traditions does not provide a separate category for the Islamic legal tradition. We strongly believe that Islamic law states have unique preferences with respect to international PR methods. Indeed, many modern Islamic law states have organized their domestic dispute resolution infrastructure to reflect Islamic law's traditional preference for informal settlement (Powell 2020). This reality—we argue—has a direct bearing on these states' forum choices in the context of their territorial disputes.

Powell and Mitchell (2007) use Gamal Moursi Badr's definition of domestic legal traditions. According to this definition, a major domestic legal system is one whose "application extended far beyond the confines of their original birth places and whose influence, through reception of their principles, techniques or specific provisions has been both widespread in space and enduring in time" (Badr 1978, 187). The civil law category includes legal traditions that either (1) stem directly from the Roman law that have been codified (Germany, France), (2) indirectly retained characteristics of Roman legal reasoning, such as the tradition of a written reason (Ecuador, Laos), or (3) have a weaker influence of Roman law, but whose law rests on the notion of legislated law (Scandinavian states). The common law category contains legal traditions based on English common law concepts, which endow judge-made case law with great importance (United Kingdom, United States, Australia, New Zealand). An Islamic law state is "a state with an identifiable substantial segment of its legal system that is charged with obligatory implementation of Islamic law, and where Muslims constitute at least 50 percent of the population" (Powell 2020, 42). Importantly, the Islamic law definition does not center merely on the religion of a state's citizenry, but rather hinges on whether a state in an obligatory way strives to incorporate Islamic law as a "substantial part of personal, civil, commercial, or criminal law" (Powell 2020, 42).[51] Mixed legal systems incorporate features of two or more legal traditions in their governance. Recall that while we have clear expectations

---

[51] For a detailed discussion of this categorization, and how it contrasts with other categorizations used in the scholarship, see Powell 2020. For more discussion, see Fadel 2009; Feldman 2008; Hallaq 2013; Hamoudi 2010; Mallat 2007; and An-Na'im 2008.

about the relationship between civil law, common law, and Islamic law states' preferences for different PR methods (Hypotheses 5, 6, and 7), we do not have any hypothesis about mixed law states or dyads. Indeed, it is reasonable to expect that the amalgamation of legal principles stemming from a variety of legal systems does not clearly translate into strong preferences for specific international PR methods. Table 5.2 provides descriptive statistics for all of our explanatory variables.

Control Variables

We recognize that simplifying the rich contexts of territorial disputes into data points limits the historical, geographic, and political aspects of these disputes, which may influence state strategies. Although it would be ideal to include many control variables to account for the breadth of potential factors unique to each of the 166 disputes, we are cognizant of our models' degrees of freedom. Thus, for empirical reasons, we have to limit the number of control variables to those that operationalize the most important alternative explanations provided by the existing scholarship on territorial and maritime disputes. Our theory builds on and is inspired by a wealth of previous research about the peaceful management of these contentions, examining structural factors, domestic factors, and a variety of characteristics of the disputes such as salience or value of the disputed territory. To account for these alternative explanations, we include a number of control variables in our empirical models: variables that capture the salience or value of the disputed territory—*Economic Salience*, *Strategic Salience*, and *Identity Salience*; and variables that capture the dyadic nature of the disputants— *Shared Alliance*, *Past Conflict*, *Shared IGO Membership*, *Democratic Dyad*, and *Power Asymmetry*.

Salience of Territory

Our first control variables, *Economic Salience*, *Strategic Salience*, and *Identity Salience*, account for the salience or value of the disputed territory (Hensel 2001; Huth 1996). To capture the three types of territorial salience, we use Huth and Allee's (2002) data, which we extended to 2015. Territory is considered to have economic value if it is located at or near a significant

Table 5.2 Descriptive statistics for explanatory variables

Variable	Measure	Mean Value	Standard Deviation	Minimum Value	Maximum Value
Proposer/ Nonproposer Win-Loss Bilateral Negotiations	Categorical	.54/.55	.22/.20	0	1
Proposer/ Nonproposer Win-Loss Nonbinding Third-Party	Categorical	.51/.50	.12/.10	0	1
Proposer/ Nonproposer Win-Loss Binding Third-Party	Categorical	.54/.53	.15/.14	0	1
Proposer Win-Loss Bilateral Negotiations Region	Categorical	.63	.21	0	1
Proposer Win-Loss Nonbinding Third-Party Region	Categorical	.60	.31	0	1
Proposer Win-Loss Binding Third-Party Region	Categorical	.60	.31	0	1
Canon of Interpretation Dyad	Dummy	.07	.26	0	1
Direct Effect Dyad	Dummy	.06	.25	0	1
High Court Compliance Dyad	Dummy	.41	.49	0	1
High Court Independence	Dummy	.20	.40	0	4
Judicial Constraints on the Executive Dyad	Dummy	.31	.46	0	1
Rule-of-Law Index Dyad	Dummy	.25	.43	0	4
Civil Law Dyad	Dummy	.24	.30	0	1
Common Law Dyad	Dummy	.05	.21	0	1
Islamic Law Dyad	Dummy	.10	.43	0	1

amount of natural resources such as fishing grounds, oil, iron, copper, or diamonds. Disputed territory has strategic value if it is located at or near military bases, major shipping lanes, or choke points for ships. The territory has ethnic value if there are ethnic minorities living on the other side of the border. Each of these dummy variables is coded 1 if the disputed territory has a particular value to at least one of the disputants, and 0 otherwise.

The existing findings about how the value of land affects the dynamics of territorial disputes are mixed. Several studies examine types and levels of salience/value and interests associated with the disputed territory. Hensel (2001) shows that higher cumulative levels of territorial salience increase the likelihood of bilateral negotiations. At the same time, salience does not necessarily affect the choice of third-party resolution methods. Gent and Shannon (2010) find that increased salience discourages leaders from resorting to binding resolution methods. In a subsequent study, Gent and Shannon (2011) show that as the value of the disputed territory increases, states try to avoid nonbinding third-party resolution methods. However, some studies provide rather contradictory arguments and findings to those of Gent and Shannon (2011) by demonstrating that higher salience levels may be associated with attempts at conflict management methods involving an intermediary (Allee and Huth 2006; Mitchell, Kadera, and Crescenzi 2009). For example, Australia felt pressure to agree to compulsory conciliation with Timor Leste in its maritime dispute because both states—but Timor Leste in particular—sought access to the immense oil and gas fields in the disputed maritime area.[52] Resolving the dispute through conciliation was deemed the quickest means to access these resources (Wolfrum 2018c). This case demonstrates that third-party methods are likely where salience levels are high. It is clear that states perceive certain kinds of territorial disputes as inapt for specific resolution methods. When asked why states are reluctant to accept the ICJ's compulsory jurisdiction, one of our interviewees answered, "Because they just don't want to have a particular

---

[52] The Report and Recommendations of the Compulsory Conciliation Commission between Timor-Leste and Australia on the Timor Sea (TSCR), May 9, 2018.

case or category of cases decided by the Court. They regard them as too delicate or too important."[53]

Shared Alliances

We include the *Shared Alliance* variable to measure whether proposer and nonproposer states are part of an alliance treaty in any given year during the lifespan of a dispute. We use the Alliance Treaty Obligations and Provisions (ATOP) dataset (version 3.0) for this variable.[54] The ATOP dataset includes information about the alliance commitments shared by a pair of states in the same year (Leeds et al. 2000). Several studies have examined the role of military alliances in shaping states' preferences with respect to PR methods. This literature suggests that disputants are less likely to attempt binding resolution forums when they share common security interests. At the same time, it seems that shared membership in military alliances encourages bilateral negotiations (Allee and Huth 2006; Huth 1996; Leeds et al. 2000). Interestingly, focusing specifically on mediation, Frazier (2006) finds that when a third party is allied with one of the disputing states, this relationship does not influence the likelihood of third-party mediation in territorial MIDs (militarized interstate dispute).

Past Conflict

To account for past conflictual relations, we include a dummy variable called *Past Conflict*, constructed using the Correlates of War data set (Jones, Bremer, and Singer 1996). This variable is coded 1 if the states in the dyad have engaged in armed conflict in the last 50 years. Because past conflict is a sign of low trust, we expect that if the proposer and nonproposer states have been involved in a past MID, they will be more likely to turn to third parties for settlement. At the same time, bilateral negotiations will be unlikely. In this context, Hensel et al. (2008, 127) find that states are more likely to pursue peaceful settlements "when they have a history of recent militarized conflict

---

[53] Author's interview (EJP) with an anonymous ICJ state advocate and international arbitrator, United Kingdom, October 2013.
[54] The website for the project is available at http://www.atopdata.org/.

over the same issue," compared to when they lack such shared experiences. Ellis, Mitchell, and Prins (2010) argue that a history of militarized conflict encourages democratic states specifically to seek third-party dispute resolution.[55]

International Organizations

We use the variable *Shared IGO Membership* to measure the combined number of pacific settlement commitments (global and regional treaties) of which both states are members in the same year. The data for this control variable come from the Multilateral Treaties of Pacific Settlement (MTOP) Data Set in the ICOW project (Hensel 2001). It is likely that states that are part of many pacific settlement treaties—and thus deeply embedded in the international community—may be more open to third-party settlement methods. States' memberships in international governmental organizations (IGOs) can also influence the likelihood and choice of resolution methods. This is an important consideration since international organizations often play the role of mediators or arbitrators in conflict management (Abbott and Snidal 1998; Bercovitch and Schneider 2000). The existing literature is relatively consistent in demonstrating that increased IGO membership—especially in IGOs whose mandate calls for peaceful dispute settlement among their members— encourages disputing states to seek an intermediary's help. Disputing states that sign and ratify a higher number of such peace-promoting agreements are more acceptant of all third-party conflict management methods (Hensel 2001; Mitchell, Kadera, and Crescenzi 2009).[56] In the context of territorial, maritime, and river disputes, Hansen, Mitchell, and Nemeth (2008) show that regional and global international organizations are more effective as intermediaries when they are institutionalized, and if their membership includes high numbers of democracies with like interests. Shannon (2009) empirically demonstrates that increased membership in such treaties boosts a state's support for binding settlement methods. More specifically, Nemeth et al. (2014) find that membership in the UN Convention on the Law of the

---

[55] In fact, these authors show that democratic dyads are 50 percent less likely to pursue third-party assistance in disputes in which the disputants have been involved in no or little past militarized conflict.

[56] Shared regional and global IGO memberships seem not to hold with Islamic law states in territorial dispute management (Powell 2020).

Sea (UNCLOS) increases the likelihood of third-party binding resolution for states involved in maritime disputes.

Democracy

We include a measure of democracy for two reasons. First, we must acknowledge and control for the extensive findings about the role of regime type in the research on conflict management and dispute resolution. Second, we include this measure to partially account for the possibility that shifts in regime type from one government to another—especially the more radical shifts—could affect strategies of subsequent leaders.[57] *Democratic Dyad* indicates whether the proposer and nonproposer states have similar Polity IV democracy scores in any given dyad year (Marshall, Gurr, and Jaggers 2019). The variable is coded 1 if both states score 6 or higher on the Polity IV scale, and 0 otherwise. In the PRTD dataset, only 19 percent of dyads share a democratic regime type. However, the Polity IV democracy scores of states engaged in territorial disputes vary considerably. Our decision to include both the *Democratic Dyad* and the *Rule of Law Index* is based on the reality that rule of law—one of our key independent variables—and democracy constitute distinct concepts that can exist independently of one another. As Gutmann and Voigt (2018, 346) write, "Democracy refers to the citizens choosing their own policies or electing representatives to take these decisions for a limited period of time; the simplest definition of what makes a country democratic is, hence, majority-decision-making. The rule of law, in contrast, sets constraints on political decision-making; decisions have to be taken within the legal framework of a country." Thus, in theory, rule of law can exist outside of a democratic environment (Powell et al. 2020).

The scholarship does not identify a unified relationship between regime type and states' preferences for the various peaceful settlement methods. While some literature suggests that democracies are more willing to resort to legalized conflict management venues such as international courts (Simmons 1999), other studies question this relationship. It is also possible

---

[57] We recognize that it would be ideal to account for shifts in regime type between individual leaders within one state, but this is beyond the scope of this study. Our quantitative tests follow the standard approach in the quantitative conflict management literature by adapting the state level, and not the individual-leader level, of analysis. Inclusion of a measure using the Polity IV score allows us to treat all state leaders equally.

that the effects of democracy may wane or altogether disappear when other factors—such as domestic culture of dispute resolution—are taken into consideration. This seems to be the case for Islamic law states (Powell 2020). Some scholarship also shows that the effects of democracy disappear in the presence of territorial claims with high salience (Park and James 2015).[58] Hensel (2001) demonstrates that democratic dyads are much more likely to use bilateral negotiations for peaceful dispute resolution. At the same time, these dyads are shown to be less attracted to any third-party methods.

Shannon's (2009) study finds that democracies have a somewhat ambivalent relationship to the idea of third-party conflict management. She empirically determines that these states are no more or less likely to attempt third-party resolution methods compared to other dyads. Interestingly, the literature has been relatively consistent in arguing that democratic dyads are "more likely to adopt compromise solutions to problems as a matter of course" (Ellis, Mitchell, and Prins 2010, 374). Extending the democratic argument to the systemic level, Mitchell (2002) finds that a higher proportion of democracies in the international system is associated with more frequent usage of third-party resolution methods by nondemocratic dyads. It seems that democracies' respect for in-court proceedings carries over into international dispute resolution and affects other states' behavior.[59]

An interesting argument advanced in the literature explains democracies' attraction to legally binding third-party resolution methods by focusing on the structural characteristics of democratic domestic institutions. Because leaders in democracies have larger winning coalitions than leaders in nondemocracies, they are more accountable to their constituencies than the latter. Thus, to remain in office, or have their political party remain in office, democratic leaders are more cautious about their decisions (Huth and Allee 2002). Consequently, these policymakers are hesitant to engage in any unpopular policies that may threaten their reputation and make them vulnerable to domestic punishment.[60] In the context of territorial disputes, this

[58] James, Park, and Choi (2006) find limited support for the democratic peace argument, showing that democratic dyads are not very likely to seek peaceful resolution in territorial disputes.
[59] Many studies build on, alter, and expand this argument and examine more closely the causal relationship between democracy and arbitration and adjudication (Allee and Huth 2006; Gent and Shannon 2011; Huth and Allee 2002; Mitchell and Hensel 2007; Mitchell, Kadera, and Crescenzi 2009; Shannon 2009; Simmons 2002).
[60] Gent and Shannon (2011) argue that binding dispute resolution attempts can be just as costly to domestic audiences since leaders can be punished for giving up control to an arbiter or international court.

argument implies that leaders of democratic states will actively try to avoid settlement options that contradict domestic discourse about the disputed territory. Pursuing peaceful settlement—particularly when it involves potential concessions or compromises—can be a costly strategy. Within this genre of literature, Chiozza and Choi (2003) find that territorial dispute resolution is more likely when new democratic leaders are in power, since these leaders are less likely to be punished, having just received endorsement from their constituents.[61]

Focusing specifically on legalized dispute settlement, Allee and Huth (2006) show that the likelihood of binding third-party dispute resolution triples when the disputing states possess democratic political institutions.[62] Huth, Croco, and Appel (2011) confirm that democratic leaders with a clear need for domestic cover are more likely to reach agreements in binding methods when states have weak legal claims to the disputed territory. Brilmayer and Faure (2014) discuss how states can go to binding methods to seek political cover for losing territory. Simmons's (2002) study dovetails nicely with these arguments asserting that international arbitration and adjudication provide democratic leaders with useful means to settle a dispute when domestic political opposition is likely to block a negotiated solution. While the "domestic political cover" mechanism constitutes a plausible explanation for states' preferences toward specific dispute resolution mechanisms, we consider it to be an alternative explanation to our theory of strategic selection based on past experience and legal variables. Despite the fact that some studies use the domestic political argument, the ability to test this theory quantitatively is challenging. For example, to test domestic political cover, in addition to a variable that measures executives facing strong domestic political opposition, Allee and Huth (2006) use measures of salience of disputed territory and democratic dyad—both of which we use in our quantitative analysis.

[61] In contrast, authoritarian leaders are more likely to attempt peaceful resolution as they spend more time in office since they have accumulated political experience and are therefore less constrained by domestic audiences.

[62] The argument is based on the notion that legalized binding resolution methods can act as more legitimate political cover for leaders who anticipate potential opposition to dispute resolution attempts.

Balance of Military Capabilities

Another factor that is found to influence territorial and maritime dispute strategies is the balance of military forces. We therefore include the variable *Power Asymmetry*, which is coded using the Correlates of War National Capabilities Index (Singer, Bremer, and Stuckey 1972). We divide the larger of the two military capabilities' scores by the sum of the two. A resulting score of .5 indicates perfect parity while a value of 1 indicates total asymmetry. The primary finding in the literature is that in general, stronger military capabilities have a negative effect on the likelihood of dispute settlement (Huth 1996). Ellis, Mitchell, and Prins (2010) examine military balance as a factor that could influence the type of settlement method, specifically in the context of democratic dyads. They show that states are twice as likely to use bilateral negotiations when the dyadic power relations are characterized by power parity compared to power asymmetry. We also know that states with high power asymmetry are less likely to pursue legally binding resolution methods (Allee and Huth 2006; Gent and Shannon 2010; Hansen et al. 2008; Hensel 2001; Hensel et al. 2008; Mitchell 2002; Shannon 2009; Simmons 2002).

Qualitative Evidence

Qualitative evidence plays a crucial role in this book, insofar as it is intended to act as a bridge with quantitative analysis by providing deep insights into the intricacies of the causal story. Our conjectures deal with strategies employed by states involved in territorial and maritime disputes. Information obtained from actors who are directly involved in decision-making during these disputes is invaluable. Collectively, the qualitative evidence points to the idea that states are strategic in how they deal with their contentions. We first analyzed primary documents used to train government officials in states involved in territorial and maritime disputes. We obtained many of our materials at the library of the International Boundaries Research Unit (IBRU) in the Geography Department, Durham University, in the United Kingdom.[63] IBRU regularly hosts international training workshops related to dispute resolution of territorial and maritime boundaries. During these workshops,

---

[63] See the website of IBRU: https://www.dur.ac.uk/ibru/.

public international law experts provide training for participants—usually government representatives sent by their states to learn about the different options and best strategies of pursuing dispute resolution. We also attained much insight at the 2018 Rhodes Academy of Oceans Law and Policy, maritime law and policy for government officials, diplomats, representatives of nongovernmental organizations, lawyers, and scholars to better understand UNCLOS and the International Tribunal for the Law of the Sea (ITLOS).[64] This intensive training program is taught by international public lawyers, international law faculty, and judges that have served on ITLOS, the ICJ, and arbitration panels in territorial and maritime disputes.

In addition, we interviewed many international lawyers, judges, arbitrators, technical experts, and academics from many countries, including Algeria, Bahrain, Belgium, China, Germany, Greece, Iran, Italy, Jordan, Kuwait, Libya, the Netherlands, Pakistan, the Philippines, South Korea, the United Arab Emirates, the United Kingdom, the United States, and Vietnam. Our interlocutors have been directly involved in the management of territorial and maritime contentions during different stages of the settlement process. We drew much insight into the dynamics of within-venue strategic selection from the Philippines v. China arbitration. We conducted field research in 2016 and 2017 in the Philippines in near real time, or shortly after the Tribunal had ruled in favor of the Philippines.[65] The examination of this dispute in particular presents a sequential description and explanation of the decision-making process by the Philippine government in its decision to pursue arbitration via an UNCLOS Annex VII tribunal in the historical and time-sensitive context in which decisions were made. Our focus on the Philippines-China dispute as an in-depth illustration, along with the numerous references to other real-world disputes, also helps us provide historical, geographical, and political context for disputes while we expound on the theory and flesh out the causal mechanism.

The interviews and other materials allow us to carefully parse out mechanisms, patterns, and causal factors that determine states' strategic

---

[64] Center for Oceans Law and Policy, https://colp.virginia.edu/Rhodesacademy.
[65] One of the authors (KEW) returned to Manila as a Senior Fulbright Scholar based at De La Salle University from January to May 2017 to conduct field research, interviewing several dozen people, as discussed earlier, and learning about Philippine domestic and foreign policy in the direct environment of the country itself. In addition to interviews conducted in Manila in 2016 and 2017, this author interviewed the lawyer who represented the Philippines in the arbitration case, in Washington, DC, in 2016, and a diplomat who was one of the key players at the Department of Foreign Affairs, who was then stationed as Consul General in San Francisco, in 2017.

behavior. Conversations with people who have been personally engaged in advising countries during these disputes are the cornerstone of our empirics. Indeed, references to these in-depth interviews and training materials meaningfully connect our statistical results to real cases of dispute settlement. Furthermore, insights from our conversations enable us to capture the influence of mechanisms of strategic selection in both stages of dispute resolution: between-venue and within-venue strategic selection. We are able to observe how states' drive to control the settlement process affects their decisions to engage with specific PR methods. All our interviewees highlight the reality of step-by-step decision-making in ongoing territorial and maritime contentions. The entire settlement proceedings are conceptualized as a complex process, throughout which legal counsel and policymakers meticulously plan their country's next move. Strategic selection does not end after both disputants' preferences converge on a particular PR venue, but continues throughout the lifespan of the settlement process. Dispute resolution constitutes an intricate and drawn-out activity that evolves and changes over time.

We use our interviews in four ways. First, our interviewees shed light on the practice of dispute resolution in the context of specific PR methods and venues described in Chapter 2. Second, in our theoretical chapters, Chapters 3 and 4, our interviews elucidate the causal mechanism of both stages of strategic selection and our core conceptualizations such as winning and losing. Importantly, these conversations shed light on preferences of the disputants and their legal counsel, as well as preferences of judges and arbitrators. Third, in Chapter 6, we rely on qualitative insight to supplement our quantitative analysis of the choice-of-venue mechanisms—past experience and the relationship between domestic and international law. Lastly, in Chapter 7, these interviews provide strong stand-alone evidence of the intricate process of within-venue strategic selection. We use the interviews to demonstrate how states engaged in within-venue strategic selection—framing the claim and shaping the procedures—pursue certain strategies to reduce their uncertainty and increase their control over the proceedings.

To sum up, the book presents a breadth of qualitative evidence to understand the general patterns revealed by our statistical analyses in the setting of specific countries and specific disputes. Taken together, descriptive materials, government documents, legal documents from settlement proceedings, and interviews provide the exact context of sequential, causal events. Moreover, the plethora of qualitative evidence provides details about the specific chain of events of decision-making. Thus, we believe that our research fills a lacuna in the literature on territorial and maritime disputes by going beyond normative arguments and presenting empirical tests of a generalizable theoretical framework. Importantly, our qualitative examples provide real-world insights that are—unfortunately—often missing in studies of conflict management.

Trends in the Peaceful Settlement of Territorial Disputes, 1945–2015

In this section, we discuss very interesting trends that our PRTD dataset on the peaceful resolution of territorial disputes from 1945 to 2015 reveals. Several of these trends are predictable, while others may come as a surprise to many scholars and practitioners. While we do not focus on states' decisions to choose a peaceful route versus a conflictual one, as discussed in Chapter 1, a peaceful mode of resolution usually constitutes the preferable method for the disputants. Indeed, acquisition of disputed territory via force is more often than not costly and risky. Most importantly, military resolutions do not lead to recognition of sovereignty in international law. Looking specifically at states' behavior in the nonmilitarized realm, we see that in 67 percent of observations in our data, neither the challenger nor the target state pursues a peaceful settlement attempt (see Figure 5.2). This frequency reflects the fairly high cost of settlement versus maintaining the status quo (Huth 1996; Wiegand 2011).

Figure 5.2 shows that out of all disputant-years, 24 percent of observations are bilateral negotiations. As discussed in Chapter 2, bilateral negotiations are the least legalized, and also the least costly, method of settlement. In many circumstances, uncertainty associated with third-party settlement outweighs that of bilateral talks. Uncertainty is especially high for disputants who pursue international adjudication. As Kohen (2013, 14) writes, "Indeed, uncertainty appears to be bigger at the international level, in the case of courts or tribunals composed by such an important figure of fifteen or twenty-one judges (or even more, if one includes ad hoc judges) coming from different countries and legal traditions, such as—respectively—the ICJ or ITLOS. No doubt, a negotiated agreement is always preferable to the uncertainty of a future judgment."

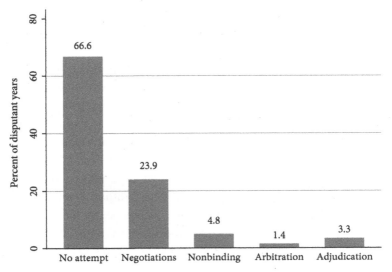

Figure 5.2. Types of proposed PR methods in territorial disputes, by disputant-year, 1945–2015.

States pursue nonbinding third-party PR methods in 4.8 percent of observations in our data. Certainly, there are contentions in which negotiations have proved unsuccessful and the parties decide to engage an intermediary to find a solution. An example is the successful mediation in the Argentina-Chile Beagle Channel dispute. After repeated failure of negotiations, Pope John Paul II mediated the contention. The Taba boundary dispute between Egypt and Israel provides another example where after the failure of bilateral talks, the disputants resorted to a third party's help.[66]

Binding methods—arbitration and adjudication—are pursued 4.7 percent of the time. When we break it down further, arbitration is attempted in only 1.4 percent of the observations and adjudication is attempted in 3.3 percent of the observations. These descriptive statistics reveal some interesting patterns that may seem unexpected. Despite the fact that arbitration allows the parties more flexibility and increased control over the resolution process, states that attempt a binding PR method usually prefer adjudication. There have been a number of territorial disputes during which any potential of a bilaterally agreed settlement was discounted. In some instances, political

[66] The parties decided to create an impartial body to help them engage in conciliation and—in case of failure—in arbitration.

factors—domestic and international—compel states to litigate. As Kohen (2013, 15) writes, specific circumstances "may indicate to a State that it is convenient to go to adjudication, particularly if, irrespective of the outcome, the State concerned will be in any way better off than it was before the proceedings." A good example is the Case Concerning Sovereignty over Pedra Branca/Pulau Batu Puteh, Middle Rocks and South Ledge.[67] Given that Singapore had control over all the geographic features, Malaysia had nothing to lose by pursuing litigation. The ICJ's judgment established that Malaysia had sovereignty over Middle Rocks, which was a clear win for Malaysia.

It is important to note that recent decades have witnessed an unprecedented growth of international courts and other quasi-adjudicative institutions. Thus, as we show later in the chapter, states have increasingly resorted to adjudication. At the same time, however, negotiations continue to be the most frequently attempted PR method in territorial contentions. Reed (2013, 296) suggests that "no party wishes to relinquish control over dispute resolution to a third party for adjudication unless no other option is available. Perhaps counter-intuitively, the existence of effective courts and tribunals might well mean that States use diplomacy with renewed vigour and patience. The spectre of judicial settlement may discipline disputing parties."

Figure 5.3 provides additional insights into states' choices of PR methods. Here we exclude all observations where no proposal was made, and plot only years when either a proposer, either a challenger or target, made an explicit move toward peaceful settlement. We denote these active years "proposer years." Of proposer years, 72 percent consist of bilateral negotiations, 14 percent of nonbinding third-party methods, 4 percent of arbitration attempts, and 10 percent of adjudication attempts. Interestingly, states that prefer to secure an intermediary's help express no definite preference with regard to nonbinding and binding methods. When we break down challenger and target state proposer years, challenger states attempt peaceful settlement 51 percent of the time, while the remaining 49 percent are made by target states.

Our data show that half of all disputants propose only one PR method, usually negotiations. However, 31 percent of disputants propose two or more methods, with 9 percent of disputants proposing three or more methods.

---

[67] Sovereignty over Pedra Branca/Pulau Batu Puteh, Middle Rocks and South Ledge, Malaysia v. Singapore, ICJ Rep. 2008, 9, Judgment of May 23, 2008.

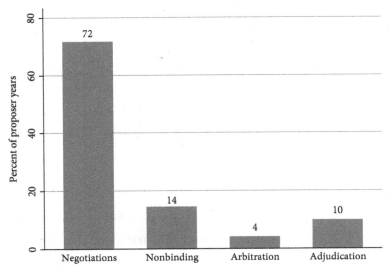

Figure 5.3. Types of proposed PR methods in territorial disputes, by proposer-year (only years with proposals made), 1945–2015.

Once a dispute ensues, states usually propose bilateral negotiations as the first method (69 percent of observations). Many of these entries pertain to claims that began before 1945 as well as brief territorial settlement claims arising out of the end of World War II.[68] The other first proposals break down into 9 percent nonbinding methods and 3 percent binding methods. In the second category, 1 percent of initial attempts are for arbitration and 2 percent for adjudication. Again—similar to patterns displayed in previous figures—these descriptive statistics reflect a significant source of variation in states' preferences that remains underexplored by the literature. Indeed, states seem to be strategic with regard to the initial attempts at resolving their territorial contentions. During the opening stages of disputes, proposals of bilateral negotiations are dominant. Frequently, during the initial negotiations, the parties put forth contradictory claims over a piece of land—a process that often crystallizes the contention. Importantly, exhaustion of bilateral negotiations does not automatically constitute a precondition for other,

---

[68] Note that percentages displayed in Figures 5.3 and 5.4 are calculated in terms of proposer-years. In contrast, percentages plotted in Figures 5.5 and 5.6 are calculated in terms of disputants—challenger and target states. In the context of most territorial disputes, there are some years in which disputants make no settlement proposals. A total of 19 percent of disputants in our data engaged in no settlement activity throughout the observation period, shown in Figure 5.5.

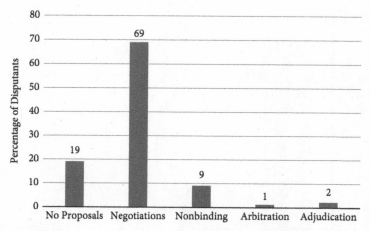

Figure 5.4. First PR proposal by a disputant in a territorial claim by type, 1945–2015.

more formal PR methods. Of course, as we explain in Chapter 2, the requirement for negotiating is often included in a treaty. However, there are situations where settling the dispute via bilateral talks is impossible. In some cases, a state may deny the very existence of a dispute with a particular opponent. A good example is the ICJ case involving Portugal making a claim on behalf of East Timor as its former colonizer, against Australia.[69] Portugal initiated ICJ proceedings against Australia concerning a 1989 treaty between Australia and Indonesia. The treaty created a Zone of Co-operation in a maritime area located between northern parts of Australia and East Timor, one of Indonesia's former provinces. Australia objected to Portugal's claim by asserting that it had no direct dispute with Portugal. Though eventually the ICJ found that it could not rule on Portugal's claims, there was no possibility of preadjudication bilateral talks.

In the initial attempts to settle a dispute, states rarely propose nonbinding third-party PR methods (9 percent). In light of these patterns, it is useful to take a closer look at specific PR methods that fall into this category. Only a handful of territorial disputes between 1945 and 2015 have successfully ended via mediation. Previous research argues that territorial disputes in particular are appealing to third-party mediators (Wilkenfeld, Young, Asal, and Quinn 2003). Moreover, some scholars posit that mediation is likely to

[69] East Timor, Portugal v. Australia, ICJ Rep. 1995, 90, Judgment of June 30, 1995.

succeed in the context of territorial disputes because of the tangible nature of these contentions (Bercovitch, Anagnoson, and Wille 1991). Interestingly, in comparison with territorial disputes, mediation occurs much more often in the context of civil wars and other interstate disputes. In fact, as Wiegand (2014) shows, mediation accounts for more than 28 percent of resolution attempts in civil wars, with much fewer in interstate territorial disputes. It is interesting to consider why attempts at mediation occur relatively seldom. First, research shows that mediations are more frequent in severe conflicts, especially those that involve armed activities and rivalries (Bercovitch and Diehl 1997; Goertz, Diehl, and Balas 2016). In fact, more than 80 percent of mediations are attempted in a rivalry. In contrast, as dyadic relationships become more peaceful, the number of mediations drops considerably.[70] Like mediation, inquiry has been used relatively rarely in territorial disputes. In comparison with other methods—binding and nonbinding—there are very few instances of successful inquiries. This fact elevates states' uncertainty about inquiry as a viable option for settlement. Conciliation, another nonbinding third-party method, usually entails a relatively elaborate procedure, more formality, and high costs. These factors are likely to diminish states' enthusiasm for this method. As Merrills (2017, 85) suggests, "since to operate a conciliation commission is neither easy nor cheap, even states with legal disputes will often have reason to prefer the tried and tested procedures of arbitration to the uncertainties of conciliation."

In contrast to Figure 5.4—which focuses on the initial settlement proposal—Figure 5.5 plots all proposals put forth in the context of all territorial disputes (1945–2015). While some disputes experience relatively few proposals, during many contentions both parties make numerous settlement proposals that are subsequently rejected by the opponents. When we aggregate the number of different PR methods proposed by disputants during the span of territorial claims, we find some interesting patterns. The PRTD data show that preferences of many disputants change over time in a large number of territorial contentions. In many instances, the inability of one PR method to produce a definitive distribution of territory leads states to propose alternative PR methods.

---

[70] Goertz, Diehl, and Balas (2016) classify good offices, mediation, and conciliation as "mediation" for the purpose of their analyses. In contrast to their data, we measure proposals at resolution, and not whether the particular method actually ensued. Thus, it is important to keep these measurement issues in mind while comparing patterns revealed by our data with those presented by Goertz, Diehl, and Balas (2016).

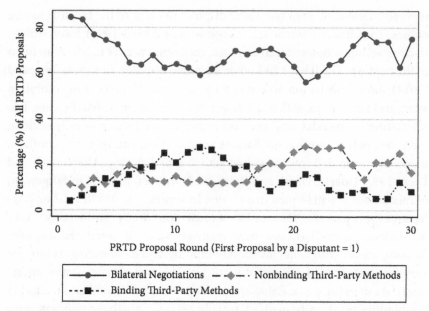

Figure 5.5. Proportion of all proposals by type and count—1st to 30th proposal made, 1945–2015.

Figure 5.5 also shows how states propose different PR methods in the second, third, and any additional rounds of proposals within the same dispute, all the way to the thirtieth round. This variation demonstrates that once a third-party proposal is made, there is a nonlinear decline of attempts at negotiations, nonbinding, and binding methods, as many bargaining models suggest. Interestingly, if a state proposes settlement up to the twelfth round of proposals, the percentage of negotiations declines, while there is an increase in binding third-party methods. However, after the twelfth round of proposals, there is a typical return back to negotiations and a decline in the percentage of binding methods proposed (Wiegand, Powell, and McDowell 2020). This suggests that states strategically propose certain methods in a way that changes over time.

As Figure 5.6 demonstrates, patterns of attempts at the various PR methods have changed over time in our observation period. Importantly, this figure displays only the proportion of proposals for all third-party methods, both nonbinding and binding. Over-time changes are especially pronounced for adjudication. Even though settlements via international courts occurred regularly between 1951 and 1962, after this time, there were

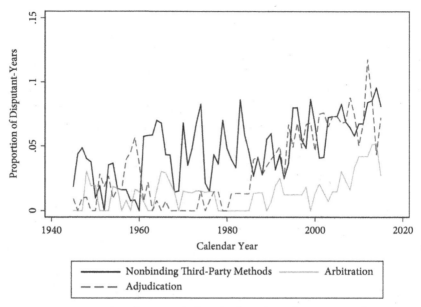

Figure 5.6. Proportion of proposals for adjudication, arbitration, and nonbinding third-party methods over time, 1945–2015.

no cases of adjudication in territorial disputes until 1983. States proposed adjudication and arbitration roughly at a similar frequency up to 1980. While adjudication has become more popular since the early 1980s, arbitration has been proposed much less often. Note that the year 2014 shows convergence between the frequencies of adjudication and arbitration proportions. The recent popularity of the PCA signals that states have become more enthusiastic about resolving their territorial disputes via arbitration. Interestingly, the case docket of the PCA has exceeded that of the ICJ in recent years.

In a way, legalized dispute settlement is exceptional in state relations.[71] States frequently shy away from adjudication because they "are unwilling to relinquish control over certain of their interests, especially those which were previously captured by the category of 'non-justiciable disputes'" (De Brabandere 2018, 467). Taken together, instances of arbitration and adjudication in territorial disputes are significantly outnumbered by negotiations and third-party nonbinding methods, especially mediation. With time, however, states have become more acceptant of international courts and arbitral

[71] For discussion, see Crawford 2012; and Kingsbury 2012.

tribunals.[72] Since the year 2000, the ICJ has had a relatively full docket, a pattern that is quite likely to continue.[73] Interestingly, nonbinding and binding third-party methods show a detectable, though less striking, increase over time, from a relatively minor proportion of disputant-years in 1945 to approximately 10 percent each in 2015. This growth in popularity reflects the reality that with time legitimacy of international mediation and/or international courts increases (Alter 2014).

Conclusions

In this chapter, we have provided an overview of the research methods used to explore the intricate dynamics of the causal mechanisms embedded in our theory. We have introduced the quantitative and the qualitative data. We have discussed the benefits and shortcomings of our data sources and each type of method, highlighting their complementarity. This chapter has also examined trends of territorial dispute settlement over the past several decades in the various geographical regions of the world. In addition to patterns uncovered by quantitative analysis, delving into the details of our causal theory through the lens of expert interviews and primary documents adds a layer of credibility and depth to our study. In particular, these data allow us to examine the intricate dynamics of the dispute resolution process from beginning to end. Using a comprehensive, multimethod approach allows us to shed light on the mechanisms of choice-of-venue strategic selection by highlighting the effects of past experience and the importance of the relationship between domestic and international law. The qualitative data illustrates well how our theory works in the context of within-venue strategic selection: the mechanisms of uncertainty about the resolution process and uncertainty about legal claims.

In addition to the technical aspects of our research design, the extensive discussion of patterns and trends of territorial disputes can be helpful to scholars and practitioners interested in the study of international dispute settlement. Our data reveal interesting patterns about dispute resolution over time and space. The discussion of regional past experience adds unique

---

[72] See De Brabandere 2018.
[73] Goertz, Diehl, and Balas (2016) show that in the last 30 years, arbitration and adjudication come in second place as methods of choice for the settlement of territorial claims. Also see Owsiak and Mitchell (2019) for discussion of nonformal and legal mechanisms in land, river, and maritime claims. For the exact timing of litigation attempts, see McDowell 2018.

insights to our knowledge of regional trends in dispute resolution. Indeed, dispute settlement preferences vary substantially by region, and to a large extent, this variance is attributable to the distinctive conflict resolution norms that prevail in each region. Consequently, when policymakers choose particular modes of dispute resolution for their own countries, it is of utmost importance that these distinctive regional norms of conflict resolution be taken into consideration. Another vital insight provided by this chapter is that states' preferences with respect to various PR methods change over time for all geographic regions. Though large-N quantitative cross-sectional data provide insights into the global patterns, much of the variation between regions is lost. For instance, as this chapter shows, Middle Eastern states, to large extent, embrace mediation and other nonbinding third-party PR methods. In Europe, these methods are used more rarely, as an overwhelming proportion of attempts at resolution in this region consist of negotiations.

6

Testing Choice-of-Venue
Strategic Selection

In this chapter, we focus on the choice-of-venue strategic selection and empirically explore proposer states' behavior in the context of territorial disputes. In Chapter 3, we linked several mechanisms to states' preferences with respect to the various peaceful resolution (PR) methods. We noted that each mechanism—past experience and the relationship between domestic and international law—has a bearing on these preferences. If our theory has any purchase, we should observe several distinctive patterns in both our quantitative analysis and qualitative interviews. First, states with a positive win-loss record in certain resolution methods should be more likely to return to these methods in their subsequent territorial contentions than if the state did not have such a positive record. In a similar way, an overall positive regional win-loss record should have a similar effect on state's preferences. We expect that states are more likely to resort to a particular PR method when the regional win-loss record with this method is encouraging.

Our second set of hypotheses deals with the relationship between domestic law and international law. We believe that states whose domestic legal system fully embraces international law should be more willing to pursue binding third-party methods, as these methods entail in-depth utilization of international law. Importantly, with regard to rule of law, Chapter 3 presented two contrasting hypotheses. Thus, our goal in the present chapter is to decipher which one better reflects reality. Do states with high levels of rule of law gravitate toward arbitration and adjudication? Or do domestic levels of rule of law have no bearing on the choice-of-venue strategic selection? Finally, the last question that we tackle in this chapter is whether domestic legal traditions—civil law, common law, or Islamic law—influence states in their decisions about conflict management. As we explained in Chapter 3, there are strong theoretical reasons to expect that common law states will gravitate toward bilateral negotiations, while civil law states will gravitate toward the more legalized venues, especially adjudication. We also expect that states

The Peaceful Resolution of Territorial and Maritime Disputes. Emilia Justyna Powell and Krista E. Wiegand,
Oxford University Press. © Oxford University Press 2023. DOI: 10.1093/oso/9780197675649.003.0006

representing the Islamic legal tradition will be most frequently drawn to the nonbinding third-party methods. Taking all of these expectations together, we want to know under what configuration of mechanisms proposer states choose negotiations, nonbinding third-party methods, and binding third-party methods.

Even controlling for a multitude of alternative factors, our quantitative evidence, presented below, suggests that there is much support for our theoretical expectations.[1] Interestingly, while all of our hypotheses that convey clear expectations (past experience, international law's position in the domestic legal systems, domestic legal traditions) receive empirical support, the results do not convey unequivocal answers in the context of the rule of law variables. Throughout this chapter, insights from our in-depth qualitative interviews shed light on the various aspects of proposer states' behavior while choosing an appropriate forum for conflict resolution of territorial disputes.

We start our analysis by examining our qualitative evidence that speaks to the broad phenomenon of choice-of-venue strategic selection. Overall, our interviews and primary documents elucidate the causal mechanisms at work and provide strong support for our expectations regarding states' choices of the various settlement venues. The main message stemming from all our conversations with a variety of interlocutors—international judges, arbitrators, lawyers, state counsel, and legal experts—is that states are indeed strategic when selecting their PR venues, particularly the legal venue—arbitration and adjudication. Any government that is considering a decision to litigate or seek arbitration must determine strategic objectives beforehand. In other words, it is of the utmost importance to "know what you want to get out of the case" (Martin 2018). Importantly, states are unable to predict the outcome of any settlement with certainty. This is especially the case when states decide to delegate their contentions to international courts. Indeed, in the process of adjudicating, international courts can create new interpretations of existing rules, or, in essence, create new rules. When asked whether in its jurisprudence the International Court of Justice (ICJ) has created new rules, one of our interlocutors answered, "Constantly. It's jurisprudence. For example, the law of state responsibility, the law of nationality of

---

[1] As with all studies that use quantitative analysis in international relations, the purpose of large-N quantitative studies is to confirm whether the direction of the relationships suggested in the theory is predicted correctly—in the language of likelihood and not certainty—and whether there is a substantive shift in the likelihood of an outcome owing to a change in an independent variable.

claims, that sort of things. In every case, it is in a sense making a law."[2] Larry Martin (2018) recommended that when determining strategic objectives in peaceful resolution, states should consider what is the most desired outcome of the settlement and what are some acceptable alternatives: "States should think about what is the likely outcome of the case before dispute settlement."[3]

As an example, the Philippines was highly strategic in selecting arbitration over bilateral negotiations, mediation, and—most of all—adjudication in its decision to seek resolution in the South China Sea dispute. The primary goal for the Philippines was to retain the highest amount of control over the contention, and to increase the probability of winning the case. One of the leading proponents of pursuing arbitration, former Department of Foreign Affairs Assistant Secretary Henry Bensurto, told us frankly that "there was a consideration of menu options—ICJ, conciliation, etc., based on what outcome the Philippines wanted to achieve."[4] Former Department of Foreign Affairs Secretary Albert Del Rosario spoke directly about the importance of strategy: "We made an assessment of various avenues to seek a peaceful settlement of the dispute. In arriving at a potential legal strategy, studies were also conducted on security and economic consequences."[5] As noted by a high-ranking Philippine government official, "on balance it was decided that the pros outweighed the cons."[6] In the end, arbitration emerged as the optimal strategy for the Philippines.

Martin (2018) also noted that "within certain margins, parties can generally predict outcomes. Sides are rarely surprised by outcomes." Therefore, it is to be expected that some states choose to avoid the ICJ. When asked why states are reluctant to accept the ICJ's compulsory jurisdiction, one of our interviewees answered, "Because they just don't want to have a particular case or category of cases decided by the Court. They regard them as too delicate or too important."[7] In the Philippines-China case, the legal team led

---

[2] Author's interview (EJP) with an anonymous ICJ state advocate and international arbitrator, United Kingdom, October 2013.

[3] Larry Martin is cochair of the International Litigation and Arbitration Department of Foley Hoag LLP in Washington, DC. He has worked with Paul Reichler representing many states in territorial and maritime disputes.

[4] Author's interview (KEW) with Henry Bensurto, former Department of Foreign Affairs Assistant Secretary and Consul General, San Francisco, CA, USA, August 31, 2017.

[5] Author's interview (KEW) with Albert Del Rosario, former Secretary of Foreign Affairs, Department of Foreign Affairs and former Ambassador of the Republic of the Philippines to the United States of America, Manila, Philippines, March 18, 2017.

[6] Author's interview (KEW) with an anonymous high-ranking Philippine government official, Manila, Philippines, March 9, 2017.

[7] Author's interview (EJP) with an anonymous ICJ state advocate and international arbitrator, United Kingdom, October 2013.

by counsel Paul Reichler presented the option of going to the ICJ as suboptimal. According to their evaluation, if it had been possible to take the case
to the ICJ, the chance of winning in that venue was rather slim.[8] The legal
team assessed that the Court would not have ruled in favor of the Philippines
in crucial aspects of the case, and the Philippines could have lost the case
to China (Kingdon 2015). The Philippine legal team was leery of pursuing
sovereignty claims for islands because China could potentially provide some
evidence indicating historic Chinese control—and thus territorial sovereignty based on historic title—over the Spratly (Nansha) islands (Talmon
and Jia 2014).[9] The goal was to eliminate the possibility of any ruling with
regard to China's potentially stronger legal case for territorial claims. The ICJ
option was therefore deemed too risky since the outcome would not necessarily be favorable to the Philippines.[10] In the perception of the Philippines,
the decision to pursue arbitration would reduce China's chances of winning. Together with the legal team led by Paul Reichler of Foley Hoag, a
Washington, DC, law firm, advisors from the Department of Foreign Affairs,
and advisors in President Benigno Aquino's administration, particularly
Senior Associate Justice Antonio Carpio who had first suggested arbitration,
President Aquino selected it as the best venue to deliver the sought-after outcome for the Philippines.[11]

  When preparing for litigation or arbitration, all policymakers know that
each PR method provides disputants with a different level of control and settlement predictability. For example, ad hoc arbitration tribunals allow for
increased levels of state control—and thus, arguably, more predictability—
compared to the International Tribunal for the Law of the Sea (ITLOS) or
the ICJ. As an ITLOS judge explained in an interview, "States sometimes feel
more comfortable with arbitration because they have more control. States
feel a bit less nervous, anxious, with arbitration compared to courts."[12]
Judge Rüdiger Wolfrum pointed out in an interview that "some states don't
like large bodies, and prefer smaller arbitration chambers because of lesser

[8] China has not accepted the compulsory jurisdiction of the ICJ. None of the interviewees
mentioned consideration of the UN Security Council as a means of dispute resolution.
[9] China has also made claims of the South China Sea region as part of China's "historic waters." See
Talmon and Jia (2014, 49–50).
[10] Author's interview (KEW) with Paul Reichler, Partner, Foley Hoag, Washington, DC,
USA, November 7, 2016. Reichler was Lead Counsel for the Philippines in the arbitration case
against China.
[11] Author's interview (KEW) with Ambassador Albert Del Rosario, Manila, Philippines, March
18, 2017.
[12] Author's interview (KEW) with an anonymous ITLOS judge, Rhodes, Greece, July 2018.

uncertainty."[13] The ability to shape the settlement process and the hope to reduce uncertainty drive states' decisions in the choice-of-venue strategic selection. One of our interlocutors, Captain Ashley Roach, explained that there are most definitely some general patterns shaping dynamics of choice of method: "In many respects, it's hard to generalize [about strategy]. Every case is different, but there are some general factors that matter."[14] He continued: "States should be strategic about choice of venue."[15] ITLOS Judge Tullio Treves noted that "a state's big decision is whether to seek to adjudicate or not. First, [a state has to] find a venue that will take the case, that can be competent. There is a lot of complicated thinking. States have to think about what chances they have, [they] must calculate having provisional measures, which speed up a case," for example.[16] In the case of the Philippines-China arbitration, devising and executing an intricate, victory-focused strategy necessitated much research. The government knew that it "would have to be magnanimous in victory," and the Department of Foreign Affairs and National Security Council evaluated several victory scenarios.[17] According to a close advisor to President Aquino,

> the main issue for the Philippines was the nine-dash line. They [Philippines legal team] were pretty sure the Tribunal would not allow the nine-dash line because in allowing it, it would be the end of UNCLOS and the Tribunal would not make a decision that would harm UNCLOS. They studied how UNCLOS was negotiated, discussed text of the Law of the Sea and they decided they were "absolutely sure" that the Tribunal would rule in the Philippines' favor. They believed they had a good case since the main thrust of the case was the nine-dash line, and the Philippines was confident that they would win this part of the ruling. There was not any other way to do it.[18]

[13] Author's interview (KEW) with Judge Rüdiger Wolfrum, former President of ITLOS, Rhodes, Greece, July 19, 2018.
[14] Author's interview (KEW) with Ashley Roach, former Judge Advocate General, US Navy and former adviser in the Office of the Legal Adviser, US Department of State, Rhodes, Greece, July 11, 2018.
[15] Ibid.
[16] Author's interview (KEW) with ITLOS Judge Tullio Treves, Rhodes, Greece, July 15, 2018.
[17] Author's interview (KEW) with Professor Jay L. Batongbacal, Director, University of the Philippines Institute for Maritime Affairs and Law of the Sea, Quezon City, Philippines, April 20, 2017.
[18] Author's interview (KEW) with an anonymous high-ranking Philippine government official, Manila, Philippines, March 9, 2017.

Outside legal counsel had to address many issues brought to the fore by the Philippine government: "What is the scope of and what would be the viability of arbitration under UNCLOS? Is there jurisdiction? What kind of claims could survive a jurisdictional challenge? And would those claims, if they prevailed, provide meaningful relief to the Philippines?"[19] As noted by a Department of Foreign Affairs official, "The first question to answer was 'was it possible?' and 'would it be binding for China?' "[20] According to legal counsel Paul Reichler, "the Philippine government felt there would be jurisdiction and they had winning arguments, and that the Philippines would win."[21] Of course, there was some degree of uncertainty with arbitration, since at that time, UNCLOS (UN Convention on the Law of the Sea) had not yet adjudicated on maritime entitlements. Despite this reality, "they [the Philippines] were willing to take the risk."[22]

Speaking more broadly to our argument about strategic selection, public international lawyer Danae Azaria explained that "strategically, disputants are choosing jurisdictions," and that "parties use tribunals and courts strategically" (Azaria 2018). Victories and losses are at the heart of dispute resolution. This is especially the case for arbitration and adjudication. ICJ Judge Al-Khasawneh noted, "judicial decisions sometimes lack the compromises which are inherent in negotiations, and sometimes countries win or lose. But that is better than going to wars or to resort to force."[23] All of our interlocutors confirmed that winning matters greatly to states engaged in territorial and maritime disputes. According to Judge Treves, "Winning is very important. Winning does matter, especially if you are the claimant state."

To secure victory while reducing uncertainty associated with the settlement process, the Philippine government engaged in a step-by-step planning scheme. Paul Reicher, the Philippines' counsel, told us that the arbitral tribunal was definitely perceived as the optimal forum where the Philippines could potentially secure a favorable outcome.[24] Several other interlocutors confirmed these sentiments. According to Jay Batongbacal, who advised

---

[19] Ibid.
[20] Author's interview (KEW) with Romulo R. Ubay Jr., Assistant/Research Tech, Maritime and Ocean Affairs Office, Department of Foreign Affairs, Manila, Philippines, April 19, 2017.
[21] Author's interview (KEW) with Paul Reichler, November 7, 2016.
[22] Ibid.
[23] Author's interview (EJP) with Judge Awn Shawkat Al-Khasawneh, former Vice-President, ICJ and former Prime Minister of Jordan, Amman, Jordan, February 18, 2015.
[24] Author's interview (KEW) with Paul Reichler, November 7, 2016, and author's interview (KEW) with Dr. Victor Andres Manhit, Director, Stratbase-Albert Del Rosario Institute, Manila, Philippines, July 11, 2016.

the Philippine team on the case, "Certainly states choose forums where they think they can win. Look at the case of the Philippines' choice of UNCLOS [Annex VII], which was determined by the thought that it would be the best place to win a case."[25] Ioannis Konstantinidis also emphasized the importance of strategy in the Philippines' decision to pursue arbitration: "As a third party, as an observer, I believe that the decision of the Philippines to bring this case before a dispute settlement forum against China was purely a strategic decision."[26]

Judge Treves also noted that "sometimes it's more important to settle the dispute and take chances because a solution is better than no solution." At the same time, he indicated that "the choice to go to court or not [is influenced by the questions:]—do we have a chance? Why should we go if we will lose?"[27] As an example, for the Philippines, a lot was at stake. According to Francis Jardeleza, Supreme Court associate justice who represented the Philippines at the arbitration case, "President Aquino put his legacy at stake by going legal, by going through arbitration. Can you imagine if we lost? I could feel that he was really conflicted."[28]

When speaking about the ICJ, one of our interviewees stated: "Surely, you are not going to waste time and money by going to the Court if you don't want to or expect to win."[29] This expectation pertains not only to adjudication but also to arbitration, since aside from the fact that the parties can influence the selection of arbitrators and shape the procedure, arbitration is "like going to the Court, but a different court."[30] Of course, international courts and arbitral tribunals are keenly aware of the reality that the goal of each disputant is to win the dispute. Thus, "courts and tribunals will often 'split the baby' to keep both sides happy with the outcome," by considering a decision where both sides gain some territorial or maritime concessions (Martin 2018). Reliance on equity may play an important role in such situations. As one of our interviewees noted, "Yet, in some [cases], it's the function of the Court to propose a compromise. The only scope for flexibility in that direction is if the

---

[25] Author's interview (KEW) with Professor Jay L. Batongbacal, April 20, 2017.

[26] Author's interview (EJP) with Ioannis Konstantinidis, state counsel and consultant, January 11, 2021.

[27] Author's interview (KEW) with Judge Tullio Treves, July 15, 2018.

[28] Tarra Quismundo, "Victory Dinner Set for Philippines' Sea Dispute Team: So Who's Picking Up the Tab?," *Asia News Network*, July 17, 2016, https://annx.asianews.network/content/victory-dinner-set-philippines-sea-dispute-team-so-who%E2%80%99s-picking-tab-22892.

[29] Author's interview (EJP) with an anonymous ICJ state advocate and international arbitrator, United Kingdom, October 2013.

[30] Ibid. Also cited in Powell (2020, 134).

parties have agreed [that] the Court shall apply not law but decide *ex aequo et bono* and decide equitably. And then, it will consider the positions of the parties."[31]

Strategizing about chances of winning in the various forums frequently involves a convoluted process. An ITLOS judge told us that in the Peru v. Chile maritime dispute resolved by the ICJ in 2014, the Peruvian government asked at least twenty legal experts for guidance in determining "if they [Peru] have a good chance" of winning a legal case against Chile.[32] Of course, no judgment can be predicted with certainty. The best that both parties can do is to estimate the chances of winning: "It's difficult sometimes to know which way the Court will swing. After all, the plaintiff state would not stop the case if it didn't think that the Court was going to decide in its favor. But that's not always the case. Sometimes the Court decides differently. Take the major issue in Barcelona Traction. The question of the protection of shareholders. Belgium thought that the Court would decide in its favor, and the Court decided in favor of Spain."[33] As Ashley Roach noted, "It's always a calculus about chances of winning and what are the costs of losing."[34] A public international law specialist who has advised multiple states in territorial and maritime contentions told us that in a maritime dispute case about swordfish, Chile v. European Union, the parties strategically decided to split the dispute into separate stages.[35] Certain aspects of the contention were brought to the World Trade Organization, while others ended up at ITLOS, because each party was "expecting to win using these venues."[36] Indeed, as this expert explained, "In one case ITLOS could have better jurisdiction than the ICJ, if case law is slightly better for the case."[37]

It is also apparent from our interviews that the expectation of winning drives proposer states. When asked whether states go to the ICJ only if they

---

[31] Ibid.

[32] Author's interview (KEW) with an anonymous ITLOS judge, July 2018. See Maritime Dispute, Peru v. Chile, ICJ Rep. 2014, 3, Judgment of January 27, 2014.

[33] Author's interview (EJP) with an anonymous ICJ state advocate and international arbitrator, United Kingdom, October 2013. The reference is to Barcelona Traction, Light and Power Company, Limited, Belgium v. Spain; Second Phase, ICJ Rep. 1970, 3, Judgment of February 5, 1970.

[34] Author's interview (KEW) with Ashley Roach, July 11, 2018. Roach also noted that "winning the case really matters—no doubt about that. . . . It's good to prevent losing as much. [States] want the best outcome."

[35] See Case Concerning the Conservation and Sustainable Exploitation of Swordfish Stocks in the South-Eastern Pacific Ocean, Chile v. European Union, ITLOS Case No. 7, Judgment of December 16, 2009.

[36] Author's interview (KEW) with an anonymous public international law specialist, Rhodes, Greece, July 2018.

[37] Ibid.

expect victory, one of our interlocutors noted that a state's position matters greatly in this regard: "It [the choice of going to a court] depends on whether they are plaintiff or defendant. If you are plaintiff, it is because you think you will win. If you are defendant, you don't have any choice."[38] Similarly, experts agreed that states do not want to lose a case, and are strategic about selecting a PR method to avoid losing. For example, Judge Treves noted that "a state that loses a case that they lost unjustly is prone to react."[39] For instance, the United States was naturally "not happy with" losing the Gulf of Maine case, and was thus "more hesitant to go to litigation" after the loss.[40] Similarly, in the aftermath of losing its ICJ case against Nicaragua, the United States did not want to—and in fact did not—comply with the ruling.[41]

Of course, most of the time the perception of injustice is quite subjective. As Judge Treves pointed out, the role of past experiences—winning and losing—"depends on if it's an unfavorable situation, if there is a feeling [by the state] of whether the decision was right or wrong."[42] Indeed, such negative feelings may prompt the losing state to withdraw support from an international court or an international treaty. Such were the actions of France when it disagreed with the Nuclear Tests case at the ICJ in 1974, the United States when it lost against Nicaragua in 1984, and Colombia when it lost against Nicaragua in 2012.[43] The losing government's rhetoric vis-à-vis its domestic population has the potential to shape these patterns. By way of illustration, in the aftermath of the 2012 ICJ judgment in the Nicaragua v. Colombia case, both states could have claimed victory since Colombia was awarded territorial concessions and Nicaragua gained maritime rights it preferred.[44] But the Colombian government perceived the judgment as a loss and informed the Colombian people that the case was a disaster to the country. As a result, Colombia was unable to return to the ICJ without potential domestic

[38] Author's interview (EJP) with an anonymous ICJ state advocate and international arbitrator, United Kingdom, October 2013.

[39] Author's interview (KEW) with Judge Tullio Treves, July 15, 2018.

[40] Author's interview (KEW) with Ashley Roach, July 11, 2018. See Delimitation of the Maritime Boundary in the Gulf of Maine Area, Canada v. United States, ICJ Rep. 1984, 246, Judgment of October 12, 1984.

[41] Delimitation of the Maritime Boundary in the Gulf of Maine Area, Canada v. United States, ICJ Rep. 1984, 246, Judgment of October 12, 1984.

[42] Author's interview (KEW) with Judge Tullio Treves, July 15, 2018.

[43] Ibid. See Nuclear Tests, Australia v. France, Judgment, ICJ Rep. 1974, 253, Judgment of December 20, 1974; Case Concerning Military and Paramilitary Activities in and against Nicaragua, Nicaragua v. United States of America, ICJ Rep. 1986, 14, Judgment of June 27, 1986; Territorial and Maritime Dispute, Nicaragua v. Colombia, ICJ Rep. 2012, 624, Judgment of November 19, 2012.

[44] Territorial and Maritime Dispute, Nicaragua v. Colombia, ICJ Rep. 2012, 624, Judgment of November 19, 2012.

costs.[45] Instead, nine days after the ICJ judgment, Colombian president Juan Manuel Santos withdrew from the 1948 Bogota Treaty, in which Colombia recognized jurisdiction of the ICJ for dispute resolution.[46] To a large extent, policymakers usually have the power to shape the public perception of a dispute outcome. Hans Corell noted in an interview that "if you can solve a dispute through negotiations, that, in a sense, is the best way of solving it. Then, the prime ministers can meet and shake hands in front of a TV camera, and the people of both sides of the dispute will see that 'Ah, so my prime minister is on board here.' That carries legitimacy to the solution of the dispute."[47] Our discussion in this section can be summed up by an observation by Ashley Roach: "If being sued, minimize losses and maximize gains; if suing, the state wants to win."[48]

Past Experience

Our hypotheses about past experience predict that proposer states' past wins and losses and the past record of states in the region will influence their selection of a PR method in ongoing territorial disputes. Positive experiences encourage returning to the same method (Hypothesis 1), while negative experiences discourage such action. Hypothesis 2 expresses our expectation that a state involved in a dispute is likely to examine not only its own past experiences with different resolution methods, but also experiences of states in the same geographic region. Judges, arbitrators, and legal counsel who work at the ICJ, ITLOS, Permanent Court of Arbitration (PCA), and other arbitration venues agree that past experience of winning or losing affects states' decisions to seek the same methods in the future. Asked in an interview whether states strategize to win, Ashley Roach responded, "Past experience does matter."[49] An ITLOS judge admitted that "states that resolve disputes through legal procedure, hopefully in their favor, may now appreciate the value of this option more than they did before."[50] Conversely,

[45] Author's interview (KEW) with an anonymous ITLOS judge, July 2018.
[46] American Treaty on Pacific Settlement—Pact of Bogotá, Organization of American States, April 30, 1948.
[47] Author's interview (EJP) with Hans Corell, former Under-Secretary-General for Legal Affairs and the Legal Counsel of the United Nations, March 14, 2015.
[48] Author's interview (KEW) with Ashley Roach, July 11, 2018.
[49] Ibid.
[50] Author's interview (KEW) with an anonymous ITLOS judge, July 2018.

states with a negative or disappointing experience with legal mechanisms seriously consider not returning to the same PR method in the future.[51] Of course, decisions about going back to PR methods that have yielded unfavorable outcomes in the past are taken in light of the existing international jurisprudence. In the Gulf of Maine case, the advocates representing the United States noted that when preparing for their case against Canada, "we examined with great care, as one would expect, the pleadings in previous related cases before the Court" (Robinson, Colson, and Rashkow 1985, 586). These cases included the 1969 North Sea Continental Shelf Cases, the 1977 Anglo-French Continental Shelf Arbitration, and the 1981 Tunisia v. Libya Continental Shelf case.[52] In a more recent case, Paul Reicher, who served as Nicaragua's lead counsel in the Nicaragua v. Colombia case in 2012, noted that "Nicaragua had won and wanted to return to the Court after winning. Where jurisdiction fits, positive experience does matter."[53]

A public international lawyer also affirmed the role of past experience, slightly diverging from the particular focus of our theory. This legal specialist pointed to the important role past experience of winning and losing can play in states' selection of legal teams and PR methods and venues. By way of illustration, while trying to resolve its maritime dispute against Guyana, Suriname restructured its legal team involving counsel proven to have "had a good track record in maritime boundary delimitation cases in the past."[54] In the Philippines-China arbitration, past successes and experience of certain public international law firms prompted the Philippine government to hire Paul Reichler and associates of Foley Hoag as legal counsel. The legal team led by Reichler had recently represented Mauritius in its arbitration case against the United Kingdom, dealing with the disputed Chagos Marine Protected Area located in the British Indian Ocean Territory.[55] Mauritius had submitted its Notification and Statement of Claim in December 2010 to initiate proceedings against the United Kingdom via an UNCLOS Annex VII

---

[51] Ibid.

[52] North Sea Continental Shelf, Germany v. Denmark, Order, ICJ Rep. 1968, 9, ICJ 149, Judgment of April 26, 1968; Case Concerning the Delimitation of Continental Shelf between the United Kingdom of Great Britain and Northern Ireland, and the French Republic, Arbitral Award of March 14, 1978; Continental Shelf, Tunisia v. Libyan Arab Jamahzriya, Application to Intervene, 1CJ Rep. 1982, 18, Judgment of February 24, 1982.

[53] Author's interview (KEW) with Paul Reichler, November 7, 2016.

[54] Author's interview (KEW) with an anonymous public international law specialist, July 2018. Guyana v. Suriname, PCA, ICGJ 370 (PCA 2007), Arbitral Award of September 17, 2007.

[55] Chagos Marine Protected Area Arbitration, Mauritius v. United Kingdom, PCA Case No. 2011-03, Arbitral Award of March 18, 2015.

tribunal. Mauritius's legal team recommended Annex VII because the United Kingdom was unwilling to consent to legal resolution through other means. Interestingly, the timing of preparations for both cases—Philippines v. China and Mauritius v. United Kingdom—largely overlapped for the legal team. On March 18, 2015, the arbitral tribunal ruled that the Chagos Maritime Protected Area established by the United Kingdom was not in accordance with UNCLOS. Thus, Mauritius emerged as a clear winner. There is no doubt that the recent experiences of the Philippines' legal team in the Mauritius v. United Kingdom case had crucial implications for the Philippines' strategy. The past experiences of the legal team directly influenced the choice-of-venue selection for the Philippine government. Despite the Philippines' own lack of experience with arbitration in the context of territorial and maritime disputes, there was a concerted effort by the Philippines to consider what worked and what did not work, influencing the selection of the ultimate PR method and venue.

Turning to our quantitative analysis of past experience, we estimated multinomial logit and logit regression models to test Hypothesis 1 (Table 6.1) and Hypothesis 2 (Table 6.2).[56] We use a multinomial logit model because our dependent variable—a state's choice of PR method—is a categorical measure in which the separate categories (negotiations, nonbinding third-party methods, and binding third-party methods) are treated in a nonordered manner, as discussed in Chapter 2. The multinomial logit model (Model 1) presents the comparison of nonbinding and binding third-party methods with bilateral negotiations as the base category. Model 2 is a logit model that compares binding third-party methods versus the other PR methods, negotiations and nonbinding third-party methods combined. Figure 6.1 presents coefficient plots. Finally, Model 3 compares only nonbinding third-party methods to binding third-party methods, excluding bilateral negotiations. In this model, the number of observations is reduced to 811, because of the exclusion of negotiations. Predicted probabilities for nonbinding and binding third-party methods are shown in Figure 6.2 based on Models 2 and 3.

Overall, we find strong support for our hypotheses about the proposer's past experience with the binding methods. There is a modest effect of

---

[56] In all of our models we use the terms "Negotiations," "Nonbinding," and "Binding" to designate the three categories of our dependent variable. The term "Nonbinding" only refers to nonbinding third-party methods.

Table 6.1 Past experience: Selection of PR methods, 1945–2015

	Model 1 Multinomial Logit		Model 2 Logit	Model 3 Logit
	Nonbinding methods	Binding methods	Binding vs. other PR methods	Nonbinding vs. binding methods
Proposer Win-Loss Negotiations	−0.314 (0.249)	−0.238 (0.261)	−0.153 (0.253)	0.023 (0.505)
Proposer Win-Loss Nonbinding	−0.716 (0.486)	−0.425 (0.540)	−0.999** (0.498)	−1.923* (0.941)
Proposer Win-Loss Binding	−0.085 (0.361)	0.660* (0.333)	0.677** (0.321)	−0.804+ (0.424)
Nonproposer Win-Loss Negotiations	−0.642* (0.272)	−0.424 (0.281)	−0.303 (0.276)	−0.063 (0.467)
Nonproposer Win-Loss Nonbinding	−0.220 (0.543)	2.542** (0.651)	2.591** (0.642)	−2.561** (0.824)
Nonproposer Win-Loss Binding	0.783* (0.359)	0.526 (0.348)	0.374 (0.340)	−0.131 (0.455)
Economic Salience	0.856** (0.125)	0.196 (0.124)	0.637 (0.120)	1.040** (0.195)
Strategic Salience	0.210+ (0.125)	−0.678** (0.121)	−0.637** (0.116)	0.702** (0.177)
Identity Salience	0.287* (0.125)	−0.515** (0.137)	−0.580** (0.134)	0.753** (0.210)
Shared Alliance	0.251+ (0.134)	0.116 (0.146)	0.116 (0.144)	0.035 (0.206)
Past Conflict	1.377** (0.157)	0.078 (0.206)	−0.272 (0.198)	1.662** (0.254)
Shared IGO Membership	0.164** (9.019)	0.165** (0.020)	0.130** (0.019)	−0.012 (0.027)
Democratic Dyad	−0.764** (.159)	−0.155 (0.142)	0.011 (0.136)	−0.530* (0.206)
Power Asymmetry	−0.938* (0.380)	−3.072** (0.378)	−2.779** (0.365)	2.184** (0.555)
Constant	−2.250 (0.637)	−1.319* (0.610)	0.134 (0.436)	−0.189 (0.993)
N	2,983	2,983	2,983	811

Note: Robust standard errors are provided, ** < .01, * < .05, + .10.

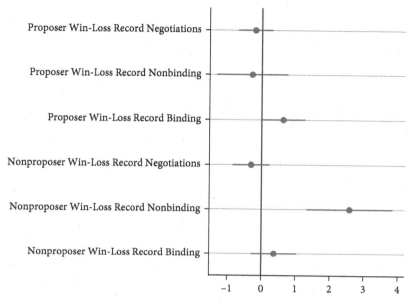

Figure 6.1. Coefficient plot for binding methods—Table 6.1, Model 2.

win-loss record for bilateral negotiations, and no effect/a negative effect for nonbinding third-party methods. Models 1 and 2 show that proposer states with a positive win-loss record in binding PR methods are more likely to return to these methods again rather than choosing bilateral negotiations. The coefficients in both models are positive—indicating the predicted direction of the relationship—and statistically significant.[57] As shown in Figure 6.2, proposer states with positive win-loss records in binding third-party methods (.029) are 93 percent more likely to resort to these methods compared to proposer states who have lost disputes in these methods in the past (.015). Compared to proposer states whose experience with arbitration or adjudication is neutral (number of wins equals number of losses), and proposer states who have never attempted binding methods before, proposer states with positive winning records in binding methods are 48 percent more likely to return to these methods. As predicted in Hypothesis 1, previous

---

[57] As a robustness check, we estimated a model to decipher whether settlement efforts are delegated or not. In this model, our dependent variable is coded as dichotomous: binding PR methods (1) and nonbinding third-party methods and negotiations combined (0). This model reflects distinctions made in the literature on delegation (Abbott and Snidal 1998, 2000). Our results with this model show a statistically significant and positive relationship between a positive win-loss record for the proposer state and the likelihood of seeking binding methods again.

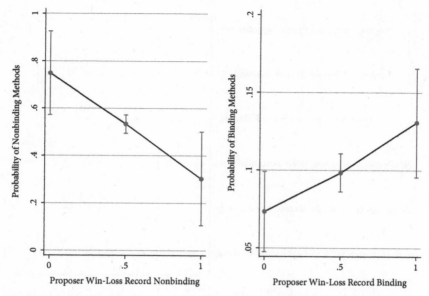

Figure 6.2. Predicted probabilities of nonbinding and binding PR methods based on past win-loss record of same methods—Table 6.1, Model 2 (right) and Model 3 (left). Adjusted predictions with 95 percent confidence intervals.

Note: These results are based on Model 2, a logit model comparing binding methods compared to bilateral negotiations and nonbinding methods combined.

success in binding methods encourages proposer states to attempt these same methods in the hope of reaching a favorable decision yet again. In this context, it is important to note that overall, values of predicted probabilities of states proposing binding methods are low. These patterns reflect the reality that states attempt arbitration and adjudication with low frequency, but when they win, they are more likely to return to these methods in future disputes. Arguably, winning or losing should matter most in the context of adjudication. As one of our interviewees noted,

Another aspect of any permanently established international court is that they have history. You have states that had a case before a particular court and lost. Maybe they lost for good reasons, maybe legally they knew we were going to lose, and understand the reasoning, but there is still a political aspect to it. You have African states after the Southwest Africa cases. You have France after the Nuclear Tests cases. These are states that don't want to put dispute resolution clauses into treaties that provide only for judicial settlement, because they had a case and it went badly, and politically it's problematic for them to be going back to the same forum where, at least in terms of public perception, they had a bad experience.[58]

Though the substantive changes in probabilities are miniscule, contrary to our expectations states with positive experience in nonbinding third-party methods are not more likely to return to these methods again. The impact of the *Proposer Win-Loss Nonbinding* variable in Model 1 is statistically insignificant, while Models 2 and 3 indicate a negative and statistically significant relationship in Model 3. Thus, the proposers' positive experience in nonbinding third-party methods does not encourage a return to any type of third-party intermediary in the future.

Quite interesting are patterns with regard to how proposer states consider the win-loss records of nonproposer states. Our models show that proposers take their opponents' win-loss record quite seriously in considering the different PR methods. Most importantly, as shown in Model 3, when nonproposers have a winning record in nonbinding third-party methods, proposers are less likely to pursue these methods compared to binding methods. Model 2 further sheds light on this effect showing that when a proposer faces a nonproposer with a positive win-loss record in mediation or conciliation, the proposer will likely gravitate toward arbitration or adjudication. In a similar manner, nonproposers' positive record in binding methods increases the likelihood that proposer states will seek nonbinding third-party methods instead of negotiations (Model 1). It is reasonable to expect that proposer states are attracted to PR methods that in the past have not yielded a record of victory for the nonproposer.

Our expectation expressed in Hypothesis 2 is that proposer states pay close attention to the win-loss record of other states in the same geographic region. This relationship holds in the context of binding third-party methods (Table 6.2, coefficient plots for Model 2, Figure 6.3). Positive regional experiences with binding methods have a powerful effect on a proposer's future binding resolution attempts. Proposers are more likely to turn to binding methods compared to negotiations when other states in the same region have won using these methods (Models 1 and 2). Predicted probabilities show a fuller picture of these effects (Figure 6.4). Proposers are 75 percent

---

[58] Author's interview (EJP) with an anonymous arbitration practitioner, February 7, 2022.

Table 6.2 Past experience of states in the same region: Selection of PR methods, 1945–2015

	Model 1 Multinomial Logit		Model 2 Logit	Model 3 Logit
	Nonbinding methods	Binding methods	Binding vs. other methods	Nonbinding vs. binding methods
Proposer Win-Loss Negotiations Same Region	−0.022 (0.273)	0.901** (0.293)	0.921** (0.288)	−1.042** (0.410)
Proposer Win-Loss Nonbinding Same Region	−0.166 (0.196)	−0.304 (0.188)	−0.281 (0.185)	0.154 (0.238)
Proposer Win-Loss Binding Same Region	0.704** (0.199)	0.608** (0.198)	0.485** (0.194)	−0.065 (0.276)
Economic Salience	0.859** (0.125)	0.171 (0.121)	0.039 (0.120)	1.068** (0.198)
Strategic Salience	0.235+ (0.125)	−0.568** (0.118)	−0.609+ (0.116)	0.603** (0.170)
Identity Salience	0.316* (0.125)	−0.516** (0.137)	−0.558** (0.135)	0.893** (0.200)
Shared Alliance	0.283* (0.134)	0.115 (0.146)	0.100 (0.144)	0.127 (0.203)
Past Conflict	1.378** (0.153)	0.125 (0.201)	−0.201 (0.196)	1.637** (0.246)
Shared IGO Membership	0.171** (0.020)	0.186** (0.021)	0.151** (0.020)	−0.026 (.028)
Democratic Dyad	−0.788** (0.154)	−0.135 (0.140)	0.013 (0.137)	−0.528** (0.559)
Power Asymmetry	−0.859* (0.381)	−2.842** (0.374)	−2.655** (0.367)	2.034** (0.559)
Constant	−3.309** (0.428)	−1.066** (0.419)	−1.040** (0.413)	−2.252** (0.618)
N	2,983	2,983	2,983	811

Note: Robust standard errors are provided, ** <. 01, * < .05, + .10.

more likely to use binding methods rather than other PR methods when other states in the same region have won in the past using these methods (.084), compared to when the regional win-loss record is negative (.048) (Model 2), or when regional states have no past experience or equal wins and losses (.064), a 30 percent increase. Past regional experiences with bilateral negotiations or nonbinding third-party methods seem not to influence the proposer's subsequent preferences in dispute resolution as one may

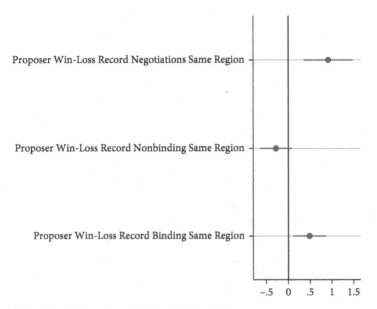

Figure 6.3. Coefficient plot—Table 6.2, Model 3.

expect. Our models show no statistically significant relationship between the regional win-loss record and the proposer state's choices vis-à-vis these methods.

Interestingly, when other states in the region have won disputes using bilateral negotiations, proposers are more likely to turn to binding methods, rather than negotiations (Models 1 and 2). Yet when we exclude attempts at negotiations from our analysis and consider only attempts at third-party PR methods, positive win-loss regional experiences with bilateral negotiations draw proposers toward the nonbinding third-party PR methods (Model 3). Proposer states are 6 percent less likely to pursue negotiations compared to other PR methods when the win-loss record of other states in the region is favorable in past negotiations (.877) rather than when it is not (.937) (Model 1). This is not surprising given that the dynamics of bilateral negotiations in the context of each contention are unique. Therefore, outcomes for bilateral talks may or may not provide hints about a state's ability to persuade its opponent in a subsequent dispute. In other words, there is much idiosyncrasy embedded in bilateral negotiations within a specific dyad.

It is important to add in this context that proposer states with positive experiences do not necessarily return to the same third party—the same

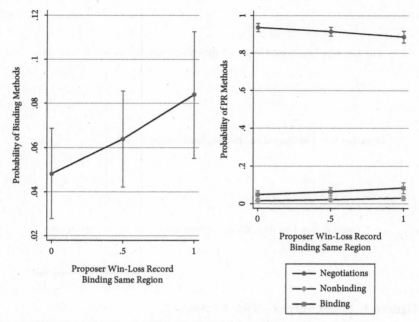

Figure 6.4. Predicted probabilities of binding methods, Table 6.2, Model 2 (left), and all PR methods based on regional win-loss record of binding methods, Table 6.2, Model 1 (right). Adjusted predictions with 95 percent confidence intervals.

Note: Model 1 is a multinomial logit model, and Model 2 is a logit model.

international court or the same arbitration panel. Instead, positive past experiences with binding methods make states more readily acceptant of these genres of PR forums. By way of illustration, Chile won a dispute with Argentina through arbitration awarded by the United Kingdom in 1977.[59] Later in 1984, Chile agreed to arbitration again in another territorial dispute with Argentina. This time, the Vatican was invited to help with the resolution.[60]

Our findings about proposer states' past experience and the regional past experiences would be incomplete without accounting for several control variables, which add to our understanding of the dispute resolution process. Patterns regarding control variables are similar for the six models we have presented so far, with a few exceptions. First, when we consider the effects of

[59] Dispute between Argentina and Chile Concerning the Beagle Channel, Award of the Arbitral Tribunal, February 18, 1977.
[60] Treaty of Peace and Friendship of 1984 between Chile and Argentina, November 29, 1984.

territorial salience, we find that when disputed territory has strategic value or identity value, proposer states are less likely to seek binding third-party assistance compared to negotiations.[61] Proposers are only 2 percent more likely to seek bilateral negotiations rather than other PR methods, a fairly minor impact. While disputed territory with strategic or identity salience reduces the likelihood of binding methods, such salience increases the likelihood of proposer states using nonbinding methods rather than negotiations. Economic salience encourages proposer states to seek nonbinding methods in comparison with negotiations. At the same time, economic salience seems to play no role in the proposer's decision to select the binding third-party methods and negotiations.[62] These findings are not surprising, since states are frequently unwilling to use binding third-party methods when disputes pertain to strategically valuable territory with military bases or geostrategic ports and borders or when the contested territory is culturally significant. On the other hand, it is also logical that proposer states would be more willing to turn to bilateral negotiations or nonbinding methods rather than binding methods because more divisible territory is easier to negotiate.

Conventional wisdom is that the presence of a military alliance is a sign of trust between states. Thus, the argument goes, military allies are more likely to negotiate and less likely to resort to binding third-party methods (Frazier 2006; Huth 1996; Leeds et al. 2000; Owsiak and Frazier 2014). Our results show that the presence of a military alliance between the proposer and nonproposer encourages that proposer to attempt resolution via nonbinding third-party methods (versus negotiations). The literature also shows that dyads with a conflictual past are generally more likely to engage in binding dispute resolution. Results regarding the *Past Conflict* variable suggest that conflictual dyadic relationships encourage proposers to seek nonbinding third-party methods rather than negotiate.[63] These patterns are to be expected given that mediation is usually used in the most violent conflicts.

Membership in peace-promoting international organizations encourages attempts at all third-party methods—nonbinding and binding—with statistically significant and positive relationships. This finding is consistent with the existing literature (Hansen et al. 2008; Shannon 2009). Our models

---

[61] These findings hold for both proposer states' own experience and regional past experience records as shown in Table 6.1, Models 2 and 3, and Table 6.2, Models 2 and 3.

[62] Table 6.1, Model 1 and Table 6.2, Model 1 show the likelihood of nonbinding methods, while predicted probabilities from Table 6.1 determine the effect on negotiations.

[63] When comparing only nonbinding to binding third-party methods, conflictual past encourages proposers to seek nonbinding methods.

suggest that when both disputants are democracies, proposers are less likely to suggest the use of nonbinding third-party methods, instead preferring negotiations. Though the sign for the *Democratic Dyad* variable is negative, in the context of comparing binding third-party methods with negotiations (column 2, Tables 6.1 and 6.2), it is statistically insignificant. These findings are consistent with several studies, including Mitchell, Kadera, and Crescenzi (2009), who find that democratic dyads are not more likely to choose third-party resolution methods. Ellis, Mitchell, and Prins (2010) show that democratic dyads seek bilateral negotiations rather than third-party methods, specifically when the disputants have not fought each other militarily, the issues at stake are salient, and military balance is closer to power parity.

Finally, the coefficient for the *Power Asymmetry* variable is negative and statistically significant in all models, indicating that power asymmetry between states in a dyad encourages proposer states to seek bilateral negotiations over any third-party methods. This result is in line with many previous studies that examine the relationship between power and states' choice of resolution methods (Allee and Huth 2006; Gent and Shannon 2010; Hansen et al. 2008; Hensel 2001; Hensel et al. 2008; Mitchell 2002; Powell 2020; Shannon 2009; Simmons 2002). All these studies show that arbitration and adjudication are more likely if the disputing states are somewhat equal in power.

Domestic and International Law

We now examine our second set of hypotheses—Hypotheses 3 to 7—that address the significance of the domestic law/international law relationship to proposer states' choices of different PR methods. As we explain in Chapter 3, it is crucial to consider whether proposers in territorial disputes pursue PR methods that are complementary to legal values and procedures characteristic of their own domestic legal systems. We anticipate that shared beliefs about law, and especially law's role in a society, provide an influential force linking domestic and international levels. There is a consistent message coming from many of our interviewees concerning the importance of examining the nexus between domestic law and international law. Indeed, the domestic legal system, and in particular, how it regulates the position of international law, constitutes a credible signal of a state's commitment to global order. In our theory, we focus on three separate, though deeply interconnected, aspects of a domestic legal system: international law's position in the domestic legal system, rule of law, and the type of domestic legal tradition. We anticipate that all these factors collectively signal a state's general attitude toward the legal aspects of the global order.

International Law's Position in the Domestic Legal System

In a way, constitutions, legislation, and other forms of legal expression operating within a domestic jurisdiction predetermine a state's relation to the global order. Thus, it is important to consider how these domestic rules of the game factor into the proposer's strategic choices of particular PR methods. In general—and despite the many differences among states in how they regulate coordination between domestic and international law—considerable hurdles in translating international law into domestic law signal a more cautious attitude toward international law. By contrast, states with a more open domestic legal system—where many international rules apply directly, or where there are few barriers to their implementation—should be friendlier toward international law. More specifically, we anticipate that proposer states that apply international treaties directly and consider international treaties as holding a higher position than domestic legislation are more likely to seek legally binding PR methods. In the context of territorial disputes, proposers with more open domestic legal systems are, simply put, less uncertain—and thus more confident—in delegating control over a territorial contention to legalized methods.

A state legal counsel whom we interviewed explained that there is an intricate link between domestic attitudes toward law and international law, "and so, it's just a matter of what your attitude is to the law. If you see advantage in obeying the law or having the law obeyed in the relations of other states with you, you are willing to go to the Court."[64] Another interviewee also pointed out: "If you want a dispute settled, and you are willing to lose it, and accept that, it is the best way because you can step down with honor and say 'oh what a law-abiding state I am.'"[65] In the context of the Philippine contention with China, international law's position in the disputant's domestic legal system

[64] Author's interview (EJP) with an anonymous ICJ state advocate and international arbitrator, United Kingdom, October 2013.
[65] Author's interview (EJP) with Lorna Lloyd, international relations scholar, United Kingdom, May 20, 2022.

had a bearing on how these states navigated the choice-of-venue stage of the settlement process. Article II.2 of the Philippine Constitution states: "The Philippines . . . adopts the generally accepted principles of international law as part of the law of the land."[66] The Philippine Supreme Court has taken the position that international custom falls under the doctrine of incorporation. As noted by Supreme Court Associate Justice Antonio Carpio, this doctrine "mandates that the Philippines is bound by generally accepted principles of international law which automatically form part of Philippine law by operation of the Constitution" (Agpalo 2006). Throughout the arbitration, there was an ongoing dialogue between the Philippine domestic legal system and international law. During this time, Philippine policymakers emphasized the strong relationship between the two. In fact, the country's respect for international law—and more specifically, international rule of law—was frequently cited as the rationale for the Philippines' decision to pursue arbitration. By way of illustration, in response to the 2016 arbitral ruling, Justice Carpio (2016) declared, "The ruling further re-affirms the wisdom of the Philippine Constitution in renouncing war as an instrument of national policy, and in adopting international law as part of the laws of the Philippines. The ruling manifests the faithful compliance by the Philippine Government to the Philippine Constitution." Secretary of Foreign Affairs Albert Del Rosario (2017) confirmed these sentiments:

> When we agree to rules and commit to upholding them, we create predictability, promote stability, foster a peaceful environment conducive to resolving disputes, and maintain the dignity of our independence as a nation. . . . The law itself, and the rules-based order that it comes from lies at the very heart of Philippine interests. Because of this, we cannot pick and choose when to promote the law and when to ignore it. Instead, we must ensure that the whole of the rules-based system succeeds. . . . Ultimately, advocating a rules-based regime is deeply embedded in who we are and what we must do.

Our quantitative analysis of territorial disputes pertaining to Hypothesis 3 reveals some interesting patterns (Table 6.3, Model 1; Figure 6.5, the coefficient plot; Figure 6.6, predicted probabilities).[67] We use a logistic regression

---

[66] Constitution of the Philippines, 1986. Available at https://www.officialgazette.gov.ph/constituti ons/1987-constitution/.

[67] Results for control variables in Table 6.3 are very similar to the results from our previously presented models. Strategic and identity territorial salience are negatively correlated with binding

Table 6.3 Direct effect and canon of interpretation: Selection of PR methods, 1945–2015

	Model 1 Logit
	Binding vs. other methods
Canon of Interpretation Dyad	0.639** (0.193)
Direct Effect Dyad	0.103 (0.195)
Economic Salience	0.123 (0.122)
Strategic Salience	−0.656** (0.118)
Identity Salience	−0.602** (0.137)
Shared Alliance	0.079 (0.146)
Past Conflict	−0.236 (0.198)
Shared IGO Membership	0.137** (0.019)
Democratic Dyad	−0.188 (0.147)
Power Asymmetry	−2.842** (0.368)
Constant	−0.109 (0.332)
N	2,983

Note: Robust standard errors are provided, ** < .01, * < .05, + .10.

model to test Hypothesis 3 because our expectation deals with the proposer state pursuing binding PR methods compared to the other PR methods. At the same time, Hypothesis 3 expresses no prediction about proposer's choices between bilateral negotiations and nonbinding third-party methods. We anticipate that proposer states whose domestic legal systems incorporate more features of the monist approach are more likely to use binding PR methods in

methods. Coefficients for shared alliances, past conflict, and democratic dyad are statistically significant. Finally, shared IGO membership encourages attempts at binding methods, which is true in all our models, and power asymmetry reduces the likelihood of binding methods.

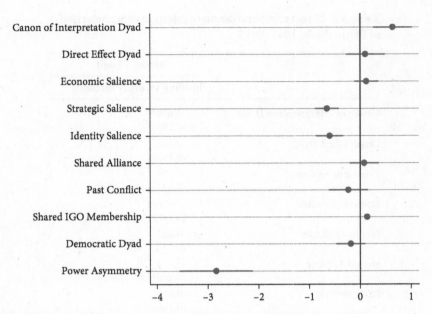

Figure 6.5. Coefficient plot for binding methods—Table 6.3, Model 1.

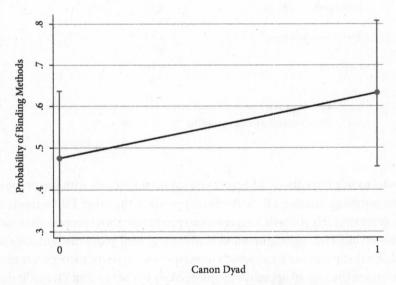

Figure 6.6. Predicted probabilities of binding methods based on canon of interpretation—Table 6.3, Model 1. Adjusted predictions with 95 percent confidence intervals.

comparison with other states. We use two measures: *Canon of Interpretation Dyad* and the *Direct Effect Dyad* variable, discussed in Chapter 5. While the coefficient for the *Direct Effect Dyad* variable is statistically insignificant, we see a positive relationship between *Canon of Interpretation Dyad* and the selection of binding methods by proposer states. In contrast to other dyads whose domestic legal systems incorporate canon of interpretation, proposers are 33 percent more likely to pursue binding methods (.632 versus .475). Thus, it seems as though the two separate mechanisms that enable the domestic judiciary to apply international treaties directly within domestic jurisdictions have distinct effects on proposer states' preferences vis-à-vis international conflict management. Per our discussion in Chapter 5, these results demonstrate the importance of going beyond the rough dichotomous distinction between monist and dualist legal systems. The simultaneous presence of canon of interpretation in jurisdictions of the proposer and nonproposer states encourages the proposer to attempt binding third-party methods.

Rule of Law

We now turn our focus to the relationship between domestic levels of rule of law and proposers' propensity to pursue specific PR methods. As we explain in Chapter 2, international dispute settlement—in particular arbitration and adjudication—is a fundamentally legal phenomenon. Thus, in the course of choice-of-venue strategic selection, there is an ongoing interchange between domestic and international legal structures. Domestic levels of rule of law constitute a crucial part of this process. Arguably, when a proposer state decides to engage any intermediaries in conflict management, such decision is based on the belief that law and legal considerations play an important role in the settlement. Yet, the scholarship has produced mixed findings with regard to the relationship between regime type, rule of law, and international institutions. While there is some substantiating evidence that democratic commitment to rule of law attracts these states to binding PR methods, several studies question the existence as well as the nature of this relationship.[68] To reflect this disagreement in the literature, we are testing two competing hypotheses. Hypothesis 4a expresses the expectation of a positive

---

[68] For an extensive review of the literature on this topic, see Chapter 3.

relationship between domestic levels of rule of law and states' propensity to attempt binding PR methods of peaceful settlement. In contrast, Hypothesis 4b asserts that domestic levels of rule of law are unrelated to states' decisions regarding these methods.

One of our interviewees, an ITLOS judge, pointed to the difficulty of using rule of law as a determinant of choice-of-venue selection: "[for] states with general regard for rule of law, it is difficult to expect them to submit to international courts, but there are many other factors that affect decisions of states."[69] Remarks by Alan James were similar in tone: "I wouldn't put very much weight on any such arguments [high rule-of-law democracies preferring international courts]. The calculations that a democracy would make would be much the same as any non-democratic state would make in terms of calculating 'am I likely to win it, am I likely to lose it? What do I think about those possibilities?' If they think that they are not likely to win it, and very possibly could lose, they would very much prefer going to a forum where they have a certain amount of leeway, where they can press this in exchange for that, rather than to a court where they have to leave things to so many justices up on the bench."[70]

Several other interlocutors, on the other hand, acknowledged a deep connection between domestic attitudes toward law and states' outlook on international law and the global order. For instance, Albert Del Rosario, former Philippine Secretary of Foreign Affairs, who sought arbitration against China in 2013, believes that good domestic governance matters greatly in the process of selecting PR methods.[71] Secretary Del Rosario noted that rule of law should be highly valued: "Our commitment of adhering to the rule of law is embedded in our national core values."[72] Hans Corell noted in an interview that the culture toward law—"the role that courts play in a country, and the responsibility that the judges must assume to assist in creating a state under the rule of law"—plays an important role in a country's decision to choose binding PR methods. He stated that philosophy of domestic dispute resolution matters, and that at times, "to go to Court [i.e., the ICJ] would be a very natural solution."[73]

[69] Author's interview (KEW) with an anonymous ITLOS judge, July 2018.

[70] Author's interview (EJP) with Alan Morien James, scholar of peacekeeping, diplomacy, and the international order, former chairman of the British International Studies Association, Congleton, UK, May 20, 2022.

[71] Author's interview (KEW) with Victor Andres Manhit, Director, Stratbase—Albert Del Rosario Institute, Manila, Philippines, July 11, 2016.

[72] Ibid.

[73] Author's interview (EJP) with Hans Corell, March 14, 2015.

Table 6.4 Rule of law: Selection of binding methods vs. other PR methods (logit models), 1945–2015

	Model 1	Model 2	Model 3	Model 4
High Court Compliance Dyad	0.451** (0.127)			
High Court Independence Dyad		−0.162 (0.121)		
Judicial Constraints on Executive Dyad			0.248+ (0.137)	
Rule of Law Index Dyad				0.157 (0.160)
Economic Salience	0.103 (0.120)	0.053 (0.119)	0.068 (0.119)	0.082 (0.121)
Strategic Salience	−0.618** (0.116)	−0.602** (0.116)	−0.615** (0.115)	−0.608** (0.116)
Identity Salience	−0.625** (0.136)	−0.591** (0.134)	−0.601** (0.135)	−0.592** (0.135)
Shared Alliance	0.102 (0.145)	0.120 (0.144)	0.108 (0.144)	0.120 (0.144)
Past Conflict	−0.124 (0.198)	−0.186 (0.196)	−0.167 (0.197)	−0.204 (0.196)
Shared IGO Membership	0.128** (0.019)	0.128** (0.019)	0.133** (0.019)	0.133** (0.019)
Democratic Dyad	−0.225 (0.147)	0.021 (0.139)	−0.152 (0.155)	−0.102 (0.163)
Power Asymmetry	−2.646** (0.365)	−2.287** (0.367)	−2.682** (0.367)	−2.781** (0.363)
Constant	−0.359 (0.337)	0.051 (0.339)	−0.244 (0.341)	−0.144 (0.336)
N	2,983	2,983	2,983	2,983

Note: Robust standard errors are provided, ** < .01, * < .05, + .10. We use logit models since our hypotheses only make predictions about binding methods versus other PR methods.

To test our two competing hypotheses about the influence of rule of law on states' preferences vis-à-vis PR methods, we estimated four logistic regression models (Table 6.4).[74] Hypothesis 4a predicts that proposers with high levels of domestic rule of law are more likely to attempt binding PR methods,

[74] To decipher whether our rule of law variables—*Rule of Law Index, High Court Judicial Independence, Judicial Constraints on Executive,* and *Compliance with High Court*—are strongly correlated with the *Democratic Dyad* variable, we estimated correlation matrices for proposer states. All correlations are relatively low and range from .35 to .42.

while Hypothesis 4b predicts that domestic levels of rule of law have no effect on proposers' decisions to attempt binding PR methods. As in the case of Hypothesis 3, we use logit models because our hypotheses 4a and 4b address proposer's choices between binding methods versus all other PR methods, and we have no predictions regarding negotiations and nonbinding methods specifically. Following the logic of our theory with regard to rule of law, our expectations expressed in both hypotheses should have strongest support in the dyadic setting—when the proposer and nonproposer share the same rule of law features. Our variables, which take into consideration features of both states, reflect this expectation.

As we noted in Chapter 5, our rule of law indicators are designed to empirically gauge the overall quality of domestic legal systems. Thus, we not only use the *Rule of Law Index Dyad* variable, but also measure the relationship between the judiciary and the executive. Naturally, all aspects of a domestic legal system's quality are deeply interconnected. Because of relatively high correlations between our rule of law variables, each model contains only one of the four variables.

Our rule of law models yield limited support for Hypotheses 4a and 4b. Coefficients for two rule of law measures are statistically insignificant (*High Court Independence Dyad, Rule of Law Index Dyad*), one measure is statistically significant at the .10 level (*Judicial Constraints on Executive Dyad*), and one is significant at the .05 level (*High Court Compliance Dyad*). Figure 6.7 presents the coefficient plot and Figure 6.8 presents predicted probabilities). When both disputing states have higher levels of high court compliance or judicial constraints on the executive, proposer states are more likely to turn to binding methods than other PR methods. Substantively, the proposer state is 45 percent more likely to turn to binding PR methods when government compliance with high courts is higher for both states (.202), compared to when there is noncompliance in both states (.139). The substantive effect of judicial constraints on the executive are lower. High levels of these constraints in both states (.501) increase the likelihood of proposers using binding PR methods by 14 percent (.439). Overall, these results provide only partial support for Hypothesis 4a, which expresses the arguments advanced by the democratic peace scholarship, especially the legalistic perspective. In light of the fact that the most comprehensive measure we use, the *Rule of Law Index Dyad*, lacks statistical significance, and the *High Court Independence Dyad* has a negative sign, we can conclude that it seems unclear whether

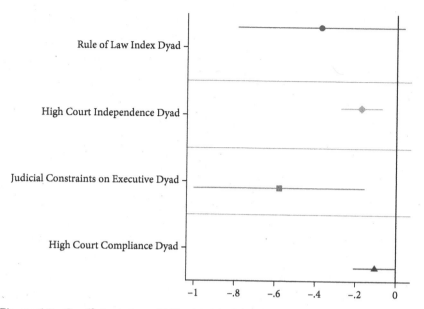

Figure 6.7. Coefficient plot—Table 6.4, Models 1–4.

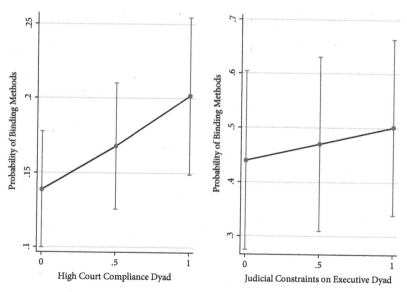

Figure 6.8. Predicted probabilities of binding PR methods based on canon of interpretation—Table 6.4, Models 1 and 3. Adjusted predictions with 95 percent confidence intervals.

disputants' affinity for courts and, more generally, legalized dispute resolution carries over into the international arena.

Together, these findings point to the lack of a robust relationship between democratic regimes and preference for specific international PR methods (Park and James 2015; Powell 2020).[75]

Domestic Legal Traditions

This section focuses on the relationship between domestic legal traditions and proposer states' preferences for specific PR methods. To understand the intricate and contested nature of the Islamic law/international law nexus specifically, we have conducted a substantial number of in-depth qualitative interviews with Islamic law states' policymakers and scholars of Islamic law. All else equal, states representing the Islamic legal tradition encounter additional hurdles when interacting with international conflict management. Indeed, in contrast to civil and common law, there is "no automatic international equivalent for sharia-based domestic conflict management" (Powell 2020, 11). At the same time, Islamic logic of dispute resolution restricts venue options for these states and amplifies their uncertainty with international PR methods.

Insights from interviews are followed by quantitative tests. Before going any further, one feature of our account needs explanation: the relative length of our discussion about domestic legal traditions. As explained in Chapter 3, there are strong theoretical reasons to believe that each of the three major legal traditions—civil, common, and Islamic—dictates a unique attitude toward PR methods. Indeed, each tradition provides an institutional space filled with substantive and procedural rules that interact with international law and international institutions. In an important way, the nature of this interaction shapes proposers' perception of uncertainty associated with international conflict management. Though in no case can a disputant be entirely confident about the resolution outcome, domestic legal traditions provide states with clues about which PR method to choose.

Our interviewees confirm that the relationship between domestic legal traditions and characteristics of specific PR methods and venues constitutes

---

[75] Results concerning control variables are almost identical to those presented in our past experience model (Model 2, Table 6.1).

an important factor in choice-of-venue strategic selection. Judge Rüdiger Wolfrum, former president of ITLOS, noted that domestic legal traditions mattered greatly in Ivory Coast's maritime dispute with Ghana.[76] Ivory Coast hired legal counsel who completed their legal education in France—a state representing the civil legal tradition. This choice of legal representation had important effects on Ivory Coast's eventual forum choice of ITLOS.[77] According to Wolfrum, just as French-trained lawyers have a better understanding of the civil legal tradition—and how it operates in international law—lawyers educated in the United States have a better understanding of common law. "A common law [trained] lawyer has a different view of what is 'reasonable' compared to a [lawyer or] judge of civil law, [such as] how to use evidence."[78] He also noted that "there [is] a clear rift between civil law and common law" when it comes to international adjudication and arbitration.[79]

The relationship between domestic legal traditions and international law is crucial when one considers the relatively incomplete nature of international law. Some areas of international law have significant gaps. Thus, with regard to many norms and rules, the jurisprudence of international courts and arbitration tribunals may promote diverging—even contrasting—interpretations. These bodies frequently decide which interpretation of a norm should prevail in the context of a specific case. Moreover, domestic legal traditions may themselves inform decisions of international adjudicative bodies. An ITLOS judge noted in an interview that "it's really international law, customary law that matters, but parties can agree together to apply for use of an applicable law [such as] Islamic law."[80] This judge explained that "they [the parties] can ask the Court to apply certain laws in addition to international laws that may not reflect domestic legal traditions."[81]

As we explain in our theory, to increase the predictability of the resolution outcome, proposers prefer to use PR methods that bear a resemblance to their own legal tradition. Many of our interlocutors emphasized that the relationship between Islamic law states in particular and PR methods is very unique. This relationship reflects the reality that an overwhelming part of international law—its substance and practice—mirrors Western legal logic

[76] Author's interview (KEW) with Judge Rüdiger Wolfrum, Rhodes, Greece, July 19, 2018.
[77] Guyana v Suriname, ICGJ 370 (PCA 2007), Arbitral Award of September 17, 2007.
[78] Author's interview (KEW) with Judge Rüdiger Wolfrum, Rhodes, Greece, July 19, 2018.
[79] Ibid.
[80] Author's interview (KEW) with an anonymous ITLOS judge, July 2018.
[81] Ibid.

and the Western notion of justice. As ICJ Judge Al-Khasawneh noted, "So there is a lot of truth in the fact that international law reflects what is now a predominant culture and that's Western culture, not only Western post-industrialist-capitalist values."[82] A diplomat from Jordan noted that the Islamic way of resolving disputes relies on a different logic of justice than the Western culture:

> When you go to a court, you are talking to an enemy. . . . Western people love to go to courts. It's a culture because you don't want to go into a house so you take it to a court. And let the lawyers take care of it and so on and so forth. I think . . . Muslims are less prone to go to courts unless nothing else is going to work. . . . But going to court is always the last measure, and [in] Europe it's the first measure. . . It's less public, it's less of a hassle, and it's quicker.[83]

Our interviewees also confirmed that much of the Islamic philosophy of nonconfrontational dispute resolution carries over to the state level. One of our interlocutors noted that "when there are disputes among the Middle East[ern] states, they use . . . mediation. They use reconciliation, they use conciliation because they think that by doing this, they do two jobs. One: they resolve their problem. Second: they have complied with the teachings of [the] Quran and sayings of the Prophet."[84]

Statistical analyses confirm many of the points brought up by our interviewees about domestic legal traditions. Descriptive statistics (Table 6.5) show that proposer states representing the common legal tradition most often attempt bilateral negotiations (76 percent). In fact, of all major legal traditions, common law proposers attempt resolution via bilateral negotiations most frequently. Against that background, it is imperative to keep in mind that common law states account for a relatively small percentage of all states in the world—since 1920, roughly anywhere between 12 and 26 percent (Mitchell and Powell 2011, 28). At the same time, these states attempt the nonbinding and binding third-party methods much less

[82] Author's interview (EJP) with Judge Awn Shawkat Al-Khasawneh, Amman, Jordan, February 18, 2015.

[83] Author's interview (EJP) with Omar Rifai, former Hashemite Kingdom of Jordan Ambassador to Israel, Italy, Egypt, Secretary-General of the Ministry of Foreign Affairs, Permanent Representative to the Arab League, Amman, Jordan, February 19, 2015.

[84] Author's interview (EJP) with Naser Abdul Rahmani, former Head of Culture and Publications Committee of the Shahrak Area Community Council, Afghanistan, April 24, 2018.

Table 6.5 Domestic legal traditions: Frequency of selection of PR methods, 1945–2015

	Bilateral Negotiations	Nonbinding Methods	Binding Methods
Common Law	76%	13%	11%
Civil Law	68%	17%	15%
Islamic Law	66%	16%	18%
Mixed Law	83%	8%	8%

often (13 percent and 11 percent respectively). Interestingly—and in line with our expectations—Islamic law proposers seek to use nonbinding third-party methods quite frequently (16 percent). It is crucial to note that the nonbinding third-party methods—mediation, conciliation, inquiry, and good offices—fulfill Islamic law states' preferences for a certain style of dispute resolution. Additionally, these PR methods allow Islamic law states to request help from Islamic intermediaries. In fact, the majority of these states' attempts at peaceful resolution of territorial disputes involved policymakers from other Islamic law states or Islamic organizations such as the Arab League, the Islamic Conference Organization, and the Gulf Cooperation Council. Arguably, beliefs and paradigms about dispute resolution are "sometimes deep-seated and strongly engrained in the fabric of a state, reflecting not only its domestic legal system, but also culture and religion" (Powell 2020, 125). In the context of Islamic law states, Islam is engrained in the everyday lives of most citizens, and much of the population "believes [that] sharia law is more supreme than the secular law."[85]

Proposers representing the civil legal tradition attempt binding methods 15 percent of the time, which is slightly below Islamic law states (18 percent), but is higher than common law states (11 percent). However, the Bahrain v. Qatar dispute accounts for considerable number of attempts at the binding methods by Islamic law states.[86] It is crucial to note that overall, civil law proposers pursue peaceful settlement much more often than their common law or Islamic law counterparts. Patterns of attempts at binding PR methods reflect these trends. Civil law proposers put forth 1,528 settlement

[85] Author's interview (EJP) with an anonymous Bahraini women's rights activist, Manama, Bahrain, December 30, 2019.
[86] Maritime Delimitation and Territorial Questions between Qatar and Bahrain, Qatar v. Bahrain, ICJ Rep 2001, 40, Judgment of March 16, 2001.

attempts in our dataset, compared to 585 attempts issued by Islamic law states, 535 attempts for common law states, and 525 attempts for mixed law states. Out of all attempts at arbitration and adjudication, civil law proposers are responsible for 52 percent, while the remaining 48 percent include proposers representing other legal traditions combined. Of course, these patterns can be partially explained by the sheer proportion of civil law states in the world. Indeed, since 1920, the civil legal tradition has been dominant, with 48 to78 percent of countries representing it (Mitchell and Powell 2011, 27). Yet, it is also interesting to note that despite their preponderance in the international system, civil law states are not as fond of bilateral negotiations as common law states. Civil and Islamic law proposers attempt bilateral negotiations less frequently than common law states (8 and 10 percent less, respectively).

Turning to multivariate analysis, we estimated a multinomial logistic regression model with the three PR methods as the categories of dependent variable. As noted in our theory, our expectations expressed in Hypotheses 5, 6, and 7 should have strongest support in the dyadic setting—when the proposer and nonproposer share the same domestic legal tradition. Thus, while investigating domestic legal traditions, it is key to consider whether the presence of shared legal tradition in a dyad influences states' choices of PR methods. Indeed—as we discuss in Chapter 3—while making decisions about PR methods, each disputant considers the opponent's domestic legal tradition in addition to its own. Dispute resolution constitutes an inherently dyadic process and, arguably, it is the interface between both disputants' preferences that leads to specific choices of PR methods.

Our variables reflect these expectations. Mixed legal dyads and dyads composed of states that do not represent the same legal tradition are combined as the omitted legal type category for Model 1 in Table 6.6. Model 2 in the same table displays a logit model that compares binding methods with all other PR methods. Although we tested a logit model comparing nonbinding to binding methods (excluding bilateral negotiations) similar to the models for past experience variables, we do not report the results in Table 6.6 because all three legal tradition variables were statistically insignificant.

Overall, we find solid support for all three hypotheses about the impact of domestic legal traditions on the proposer state's selection of PR methods (see coefficient plots in Figure 6.10). As predicted by Hypothesis 5, the coefficient for the *Common Law Dyad* variable is statistically significant at the .10 level in Models 1 and 2 for binding methods. These results suggest that common

Table 6.6 Dyadic domestic legal traditions: Selection of PR methods, 1945–2015

	Model 1 Multinomial Logit		Model 2 Logit
	Nonbinding methods	Binding methods	Binding vs. other methods
Civil Law Dyad	0.702** (0.145)	0.555** (0.154)	0.414** (0.152)
Common Law Dyad	0.205 (0.406)	−1.308+ (0.737)	−1.346+ (0.734)
Islamic Law Dyad	1.008** (0.217)	0.839** (0.206)	0.699** (0.202)
Economic Salience	0.745** (0.128)	0.040 (0.127)	−0.066 (0.125)
Strategic Salience	0.282 (0.126)	−0.548** (0.119)	−0.589** (0.117)
Identity Salience	0.450** (0.134)	−0.469** (0.143)	−0.502** (0.142)
Shared Alliance	−0.016 (0.142)	−0.141 (0.156)	−0.106 (0.154)
Past Conflict	1.412** (.154)	0.108 (0.203)	−0.238 (0.198)
Shared IGO Membership	0.172** (.200)	0.164** (0.022)	0.128** (0.021)
Democratic Dyad	−0.759** (0.162)	−0.061 (0.147)	0.094 (0.143)
Power Asymmetry	−0.547 (0.405)	−2.659** (0.383)	−2.502** (0.377)
Constant	−3.405** 0.387	−0.342 (0.346)	−0.338 (0.342)
N	2,983	2,983	2,983

Note: Robust standard errors are provided, ** < .01, * < .05, + .10.

law dyads are less likely to seek binding methods compared to negotiations (Model 1) and other PR methods (Model 2).[87] Specifically, the likelihood of a proposer state in a common law dyad attempting negotiations (.953) compared to other PR methods is higher than for proposer states in civil law

---

[87] Our results concerning control variables in Table 6.5 are identical to the findings in Table 6.4 about rule of law.

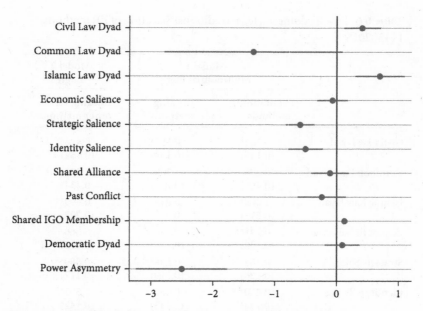

Figure 6.9. Coefficient plot of binding methods—Table 6.6, Model 3.

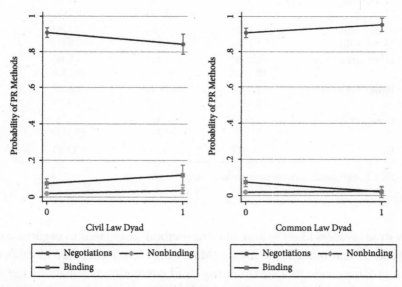

Figure 6.10. Predicted probabilities of proposals of PR methods based on civil and common law dyads—Table 6.6, Model 1. Adjusted predictions with 95 percent confidence intervals.

and Islamic law dyads (.843 and .801, respectively) (Model 1). At the same time, attempts at arbitration and adjudication compared to negotiations are much less likely for common law proposer states disputing with other common law states (.021)—470 percent less likely than civil law dyads (.120) and 600 percent less likely than Islamic law dyads (.152).

Proposers in civil law dyads are clearly drawn to binding PR methods compared to negotiations (Model 1) and compared to all other PR methods (Model 2). As stated in Hypothesis 6, we anticipate that proposer states in civil law dyads prefer third-party binding methods, given that the level of formality, rules, and procedures of legally binding PR methods strongly resemble the civil law tradition. The *Civil Law Dyad* variable is positive and statistically significant in Models 1 and 2. Overall, proposers in civil law dyads are 62 percent more likely to pursue binding methods rather than negotiations compared to all other legal traditions combined (.120 versus .074) (Model 1). Focusing on specific legal tradition dyads, proposer states in civil law dyads (.120) are 82 percent more likely than proposers in common law dyads (.021) to attempt arbitration or adjudication instead of negotiations (Model 1). Proposers in civil law dyads (.133) are 44 percent more likely than proposers in other legal tradition dyads (.092) to seek binding methods rather than other PR methods (Model 2).

We also find that proposer states in civil law dyads are more likely to turn to nonbinding third-party methods than negotiations (Model 1). These proposers are also 13 percent less likely to turn to bilateral negotiations compared to proposers in common law dyads (.843 versus .953). Together, these findings provide support for the existing literature. For instance, Mitchell and Powell (2011) argue and empirically demonstrate that civil law states are more likely than other states to accept the compulsory jurisdiction of the ICJ. As originators—or, creators of the Court—these states perceive the ICJ as an unbiased and fair adjudicator. The ICJ utilizes legal principles and procedures deeply embedded in the civil legal tradition. Thus, civil law dyads are more willing to allow the Court to intervene in their territorial disputes.

In support of Hypothesis 7, we find in Model 1 (Table 6.6) a statistically significant and positive relationship between the *Islamic Law Dyad* variable and nonbinding third-party methods versus negotiations. Proposers in Islamic law dyads are 148 percent more likely to use nonbinding third-party methods than negotiations when compared to dyads representing other

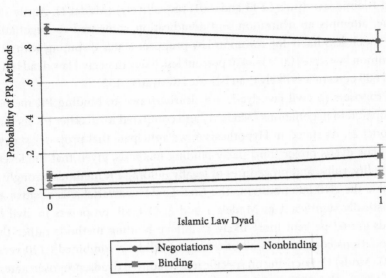

Figure 6.11. Predicted probabilities of proposals of PR methods based on Islamic law dyads: proposals of PR methods—Table 6.6, Model 1. Adjusted predictions with 95 percent confidence intervals.

legal traditions (.047 versus .019) (Model 1, see Figure 6.11). Compared to proposer states in common law dyads (.025), proposer states in Islamic law dyads (.047) are 88 percent more likely to turn to nonbinding methods instead of negotiations. Similarly, Islamic law dyads are 31 percent more likely than proposer states in civil law dyads (.036) to attempt nonbinding methods instead of negotiations. These findings clearly indicate that of the three major legal traditions, proposer states in Islamic law dyads gravitate toward the nonbinding third-party methods. These proposers are also 13 percent less likely that other dyads (.801 versus .906) to turn to bilateral negotiations compared to other PR methods (Model 1).

Perhaps the most interesting results pertain to Islamic law states' preferences with regard to arbitration and adjudication. Proposers in Islamic law dyads are relatively likely to attempt resolution via the binding methods. However, as noted earlier, the dispute between Bahrain and Qatar—an Islamic law dyad—was a protracted contention, during which both sides issued numerous calls for third-party resolution, thus contributing many observations to our data. It is also crucial to consider that there are many more civil law and common law dyads than Islamic law dyads in the world.

In fact, the Islamic legal tradition has the smallest state membership among the three major legal traditions. This is all the more reason to highlight proposer states in Islamic law dyads' commitment to third-party PR methods. Though Islam, like other legal traditions, embraces justice, the notion of justice has a unique status and connotations. According to Radwan Ziadeh, "Islam in the *Qur'an* puts justice exactly on the level of belief, which is the highest level."[88]

Overall, our results strongly suggest that proposer states in dyads sharing the same domestic legal tradition follow predicted patterns of dispute resolution. Proposer states in common law dyads are clearly hesitant to use arbitration and adjudication, and instead prefer bilateral negotiations. This result can readily be explained by the lack of formality in negotiations, a feature highly valued by the common law tradition. Proposer states in civil law dyads resort to binding PR methods. These methods' high level of formality and relatively strict adherence to international law resemble the underlying logic of the civil legal tradition. Proposer states in Islamic law dyads prefer nonbinding third-party methods compared to all other legal tradition dyads because these methods bear a resemblance to the Islamic institution of *sulh*, a nonconfrontational, informal settlement between the disputants. At the same time, however, our results demonstrate that proposer states in Islamic law dyads are relatively open to arbitration and adjudication.

Conclusions

In this chapter we examined the mechanisms of choice-of-venue strategic selection in territorial disputes. Throughout the twentieth and twenty-first centuries, the judicialization of the international realm necessarily resulted in the increased presence of international PR methods. This reality, in turn, has generated the possibility for states to engage in choice-of-venue strategic selection, whereby state leaders strategically cherry-pick between the existing PR methods. As this chapter demonstrates, the various PR methods do not appear equally attractive to all proposer states. Quite the opposite: there are important forces of attraction and repulsion at work when states attempt to

---

[88] Author's interview (EJP) with Radwan Ziadeh, former Director and Founder of the Damascus Center for Human Rights Studies (Syria), Senior Fellow, U.S. Institute for Peace, Notre Dame, IN, January 22, 2016.

peacefully settle their territorial and maritime disputes. The combination of qualitative interviews and statistical analyses suggests that these forces have not faded away with time, but instead continue to affect states' perceptions of international conflict management. In an important way, the mechanisms of choice-of-venue strategic selection—past experience and the relationship between domestic and international law (international law's position in the domestic legal system, rule of law, and the type of domestic legal tradition)—are an intricate part of a state's fabric, and thus are strong predictors of proposer states' preferences. Importantly, the impact of these mechanisms is stronger when we consider the dyadic setting.

As we predicted, proposer states deeply value their previous interactions with binding PR methods, and are encouraged to return to methods that have yielded positive experiences in the past. Regional experiences in arbitration and adjudication are also influential in the process of choice-of-venue strategic selection. Our results regarding the domestic law/international law relationship also reveal some interesting patterns. First, our models demonstrate the necessity of going beyond the rough distinction between monist and dualist legal systems. It seems that in the context of territorial disputes, the presence of the direct-effect mechanism in domestic law does not encourage proposer states to use the binding PR methods. In contrast, when canon of interpretation is present in the domestic legal system of both disputants, proposers tend to prefer arbitration and adjudication. Next, it is important to highlight that the quality of domestic legal systems—measured as levels of rule of law and the judiciary/executive relationship—does not unequivocally and consistently influence proposers' attempts at binding PR methods. Lastly, owing to their distinctive characteristics, domestic legal traditions of both disputants deeply impact proposer states' preferences vis-à-vis the various PR methods.

Results presented in this chapter confirm that international dispute resolution is an inherently legal phenomenon through which states' legal rights are determined by means of many legal procedures. This reality implies that there is an ongoing dialogue between disputants' domestic legal systems and international law. These findings suggest important conclusions with regard to territorial and maritime disputes—contentions that are known for their seriousness. In short, proposer states in different combinations of dyads are naturally predisposed to employ specific PR methods offered on the international level. The international community must be aware of the fact that not all of its members have similar preferences with respect to international dispute management. The qualitative and quantitative evidence presented here, consistent with our theory, suggests that selection of PR methods depends in a crucial way on the specific amalgamation of proposer states' past experiences and the characteristics of their domestic legal systems vis-à-vis nonproposer states.

7

Application of Within-Venue Strategic Selection

[In arbitration] there is more flexibility and states feel that they can control one way or another the dispute process. Sometimes this is true and sometimes this is not true at all.

—Ioannis Kostantinidis[1]

The previous chapter, Chapter 6, delved into general patterns of states' behavior in the context of choice-of-venue strategic selection. Yet, there are interesting and quite unique mechanisms that our quantitative data are not able to capture—mainly, the within-venue strategic selection—elements of which are, simply put, hard to express and operationalize in numbers. Thus, the goal of the present chapter is to further illustrate and contextualize causal mechanisms of our theoretical discussion regarding within-venue strategizing. While our statistical analyses capture information at the proposer's level—rule of law, past experience, characteristics of the domestic legal system, alliances, and so on—the discussion here focuses on the dynamics at the individual level. Our in-depth qualitative interviews with policymakers, state counsel, international judges, mediators, and arbitrators allow us to expound on the specifics of our causal story, going beyond what aggregates at the state level. This chapter shows how important the messiness of territorial and maritime disputes is. It is the amalgamation of human experiences, preferences, strategies, and many individual-level decisions that combine to produce the disputants' moves in the context of peaceful resolution (PR) methods and specific venues. Thus, while there are several

[1] Author's interview (EJP) with Ioannis Kostantinidis, state counsel and consultant, January 11, 2021.

important patterns that most territorial and maritime disputes seem to follow, there is much idiosyncrasy in how states behave.

As our theoretical chapters explain, uncertainty associated with the settlement process does not subside once the disputants' preferences converge on a PR method and a specific venue, such as the International Court of Justice (ICJ) or an arbitration tribunal. To reduce uncertainty, to minimize their perceived risk of losing, and to navigate the myriad rules and mechanisms associated with each PR method, each disputant engages in an elaborate planning scheme—a strategy—during the within-venue stage of settlement. The two mechanisms of strategic selection at work during this stage of settlement—framing legal claims and shaping the procedures—are at work regardless of any external factors that may simultaneously influence states' behavior. Adapting their strategies to the chosen method and venue, states put considerable effort into maximizing their control over the progression of the settlement. They attempt to shape the execution of the venue's rules and procedures, and they go to great lengths in selecting counsel, arbitrators, mediators, and judges. To further expound on our causal story, and contextualize the dynamics of within-venue strategic selection, we use two types of evidence, as laid out in Chapter 5: primary documents and interviews. Taken together, descriptive materials, government documents, legal documents from settlement proceedings, and interviews highlight the specifics of decision-making during the settlement process. Strategic planning is crucial: "States need to assess all this—what is the outcome that will be most beneficial for their interest?"[2] Recognizing that there are many influential factors shaping within-venue strategic selection, in line with our theory, the discussion below homes in on framing the claim and shaping the procedures.

Framing the Claim

Regardless of which PR method and, subsequently, specific venue is selected at the choice-of-venue stage, a legal strategy—especially strategic framing of territorial/maritime claims—is just as important as political considerations. Every PR method has a strong legal component that manifests itself either in its structure or in the arguments and strategies undertaken by the disputants.[3]

---

[2] Author's interview (KEW) with an anonymous public international law expert, Rhodes, Greece, July 19, 2018.

[3] We discuss this issue in great detail in Chapter 2.

In bilateral negotiations, disputants seek to limit the information they share with their opponents, and strategize about which demands to make regarding sovereignty or maritime rights. Similarly, in mediation or other nonbinding third-party methods, disputants must consider the legal claims and demands they will bring to a mediator. In the binding third-party methods, the legal strategy is dominant, regardless of political considerations. The legal counsel, in cooperation with government lawyers and policymakers, build their client's legal case. This process entails deliberate, careful strategizing about each step of the case's progression through a particular PR method and a specific venue. Legal teams, government lawyers, and policymakers spend months, and in some cases years, meticulously outlining the details of their legal strategy. As one of our interviewees noted:

> All ministries provide recommendations, must ask for guidance from top decision makers, and must consult with all relevant ministries. The government discusses strategies, and may stop and ask for political guidance from political bureaus. The boundary division gives an assessment about the issue, then they seek approval from political bureaus. The strategy can change over time, depending on other factors. They may recommend one or several choices, establish scenarios about possible strategies, [and] write really detailed reports sent to political bureaus.[4]

Larry Martin, state counsel in many territorial and maritime dispute cases, emphasized that a strong relationship exists between formulating the claim and a disputant's strategic objectives (Martin 2018). According to International Tribunal for the Law of the Sea (ITLOS) judge Rüdiger Wolfrum (2018b), "how a case is presented can sometimes matter. The perspective on facts can be influential." Indeed, as we explain in Chapter 4, there usually are several ways to view and interpret the dispute's patterns. Most, though not all, aspects of any dispute—its historical background, the sides' perspectives, legal arguments, and so on—can strategically be prioritized or made insignificant. For instance, not all possible aspects of a case will be submitted to the ICJ. Instead, states strategically select specific aspects of a case—those that in their one-sided estimation are strongest and, therefore, most likely to succeed. In other words, a dispute's aspects that make it to the

---

[4] Author's interview (KEW) with an anonymous official, Philippines Department of Foreign Affairs, 2018.

Court's docket usually constitute a judiciously built skeleton of all potential territorial or maritime claims.

In preparing for any boundary case, the first step for the legal counsel is to identify the relevant claim and to assess its strengths and weaknesses by determining whether some assertions are perhaps exaggerated. In training materials for counsel and government officials, public international law expert and state counsel William Thomas asserts that the "practitioner's role is to: 1) marshal facts, 2) apply law, 3) determine strategy, and 4) advocate [the] State's case." He continues that it is crucial to recognize that "states need to be legally, factually, and technically informed." Thomas also identifies several key questions that all disputants must ask themselves when attempting to strategically frame their claim: "What is your claim? How will you make your case? and What steps will the case entail?" (Thomas 2015).

Legal counsel provide their client initial evaluation of their case, which begins the process of framing the claim:

Good counsel in most cases should be able to look at a dispute and say, "ok, well if you take this to a court or a tribunal, the range of outcomes that you are likely to end up with out of all possible outcomes is somewhere between here and here. So these outcomes we think are really unlikely. We don't think a court or tribunal would go there. These other outcomes, likewise we think would be unlikely. We think your range of potential outcomes is between this and that." This narrows down your uncertainty a lot.[5]

State counsel Rodman Bundy (2015) advises government officials that it is possible that only a small portion of claims will become the focus of arbitral or judicial proceedings because it is up to each disputant to decide whether to focus on all sovereignty-related claims, or merely a portion of them, or whether to, for instance, limit the claim to maritime aspects. The manner in which states frame their claims betrays a deep connection between politics and law. As one of our interlocutors noted, "sometimes, certain claims or points cannot be made for political reasons, even if it would help to win."[6] While talking about the role of politics in formulating strategies, another of our interviewees brought up the negotiations between Sweden and the Soviet

---

[5] Author's interview (EJP) with an anonymous arbitration practitioner, February 7, 2022.
[6] Author's interview (KEW) with an anonymous public international law expert, Rhodes, Greece, July 2018.

Union concerning the delimitation of the maritime boundary in the Baltic Sea, specifically around the Island of Gotland.[7] According to Hans Corell, although Sweden had other preferences, the outcome—the Agreement—"was a political solution. We [Sweden] came to the conclusion that we could take 75 percent of the area and the Russians could have 25 percent. And that became a political decision. Then my colleague—the Chief Legal Advisor in the Russian Foreign Ministry—and I negotiated the exact border line and this was then established on both sides and signed by ministers of foreign affairs."[8] Thus, understandably, political considerations factor into states' legal decisions in all stages of the peaceful settlement process.

Designing a successful legal strategy entails avoiding potentially problematic issues. This is confirmed by legal training documents composed by state counsel Loretta Malintoppi (2015), who writes that states are able to "define with precision the issues that are to be decided by the arbitral tribunal in their arbitration agreement. Accordingly, an arbitral tribunal [or court] has the authority only to answer those issues that the parties have referred to it." All other issues—notwithstanding their deep relevance to the matter at hand—fall outside the particular case. But the framing of the claim constitutes an inherently dynamic process and states may alter the particulars of their claims while the settlement procedure is under way. As Ioannis Konstantinidis, state counsel and legal consultant, told us:

> Normally, before a decision is made as to whether to bring a case before a court or tribunal, there is a preliminary assessment of the case. . . . If, pursuant to this preliminary assessment, a case proves to be strong, then the case may proceed. The preliminary assessment is an exercise that helps states understand the strong and the weak parts of their claims. As a result, they are—or should be—ready to support the "weak" part of their claims throughout the procedure (written and oral pleadings). Hiring experienced counsel play[s] a pivotal role. In territorial claims, states tend to follow a minimalistic approach. After all, they know that part of their claims may be rejected by a court/tribunal. Throughout the proceedings, a claimant may decide to downplay certain parts of its claims. I have seen cases where the

---

[7] The Agreement on the Principles for the Delimitation of Sea Area in the Baltic Sea, signed in Stockholm, January 1988.

[8] Author's interview (EJP) with Hans Corell, former Under-Secretary-General for Legal Affairs and the Legal Counsel of the United Nations, January 13, 2021.

claimant, at a certain stage of the proceeding, decides to silently and discreetly abandon certain claims.[9]

Since all boundary disputes, whether territorial or maritime, engage expertise from numerous disciplines beyond international law—geography, cartography, history, geology, etc.—most cases require input from many sources. In the words of William Thomas (2015), "what you need to prove determines whose help you need. Cooperation and coordination are paramount." If the contention mainly deals with issues of territorial sovereignty, framing the claim likely involves decisions regarding specific tracts of land, boundaries, alternative boundary delimitation, and so forth. Maritime contentions prompt choices about coastlines, baselines, and definitions of maritime features. The parties must also consider whether to seek delimitation of territorial seas, or whether to focus on specific maritime zones such as an exclusive economic zone (EEZ) or a continental shelf. Moreover, each disputant must contemplate the different aspects of the UN Convention on the Law of the Sea (UNCLOS) that may be pertinent to the dispute at hand. As our theory explains, maps—a powerful visualization tool—can aid the disputants in framing their respective claims. A map "anchor[s] things down," but "[sometimes] takes on a life of its own, even though its purpose is to illustrate the treaty or to illustrate reality. . . . The map ends up defining reality. Reality actually has to move to fit the map, which is crazy when you think about it. But it becomes a legal benchmark you can point to."[10] Through different versions of a map, policymakers and state counsel can, depending on their preferences, promote either certainty or uncertainty with regard to the issue at stake: "maps can be both a vehicle for certainty and a vehicle for uncertainty. . . . They kind of promote the ambiguity, but in a different situation, they can be used to . . . anchor down the negotiation."[11]

Loretta Malintoppi (2015) explains that organizing the claim in two separate stages may frequently be beneficial for the parties. The first stage could focus on the scope of the dispute and issues of sovereignty, the second stage on maritime delimitation issues, if pertinent to the case. Such was the progression of the Eritrea v. Yemen arbitration case.[12] The parties asked the

[9] Author's interview (EJP) with Ioannis Kostantinidis, January 11, 2021.

[10] Author's interview (EJP) with Philip Steinberg, Director of International Boundaries Research Unit, University of Durham, Durham, UK, March 9, 2022.

[11] Ibid.

[12] Sovereignty and Maritime Delimitation in the Red Sea, Eritrea v. Yemen, PCA, phase I (1998), phase II (1999), 2001, 40 ILM 900 and 983, Arbitral Awards of October 9, 1998, and December 17, 1999.

tribunal to initially define the scope of the dispute. At a later stage, the tribunal was asked to address issues of sovereignty and maritime boundaries. This structure—whereby an intermediary deals merely with one aspect of claims at a time—can be beneficial to both disputants. Indeed, by splitting issues into several stages, disputants can update their information during the settlement, tactically shaping their behavior in a stage-by-stage manner based on the intermediary's preceding decision. The Gulf of Maine case illustrates the importance of framing the claim.[13] In 1981 the United States and Canada signed a Special Agreement, in which they consented to submit the dispute to the ICJ.[14] The parties specified "the question that the tribunal is asked to decide," and the United States insisted on using the term "single maritime boundary" to ensure that the Court considered all boundary decisions as one package (Robinson, Colson, and Rashkow 1985, 583). The American legal team "believed that it was in the U.S. interest not to limit considerations in this case" to merely certain aspects (584).[15] This approach was pursued to prevent Canada from picking and choosing certain claims.

Strategic design of a claim is absolutely decisive at the formative stages of dispute settlement. A claim's substantive and procedural aspects largely determine whether the specific venue has jurisdiction. In the words of one of our interviewees, "first, [states] think about the scope of jurisdiction and reflect on how the merits of [of the case] are perceived. . . . The [main question is] how will you [the state] bring the claim under jurisdiction? The state must be strategic about how the issue fits with jurisdiction [of a forum]—i.e. [using] LOSC [treaty first], then applicable law, etc."[16]

The Philippines v. China case provides a good in-depth examination of these dynamics.[17] To ensure that the UNCLOS Annex VII tribunal had jurisdiction, the Philippine government strategically singled out certain claims that fell under the jurisdiction of the tribunal. At the same time, other

---

[13] For a detailed description of the case, see Terres 1985.

[14] The Special Agreement, or The Letter from the Ambassadors of Canada and the United States of America to the Netherlands to the Registrar, The Hague, November 25, 1981, available at https://www.icj-cij.org/en/case/67.

[15] Delimitation of the Maritime Boundary in the Gulf of Maine Area, Canada v United States, ICJ Rep. 1984, 246, Judgment of October 12, 1984. It is also important to highlight that as part of their strategy, the disputants did not request that the ICJ draw "the line to the permissible outer limit of the continental shelf, an issue that was unsettled when the Special Agreement was negotiated in 1979" (Robinson, Colson, and Rashkow 1985, 585).

[16] Author's interview (KEW) with an anonymous public international law expert, Rhodes, Greece, July 19, 2018.

[17] South China Sea Arbitration, Philippines v. China, PCA Case No. 2013-19, ICGJ 495 (PCA 2016), Arbitral Award of July 12, 2016.

claims—especially those that were likely to fall under China's 2006 optional exception from compulsory dispute settlement (Article 298 of UNCLOS)—had to be avoided. In 2006 China placed an optional exception from compulsory dispute settlement regarding territorial sovereignty and maritime boundary delimitation. According to an anonymous Philippine Department of Foreign Affairs official whom we interviewed, the legal team "was very strategic, so China could not claim they were exempted from the Tribunal's jurisdiction."[18] Most significantly, China exempted itself from any legal ruling about "whether the 'historic title' of one of the parties should be taken into account in territorial sea boundary delimitation" (Beckman and Bernard 2011, 15). This meant that the Philippines could not request a ruling on historic title or maritime boundary delimitation. According to Paul Reichler, lead counsel for the Philippines, "The difficulty facing the Philippines was how to frame a case under the Law of the Sea Convention that would accomplish two critical objectives: 1) survive anticipated jurisdictional objections by China; and 2) enable the Philippines to obtain meaningful relief," or win the case.[19]

The Philippine Notification and Statement of Claim issued on January 22, 2013, was emphatic: "It follows that the Philippines' claims do not fall within China's Declaration of 25 August 2006, because they do not concern the interpretation or application of Articles 15, 74, and 83 [of UNCLOS]."[20] This choice of legal language allowed the Philippines' legal team to sidestep any claims that fell under China's optional exceptions from jurisdiction. As noted by Reichler, there were obstacles about jurisdiction that were "looming over the case," and "the solution, after much thought, analysis, and debate, was to bring a case about maritime entitlements rather than sovereignty over islands or delimitation of boundaries."[21] Reichler continued by noting that the legal team "became creative in that they felt they could still litigate what

[18] Author's interview (KEW) with an anonymous official, Philippines Department of Foreign Affairs, 2018.

[19] Author's interview (KEW) with Paul Reichler, Washington, DC, USA, November 7, 2016.

[20] Notification and Statement of Claim, Department of Foreign Affairs, January 22, 2013. China's declaration is: "The Government of the People's Republic of China does not accept any of the procedures provided for in Section 2 of Part XV of the Convention with respect to all the categories of disputes referred to in paragraph 1 (a) (b) and (c) of Article 298 of the Convention." See Declaration under Article 298 by the Government of the People's Republic of China, August 25, 2006, UN Division for Ocean Affairs and the Law of the Sea, http://www.un.org/Depts/los/convention_agr eements/convention_declarations.htm#China after ratification. UNCLOS Articles 15, 74, and 83 address maritime boundary delimitations, particularly territorial seas, EEZs, and continental shelves, as well as military activities and disputes dealt with by the UN Security Council.

[21] Author's interview (KEW) with Paul Reichler, November 7, 2016.

the entitlements of the features were and their status . . . without deciding what is sovereign."[22] Secretary of Foreign Affairs Albert Del Rosario confirmed this, pointing out that "we selected compulsory arbitration, which asked the Tribunal to rule on the extent of maritime entitlements on various features, regardless of what state exercises sovereignty over them."[23] Another high-ranking Philippine government official directly involved in the decision-making about the arbitration process stated that "the Philippine government made it clear to the Tribunal and to China that the case was not about sovereignty, but maritime issues, specifically entitlements relating to 12nm, EEZ. They were quite sure they had a very strong case."[24] General Emmanuel Bautista stated that "we felt we were on the right track; we had a strong case."[25] Assistant Secretary Henry Bensurto explained that "much depended on how the issues were phrased about the features and questions of ownership."[26] The Philippines' statement of claim therefore noted that "the Philippines does not seek in this arbitration a determination of which Party enjoys sovereignty over the islands claimed by both of them. Nor does it request a delimitation of any maritime boundaries."[27]

A Vietnamese Ministry of Foreign Affairs official who carefully observed the Philippine legal strategy noted that "how the question is framed matters to establish jurisdiction of a tribunal. It cannot depend on any incident, but specific questions. There was a very thin window to get jurisdiction without China's consent."[28] The Philippine strategy of framing the claim was successful. The Tribunal considered many of the issues brought by the Philippines, and subsequently the award emphasized the distinction made by the Philippine framing of their legal claims. According to one of the arbitrators, Judge Rüdiger Wolfrum (2018d), "The Arbitral Award honored

[22] Ibid.

[23] Author's interview (KEW) with Albert Del Rosario, former Secretary of Foreign Affairs, Department of Foreign Affairs and former Ambassador of the Republic of the Philippines to the United States of America, Manila, Philippines, March 18, 2017.

[24] Author's interview (KEW) with an anonymous high-ranking Philippine government official, Manila, Philippines, March 9, 2017.

[25] Author's interview (KEW) with General Emmanuel Bautista, Manila, Philippines, April 17, 2017.

[26] Author's interview (KEW) with Consul General Henry Bensurto, former Department of Foreign Affairs Assistant Secretary and Consul General, San Francisco, CA, USA, August 31, 2017.

[27] Notification and Statement of Claim, Philippines Department of Foreign Affairs, January 22, 2013. In the ICJ case between Indonesia and Malaysia, both states agreed to request a ruling by the Court only over territorial sovereignty, not maritime boundaries, similarly demonstrating selective claims submitted to legal dispute resolution. Sovereignty over Palau Ligitan and Palau Sipadan, Indonesia v. Malaysia, Philippines Application for Permission to Intervene, Judgment, ICJ Rep. 2001, 575, Judgment of March 13, 2001.

[28] Author's interview with an anonymous official, Vietnam Ministry of Foreign Affairs, 2018.

the declaration of China; it did not attempt to delimit the marine spaces be-tween China and the Philippines and did not decide on an incident which had a military character."

Of course, as we noted earlier, the Philippines' legal team was simulta-neously involved in the Chagos dispute arbitration via another UNCLOS Annex VII tribunal. Thus, much of the Philippines' claim was designed with an eye on the legal team's experiences in the Chagos arbitration.[29] For in-stance, while dealing with the Chagos dispute, the legal team learned that pursuing sovereignty claims would preclude Mauritius from using ITLOS, since the tribunal does not have jurisdiction over territorial boundary de-limitation (Wolfrum 2018a). The same legal strategy was then adopted in the Philippine v. China arbitration. Reichler provided us with much insight into the dynamics of claim framing. For instance, he noted that "the Philippines had taken pains not to raise issues of land sovereignty or boundary delim-itation. . . . That left us with the question of whether a case about maritime entitlements alone would be enough to justify the Philippines' recourse to arbitration."[30] Framing the claim was also noticeable in the Philippine Memorial submitted to the Tribunal on March 30, 2014: "For the avoid-ance of all doubt, the Philippines does not seek any determination by the Tribunal as to any question of sovereignty over islands, rocks or any other maritime features. The Tribunal is not invited, directly or indirectly, to adju-dicate on the competing sovereignty claims to any of the features at issue (or any others)."[31] In his statement to the Tribunal, Secretary Del Rosario (2015) stated: "Mr. President, allow me to respectfully make it clear: in submitting this case, the Philippines is NOT asking the tribunal to rule on the territorial sovereignty aspect of its dispute with China. We are here because we wish to clarify our maritime entitlements in the South China Sea, a question over which the Tribunal has jurisdiction." The Philippines' deliberate strategy was also clear to scholars who argued in favor of China's claims. For instance, Talmon and Jia (2014, 37) stated clearly that the Philippines tried "to circum-vent the question of sovereignty and other rights over land territory."

Reichler and the legal team were "confident that by asserting claims based on entitlements, rather than sovereignty or delimitation, we would survive

---

[29] Chagos Marine Protected Area Arbitration, Mauritius v. United Kingdom, PCA Case No. 2011-03 Arbitral Award of March 18, 2015.

[30] Author's interview (KEW) with Paul Reichler, November 7, 2016.

[31] Memorial of the Philippines, Volume 1, Arbitration under Annex VII of the United Nations Convention of the law of the Sea, March 30, 2014.

China's anticipated jurisdictional challenges, and this proved correct."[32] The legal team focused on rights and obligations in the waters, seabed and maritime features of the South China Sea, classification of maritime features as islands, low-tide elevations or submerged banks, capability of these features to generate entitlement to maritime zones greater than twelve nautical miles, and perhaps most importantly, the invalidity of China's nine-dash line claims.

China has attempted to turn several maritime features into islands. Therefore, another key part of the legal team's effort to frame the claim in an optimal way was to focus on the definition of an island—as distinct from rocks, reefs, banks, and shoals. Article 121 of UNCLOS defines an island as "a naturally formed area of land, surrounded by water, which is above water at high tide."[33] Most importantly, rocks, reefs, banks, and shoals that cannot "sustain human habitation or economic life of their own" can generate no EEZ or continental shelf, and only a twelve nautical mile territorial sea.[34] But the Tribunal ruled that "human modification cannot change the seabed into a low-tide elevation or a low-tide elevation into an island. A low-tide elevation will remain a low-tide elevation under the Convention, regardless of the scale of the island or installations built atop it" (Merits, para. 305). Thus, islands are created via natural processes. The Tribunal also ruled that, in this context, the size of a maritime feature is not a relevant factor on its own.

The Philippine legal team creatively argued that the maritime features claimed both by the Philippines and China were not islands, and thus neither state could claim rights to EEZs and the continental shelf. Though seemingly detrimental to Philippine interests, the main Philippine objective was to prevent China from claiming maritime entitlements. In the January 2013 Notification and Statement of Claim, the Philippine government issued a claim that "submerged features in the South China Sea that are not above sea level at high tide, and are not located in a coastal State's territorial sea, are part of the seabed and cannot be acquired by a State, or subjected to its sovereignty, unless they form part of that State's Continental Shelf under Part VI of the Convention."[35] This classification was upheld by the subsequent ruling: "none of the features in the Spratly Islands is capable, based on its own

---

[32] Author's interview (KEW) with Paul Reichler, November 7, 2016.

[33] United Nations Convention for the Law of the Sea, 10 Dec. 1982, 1833 U.N.T.S. 397.

[34] If the maritime feature is indeed a naturally formed area of land, "the state gets the full house of maritime zones" (Gavouneli 2018).

[35] Notification and Statement of Claim, Philippines Department of Foreign Affairs, January 22, 2013.

natural elements, of sustaining both human habitation and economic life of their own" (Merits, para. 426).[36]

Instead, the Philippines framed its claim to focus only on territorial seas, EEZs, and a continental shelf as measured from its archipelagic baselines— the mainland islands in the Philippine archipelago. As noted directly by Reichler, "if we could get the Tribunal to declare for most of these features that they were either low-tide elevations or submerged, then there is no maritime entitlement. The idea would be to reduce to a minimum the maritime entitlements of the Spratly features. So our approach was to say 'we can't contest sovereignty, we can't have sovereignty resolved, but we can determine the entitlements of these features,' and that was something we felt would be in the jurisdiction of the Tribunal."[37] Most importantly, Reichler noted that "the Philippine government was willing to live with zero maritime entitlements for the low tide features and twelve nautical miles from the features above water at high tide" for their own maritime features not claimed by China.[38] Assistant Secretary Bensurto noted that "the bigger issue was maritime— 85 percent of the problem. [They] could live with losing 15 percent territorial [issues]."[39] Though partially disadvantageous to the Philippines, this approach was clearly strategic. If the Tribunal ruled that the contested maritime features did not constitute islands, China would not be able to claim rights to EEZs or the continental shelf around these martitime features. The Philippines pursued this claim partially because the country already had 200 nautical miles of its EEZ from the coast of the archipelagic island of Palawan. As Reichler noted, by taking this approach, "there was no need to delimit a boundary since there were no overlapping maritime entitlements" between China and the Philippines.[40]

The Philippines v. China arbitration was not the first case in which an international adjudicator was asked to determine whether a maritime feature was a rock or an island. In the Denmark v. Iceland contention, both states claimed that the Norwegian island of Jan Mayen constituted an island to better make their case regarding delimitation of maritime zones.[41] Arguably, in two

---

[36] Memorial, paras. 5.96–5.114; Supplemental Written Submission, Vol. I, pp. 117–118, paras. 1–4; Schofield Report, p. 18.

[37] Author's interview (KEW) with Paul Reichler, November , 2016.

[38] Ibid.

[39] Author's interview (KEW) with Consul General Henry Bensurto, August 31, 2017.

[40] Author's interview (KEW) with Paul Reichler, November 7, 2016.

[41] Maritime Delimitation in the Area between Greenland and Jan Mayen, ICJ Rep. 1993, 38, Judgment of June 14, 1993.

other cases the ICJ came close to defining an island: Ukraine v. Romania and Nicaragua v. Colombia.[42] In the end, however, judgments delivered in these contentions did not provide such a definition. In contrast, the Philippines v. China arbitral award contained nearly 130 pages of details concerning the application of Article 121 of UNCLOS—about the definition of islands. As a result, this award sets an important guideline for future cases dealing with maritime entitlements and maritime boundary delimitation.

The decision about whether to inquire about the status of Itu Aba, a maritime feature controlled and built up by Taiwan, was a particularly controversial aspect in the legal strategy designed by the Philippines' legal team. The process leading up to the unfolding of the eventual legal strategy illustrates well how uncertainty about winning influences the framing of the claim. When preparing to submit the Philippines' Memorial to the Tribunal (March 2014), Philippine agents Francis Jardeleza and Florin Hilbay planned to keep Itu Aba out of the Philippine legal claims. In their estimation, it was feasible that the Tribunal could classify Itu Aba as an island. If so, then the Tribunal would lack jurisdiction, given its inability to determine territorial sovereignty and such an outcome would be in China's favor. As Jardeleza noted, "Nobody wanted to mention Itu Aba because the risk was, if the Tribunal ruled that it was an island, there would be an overlap of the EEZs" (Hofilena and Vitug 2016). Consideration of risks are clear in Hilbay's statement: "I saw the Itu Aba issue as belonging to the baskets where there was a need to reduce the impact of a potential loss and protect the President.... The Itu Aba issue is one where the *entire* team's level of confidence was not at its highest. This explains why that feature was not included in our 'complaint' in the first place" (Esmaquel 2016). In defending his initial decision to omit Itu Aba from the Philippine claims, Hilbay noted, "we should not signal to the Tribunal that we think we might lose. We needed to focus our firepower on winning that issue.... I told everyone I will not be the Solicitor General who sold this case to China" (Esmaquel 2016). Eventually, high-ranking Philippine officials along with Reichler persuaded President Aquino to include Itu Aba in the claims submitted to the Tribunal. In the end, the Tribunal ruled that Itu Aba and the Spratly maritime features were not islands. The strategy of focusing on the classification of maritime features in the Spratlys secured victory for

[42] Maritime Delimitation in the Black Sea, Romania v. Ukraine, ICJ Rep. 2009, 61, Judgment of February 3, 2009; Territorial and Maritime Dispute, Nicaragua v. Colombia, ICJ Rep. 2012, 624, Judgment of November 19, 2012.

the Philippines. The ruling effectively challenged all of China's claims for maritime entitlements.

Shaping the Procedures

As we explained in Chapter 4, more often than not, states have the option to shape procedures in two ways: through influencing specific rules and procedures, and through the selection of decision makers involved in the settlement—mediators, legal counsel, arbitrators, and judges. Although the various PR methods differ in levels of legality, our in-depth qualitative interviews overwhelmingly substantiate our supposition that states strategize via these two mechanisms in all methods. Of course, this strategizing becomes increasingly constricted as we move from negotiations, through the nonbinding third-party methods, to arbitration and, finally, adjudication.

Rules and Procedures

To a large extent, the degree to which the disputants can influence a venue's rules and procedures determines states' decisions at the choice-of-venue stage. Usually, states believe that controlling—shaping, altering, adjusting—the venue's rules and procedures diminishes uncertainty about the settlement process. As an ITLOS judge told us, "There are two questions [for states]: 1) Why states decide [to pursue a] legal method other than a political method. Whichever court it may be, it is a big deal to [resolve a] dispute [legally]. And 2) when states decide to submit to courts, they have a choice of procedures."[43] Frequently, states influence the rules by specifying the basis for the intermediary's decision: international law, a particular subset of international rules, specific treaties, a domestic legal system, international practice, and equity. It may be that the parties disagree over which set of rules is most beneficial for the resolution of their dispute. In the words of one of our interlocutors, "although one party may say *ex aequo et bono* the other party will not. The other party wants to be decided on law. For example, there has been a public issue that has been there for many years, between Belize and Guatemala, about the boundary. Guatemala says it will go to the Court only

---

[43] Author's interview (KEW) with an anonymous ITLOS judge, July 2018.

ex aequo et bono and Belize says no, the law is clear and we go to the Court to get a decision on the law."[44]

Arbitration constitutes a particularly attractive option in the event that states are adamant on specifying the applicable law. In general, given the ad hoc nature of arbitral tribunals, disputants tend to have a significant amount of influence on the procedures, much more so than in ICJ or ITLOS. As noted by an arbitration practitioner, "You can customize the procedure in all kinds of ways. You can have more confidentiality, or less confidentiality. You can do different things with witnesses and experts. . . . If you go to an international court, then by and large you get their procedure. You'll have some input, but generally you get their standard procedure."[45] Though the specifics depend largely on the subject matter of the dispute, prior to the arbitral proceedings states must agree with regard to applicable procedural rules, exchange of written pleadings and evidence, oral hearings, deliberations, and delivery of an award. Though for over a century the Permanent Court of Arbitration (PCA) has hosted and provided administrative assistance to arbitration tribunals, at times states prefer arbitration outside the PCA framework. In such cases, the PCA merely appoints the Registrar to record the details of the award. States' decisions to arbitrate outside the PCA framework are, of course, strategic, as absolute control over rules and procedures is not possible in the PCA. Examples of territorial and maritime disputes arbitrated outside the PCA framework include the Rann of Kutch arbitration between India and Pakistan in 1968, Delimitation of the Continental Shelf arbitration between France and the United Kingdom in 1978, the Beagle Channel arbitration between Chile and Argentina in 1978, the Dubai-Sharjah arbitration in 1981, and the Taba arbitration between Egypt and Israel in 1988 (Malintoppi 2015).[46]

There are some features of adjudication that can be controlled to some extent, or influenced by the disputants: submission of memorials, use of

[44] Author's interview (EJP) with an anonymous ICJ state advocate and international arbitrator, UK, October 2013.
[45] Author's interview (EJP) with an anonymous arbitration practitioner, February 7, 2022.
[46] The Indo-Pakistan Western Boundary (Rann of Kutch) between India and Pakistan, Volume XVII pp. 1–576, February 19, 1968; Delimitation of the Continental Shelf between the United Kingdom of Great Britain and Northern Ireland, and the French Republic, United Kingdom v. France, Volume XVIII pp. 3–413, June 30, 1977–March 14, 1978; Dispute between Argentina and Chile concerning the Beagle Channel, Volume XXI pp. 53–264, February 18, 1977; Dubai/Sharjah Border Arbitration, 91 ILR 543, Arbitral Award of October 19, 1981; Case Concerning the Location of Boundary Markers in Taba between Egypt and Israel, Volume XX pp. 1–118, Arbitral Award of September 29, 1988.

evidence, timing and organization of oral arguments, and use of expert witnesses (Malintoppi 2015). In fact, many training documents highlight the reality that the complicated procedure of international adjudication makes the within-venue strategic selection possible: "The procedure in international courts is quite extended. Usually there are memorials and counter-memorials, replies and response. In a domestic court, it's not quite the same. In domestic court, more of the proceedings are oral and not always so."[47]

Shaping the rules of procedure can be interconnected with initial choice of venue. In fact, anticipating the ability to influence settlement procedures in the within-venue stage can be influential when states select a PR method and a specific venue. The Gulf of Maine ICJ case between the United States and Canada provides a good example.[48] According to the advocates who represented the United States—Davis Robinson, US agent; David Colson, deputy US agent; and Bruce Rashkow, assistant legal advisor—the United States favored resolution by a smaller ICJ Chamber of five judges instead of the regular panel of fifteen judges. The US legal team was particularly influenced by a 1973 article written by ICJ Judge Eduardo Jimémez de Aréchaga about amendments to the Court's Rules (Robinson, Colson, and Rashkow 1985). The article asserted that "recourse to *ad hoc* Chambers would prove more attractive to potential litigants" (Aréchaga 1973, 2). The novel procedure drew on several features of arbitration: the parties' ability to influence the procedure and the composition of the bench—while providing many benefits of a long-standing international court (Robinson, Colson, and Rashkow 1985, 581). Thus, in this case, the anticipation of the ability to shape rules and procedures was influential in the choice-of-venue stage and the within-venue stage.

In maritime disputes, during the within-venue stage, dissatisfaction with rules and procedures can prompt the parties to resort to a different PR venue. As noted by one of our interviewees, an ITLOS judge, "if one state says [it chooses] ITLOS and the other disagrees, the dispute goes to Annex VII arbitration as the default PR settlement and residual procedures are automatically applied if there is a disagreement."[49] In the event that a dispute is submitted to an Annex VII tribunal, UNCLOS provides the parties the prerogative to

[47] Author's interview (EJP) with an anonymous ICJ state advocate and international arbitrator, UK, October 2013.
[48] Delimitation of the Maritime Boundary in the Gulf of Maine Area, Canada v. United States, ICJ Rep. 1984, 246, Judgment of October 12, 1984.
[49] Author's interview (KEW) with an anonymous ITLOS judge, July 14, 2018.

subsequently transfer the contention to ITLOS. At times, such a move may be perceived as strategic by one or both parties. For example, Bangladesh agreed to shift the resolution of its case against Myanmar to ITLOS, though initially both parties selected an Annex VII tribunal. Confronted with a specific venue with a set procedure—such as an Annex VII tribunal—disputants may revert to the choice-of-venue stage and adjust their subsequent strategies. In the words of the ITLOS judge, "States think about if this [ITLOS] is the best option, but they may not have thought about which procedure is the best option."[50]

According to legal experts, timing—initiation and duration—of the proceedings, an intricate part of a settlement's rules and procedures, constitutes an important aspect of within-venue strategic selection. In a way, when a settlement procedure ensues, or how long it lasts, may determine the outcome. Either way, exercising some control over the duration of a case has the indirect effect of helping states feel they have more control. Thus, states make the timing of settlement a key part of their strategies: "Does a state want an expeditious resolution of its dispute by a third-party forum, a court or a tribunal? Yes or no? . . . If you take a look at the docket of the International Court of Justice, you will realize that the ICJ is extremely busy. This means that it will take more time, theoretically, for the case to move on. When it comes to ITLOS, ITLOS is not as busy as the International Court of Justice. . . . With regard to an arbitral tribunal, things can move even faster."[51] States may adapt expedited timetables and put explicit limits on a tribunal's deliberations (Thomas 2015). Relatedly, it may be beneficial to set up a tribunal or a panel consisting merely of a few arbitrators. Such limited panels bring about fewer disagreements and thus usually render quicker decisions (Malintoppi 2015). Shorter cases reduce charges and provide states with an increased amount of influence.

It is often said that states that prioritize speed in the context of a particular case are drawn to arbitration (Kingdon 2015). For example, Philippine President Benigno Aquino hoped that the South China Sea arbitration proceedings would commence and end relatively quickly. The fear was that his successor might decide to withdraw the case three years after its submission.[52] It is also important to consider that in some cases, arbitration

---

[50] Ibid.

[51] Author's interview (EJP) with Ioannis Kostantinidis, January 11, 2021.

[52] Author's interview (KEW) with an anonymous official, Philippines Department of Foreign Affairs, 2018. South China Sea Arbitration, Philippines v. China, Award, PCA Case No. 2013-19, ICGJ 495, July 12, 2016. The tribunal ruled on the case less than two weeks after President Benigno

may be slower than established courts, as one of our interviewees—an ITLOS judge—noted.[53] Indeed, commencing an UNCLOS Annex VII arbitration means, for the most part, starting the settlement procedure from scratch. The process of setting up such a tribunal can prolong the proceedings when compared to an established adjudicator, because the ad hoc tribunals do not have their own permanent facilities and structure. The situation is slightly better in cases of arbitrations that take place in the framework of the PCA, since the PCA provides a multiplicity of dispute resolution services to the disputants, and has access to several hearing facilities. The Court maintains many specialized panels of experts and arbitrators, and has a considerable financial assistance fund.[54] Nonetheless, as a general pattern, and based on recent trends in practice, disputes delegated to ITLOS and Annex VII arbitral tribunals get settled faster than the majority of ICJ cases (Martin 2018).

Costs associated with proceedings at a chosen venue are immensely important to all states.[55] That was a message conveyed by several of our interviewees, including an ITLOS judge.[56] The judge noted that ITLOS and the ICJ offer free services to states, with the exception of legal fees and travel. In contrast, he continued, the price for most instances of arbitration is high, owing to its ad hoc nature. Indeed, when using ad hoc arbitration tribunals, states have to pay for use of the facility and for the arbitrators and cover all legal fees and costs of the registry.[57] But, in general, proceedings in any third-party venue usually accrue significant costs, including the costs to be paid to a venue—PCA, a specific mediator, or conciliator, etc.—as well as the costs of hiring legal counsel and pertinent experts. As legal expert Alex Oude Elferink noted, "Litigation isn't always the best method, [because] it

---

Aquino left office and President Rodrigo Duterte took office. President Aquino's fears were confirmed when President Duterte played down the ruling, all but ignoring it, followed by a visit to China, the new president's first official state visit to a foreign country.

[53] Author's interview (KEW) with an anonymous ITLOS judge, July 2018.
[54] For more information, see the website of PCA at https://pca-cpa.org/en/home/. The PCA can provide space and administrative support to Annex VII arbitration tribunals.
[55] For discussion of this important issue in the context of specific cases, see Rowland A. Parks, "COLA Hosts Negotiators of the Belize-Guatemala Differendum," *Amandala*, September 30, 2008, https://amandala.com.bz/news/cola-hosts-negotiators-of-the-belize-guatemala-differendum/; Willard 2009; Robinson, Colson, and Rashkow 1985.
[56] Author's interview (KEW) with an anonymous ITLOS judge, July 2018.
[57] A secretary/registrar is often appointed by the Tribunal after consulting with disputing parties, acting as the official conduit for communications/pleadings, providing assistance to the Tribunal, and conducting financial administration and logistics (meetings places, hearings, transcripts, etc.). See Bundy 2003.

be can be costly."[58] Charges tend to be highest for maritime boundary cases, because, according to legal expert Konstantinidis, "the composition of a maritime boundary delimitation case is different. It requires people with technical expertise and this entails additional costs."[59] The reality is that "not all states have the financial capacity to hire counsel and to come up with a team."[60] As legal experts confirm, costs can be controlled through efficient case management: hiring small but experienced teams, ensuring that a case is carefully organized and coordinated, avoiding duplication, and limiting plenary meetings, written pleadings, and documentary annexes. Yet, since winning is usually the most important goal for each disputant, if the more expensive venue is simultaneously deemed more advantageous, considerations of cost become secondary in importance.[61] According to Coalter G. Lathrop, "I think that decision [about which resolution forum to choose] is probably less about cost and more about the party autonomy side of that equation. Being able to choose the rules, choose the people, choose the place, you know, those considerations are important ones. . . . And in terms of pulling out of something, I've never run into a situation where the budget dried up and the country said 'we can't appear.' These are core sovereignty issues. . . . They [states] find the money to defend their core sovereignty interests. And it's public, when a state is litigating these matters, reputation is at stake on a very public international stage."[62]

Selection of Actors

The process of selecting actors involved in dispute resolution plays a crucial role in all PR methods. Though negotiations do not entail participation of intermediaries, governments have the prerogative to choose specific people to prepare and carry out bilateral talks. These decisions involve input from applicable ministries, agencies, and bureaus. Not all recommendations are treated equally, and politics—within the dyad, on the regional and global levels—are instrumental in these decisions. According to an anonymous

---

[58] Author's interview (KEW) with Alex Oude Elferink, Director of the Netherlands Law of the Sea Institute, School of Law, Utrecht University, Rhodes, Greece, July 11, 2018.

[59] Author's interview (EJP) with Ioannis Kostantinidis, January 11, 2021.

[60] Ibid.

[61] Author's interview (KEW) with an anonymous ITLOS judge, July 2018.

[62] Author's interview (EJP) with Coalter G. Lathrop, Sovereign Geographics, International Boundary Consultancy, March 14, 2022.

foreign affairs department official, "It takes a long time [for the government] to choose a strategy, it depends on the political bureau. Every question of political importance must be addressed by the political bureau of a government."[63] It is crucial for each side to select individuals who are likely to be effective in securing the best outcome. Of course, in its everyday activities, each government relies on a host of legal advisors. The same is true of decisions that pertain to any territorial and maritime disputes a state is involved in. As one of our interviewees pointed out, "First of all, in a country, there are always legal advisors in the government. In particular in these kinds of situations, you have the legal advisor in the Ministry of Foreign Affairs. And this person, of course, will be asked to give advice in these situations."[64] Factors such as diplomatic experience, personal relations, and a successful record in past negotiations carry a lot of weight in who is chosen to participate in negotiations (Wiegand, Keels, and Rowland 2021). Lorna Lloyd noted in an interview that she "never came across a diplomat who didn't believe personal relations make a difference. It's not going to alter the overall scheme of things, but they all felt personal relationships helped things along."[65] Ability to think strategically is of the utmost importance. According to Hans Corell, "As a negotiator, I always say that you should never try to score a point at the expense of the other party. You should really be very serious and think about how your counterparts think about the situation. You should try to imagine how they reason and see what are the reasons for them taking this particular position."[66]

A key strategic decision deals with the selection of government officials, legal counsel, and other experts involved in preparing the case. The importance of these decisions cannot be overestimated.[67] In the context of arbitration, one of our interviewees noted,

If you're in a situation where you have sophisticated counsel—and I don't necessarily mean outside counsel because I think that foreign ministry, internal lawyers can be perfectly sophisticated on these issues—if you have

---

[63] Author's interview (KEW) with an anonymous official, Philippines Department of Foreign Affairs, 2018.

[64] Author's interview (EJP) with Hans Corell, January 13, 2021.

[65] Author's interview (EJP) with Lorna Lloyd, international relations scholar, United Kingdom, May 20, 2022.

[66] Ibid.

[67] Author's interview (KEW) with Judge Rüdiger Wolfrum, July 19, 2018, and with Alex Oude Elferink, July 11, 2018.

sophisticated counsel who can look at those elements of flexibility in arbitration and consider how the proceedings can be adjusted in a way that
would favor their case—for instance in selecting a tribunal that is perhaps
more favorable to their position than not—you can try to use those tools
strategically.[68]

A weak legal counsel may make costly mistakes. As Ioannis Konstantinidis
noted, "the first thing that a state dissects when it comes to all types of interstate disputes—including territorial and/or maritime disputes—is the question of consent. What are the available dispute settlement fora? What are the
available courts and tribunals? . . . Sometimes states do not proceed this way
because of lack of expertise . . . because they do not hire counsel . . . because
they do not consult the right people."[69] Acquiring good legal counsel ensures
that a country's claims are framed strategically with full consideration of
rules and procedures specific to a chosen venue.

Upon completing background research related to the case at hand, legal
counsel is "instructed by a state, or should be instructed, to prepare a legal
memorandum focusing on the available options and what is the best option. So, these are strategic considerations, one hundred percent."[70] A good
legal counsel is composed of highly credible international law experts, who
are educated in more than one legal system, and speak multiple languages.
In general, effective interstate case management involves "selecting a be-
spoke team made up of a range of different specialists, and then trying to
get them all facing in the same direction."[71] Thus, the position of a lead
legal counsel is particularly important. The lead legal counsel is "an overall
team leader, a 'conductor' of the orchestra. . . . Their biggest job is making
sure that all of these different cogs in the machine fit and work harmoni-
ously together."[72]

Every person assisting in dispute settlement is responsible for a specific
aspect of the proceedings. The ability to strategically manage the entire team
is of the utmost importance. The selection of experts depends on the relevant
factual and legal circumstances of the contention. Academics, historians,
archival specialists, cartographers, geographers, and hydrographers may

---

[68] Author's interview (EJP) with an anonymous arbitration practitioner, February 7, 2022.
[69] Author's interview (EJP) with Ioannis Kostantinidis, January 11, 2021.
[70] Ibid.
[71] Author's interview (EJP) with William Thomas QC, Freshfields Bruckhaus Deringer, March
9, 2022.
[72] Ibid.

need to be consulted. In general, the "management of boundary and territorial sovereignty disputes is a particular and demanding exercise, requiring various different skill sets—for example, lawyers, historians, archivists, cartographers, and hydrographers. It therefore becomes a project- and people-management exercise as much as a litigation exercise."[73] The counsel works on behalf of the state and presents options regarding the settlement process and specific PR methods, highlighting issues associated with each venue and prospective within-venue plan of action. The role of the legal counsel is to "think strategically" about legal and political issues surrounding the case.[74]

Hiring a firm that specializes in public international law helps a government in multiple ways. There are a few firms that have developed an expertise in the field of interstate dispute resolution, and "sometimes those firms get recruited because they have an existing relationship with a government, not necessarily for their boundary expertise, but, obviously, they are smart enough to reach out and find the relevant experts to work with them. Only two or three have really been able to develop it into a repeat business."[75] The legal teams can assist with formal communications between the disputant—their client—and the court or tribunal. Also, it is usually the firm's responsibility to organize the logistics of written and oral proceedings, research factual evidence, and, if needed, hire pertinent experts: "governments sound out experts usually through the lawyers they've hired and the lawyers who have worked with me either through negotiations or cases tend to recommend individuals to be part of a government team preparing for negotiations or for a third-party settlement of a dispute."[76]

All of these tasks may seem bureaucratic, but each task can help the state feel it has greater control over the resolution process. The counsel who represents a government plays an absolutely critical role in the settlement proceedings. Of course, the counsel receives instructions from the client state and must respect the state's wishes (Martin 2018). Strategies adopted by the agent, legal counsel, and the government must align to reflect the goals and preferences of the state. Usually, there is an ongoing dialogue between all these actors, since the details of strategizing, and thus the best way

---

[73] Ibid.
[74] Author's interview (KEW) with Ashley Roach, former Judge Advocate General, U.S. Navy and adviser in the Office of the Legal Adviser, US Department of State, Rhodes, Greece, July 11, 2018.
[75] Author's (EJP) interview with Martin Pratt, Bordermap Consulting, January 27, 2022.
[76] Ibid.

to proceed, may change with time.[77] To ensure that an optimal counsel is selected, governments "really have to ask around [since] states don't know who to turn to."[78] ITLOS judge Tullio Treves noted that states tend to inquire with multiple law firms about the best approach to a case, indicating the selection of counsel is strategic.[79]

According to our interviewees, the counsel's positive personal experiences with certain venues and/or judges and arbitrators play a vital role in states' selection of lawyers. One interviewee noted, "Obviously they [states] want to win. It's a question of what they want to win, but no matter what it is, yes they want to win. So if they're going into a forum that has a list of folks who have had success there, that's who you want to hire. You don't really want to roll the dice on the new guy."[80] As Hans Corell explained, "if you go before a court, both sides look around for people who have experience of appearing before international courts and arbitral tribunals."[81] This was the case with counsel representing Nicaragua in its dispute with Honduras.[82] The counsel had "personal experience and knew people at The Hague."[83] These considerations were crucial in Nicaragua's decision to suggest the ICJ as its preferred venue. In other cases, states strategically use the same team of lawyers for two different contentions against the same disputant, as happened in the context of the Bangladesh v. Myanmar and Bangladesh v. India contentions. Myanmar and India both used the same legal team for their ITLOS cases against Bangladesh (Martin 2018).[84] By using the same legal team against the same target state, India and Myanmar were able to rely on their legal teams' strategy in substantially similar disputes dealing with maritime boundary delimitation. Arguably, these decisions gave India and Myanmar some degree of leverage when presenting their claims to ITLOS.

---

[77] Author's interview (KEW) with an anonymous public international law expert, Rhodes, Greece, July 2018. An agent is the legal representative of the government, while counsel is an external member of the legal team from a law firm who represents the government at the Court or tribunal.

[78] Ibid.

[79] Author's interview (KEW) with ITLOS Judge Tullio Treves, Rhodes, Greece, July 15, 2018.

[80] Author's interview (EJP) with Coalter G. Lathrop, March 14, 2022.

[81] Author's interview (EJP) with Hans Corell, January 13, 2021.

[82] Territorial and Maritime Dispute between Nicaragua and Honduras in the Caribbean Sea, Nicaragua v. Honduras, ICJ Rep. 2007, 659, Judgment of October 8, 2007.

[83] Author's interview (KEW) with an anonymous public international law expert, Rhodes, Greece, July 2018.

[84] Dispute Concerning Delimitation of the Maritime Boundary between Bangladesh and Myanmar in the Bay of Bengal, Bangladesh v. Myanmar, ITLOS Case No. 16, 52014XC0830(01), ICGJ 448 (ITLOS 2012), Judgment of March 14, 2012; Bay of Bengal Maritime Boundary Arbitration between Bangladesh and India, Bangladesh v. India, ICGJ 479 (PCA 2014), Arbitral Award of July 7, 2014.

Our conversations with several interlocutors connected to the South China Sea arbitration case shed light on the chain of events leading the Philippines to select Paul Reichler as lead legal counsel. Shortly after the Scarborough Shoal incident in April 2012, President Aquino's office contacted multiple law firms in May 2012—including Foley Hoag in Washington, DC—to inquire about the best legal venue to pursue. President Aquino's advisors, in particular Assistant Secretary Henry Bensurto and Secretary of Foreign Affairs Alberto Del Rosario, knew Paul Reichler, who at that time had already represented multiple states at the ICJ and arbitration tribunals. According to Bensurto, his friend Robert Beckman, a maritime legal expert who had suggested the potential use of UNCLOS Annex VII arbitration in the South China Sea disputes, provided Bensurto with Reichler's name. Subsequently, Bensurto met with Reichler in Washington, DC. In Bensurto's view, "he [Reichler] understood it. He was the only lawyer who said it could be done."[85] Another interviewee noted that of the four counsel asked to advise the Philippine government, two of the counsels' recommendations were opposed to each other, and two highlighted the possibilities. Reichler provided one of the latter opinions.[86] His substantial experience at the ICJ—especially as Nicaragua's counsel in its case against Colombia—shaped the Philippine government's decision to hire Reichler as lead counsel. President Aquino had been "waffling before, but after the victory in Nicaragua-Colombia," in November 2012, the Philippine government decided to move forward with hiring Reichler and his colleagues to pursue a legal case against China.[87]

A legal counsel's previous experience in litigating similar cases is a source of information about PR methods and specific venues, and thus reduces states' uncertainty with the settlement process. Such experience simultaneously increases states' confidence in winning the contention. Simply put, experts with prior litigation experience "are an asset to a case" (Martin 2018). The counsel's role is to fulfill the client's preferences to the greatest extent possible. Some states are not comfortable with large settlement forums and prefer smaller arbitration chambers "because of lesser uncertainty," according to former president of ITLOS Judge Rüdiger Wolfrum.[88] In such cases, the

---

[85] Author's interview (KEW) with Consul General Henry Bensurto, San Francisco, CA, USA, August 31, 2017.

[86] Author's interview (KEW) with Jay L. Batongbacal, Director, University of the Philippines Institute for Maritime Affairs and Law of the Sea, Quezon City, Philippines, April 20, 2017.

[87] Ibid. Territorial and Maritime Dispute, Nicaragua v. Colombia, ICJ Rep. 2012, 624, Judgment of November 19, 2012.

[88] Author's interview (KEW) with Judge Rüdiger Wolfrum, July 19, 2018.

counsel should steer the case away from the ICJ, unless there are strategic reasons for doing otherwise. On the individual level, some lawyers feel comfortable working with the ICJ. In this context, it is worth adding that usually people in decision-making capacities at the ICJ, ITLOS, and PCA rotate from one function to another. As one of our interlocutors noted, "We have the same people deciding the same disputes, but sometimes these people wear a different hat."[89] Thus, it is possible—and indeed a frequent occurrence—that a lawyer's positive personal connection with a judge or an arbitrator will lead to a subsequent PCA, ICJ, or ITLOS submission. Regardless, "established relationships between counsel and the state matter."[90] There is no doubt that the "choice of counsel matters. It's a matter of appearance. A lot has to do with trust."[91] Of course, at times, legal counsel faces obstacles in trying to decipher the client's—a state's—preferences and instructions. Various state officials may have different objectives, and thus expect different things from the legal counsel. In such cases, "managing that dynamic then becomes one of the key jobs of whoever is leading the legal team. You've first got to make sure all relevant stakeholders are (and feel) heard, then bring differing views together and thereafter formulate an agreed approach. And then you have to ensure a consistent and coherent case strategy is bought into and executed by all the stakeholders and team members."[92]

In most cases, specialist outside counsel—in particular counsel trained in international law in the context of foreign jurisdictions—is brought in for strategic reasons. Mirroring the diverse backgrounds of the judges on international courts and tribunals, states may prefer "to select their international counsel from a range of jurisdictions (both common and civil law), and potentially speaking different languages. For example, if you're [a State] before the ICJ—the official languages of the court are both English and French, so you usually want your counsel team to plead in a mix of the two languages."[93] In the Gulf of Maine case, just months before the November 1981 submission of the case to a special Chamber of the ICJ, the US government decided to bring in legal experts outside the US government as well as foreign legal consultants.[94] According to the US agents, "there were several considerations

[89] Author's interview (EJP) with Ioannis Kostantinidis, January 11, 2021.
[90] Author's interview (KEW) with Judge Rüdiger Wolfrum, July 19, 2018.
[91] Author's interview (KEW) with an anonymous public international law expert, Rhodes, Greece, July 19, 2018.
[92] Author's interview (EJP) with William Thomas QC, March 9, 2022.
[93] Ibid.
[94] Delimitation of the Maritime Boundary in the Gulf of Maine Area, Canada v. United States, ICJ Rep. 1984, 246, Judgment of October 12, 1984.

that went into U.S. thinking in this regard. We wanted to obtain the widest and most sophisticated insight into practice before the Court" (Robinson, Colson, and Rashkow 1985, 588). Though in the end, the US legal team decided to use only US agents to present the oral arguments at the Court, the US team was "originally concerned that if we did not use foreign counsel, Canada, which had determined that foreign counsel would participate in its oral presentation, might gain some edge" (593).

The strategy of involving foreign legal teams is particularly important in disputes involving Islamic law states. These states tend to draw expertise from Western legal firms and Western lawyers. When asked specifically about whether, and if so why, Islamic law states try to hire Western international lawyers to represent them, one of our interlocutors responded,

> They do, in fact. That's intrinsic because it [the proceedings] happens in the West. There are a number of highly qualified practitioners. And each side would like to have the benefit of their help. They don't choose them by reference to their nationality but their standing in the practice of international law. I have been instructed and appeared in a number of cases for Muslim states. It does not bother me, it does not bother them. What matters is that they can draw on my experience.[95]

Speaking about Islamic law states, ICJ judge Al-Khasawneh confirmed that when these states are considering international adjudication, "much depends on their counsel, who are usually British, French, or American."[96] Thus, thinking strategically, these states "hire Western lawyers in the assumption that they are much more experienced than the lawyers from their region."[97] In fact, the assumption frequently is that US- or European-based legal teams have more powerful and well-informed experts, and thus are more likely to efficiently steer the case toward victory.

In nonbinding third-party methods—mediation, conciliation, good offices, and inquiry—the disputants usually have the prerogative to designate the intermediary, or can bilaterally agree to an offer issued by a specific person or a body. Strategy is critical in these decisions. For instance,

---

[95] Author's interview (EJP) with an anonymous ICJ state advocate and international arbitrator, UK, October 2013. Cited in Powell 2020, 208.

[96] Author's interview (EJP) with Judge Awn Shawkat Al-Khasawneh, former Vice-President, ICJ, and former Prime Minister of Jordan, Amman, Jordan, February 18, 2015.

[97] Author's interview (EJP) with an anonymous international law expert and legal counsel, Brussels, Belgium, July 4, 2014.

the best mediators are those who are deeply familiar with mediation as a PR method, have ample past experience with mediation, and are acquainted with disputants, their preferences, and their cultural traditions (Wiegand, Rowland, and Keels 2021). Equally important, in the context of arbitration and adjudication, is the selection of arbitrators and judges involved in a case. Since "litigation is always risky and [states] can't control the outcome, there are ways to avoid risks," as emphasized by one of our interlocutors.[98] States view their ability to influence the selection of arbitrators and judges as key to minimizing their uncertainty. According to Alex Oude Elferink, "there are people you may want as a judge or arbitrator, and this matters, especially with a five-person arbitration, since there are so few deciders." Indeed, states should "look carefully at who should be selected as arbiters."[99] Counsel Loretta Malintoppi (2015) also confirms that states select arbitrators to reduce uncertainty:

> State parties are often attracted to the idea of selecting the entire panel that will be called upon to decide their dispute and controlling the method of their appointment. The idea of managing the process of selection and appointment of arbitrators is indeed appealing, not only because states may wish to appoint an individual who is familiar with a particular legal culture or who comes from a specific region of the world, but also because they may wish to retain a certain measure of control in the appointment of the Chairman of the panel and determine from the outset the mechanism of decisions upon challenges and replacements of arbitrators.

More broadly, states frequently prefer arbitration to adjudication since they can control who serves as an arbitrator. This is especially crucial in highly technical cases. According to one of our interviewees,

> Sometimes if you have a particularly technical case you may have more confidence in an arbitration setting where you have more control over the choice of decision makers and how the process works. For instance, you may be afraid that if you take something very technical into a court of general international lawyers, they may not understand the technical aspects of it. But I think there's a lot of strategic elements that probably go into those

---

[98] Author's interview (KEW) with Ashley Roach, July 11, 2018.
[99] Author's interview (KEW) with Alex Oude Elferink, July 11, 2018.

decisions if you actually have a circumstance where you have multiple options available.[100]

Some states "believe that fifteen plus two—seventeen judges—and twenty-one plus two—twenty-three judges—are too many. That is why they go for Annex VII arbitration. And the great majority of maritime boundary delimitation cases, after the entry into force of the UN Convention on the Law of the Sea, have been decided by Annex VII arbitral tribunals."[101] In some venues, states automatically have less influence over the selection of the panel. For instance, for states seeking peaceful resolution of their maritime disputes, using ITLOS means that a state has no prerogative to select the twenty-one judges.[102] Granted, states have the ability to appoint an ad hoc judge, which "can be a reassurance for the State that appointed him or her" (Malintoppi 2015). Indeed, it is a "person that—certainly statistically, not always, but statistically—will vote in favor of the state that appointed him or her."[103]

If the idea of a predetermined panel of judges is unattractive to states in maritime disputes, governments can turn to an UNCLOS Annex VII arbitral tribunal, in which case the state has much more influence over the selection of arbitrators. According to Ioannis Konstantinidis, "In the context of Annex VII arbitration, we have five arbitrators. A party appointed arbitrator can certainly influence the majority. Dynamics are different. This is a very important strategic consideration."[104] Thus, in the Annex VII cases, as noted by an ITLOS judge, states not only name one arbitrator, but they also have some influence over the selection of three others not appointed by the opponent.[105] At the ICJ, states may nominate a judge from their own country to join the bench. Yet, as Alex Oude Elferink admitted, there could be a question about "how . . . the bench view[s] an ad hoc judge" and whether the proposed person is indeed the right person for the case.[106] After all, one-sided strategic decisions on the part of a disputant should not overshadow the overarching goals of international adjudication—seeking justice and providing unbiased decisions. Of course, states can also challenge a judge's or arbitrator's role in a case if "circumstances exist that give rise to justifiable doubts as to

---

[100] Author's interview (EJP) with an anonymous arbitration practitioner, February 7, 2022.
[101] Author's interview (EJP) with Ioannis Kostantinidis, January 11, 2021.
[102] Author's interview (KEW) with an anonymous ITLOS judge, July 2018.
[103] Author's interview (EJP) with Ioannis Kostantinidis, January 11, 2021.
[104] Ibid.
[105] Author's interview (KEW) with an anonymous ITLOS judge, July 2018.
[106] Author's interview (KEW) with Alex Oude Elferink, Rhodes, Greece, July 11, 2018.

the arbitrator's impartiality or independence" (Malintoppi 2015, 27). By way of illustration, Mauritius challenged the nomination of Judge Christopher Greenwood in the Chagos Marine Protected Area Arbitration case against the United Kingdom in 2012 because of Greenwood's work as a legal advisor for the UK Foreign Affairs office.[107]

In the process of establishing an arbitral tribunal, states have the ability to pursue within-venue strategic selection with regard to the number of arbitrators, the balance between neutral versus party-appointed arbitrators, the choice of the president/chairman, and the procedure delineating challenges or replacements (Bundy 2003). As noted by an arbitration practitioner, "you get a say over who the members of the tribunals are. There's a lot of tailoring that you can put into that."[108] When selecting specific judges or arbitrators, states and their legal counsel consider several factors, such as the candidates' professional expertise, reputation, personal qualities, character, independence and impartiality, ability to interact with the other judges or arbitrators, technical knowledge, subject-specific competence, historic or cultural familiarity, and awareness of the case's political sensitivities (Malintoppi 2015).

From several of our interviews with international judges, we received the impression that states and their legal counsel extensively analyze individual arbitrators' and judges' previous decisions, not just for precedent, but for patterns of legal preferences and certain legal positions. Though the counsel should not presume "anything about the reputations of judges, [there is] some sense of where judges would be on a position based on writings. [This] will be taken into account."[109] Of course, at the same time, no state can be certain about how a tribunal will decide. According to ITLOS judge Rüdiger Wolfrum, "Even when a state chooses an arbitrator, this does not tell [the state] how the arbitrator will decide. [But] writings [by the arbitrator or judge] can show what the arbitrator will not necessarily vote on."[110] Alex Oude Elferink agreed that the "counsel will look at what kind of position arbitrators have taken [through] writings."[111] Another interviewee—an

---

[107] The Tribunal ruled that the challenge was not justifiable and Judge Greenwood remained on the Tribunal. Chagos Marine Protected Area Arbitration, Mauritius v. United Kingdom, PCA Case No. 2011-03, Arbitral Award of March 18, 2015.

[108] Author's interview (EJP) with an anonymous arbitration practitioner, February 7, 2022.

[109] Author's interview (KEW) with an anonymous public international law expert, Rhodes, Greece, July 19, 2018.

[110] Author's interview (KEW) with Judge Rüdiger Wolfrum, July 2018.

[111] Author's interview (KEW) with Alex Oude Elferink, July 11, 2018.

international judge—brought up the Bolivia v. Chile case to illustrate states' behavior in this context. This judge confidentially recalled that in preparation for the ICJ proceedings, Chile rejected a particular judge, having carefully examined the judge's past record.[112] According to our interviewee, Chile considered the judge in question "too progressive." Moreover, Chilean legal counsel was concerned that the judge "would make conclusions that are too conciliatory, and was not hard-nosed."[113]

Influencing the selection of arbitrators—pursuant to Article 3(b) of Annex VII—was a key part of the Philippine strategy in its case against China.[114] Many of our interlocutors highlighted that the Philippine legal team went to great lengths to gather information about the preferences and jurisprudence of particular arbitrators. In the 2013 Notification and Statement of Claim, the Philippines appointed its first choice of arbitrator, Judge Rüdiger Wolfrum, former president of ITLOS. According to an anonymous legal advisor, Wolfrum was selected "because he has a specific view on territorial and maritime disputes," which were clear from his previous statements.[115] For instance, Wolfrum had previously stated that before establishing a maritime baseline, a land boundary must be determined. In the words of our interlocutor, "the Philippines deliberately chose Wolfrum from the arbitrator list for this reason."[116] Also of great importance was Wolfrum's speech at the UN General Assembly in December 2006. Referring to mixed disputes, that is, disputes over maritime and territorial boundaries, Wolfrum stated that "maritime boundaries cannot be determined in isolation without reference to territory" (Wolfrum 2006). He also emphasized that UNCLOS had "several provisions" that dealt with "issues of sovereignty and the inter-relation between land and sea" (Wolfrum 2006). These statements indicated Wolfrum's belief that UNCLOS Annex VII ad hoc tribunals were well suited to address issues of territorial sovereignty in addition to maritime rights and boundaries. Such conceptualization was critical to the strategy legal counsel Paul Reichler designed for the

---

[112] Obligation to Negotiate Access to the Pacific Ocean, Bolivia v. Chile, Preliminary Objection, ICJ Rep. 2015, 592, July 15, 2014.

[113] Author's interview (KEW) with an anonymous ITLOS judge, July 2018.

[114] Article 3(b) of Annex VII states that "the party instituting the proceedings shall appoint one member to be chosen preferably from the list referred to in article 2 of this Annex, who may be its national."

[115] Author's interview with an anonymous public international law expert, Rhodes, Greece, July 2018.

[116] Ibid.

Philippines: the argument that sovereignty—and subsequent contiguous zones and EEZs—could not be claimed by China—or the Philippines—because certain maritime features did not constitute islands.

Wolfrum was also involved in the Guyana v. Suriname Annex VII arbitration regarding maritime and territorial issues (Oude Elferink 2018).[117] Interestingly, Paul Reichler was a co-agent for Guyana in that case. In the Annex VII Chagos arbitration, Wolfrum was one of the arbitrators—chosen by Mauritius—and Reichler served as the head counsel for Mauritius.[118] It is also likely that Wolfrum's position as the president of ITLOS was a strong determinant in the Philippines' decision to propose him as their selected arbitrator. The hope was that Wolfrum would influence the nomination of the remaining arbitrators. This was an important consideration since China did not participate in the proceedings and thus did not name an arbitrator.[119] On a more personal level, the director of the Maritime and Ocean Affairs division at Department of Foreign Affairs—Assistant Secretary Henry Bensurto—met Judge Wolfrum at a summer seminar on international maritime law in Rhodes, Greece, and this also contributed to Bensurto recommending Wolfrum for the appointment at the Tribunal.[120]

When the deadline of February 22, 2013, had passed without China appointing an arbitrator, the Philippines requested that the ITLOS president, Judge Sunji Yani, appoint an arbitrator on behalf of China (Talmon and Jia 2014). After the March 25 deadline for the appointment of the three other arbitrators "by agreement between the parties" had passed, the Philippines "at the earliest possible moment" requested the ITLOS president to fill these spots (Talmon and Jia 2014, 11–12). Although the ITLOS president initially appointed Judge Chris Pinto as one of the arbitrators, there was a potential conflict of interest owing to Pinto's marriage to a Filipino national.[121] Solicitor General Francis Jardeleza of the Philippine legal team submitted a May 27 letter requesting the appointment of another arbitrator to replace Pinto to "assure that any award that might be rendered in these

[117] Delimitation of the Maritime Boundary, Guyana v. Suriname, ICGJ 370 (PCA 2007), Arbitral Award of September 17, 2007.
[118] Chagos Marine Protected Area Arbitration, Mauritius v. United Kingdom, PCA Case No. 2011-03, Arbitral Award of March 20, 2015.
[119] Authors' note: There was no implication in any interviews that Judge Rüdiger Wolfrum would be biased or privilege the Philippines in any way.
[120] Author's interview (KEW) with Ambassador Albert Encombienda, Manila, Philippines, March 8, 2017.
[121] Judge Pinto stepped down from the Tribunal in order to avoid the potential conflict of interest.

proceedings is accorded the full degree of respect to which it is entitled, and is as safe as possible from attack by anyone who might be motivated to undermine it" (Talmon and Jia 2014, 12). The goal was to avoid any potential conflicts of interest that could subsequently cause problems for the Philippines in the case.

Although the Philippines was allowed to appoint only one arbitrator, an anonymous legal advisor told us that the president of the Philippine v. China Annex VII Tribunal, Thomas Mensah, allegedly asked the Philippines to consent to the selection of another arbitrator, Alfred Soons.[122] The Philippine government agreed to this nomination, though according to our anonymous source, "China was unhappy with Soons because he deviates from academic perspectives" that could be favorable toward China.[123]

Regardless of the specific venue chosen, states engaged in adjudication and arbitration may attempt to sway the decision-making process by appealing to their own domestic legal systems. Of course, this is likely to happen if such interpretation is, in a word, strategic to the disputant. States, guided by their legal counsel, try to decipher which arbitrators or judges are open to nonstandard interpretations of international law. Since the overwhelming portion of international law is informed by Western legal values, "non-Western legal traditions provide a fertile source for contra-majority arguments" (Powell 2020, 214). As practice shows, lawyers representing Islamic law states may refer to concepts in the Islamic legal tradition when these concepts give their clients an advantage. In the words of one of our interviewees:

> The only time they [Islamic law states] will invoke Islamic law concept is not them but their lawyers who are representing them if they find something in Islamic law. For example, for the Qatar and Bahrain case, El Kosheri invokes something called the "Arabo-Islamic" tradition.... He just plucked that up from somewhere. I mean: it doesn't exist. He made it up in order to say there is an Arabo-Islamic tradition, which is different from the international law today and this is how it should be done. But it didn't work. The Court didn't accept it. It didn't refer to it.[124]

---

[122] Author's interview with an anonymous public international law expert, Rhodes, Greece, July 2018.
[123] Ibid.
[124] Author's interview (EJP) with an anonymous international law expert and legal counsel, Brussels, Belgium, July 4, 2014.

Conclusions

This chapter further illustrates and highlights the dynamics of the causal mechanisms associated with within-venue strategic selection. Uncertainty caused by dispute settlement does not subside when the disputants select a specific method and a specific venue. Both disputants remain uncertain about the outcome of the resolution process until the settlement decision is final. To further reduce their uncertainty and minimize their perceived risk of losing, states try to navigate the procedures of each venue, with regard to their claims and the venues' rules and procedures. The primary documents used to train government officials and lawyers, as well as a substantive amount of insights obtained from our in-depth interviews with policymakers, practitioners, judges, arbitrators, lawyers, and politicians, further illustrate the importance of strategizing. Indeed, within-venue strategic selection lies at the heart of international dispute settlement. States engaged in maritime and territorial disputes are willing to incur high costs in order to increase their likelihood of winning, while reducing uncertainty with the settlement process. Of course, flexibility—and thus states' ability to strategize—has its limits. Aware of this reality, states hinge their venue choices on the venue's procedures and pliability. Simply put, though required by international law to resolve their contentions in a peaceful manner, states like to stretch, shape, and push the boundaries of available PR methods and venues. Consequently, there are no unified patterns of dispute resolution that hold for every state and every territorial or maritime contention. The practice of international dispute settlement depends on the mingling of states' preferences in a context of a particular contention and a particular venue. States' preferences, in turn, emerge as a result of an intricate process whereby decisions made by individuals—state officials, lawyers, arbitrators, judges, mediators, and so on—combine to create what seems to be a coherent strategy.

8

Conclusions

This book addresses an issue of central importance to global peace: the peaceful resolution of territorial and maritime disputes; and it provides a comprehensive examination of the entire peaceful dispute resolution process: the choice of settlement methods and states' behavior within the context of the chosen method. The research is based on quantitative and qualitative methods of scientific inquiry. We focus on the various means through which states pursue peaceful settlement: negotiations; the nonbinding third-party methods—mediation, conciliation, inquiry, and good offices; and the binding third-party methods—arbitration and adjudication. We articulate, in theoretical and empirical terms, states' choices with regard to these methods, arguing that the entire resolution process consists of inherently strategic choices.

We should like to reemphasize that territorial and maritime disputes do, of course, differ in some areas. The laws outlining states' rights and obligations over land and maritime areas are distinct, and there exist partially unique sets of dispute settlement procedures applicable to each.[1] Additionally, the manner via which states acquire a title over land and over water is different (Brilmayer and Klein 2001; Shaw 2007). It is also important to add that "for maritime boundaries the political costs are often somewhat less," because of these disputes' smaller economic, ethnic, and symbolic relevance (Kingsbury 2012, 217). There are partially different considerations that drive states' strategies in the context of settling maritime and territorial disputes: "the domestic politics and human experience don't drive that decision-making quite as much in the maritime zone."[2] These differences notwithstanding, territorial and maritime contentions have much in common. Proper territorial delimitation constitutes the basis for the determination of maritime rights and entitlements of coastal states. In a significant way, therefore, the maritime

---

[1] For instance, UNCLOS includes numerous rules that regulate the determination of baselines and maritime boundaries.

[2] Author's interview (EJP) with Coalter G. Lathrop, Sovereign Geographics, International Boundary Consultancy, March 14, 2022.

The Peaceful Resolution of Territorial and Maritime Disputes. Emilia Justyna Powell and Krista E. Wiegand,
Oxford University Press. © Oxford University Press 2023. DOI: 10.1093/oso/9780197675649.003.0008

status quo follows the existing territorial situation. Most importantly, both types of disputes deal with a key aspect of statehood—sovereignty. There is a finite amount of territory and sea in the world. Thus, any sovereignty concessions for one state necessarily imply losses for other states. These are inherently zero-sum contentions, especially since it is not often the case that a state would be willing to give up its territorial or maritime claims in exchange for other gains. It is safe to say that states consider issues of sovereignty to be more important than any other issues. Both disputants cannot simultaneously secure, or win, the contested area. Instead, the settlement decision may entail division of land or a maritime area, or, alternatively, constitute a complete victory for one side. Aware of this reality, when attempting peaceful settlement, states engage in a great deal of strategizing in an effort to reduce their uncertainty with the settlement process and increase chances of securing concessions.

The theoretical conceptualization presented in this book portrays peaceful resolution of territorial and maritime disputes as a multilayered process that rests on inherently dynamic and continuously evolving interactions between many streams of influence, some of a political and some of a legal nature. A real, ongoing tension exists between the norms of international law and states' pursuit of strategies that best further their interests. Though usually there are legal limits for political decisions, as ITLOS judge Rüdiger Wolfrum (2018a) noted, "in international law, every dispute has a political aspect." Thus, the issue of peaceful resolution of territorial and maritime contentions should be studied with the recognition that domestic public affairs, diplomacy, and law are deeply intertwined. The quest for an arbitral award, a mediated outcome, or a judgment is usually merely a part of a much larger geostrategic context. Recognizing the intricate nexus between politics and law must be at the core of research on how states bargain in negotiations or third-party peaceful resolution (PR) methods and how states design their strategies during the settlement process.

Legal pronouncements made by courts and arbitration tribunals generate repercussions of a political nature for the disputants, states in the region, and beyond. Thus, long after a judgment or an award is made, the disputants in particular continue to bear the costs and the benefits of these decisions. For example, in the Ghana v. Ivory Coast case, the 2017 ITLOS decision delimiting maritime boundaries had a direct impact on the future of both states' economies.[3] Among other things, the Court's ruling that Ghana's

---

[3] Case Concerning Delimitation of the Maritime Boundary between Ghana and Côte d'Ivoire in the Atlantic Ocean, Ghana v. Côte d'Ivoire, ITLOS Case No. 23, Judgment of September 23, 2017.

exploration of oil within the disputed boundaries in the Atlantic Ocean did not violate rights of Ivory Coast opened "the way for development drilling to resume on Ghana's multi-billion dollar TEN deep-water oil and gas project."[4] Likewise, the Timor-Leste v. Australia conciliation case concerning overlapping maritime boundaries has had considerable repercussions for both states.[5] Timor-Leste, the clear winner of the dispute, now has access to gas and oil reserves, which are generating much-needed revenue for the country's poor economy.[6] Again, we return to insights offered by Judge Wolfrum (2018d, 174), who noted:

> The fact that a legal controversy is intertwined with political issues does not itself deprive a court or tribunal of jurisdiction. What matters is that the subject matter be articulated in legal terms; if this is so, the Court must exercise its jurisdiction regardless of its political implications or effects. In general, I would like to emphasize that no case before international courts and tribunals is apolitical, even the allegedly technical maritime delimitation cases are highly political. Their outcome may have a significant impact upon the states concerned as can be seen in nearly any of these disputes.

The commingling of political and legal influences shapes states' choice of the specific PR method and the strategy pursued. Our theory depicts states' preferences and strategies as rational and continuously evolving. Most importantly, we highlight the reality that international dispute settlement constitutes an irreducibly human enterprise whereby states' actions are carried out by policymakers, legal counsel, and international law practitioners. These individuals' decisions combine to generate persuasive, more often than not rationally constructed strategies that states employ when settling their contentions. In the words of one of our interlocutors, "at the end of the day, an individual advised by individuals is making a decision."[7] States are not unitary actors. We home in on the reality that resolution of maritime and territorial disputes consists of a multitude of decisions

---

[4] Emma Farge and Kwasi Kpodo, "Court Ruling Favors Ghana in Ocean Border Dispute with Ivory Coast," *Reuters*, September 23, 2017.

[5] Maritime Boundary between Timor-Leste and Australia (The Timor Sea Conciliation), PCA Case No. 2016-10, Arbitral Award of May 9, 2018.

[6] The judgment established that unilateral oil activities in a disputed maritime area are not illegal if the areas in question are determined to belong to the disputant.

[7] Author's interview (EJP) with Laurie Nathan, international mediator, former Senior Advisor to the UN Mediation Support Unit, Notre Dame, USA, January 21, 2022.

taken on the level of governments, specific ministries, bureaus, legal counsel, individual policymakers, international law practitioners, and judges. States' preferences, as expressed in their subsequent behavior, emerge as a result of ongoing conversations between multiple actors and institutions. There are deep-seated multifaceted reasons for why proposer states attempt resolution via specific PR methods.

The framework offered in this book gauges how governments attempt to address contextual forces outside of their control by strategizing throughout the settlement process. Proposer states' strategic behavior in peaceful settlement is at the core of this book. Though the management of territorial and maritime contentions ranges from the threat and use of force—including full-scale war—to peaceful settlement, we focus on how proposer states make choices about peaceful resolution. We argue that in order to fully understand the dynamics of settlement in these disputes, we must not only highlight but also unpack the intrinsically multistage nature of the settlement process. First of all, over the duration of any contention, proposers put forth several proposals for various PR methods and specific venues. Indeed, many contentions lie dormant for extended periods of time, and intermittently the situation may be interrupted by either resurfacing of the contention or an attempt at peaceful settlement. As history shows, many attempts at resolution are unsuccessful, or provide solutions with which parties may not fully agree. Consequently, any single dispute may involve many attempts at a multiplicity of distinct PR methods. Since international law offers several options, attempts at settlement entail informed, strategic forum shopping. It is unsurprising that states usually have strong a priori preferences about specific settlement mechanisms. Of course, each proposer state pursues strategies aimed at achieving the ultimate goal: securing territorial or maritime concessions via a method that, in the state's own estimation, is most likely to engender the least amount of uncertainty and most likely to yield the preferred outcome.[8]

A unifying feature of all PR methods is that states cannot predict the settlement outcome with absolute certainty. When a contention is delegated to a third-party venue, either binding or nonbinding, disputants experience the

---

[8] This reality has important repercussions for all PR methods, especially arbitration and adjudication bodies. As Alter, Helfer, and Madsen (2018, 459) write, "Unlike national judges in stable rule-of-law systems, ICs [international courts] operate in a contested legal and political space where multiple judicial venues are often available, where the legal and extralegal alternatives to litigation are many, and where the political winds can shift quickly and radically."

highest levels of uncertainty. But even during negotiations, neither party can be sure about the other's motivations and decisions concerning the settlement process. Though binding PR methods, arbitration and adjudication, come with more stringent frameworks of rules and procedures that guide resolution, the informal structure of negotiations provides a fertile environment for politics and strategy-based solutions. Any time there is a risk that power—rather than law—becomes the basis for settlement, uncertainty is present.

States dislike uncertainty. Stakes in territorial and maritime disputes are high and no disputant wants to lose sovereignty over land or entitlement to a maritime area, however small. Our book explains that states can reduce this uncertainty in a number of ways, thereby increasing the control they have over how the settlement proceeds. To diminish uncertainty, states strategize with regard to the initial choice of a specific PR method and, furthermore, about tactics to be used within the setting of the selected method. Our theoretical argument rests on the conceptualization of the entire resolution process— from the proposer's initial resolution attempt to the dispute's conclusion—as strategic. Uncertainty about the settlement and the drive to win a dispute push states to pursue what we call strategic selection. States pursue strategic selection in two distinct though deeply interrelated stages. The goal of the choice-of-venue strategic selection stage is to pursue a PR method that will provide the best outcome for the state, which usually involves securing all or the majority of territorial/maritime concessions. The within-venue strategic selection stage describes states' choices with regard to framing of their claims and shaping the settlement rules and procedures. As the settlement proceeds through its various stages, states continuously reconsider and reframe their strategies to optimally navigate rules and procedures. Designing intricate strategies comes with considerable costs. Yet, states usually spare no expense to secure the best legal counsel that, in the states' estimation, will successfully navigate the settlement process. It is the job of the legal counsel to engage in intense gathering of information about specific PR methods, the opponent's strategies, and preferences of individual negotiators, mediators, arbitrators, and judges. Such a comprehensive, usually time-consuming process of fact finding precedes the emergence of any strategy subsequently adopted by a disputant.

For both stages of strategic selection, we identify several mechanisms that determine proposer states' strategies. The combination of quantitative and qualitative evidence sheds much light on how these mechanisms factor into the process of decision-making on the state level. In the context of choice-of-venue strategic selection, we argue that past experience in PR methods—winning and losing—influences proposer states' strategies. Obviously, to say these factors influence states' willingness to favorably assess PR methods is in no way to suggest that other mechanisms and influences play no role. This reality is a mainstay of this book. The nature, character, and value of the disputed territory or a maritime area matter in how states strategize at the choice-of-venue selection stage. We find that outcomes of previous interactions with the various PR methods convey crucial data to states. These data help proposer states formulate strategies in future disputes. Interestingly, proposers pay attention not only to their own past experiences, but also to experiences of other states, especially those within the same geographic region. In particular, it is clear that regional- and disputant-level positive, as well as negative, experiences in arbitration and adjudication are quite influential in the process of choice-of-venue strategic selection. Consequently, it seems that when strategizing, states, guided by their legal counsel, are a priori predisposed to view certain PR methods as better suited for the resolution of the dispute at hand. The importance of the regional win-loss record demonstrates that, to some extent, proposer states engaged in territorial and maritime contentions adopt practices and patterns that have proved beneficial to other states. States located in the same geographic region have many shared experiences, needs, and cultural traditions that influence their attitude toward peaceful settlement. Indeed, as Goodman and Jinks (2013) write, with time, regional states become acculturated into specific patterns of behavior. In a crucial way, outcomes occurring on the international level—previous victories and losses via the various PR methods—systematically shape state-level decisions.[9]

Our theory and empirical tests also gauge the intricate connection between the deeply legal nature of international disputes and domestic law. To some extent, disputants perceive international law through the lens of their own domestic legal traditions and their own beliefs about justice. We have focused on three separate, though interrelated, aspects of the domestic law/international law relationship: international law's position in the domestic

---

[9] Also see Goodman and Jinks (2013, 40), for discussion of how "macro-level developments influence relevant actors within states, including government officials, members of the national and local media, issue-specific activists, and even ordinary citizens." Interestingly, these authors also talk about "a macro-micro-macro causal explanation," via which actors within states play a key role in state-level decision making (citing Coleman 1990).

legal system, rule of law, and type of domestic legal tradition. To reduce uncertainty with dispute resolution, proposer states construct their strategies in light of the nexus between domestic law and international law. At the core of this argument is states' familiarity and confidence in specific ways of carrying out justice. Insights from our qualitative and quantitative data are quite revealing with regard to all these factors. We find that when trying to understand the intricate dialogue between domestic legal systems and international law, it is necessary to go beyond the rough distinction between monist and dualist legal systems. Attention to more fine-grained features, such as the domestic presence of the canon of interpretation, is needed.

We also discover that the quality of domestic legal systems—levels of rule of law and the judiciary/executive relationship—may not always relate to states' choices vis-à-vis the binding PR methods. This finding is important because the political science and international law scholarship has long pondered the nature of the relationship between the quality of domestic law/ regime type and states' support for international courts. Yet, the nature of the relationship remains still largely contested. It is worth highlighting that notwithstanding the complexity of the rule of law/international law nexus, features of domestic legal systems "differ widely between states, and in many cases are in flux, creating dynamic and shifting cross-influences between the national and international levels" (Mackenzie et al. 2010, 26). Also, as the Philippines v. China arbitration dispute reveals, some states work hard to create an image of a champion of international commitments. Frequently, Philippine policymakers emphasized the point that China would not comply with a UN Convention on the Law of the Sea (UNCLOS) Annex VII tribunal arbitration ruling, but the Philippines would. Clearly, the Philippines' goal was to demonstrate that the country's reputation as a promoter of the global rule of law is at the core of Philippine legal identity. Arguably, several aspects of the Philippine political and legal realities were in part misrepresented, or even concealed in order to score rhetorical points by the government. Some might even argue that the arbitration from beginning to end had elements of a theatrical exercise, however effective.

Our quantitative tests show that, owing to their distinctive characteristics, domestic legal traditions may at times affect proposer states' preferences toward the various PR methods. With regard to the Western legal traditions, civil law and common law, our analyses reveal interesting patterns. Proposer states in common law dyads are more drawn to simple bilateral negotiations while proposer in civil law dyads are more likely to propose binding third-party methods. Interestingly, there is a natural synergy between the international nonbinding third-party PR methods and the Islamic legal tradition. To an extent, mediation and conciliation resemble the Islamic institution of *sulh*, a nonconfrontational, informal settlement. This is why Islamic law states find these methods quite attractive. It seems that these states, while making decisions concerning optimal PR methods and PR venues, include the International Court of Justice (ICJ), Permanent Court of Arbitration (PCA), and International Tribunal for the Law of the Sea (ITLOS), as viable alternatives, notwithstanding that "the ICJ is the choirmaster for Western legal values, values that have been projected onto the global level from within the Western jurisdictions" (Powell 2020, 280). Our findings also suggest that there is a continuous need to make PR methods, especially the binding ones, more inclusive of the various domestic legal systems. As Mackenzie et al. (2010, 41) write in the context of international courts, "The inclusion of judges who have developed their skills in a broad range of legal cultures may extend the reach or acceptability of the court's findings, as they will be developed and explained in a manner that takes into account the full range of legal systems." Indeed, it is urgent to ensure that modern international law is truly universal, and its "Eurocentric, Western-centric" ideas and practices include thoughts or interpretations embedded in all existing legal traditions.[10]

A major insight from this book is that the various PR methods offered by international law are not equally attractive to all proposer states. Instead, many factors combine to engender powerful forces of attraction and repulsion vis-à-vis negotiations, and nonbinding and binding third-party methods. Some of these factors are entrenched in the state fabric, such as international law's position in the domestic legal system. Other features, such as states' past experiences with the various PR methods, are external to states and accumulate over time. These findings should be considered during negotiations of international treaties that establish international courts or arbitration tribunals. How can the structure of these institutions be improved to encourage participation from a variety of states?

Our book speaks directly to the reality of forum shopping on the international level. We agree with one of our interviewees, who noted that "plurality of options, is, ultimately, the best for international dispute resolution."[11] Availability of multiple PR methods is, first of all, necessary to suit

---

[10] Author's interview (EJP) with Judge Awn Shawkat Al-Khasawneh, former Vice-President, ICJ, and former Prime Minister of Jordan, Amman, Jordan, July 1, 2022.

[11] Author's interview (EJP) with an anonymous arbitration practitioner, February 7, 2022.

preferences of a variety of differently predisposed potential states: "You're going to have a bunch of states that strongly favor international courts. . . . And then you have a group of states that just don't like this whole courts thing at all, and prefer arbitration."[12] It is also worth highlighting that the plurality of settlement options also serves to sustain the quality of international jurisprudence: "There is an element of competition [between forums]. In general, I think that's a good thing because it keeps everybody sharp. You [a forum] do your best work when you're not guaranteed that there will necessarily be more of it."[13] Granted, as we discuss in Chapter 3, there are also downsides of forum shopping on the global level.

Interesting and multifaceted dynamics of strategic selection take place in the context of the within-venue selection stage. Our qualitative interviews demonstrate the importance of disputants' efforts to frame their claims and shape rules/procedures of settlement methods. By selecting stronger claims and avoiding weaker claims, policymakers and legal counsel are hoping to decrease uncertainty with the settlement process and increase the likelihood of winning the contention. Of course, there are many ways in which states can frame their claims and attempt to shape rules/procedures of a selected PR method. Particulars of strategizing vary considerably across disputes, states, and issues. As one of our interviewees noted, "I don't think there is a one-size-fits-all strategy here."[14] Though some important patterns emerge when we take an empirical look at a multiplicity of contentions, to some extent, each territorial and maritime contention entails a "completely different story."[15] Consequently, how states strategize "is driven by the scenario and by the actors, and maybe by the type of dispute, more than it is a model approach."[16]

There are numerous, quite nuanced, policymaker-level influences that subsequently affect the dyadic relationship between the disputants. The qualitative aspects of our research shed considerable light on these influences, because in the end, these influences—perhaps as much as the state-level characteristics—shape strategic, rational, and victory-driven decisions made by the disputants. One cannot set aside the human element as unimportant to peaceful resolution of territorial and maritime contentions. States' decisions

---

[12] Ibid.
[13] Ibid.
[14] Author's interview (EJP) with Sean D. Murphy, professor of international law, George Washington University, January 28, 2022.
[15] Ibid.
[16] Ibid.

with regard to international PR methods emerge as a result of a multitude of individual-level decisions, preferences, and core values. Only when we take these forces into account does a vivid picture emerge. Importantly, the effects of factors related to idiosyncratic preferences of policymakers, international judges, and legal counsel cannot be adequately gauged via large-N quantitative analyses. Many of our in-depth interviews suggest that the selection of legal counsel and specific intermediaries plays a substantial role in the conduct of conflict management. By way of illustration, personal positive past interactions between key members of the legal counsel or a policymaker with particular international practitioners can determine the membership of an arbitral panel. Leaders' preferences matter greatly. Some want to be remembered as leaders who brought to an end a dispute that "has been a thorn in the side of diplomatic relations between the two states for decades."[17] Thus, "on the traditional boundary side . . . there may be some consideration of the legacy of individual leaders as they think about how to resolve a long-standing dispute."[18]

Our book provides valuable insights into the reality of the day-to-day practice of international law. While theorizing about the normative status, origins, and benefits of international law is certainly useful, and thus should occupy a central place in the scholarship, it is also of utmost importance that we understand how the global order operates. As the literature devoted to comparative international law shows, theory and the written letter of international law frequently differ from state practice (Powell 2020, 2021; Roberts et al. 2015, 2018; Roberts 2017; Zartner 2014). States view international rules and institutions—including PR methods—through the lens of their own domestic legal systems, geopolitical positions, cultures, and notions of justice. Thus, the practice of international law is far more complicated, multifaceted, and multilayered and far less uniform than is often recognized. Different states have distinct goals and preferences, and these preferences lead to different policy choices in the domestic and international realms. This reality is reflected in how states strategize when dealing with peaceful resolution of territorial and maritime disputes.

As we explain, resolution of these contentions involves dealing with an intricate international legal regime regulating territorial sovereignty and maritime delimitation, entitlements, and so on. In fact, perhaps more than any

---

[17] Author's (EJP) interview with Coalter G. Lathrop, March 14, 2022.
[18] Ibid.

other issue area, law of territorial sovereignty and maritime law comprise a multitude of detailed rules, norms, and regulations. It is a highly judicialized environment, in which the ICJ, PCA, ITLOS, and other international adjudicators and arbitrators thrive. Though a relatively small portion of territorial and maritime disputes make it to the docket of an international court or an arbitration tribunal, all states bargain in the shadow of these institutions (Bilder 1981). As Scott (2014, 36) writes, "the introduction of a litigation phase into a dispute may be enough to bring a state—including those relatively powerful—to the negotiating table." The prominent direct and indirect role of the binding PR methods is a clear sign of considerable legalization and judicialization of the global order (Shapiro and Stone Sweet 2002). It is vis-à-vis such an intricate normative and complex regime that states, guided by their legal counsel, construct their strategies. By capturing these practices empirically, our book directly contributes to the burgeoning empirical study of international law that uses tools of social science to inquire about the various aspects of the global order (Alter 2014; Alter and Helfer 2017; Chilton, Ginsburg, and Abebe 2021; Koremenos 2016; Simmons 2002, 2009; Powell 2021).[19]

All PR methods—ranging from bilateral negotiations through the nonbinding third-party methods to the binding methods of arbitration and adjudication—are in some ways flexible. To an extent, this flexibility allows states to pursue their interests. The interface between the disputants' self-motivated, rationally preplanned strategies and structures of the various PR methods suggests that there are multiple patterns of dispute resolution. In other words, through fulfilling their distinct preferences and following unique strategies while resolving a particular dispute, states de facto create multiple paths of settlement in the context of each PR method. As much as possible, states tailor international institutions to pursue their idiosyncratic goals and desires in each phase of settlement. Though negotiations, nonbinding methods, and binding third-party methods must stay true to their fundamental characteristics, these methods—and the specific venues such as the ICJ, PCA, ITLOS, etc.—are in practice remarkably malleable. Consequently, not all arbitration proceedings are identical, and not every ICJ case follows an identical step-by-step track. Aided by their legal counsel,

---

[19] There are many more works that incorporate the social science approach into the study of global order and international law. For an in-depth review, see Chilton, Ginsburg, and Abebe 2021; Shaffer and Ginsburg 2012.

states explore and then, if possible, push and expand the boundaries of each PR method with the hope of securing victory.

At the same time, each PR method, including bilateral negotiations— which take place in the shadow of the law—reflects the efficacy and value of international law as it operates within the challenging realities of power politics. Ultimately, the success of international PR methods will depend on whether the ongoing tensions between politics, law, and the different national perspectives on international law can be reconciled. Yet, the often-conflicting domestic perspectives and strategies can largely be accommodated. As our results show, despite some shortcomings and relatively rigid frameworks of the binding third-party PR methods, many states find these methods legitimate and useful even in the context of highly contentious territorial and maritime disputes. We end this book with a deeply insightful quote from Hans Corell, one of our interlocutors. Corell here captures the importance of resolving all territorial contentions in a peaceful manner:

> What is the situation? What does the geography look like? Are there rivers, or are there lakes? What about the population? What are the main resources and so forth? So, these are things that you have to look at. You have to look at the history. And then, what you need above all is something that I am asking for all the time: you need statesmanship. Statesmen and women who can look to the horizon and realize that their responsibility is not only to their own country but also to humankind . . . to future generations. And this means that it is necessary to find solutions.[20]

---

[20] Author's interview (EJP) with Hans Corell, former Under-Secretary-General for Legal Affairs and the Legal Counsel of the United Nations, January 13, 2021.

References

Abbott, Kenneth W., and Duncan Snidal. 1998. "Why States Act through Formal International Organizations." *Journal of Conflict Resolution* 42 (1): 3–32.

Abbott, Kenneth W., and Duncan Snidal. 2000. "Hard and Soft Law in International Governance." *International Organization* 54 (3): 421–56.

Abou El Fadl, Khaled. 2003. "Conflict Resolution as a Normative Value in Islamic Law: Handling Disputes with Non-Muslims." In *Faith-Based Diplomacy: Trumping Realpolitik*, edited by Douglas Johnson, 178–209. Oxford: Oxford University Press.

Abou El Fadl, Khaled. 2012. "Conceptualizing Shari'a in the Modern State." *Villanova Law Review* 56 (5): 803–16.

Agpalo, Ruben E. 2006. *Public International Law*. Quezon City, Philippines: Rex Book Store.

Alexandrov, Stanimir. A. 1995. *Reservations in Unilateral Declarations Accepting the Compulsory Jurisdiction of the International Court of Justice*. Leiden: Martinus Nijhoff.

Aljaghoub, Mahasen M. 2006. *The Advisory Function of the International Court of Justice 1946–2005*. Heidelberg: Springer-Verlag.

Allcock, John B. 1992. *Border and Territorial Disputes*. 3rd ed. Longman Current Affairs. Harlow, UK: Longman Group.

Allee, Todd L., and Paul K. Huth. 2006. "The Pursuit of Legal Settlements to Territorial Disputes." *Conflict Management and Peace Science* 23 (4): 285–307.

Alter, Karen J. 2014. *The New Terrain of International Law: Courts, Politics, Rights*. Princeton: Princeton University Press.

Alter, Karen J., and Laurence R. Helfer. 2017. *Transplanting International Courts: The Law and Politics of the Andean Tribunal of Justice*. Oxford: Oxford University Press.

Alter, Karen J., Laurence R. Helfer, and Mikael Rask Madsen. 2018. "Conclusion: Context, Authority, Power." In *International Court Authority*, edited by Karen J. Alter, Laurence R. Helfer, and Mikael Rask Madsen, 435–60. Oxford: Oxford University Press.

Alvarez, José E. 2005. *International Organizations as Law-Makers*. Oxford: Oxford University Press.

Anderson, David. 2008. "Drafting International Boundary Agreements." Presentation at the Negotiating International Boundaries Workshop, International Boundaries Research Unit, University of Durham, Durham, UK, April 7–9.

An-Na'im, Abdullahi Ahmed. 2008. *Islam and the Secular State: Negotiating the Future of Shari'a*. Cambridge, MA: Harvard University Press.

Aréchaga, Eduardo Jiménez. 1973. "The Amendments to the Rules of Procedure of the International Court of Justice." *American Journal of International Law* 67 (1): 1–22.

ASEAN Charter. 2008. Association of Southeast Asian Nations. Jakarta: ASEAN Secretariat.

Ashworth, Scott, Christopher R. Berry, and Ethan Bueno de Mesquita. 2021. *Theory and Credibility: Integrating Theoretical and Empirical Social Science*. Princeton: Princeton University Press.

Askandar, Kamarulzaman, and Carelervin Sukim. 2016. "Making Peace over a Disputed Territory in Southeast Asia: Lessons from the Batu Puteh/Pedra Branca Case." *Journal of Territorial and Maritime Studies* 3 (1): 65–85.

Azaria, Danae. 2018. "The Use of Extraneous Rules of International Law by Law of the Sea Convention Tribunals." Rhodes Academy on Maritime Law and Policy, Rhodes, Greece, July 19.

Badr, Gamal Moursi. 1978. "Islamic Law: Its Relation to Other Legal Systems." *American Journal of Comparative Law* 26 (2): 187–98.

Bagares, Romel Regalado. 2019. "The Philippines." In *Oxford University Handbook on International Law in the Asia and the Pacific*, edited by Simon Chesterman, Ben Saul, and Hisahi Owada, 406–32. Oxford: Oxford University Press.

Baratta, Joseph Preston. 1989. *International Arbitration: Improving Its Role in Dispute Settlement*. Washington, DC: Center for UN Reform Education.

Bassiouni, Cherif M. 2014. *The Shari'a and Islamic Criminal Justice in Time of War and Peace*. New York: Cambridge University Press.

Baxter, Richard R. 1980. "International Law in 'Her Infinite Variety.'" *International and Comparative Law Quarterly* 29 (4): 549–66.

Beber, Bernd. 2012. "International Mediation, Selection Effects, and the Question of Bias." *Conflict Management and Peace Science* 29 (4): 397–424.

Beckfield, Jason. 2010. "The Social Structure of the World Polity." *American Journal of Sociology* 115 (4): 1018–68.

Beckman, Robert, and Leonardo Bernard. 2011. "Disputed Areas in the South China Sea: Prospects for Arbitration or Advisory Opinion." Presentation at the Third International Workshop: The South China Sea: Cooperation for Regional Security and Development, Hanoi, Vietnam, November 3–5.

Bell, John. 2006. *Judiciaries within Europe: A Comparative Review*. Cambridge: Cambridge University Press.

Bercovitch, Jacob, J. Theodore Anagnoson, and Donnette L. Wille. 1991. "Some Conceptual Issues and Empirical Trends in the Study of Successful Mediation in International Relations." *Journal of Peace Research* 28 (1): 7–17.

Bercovitch, Jacob, and Paul F. Diehl. 1997. "Conflict Management of Enduring Rivalries: The Frequency, Timing, and Short-Term Impact of Mediation." *International Interactions* 22 (4): 299–320.

Bercovitch, Jacob, and Allison Houston. 2000. "Why Do They Do It Like This? An Analysis of the Factors Influencing Mediation Behavior in International Conflicts." *Journal of Conflict Resolution* 44 (2): 170–202.

Bercovitch, Jacob, and Richard Jackson. 2001. "Negotiation or Mediation? An Exploration of Factors Affecting the Choice of Conflict Management in International Conflict." *Negotiation Journal* 17: 59–77.

Bercovitch, Jacob, and Richard Jackson. 2009. *Conflict Resolution in the Twenty-First Century: Principles, Methods, and Approaches*. Ann Arbor: University of Michigan Press.

Bercovitch, Jacob, and Gerald Schneider. 2000. "Who Mediates? The Political Economy of International Conflict Management." *Journal of Peace Research* 37 (2): 145–65.

Bilder, Richard B. 1981. *Managing the Risks of International Agreement*. Madison: University of Wisconsin Press.

Bilder, Richard B. 1998. "International Dispute Settlement and the Role of International Adjudication." In *International Law: Classic and Contemporary Readings*, edited by Charlotte Ku and Paul F. Diehl, 233–56. Boulder: Lynne Rienner.

Black, Henry Campbell, Joseph R. Nolan, and Michael J. Connolly. 2009. *Black's Law Dictionary*. 9th ed. St. Paul, MN: West Publishing.

Blakeslee, Merritt R. 1991. "The Distant Island Problem: The Arbitration on the Delimitation of the Maritime Zones around the French Collecti Viti Territoriale of Saintpierre-and-Miquelon." *Georgia Journal of International and Comparative Law* 21: 359–85.

Boggs, Whittemore S. 1940. *International Boundaries: A Study of Boundary Functions and Problems*. New York: Columbia University Press.

Boisson de Chazournes, Laurence, and Antonella Angelini. 2013. "Between Saying and Doing: The Diplomatic Means to Implement the International Court of Justice's Iuris Dictum." In *Diplomatic and Judicial Means of Dispute Settlement*, edited by Laurence Boisson de Chazournes, Marcelo G. Kohen, and Jorge E. Viñuales, 155–85. Leiden: Martinus Nijhoff.

Brilmayer, Lea, and Adele Faure. 2014. "Initiating Territorial Adjudication: The Who, How, When, and Why of Litigating Contested Sovereignty." In *Litigating International Law Disputes: Weighing the Options*, edited by Natalie Klein, 193–229. Cambridge: Cambridge University Press.

Brilmayer, Lea, and Natalie Klein. 2001. "Land and Sea: Two Sovereignty Regimes in Search of a Common Denominator." *NYU Journal of International Law and Policy* 33: 703–68.

Brown, Chester. 2007. *A Common Law of International Adjudication*. Oxford: Oxford University Press.

Brunet-Jailly, Emmanuel. 2015. *Border Disputes: A Global Encyclopedia*. Vol. 1. Santa Barbara, CA: ABC-CLIO.

Bueno de Mesquita, Bruce. 2004. "Negotiation in International Politics." *Conflict Management and Peace Science* 21 (3): 155–58.

Bundy, Rodman R. 2003. "Submission of a Boundary Dispute to Arbitration." Presentation at the Preparing for Boundary Litigation/Arbitration Training Workshop No. 21, International Boundaries Research Unit Workshop, Office of Eversheds Frere Cholmeley, Paris, France, December 1–3.

Bundy, Rodman R. 2014. "Asian Perspectives on Inter-state Litigation." In *Litigating International Law Disputes: Weighing the Options*, edited by Natalie Klein, 148–65. Cambridge: Cambridge University Press.

Bundy, Rodman R. 2015. "Choosing a Forum and Bringing a Case." Presentation at Preparing for Third Party Settlement of Boundary & Territorial Disputes Workshop, International Boundaries Research Unit Workshop, The Hague, Netherlands, May 4–6.

Burke, Naomi. 2014. "Annex VII Arbitral Tribunal Delimits Maritime Boundary between Bangladesh and India in the Bay of Bengal." *ASIL Insights* 18 (20). https://www.asil.org/insights/volume/18/issue/20/annex-vii-arbitral-tribunal-delimits-maritime-boundary-between.

Butler, Andrew S., and Petra Butler. 1999. "The Judicial Use of International Human Rights Law in New Zealand." *Victoria University of Wellington Law Review* 29 (1): 173–91.

Buzan, Barry, and Ole Waever. 2003. *Regions and Power: The Structure of International Security*. Cambridge: Cambridge University Press.

Carpio, Antonio. 2016. "Personal Statement on the Final Arbitral Award." *Institute for Maritime Affairs*, July 12. http://www.imoa.ph/category/statements.

Carter, David. 2010. "The Strategy of Territorial Conflicts." *American Journal of Political Science* 54 (4): 969–87.

Caselli, Francesco, Massimo Morelli, and Dominic Rohner. 2015. "The Geography of Interstate Resource Wars." *Quarterly Journal of Economics* 130 (1): 267–315.

Castellino, Joshua A., and Steve Allen. 2003. *Title to Territory in International Law: A Temporal Analysis*. Burlington, VT: Ashgate.

Central Intelligence Agency. 2018. "The World Factbook." Accessed April 1, 2018. https://www.cia.gov/library/publications/the-world-factbook/index.html.

Charney, Jonathan I. 1998. "Third Party Dispute Settlement and International Law." *Columbia Journal of Transnational Law* 36 (1–2): 65–89.

Chesterman, Simon. 2008. "An International Rule of Law?" *American Journal of Comparative Law* 56 (2): 331–61.

Chi, Sang-Hyun, and Colin Flint. 2013. "Standing Different Ground: The Spatial Heterogeneity of Territorial Disputes." *GeoJournal* 78: 553–73.

Chilton, Adam, Tom Ginsburg, and Daniel Abebe. 2021. "The Social Science Approach to International Law." *Chicago Journal of International Law* 22 (1): 1–23.

Chinkin, Christine M., and Romana Sadurska. 1991. "Learning about International Law through Dispute Resolution." *International and Comparative Law Quarterly* 40 (3): 529–50.

Chiozza, Giacomo, and Ajin Choi. 2003. "Guess Who Did What: Political Leaders and the Management of Territorial Disputes, 1950–1990." *Journal of Conflict Resolution* 47 (3): 251–78.

Ciarli, Stefano, and Keith McLachlan. 1996. "A Bibliographic Review: Studies of Libya's International Borders." *Libyan Studies* 27: 89–98.

Clarke, Kevin A., and David M. Primo. 2012. *A Model Discipline: Political Science and the Logic of Representation*. Oxford: Oxford University Press.

Cockerham, Geoffrey B. 2007. "The Delegation of Dispute Settlement: Authority to Conventional International Governmental Organizations." *International Politics* 44 (6): 732–52.

Coleman, James. 1990. *Foundations of Social Theory*. Cambridge, MA: Harvard University Press.

Collier, John G. 2009. "The International Court of Justice and the Peaceful Settlement of Disputes." In *Fifty Years of the International Court of Justice: Essays in Honour of Sir Robert Jennings*, edited by Vaughan Lowe and Malgosia Fitzmaurice, 364–72. Cambridge: Cambridge University Press.

Collier, John G., and Vaughan Lowe. 2000. *The Settlement of Disputes in International Law: Institutions and Procedures*. Oxford: Oxford University Press.

Coppedge, Michael, John Gerring, Carl Henrik Knutsen, Staffan I. Lindberg, Jan Teorell, David Altman, Michael Bernhard, M. Steven Fish, Adam Glynn, Allen Hicken, Anna Lührmann, Kyle L. Marquardt, Kelly McMann, Pamela Paxton, Daniel Pemstein, Brigitte Seim, Rachel Sigman, Svend-Erik Skaaning, Jeffrey Staton, Agnes Cornell, Lisa Gastaldi, Haakon Gjerløw, Valeriya Mechkova, Johannes von Römer, Aksel Sundtröm, Eitan Tzelgov, Luca Uberti, Yi-ting Wang, Tore Wig, and Daniel Ziblatt. 2020. "V-Dem Codebook v10." Varieties of Democracy (V-Dem) Project. https://www.v-dem.net/en/data/data-version-10/.

Crawford, James R. 2012. *Brownlie's Principles of Public International Law*. 8th ed. Oxford: Oxford University Press.

Damrosch, Lori Fisler, and Sean D. Murphy. 2019. *International Law: Cases and Materials*. West Academic Publishing.

David, René. 1985. *Major Legal Systems in the World Today: An Introduction to the Comparative Study of Law*. 3rd ed. Translated by John E. C. Brierley. London: Stevens.

Davis, Christina L. 2012. *Why Adjudicate? Enforcing Trade Rules in WTO.* Princeton: Princeton University Press.

Day, Alan J. 1987. *Border and Territorial Disputes.* 2nd ed. Essex, UK: Longman.

De Brabandere, Eric. 2018. "International Dispute Settlement—From Practice to Legal Discipline." *Leiden Journal of International Law* 31 (3): 459–68.

de La Fayette, Louise. 1993. "Award in the Canada-France Maritime Boundary Arbitration." *International Journal of Marine and Coastal Law* 8 (1): 77–104.

Del Rosario, Albert. 2015. "Statement before the Permanent Court of Arbitration on Maritime Entitlements." Peace Palace, The Hague, Netherlands, July 7.

Del Rosario, Albert. 2017. "The South China Sea: The Philippines, ASEAN, and their International Partners." Presentation at Stratbase ADRi Forum, Manila, Philippines, April 25.

Dicey, Albert Venn. 1889. *Introduction to the Study of the Law of the Constitution.* London: Macmillan.

Diehl, Paul F. 2006. "Just a Phase? Integrating Conflict Dynamics over Time." *Conflict Management and Peace Science* 23 (3): 199–210.

Diehl, Paul F., and Patrick Regan. 2015. "The Interdependence of Conflict Management Attempts." *Conflict Management and Peace Science* 32 (1): 99–107.

Dixon, William. 1993. "Democracy and the Management of International Conflict." *Journal of Conflict Resolution* 37 (1): 42–68.

Downing, David. 1980. *An Atlas of Territorial and Border Disputes.* London: New English Library.

Ellis, Glynn, Sara McLaughlin Mitchell, and Brandon C. Prins. 2010. "How Democracies Keep the Peace: Contextual Factors that Influence Conflict Management Strategies." *Foreign Policy Analysis* 6 (4): 373–98.

Esmaquel, Paterno. 2016. "Hilbay Defends Aborted Strategy vs China." *Rappler*, July 21. http://www.rappler.com/nation/140482-hilbay-itu-aba-philippines-china-case.

Essien Umoh, Ubong. 2015. "Cameroon, Nigeria and the Bakassi Conflict: Building Blocks for a Non-democratic Peace Theory." *Journal of International Relations and Development* 18 (2): 227–47.

Etekpe, Ambily. 2013. "ICJ Judgment on Bakassi Peninsula and Lake Chad: Litmus Test for Peace and Integration in Africa." *African Journal of Political Science and International Relations* 7 (6): 286–94.

Evans, Malcolm D., and J. G. Merrills. 1997. "The Land and Maritime Boundary Case (Cameroon V. Nigeria), Order of 15 March 1996." *International and Comparative Law Quarterly* 46 (3): 676–81.

Fadel, Mohammad. 2009. "Back to the Future: The Paradoxical Revival of Aspirations for an Islamic State." *Review of Constitutional Studies* 14 (1): 105–23.

Falk, Richard A. 1967. "The South West Africa Cases: An Appraisal." *International Organization* 21 (1): 1–23.

Favretto, Katja. 2009. "Should Peacemakers Take Sides? Major Power Mediation, Coercion, and Bias." *American Political Science Review* 103 (2): 248–63.

Fearon, James D. 1994. "Domestic Political Audiences and the Escalations of International Disputes." *American Political Science Review* 88 (3): 577–92.

Fearon, James D. 1995. "Rationalist Explanations for War." *International Organization* 49 (3): 379–414.

Feldman, Noah. 2008. *The Fall and Rise of the Islamic State.* Princeton: Princeton University Press.

Ferrari, Franco. 2002. "'Forum Shopping' Despite International Uniform Contract Law Conventions." *International and Comparative Law Quarterly* 51 (3): 689–707.

Franck, Thomas. 1995. *Fairness in International Law and Institutions.* New York: Clarendon.

Fravel, M. Taylor. 2008. *Strong Borders, Secure Nation: Cooperation and Conflict in China's Territorial Disputes.* Princeton: Princeton University Press.

Frazier, Derrick V. 2006. "Third Party Characteristics, Territory and the Mediation of Militarized Interstate Disputes." *Conflict Management and Peace Science* 23 (4): 267–84.

Frederick, Bryan A, Paul R. Hensel, and Christopher Macaulay. 2017. "The Issue Correlates of War Territorial Claims Data, 1816–2011." *Journal of Peace Research* 54 (1): 99–108.

Gamble, John King, Jr. 1976. "The Law of the Sea Conference: Dispute Settlement in Perspective." *Vanderbilt Journal of Transnational Law* 9 (2): 323–44.

Gamble, John King, Jr., and Dana D. Fischer. 1976. *The International Court of Justice: An Analysis of a Failure.* Lexington, MA: Lexington Books.

Gates, Douglas. 2017. "International Law Adrift: Forum Shopping, Forum Rejection, and the Future of Maritime Dispute Resolution." *Chicago Journal of International Law* 18 (1): 287–320.

Gavouneli, Maria. 2018. "Regime of Islands." Presentation at the Rhodes Academy of Maritime Law and Policy, Rhodes, Greece, July 6.

Gent, Stephen E., and Megan Shannon. 2010. "The Effectiveness of International Arbitration and Adjudication: Getting into a Bind." *Journal of Politics* 72 (2): 366–80.

Gent, Stephen E., and Megan Shannon. 2011. "Choosing the Ties That Bind: Decision Control and the Pursuit of Binding Conflict Management." *Journal of Conflict Resolution* 55 (5): 710–34.

Gerring, John. 2017. "Qualitative Methods." *Annual Review of Political Science* 20: 15–36.

Gibler, Douglas M. 2007. "Bordering on Peace: Democracy, Territorial Issues, and Conflict." *International Studies Quarterly* 51 (3): 509–32.

Gibler, Douglas M. 2012. *The Territorial Peace: Borders, State Development, and International Conflict.* Cambridge: Cambridge University Press.

Glendon, Mary Ann, Michael W Gordon, and Christopher Osakwe. 1994. *Comparative Legal Traditions: Text, Materials, and Cases on the Civil and Common Law Traditions, with Special Reference to French, German, English, and European Law.* 2nd ed. St. Paul, MN: West Pub.

Glenn, Patrick H. 2014. *Legal Traditions of the World: Sustainable Diversity in Law.* 5th ed. New York: Oxford University Press.

Goertz, Gary. 2017. *Multimethod Research, Causal Mechanisms, and Case Studies: An Integrated Approach.* Princeton: Princeton University Press.

Goertz, Gary, and Paul F. Diehl. 1992. *Territorial Changes and International Conflict.* New York: Routledge.

Goertz, Gary, Paul F. Diehl, and Alexandru Balas. 2016. *The Puzzle of Peace: The Evolution of Peace in the International System.* Oxford: Oxford University Press.

Goldsmith, Jack L., and Eric A. Posner. 2005. *The Limits of International Law.* Oxford: Oxford University Press.

Goodman, Ryan, and Derek Jinks. 2013. *Socializing States: Promoting Human Rights through International Law.* New York: Oxford University Press.

Greig, Michael J. 2001. "Moments of Opportunity: Recognizing Conditions of Ripeness for International Mediation between Enduring Rivals." *Journal of Conflict Resolution* 45 (6): 691–718.

Gutmann, Jerg, and Stefan Voigt. 2018. "The Rule of Law and Islam." In *Handbook on the Rule of Law*, edited by Christopher May and Adam Winchester, 345–56. Cheltenham, UK: Edward Elgar.

Guzman, Andrew T. 2005. "The Design of International Agreements." *European Journal of International Law* 16 (4): 579–612.

Hallaq, Wael B. 2005. *The Origins and Evolution of Islamic Law*. Cambridge: Cambridge University Press.

Hallaq, Wael B. 2013. *The Impossible State*. New York: Columbia University Press.

Hamoudi, Haider Ala. 2010. "Orientalism and the Fall and Rise of the Islamic State." *Middle East Law and Governance* 2 (1): 81–103.

Hansen, Holley E., Sara McLaughlin Mitchell, and Stephen C. Nemeth. 2008. "IO Mediation of Interstate Conflicts: Moving beyond the Global versus Regional Dichotomy." *Journal of Conflict Resolution* 52 (2): 295–325.

Hartzell, Caroline, and Matthew Hoddie. 2003. "Institutionalizing Peace: Power Sharing and Post–Civil War Conflict Management." *American Journal of Political Science* 47 (2): 318–32.

Helfer, Laurence R., and Anne-Marie Slaughter. 1997. "Toward a Theory of Effective Supranational Adjudication." *Yale Law Journal* 107 (2): 273–391.

Hensel, Paul R. 1999. "Charting a Course to Conflict: Territorial Issues and Interstate Conflict." In *A Road Map to War*, edited by Paul Diehl. Nashville: Vanderbilt University Press, 115–46.

Hensel, Paul R. 2001. "Contentious Issues and World Politics: The Management of Territorial Claims in the Americas, 1816–1992." *International Studies Quarterly* 45 (1): 81–109.

Hensel, Paul R., Michael Allison, and Ahmed Khanani. 2009. "Territorial Integrity Treaties and Armed Conflict over Territory." *Conflict Management and Peace Science* 26 (2): 120–43.

Hensel, Paul R. and Sara McLaughlin Mitchell. 2005. "Issue Indivisibility and Territorial Claims." *GeoJournal* 64 (4): 275–85.

Hensel, Paul R., Sara McLaughlin Mitchell, Thomas E. Sowers, II, and Clayton L Thyne. 2008. "Bones of Contention: Comparing Territorial, Maritime, and River Issues." *Journal of Conflict Resolution* 52 (1): 117–43.

Hensel, Paul R., and John Tures. 1997. "International Law and the Settlement of Territorial Claims in South America, 1816–1992." Paper presented at the Annual Meeting of the American Political Science Association, Washington, DC, August 30.

Hofilena, Chay F., and Marites Danguilan Vitug. 2016. "Hilbay, Jardeleza Opposed Inclusion of Itu Aba in PH Case." *Rappler*, July 22. http://www.rappler.com/newsbreak/in-depth/140182-hilbay-jardeleza-itu-aba-west-ph-sea. Accessed July 22, 2016.

Hristova, Velislava. 2020. "The Border of Slovenia and Croatia—Where the CJEU Reached the Frontier of Its Jurisdiction." *Kluwer Arbitration Blog*, April 28. http://arbitrationblog.kluwerarbitration.com/2020/04/28/the-border-of-slovenia-and-croatia-where-the-cjeu-reached-the-frontier-of-its-jurisdiction/.

Hurd, Ian. 2017. *How to Do Things with International Law*. Princeton: Princeton University Press.

Huth, Paul K. 1988. *Extended Deterrence and the Prevention of War*. New Haven, CT: Yale University Press.

Huth, Paul K. 1996. *Standing Your Ground: Territorial Disputes and International Conflict*. Ann Arbor: University of Michigan Press.

Huth, Paul K., and Todd L. Allee. 2002. *The Democratic Peace and Territorial Conflict in the Twentieth Century*. Cambridge: Cambridge University Press.

Huth, Paul K., Sarah E. Croco, and Benjamin J. Appel. 2011. "Does International Law Promote the Peaceful Settlement of International Disputes? Evidence from the Study of Territorial Conflicts since 1945." *American Political Science Review* 105 (2): 415–36.

Huth, Paul K., Sarah E. Croco, and Benjamin J. Appel. 2013. "Bringing Law to the Table: Legal Claims, Focal Points, and the Settlement of Territorial Disputes since 1945." *American Journal of Political Science* 57 (1): 90–103.

Huth, Paul K., Christopher Gelpi, and D. Scott Bennett. 1992. "System Uncertainty, Risk Propensity and International Conflict among the Great Powers." *Journal of Conflict Resolution* 36 (3): 478–517.

Huth, Paul K., Christopher Gelpi, and D. Scott Bennett. 1993. "The Escalation of Great Power Militarized Disputes." *American Political Science Review* 87 (3): 609–23.

International Boundary Research Unit. 2018. "Boundary News." https://www.dur.ac.uk/ibru/news/.

James, Patrick, Johann Park, and Seung-Whan Choi. 2006. "Democracy and Conflict Management: Territorial Claims in the Western Hemisphere Revisited." *International Studies Quarterly* 50 (4): 803–17.

Jervis, Robert. 1976. *Perception and Misperception in International Politics*. Princeton: Princeton University Press.

Johnson, Constance. 2000. "Case Analysis: Eritrea-Yemen Arbitration." *Leiden Journal of International Law* 13 (2): 427–46.

Jones, Daniel M., Stuart A. Bremer, and J. David Singer. 1996. "Militarized Interstate Disputes, 1816–1992: Rationale, Coding Rules, and Empirical Patterns." *Conflict Management and Peace Science* 15 (2): 163–213.

Jouannet, Emmanuelle. 2006. "French and American Perspectives on International Law: Legal Cultures and International Law." *Maine Law Review* 58 (2): 293–336.

Juenger, Friedrich K. 1989. "Forum Shopping, Domestic and International." *Tulane Law Review* 63 (3): 553–74.

Kacowicz, Arie M. 2005. *The Impact of Norms in International Society: The Latin American Experience, 1881–2001*. Notre Dame, IN: University of Notre Dame Press.

Kadir, Mohamad. 2015. *Malaysia-Singapore: Fifty Years of Contentions, 1965–2015*. Kuala Lumpur, Malaysia: The Other Press.

Kaura, Vinay. 2017. "The Durand Line: A British Legacy Plaguing Afghan-Pakistani Relations." *Middle East Institute*, June 27. https://www.mei.edu/publications/durand-line-british-legacy-plaguing-afghan-pakistani-relations.

Kelley, Judith. 2007. "Who Keeps International Commitments and Why? The International Criminal Court and Bilateral Nonsurrender Agreements." *American Political Science Review* 190 (3): 573–89.

Kelsen, Hans. 1952. *Principles of International Law*. New York: Rinehart.

King, Gary, Robert O. Keohane, and Sidney Verba. 1994. *Designing Social Inquiry: Scientific Inference in Qualitative Research*. Princeton: Princeton University Press.

Kingdon, Emma. 2015. "A Case for Arbitration: The Philippines' Solution for the South China Sea Dispute." *Boston College International and Comparative Law Review* 38 (1): 129–57.

Kingsbury, Benedict. 2012. "International Courts: Uneven Judicialization in Global Order." In *The Cambridge Companion to International Law*, edited by James Crawford and Martti Koskenniemi, 203–27. Cambridge: Cambridge University Press.

Klein, Natalie, ed. 2014. *Litigating International Law Disputes: Weighing the Options.* Cambridge: Cambridge University Press.

Klein, James P., Gary Goertz, and Paul F. Diehl. 2008. "The Peace Scale: Conceptualizing and Operationalizing Non-Rivalry and Peace." *Conflict Management and Peace Science* 25 (1): 67–80.

Koch, Charles H. 2003. "Envisioning a Global Legal Culture." *Michigan Journal of International Law* 25 (1): 1–77.

Kocs, Stephen. 1995. "Territorial Disputes and Interstate War, 1945–1987." *Journal of Politics* 57 (1): 159–75.

Koh, Tommy. 2011. "International Law and the Peaceful Resolution of Disputes: Asian Perspectives, Contributions, and Challenges." *Asian Journal of International Law* 1 (1): 57–60.

Kohen, Marcelo G. 2013. "Interaction between Diplomatic and Judicial Means at the Initiation of Proceedings." In *Diplomatic and Judicial Means of Dispute Settlement*, edited by Laurence Boisson de Chazournes, Marcelo G. Kohen, and Jorge E. Viñuales, 13–24. Leiden: Martinus Nijhoff.

Koremenos, Barbara. 2005. "Contracting around International Uncertainty." *American Political Science Review* 9 (4): 549–65.

Koremenos, Barbara. 2016. *The Continent of International Law: Explaining Agreement Design.* Cambridge: Cambridge University Press.

Koremenos, Barbara, Charles Lipson, and Duncan Snidal. 2001. "The Rational Design of International Institutions." *International Organization* 55 (4): 761–99.

Koskenniemi, Martti. 1990. "The Politics of International Law." *European Journal of International Law* 1 (1): 4–32.

Koskenniemi, Martti. 2007. "The Fate of Public International Law: Between Technique and Politics." *Modern Law Review* 70 (1): 1–30.

Koskenniemi, Martti, and Päivi Leino. 2002. "Fragmentation of International Law? Postmodern Anxieties." *Leiden Journal of International Law* 15 (3): 553–79.

Kritzer, Herbert M., ed. 2002. *Legal Systems of the World: A Political, Social, and Cultural Encyclopedia.* Santa Barbara, CA: ABC-CLIO.

Kwon, Edward. 2022. "The Strained International Relations between Korea and Japan: Shinzo Abe's Territorial Claim over Dokdo." Paper presented at the South Korea's Role in the Era of a U.S.-China Rivalry Workshop, University of Tennessee, Knoxville, TN, April 23.

Kydd, Andrew. 2003. "Which Side Are You On? Bias, Credibility, and Mediation." *American Journal of Political Science* 47 (4): 597–611.

La Porta, Rafael, Florencio Lopez-De-Silanes, Andrei Shleifer, and Robert W. Vishny. 1997. "Legal Determinants of External Finance." *Journal of Finance* 52 (3): 1131–50.

Lake, David A., and Robert Powell. 1999. "International Relations: A Strategic-Choice Approach." In *Strategic Choice and International Relations*, edited by David A. Lake and Robert Powell, 3–38. Princeton: Princeton University Press.

Lathrop, Colater G. 2014. "Why Litigate a Maritime Boundary? Some Contributing Factors." In *Litigating International Law Disputes: Weighing the Options*, edited by Natalie Klein, 230–59. New York: Cambridge University Press.

Lauterpacht, Elihu. 2011. "Principles of Procedure in International Litigation." In *Collected Courses of the Hague Academy of International Law*. Brill Online. https://ref erenceworks.brillonline.com/entries/the-hague-academy-collected-courses/*A97890 04185142_02.

Lauterpacht, Hersch. 1950. *International Law and Human Rights*. New York: Frederick A. Praeger.

Lauterpacht, Hersch. 1958. *The Development of International Law by the International Court*. London: Stevens.

Lee, Eric Yong-Joong. 2013. "Evolving Concept of Law in Korea: A Historical and Comparative Perspective." *Asia Pacific Law Review* 21 (1): 77–101.

Leeds, Brett Ashley, Jeffrey M. Ritter, Sara McLaughlin Mitchell, and Andrew G. Long. 2000. "Alliance Treaty Obligations and Provisions, 1815–1944." *International Interactions* 28 (3): 237–60.

Lefler, Vanessa A. 2015. "Strategic Forum Selection and Compliance in Interstate Dispute Resolution." *Conflict Management and Peace Science* 32 (1): 76–98.

Linzer, Drew A., and Jeffrey. K. Staton. 2015. "A Global Measure of Judicial Independence, 1948–2012." *Journal of Law and Courts* 3 (2): 223–56.

Lupu, Yonatan, Pierre-Hugues Verdier, and Mila Versteeg. 2019. "The Strength of Weak Review: National Courts, Interpretive Canons, and Human Rights Treaties." *International Studies Quarterly* 63 (3): 507–20.

Maas, Richard. 2021–2022. "Salami Tactics: Faits Accomplis and International Expansion in the Shadow of Major War." *Texas National Security Review* 5 (1): 33–54.

Mackenzie, Ruth, and Philippe Sands. 2003. "International Courts and Tribunals and the Independence of the International Judge." *Harvard International Law Journal* 41 (1): 271–85.

Mackenzie, Ruth, Kate Malleson, Penny Martin, and Philippe Sands. 2010. *Selecting International Judges: Principle, Process, and Politics*. Oxford: Oxford University Press.

Malintoppi, Loretta. 2015. "Methods of Dispute Resolution in the Inter-State Litigation When States Go to Arbitration Rather Than Adjudication." Presentation at the Preparing for Third Party Settlement of Boundary & Territorial Disputes Workshop, International Boundary Research Unit Workshop, The Hague, Netherlands, May 4–6.

Mallat, Chibli. 2007. *Introduction to Middle Eastern Law*. Oxford: Oxford University Press.

Maloy, Richard. 2005. "Forum Shopping? What's Wrong with That?" *Quinnipiac Law Review* 24 (1): 25–62.

Mansbach, Richard W., and John A. Vasquez. 1981. *In Search of Theory: A New Paradigm for Global Politics*. New York: Columbia University Press.

Marshall, Monty G., Ted Robert Gurr, and Keith Jaggers. 2019. *Polity IV Project: Political Regime Characteristics and Transitions, 1800–2015*. Dataset and users' manual. Center for Systemic Peace.

Martin, Larry. 2018. "Litigation and Arbitration of Disputes under UNCLOS." Presentation at the Rhodes Academy of Maritime Law & Policy, Rhodes, Greece, July 16.

Mattei, Ugo. 1997. "Three Patterns of Law: Taxonomy and Change in the World's Legal Systems." *American Journal of Comparative Law* 45 (1): 5–44.

McDorman, Ted L. 1990. "Canada and France Agree to Arbitration for the St. Pierre and Miquelon Boundary Dispute." *International Journal of Estuarine and Coastal Law* 5 (2): 357–61.

McDorman, Ted L. 2009. *Salt Water Neighbors: International Ocean Relations between the United States and Canada*. New York: Oxford University Press.

McDowell, Steven. 2018. "Law, Settlement Failure, and the Timing of Litigation in Interstate Territorial Disputes." PhD diss., University of Notre Dame.

McGinley, Gerald P. 1985. "Intervention in the International Court: The Libya/Malta Continental Shelf Case." *International and Comparative Law Quarterly* 34 (4): 671–94.

Melin, Molly M. 2011. "The Impact of State Relationships on If, When, and How Conflict Management Occurs." *International Studies Quarterly* 55 (3): 691–715.

Merrills, John G. 2005. *International Dispute Settlement*. 4th ed. Cambridge: Cambridge University Press.

Merrills, John G. 2011. *International Dispute Settlement*. 5th ed. Cambridge: Cambridge University Press.

Merrills, John G. 2014. "The Place of International Litigation in International Law." In *Litigating International Law Disputes: Weighing the Options*, edited by Natalie Klein, 3–23. Cambridge: Cambridge University Press.

Merrills, John G. 2017. *International Dispute Settlement*. 6th ed. Cambridge: Cambridge University Press.

Merry, Sally Engle. 2010 "What Is Legal Culture? An Anthropological Perspective." *Journal of Comparative Law* 5 (2): 40–58.

Merryman, John Henry. 1985. *The Civil Law Tradition*. Stanford, CA: Stanford University Press.

Mideast Mirror. 2000. "Reducing Tensions in the Arabian Peninsula." *Mideast Mirror* 14 (118). http://www.mideast-mirror.com/.

Mitchell, Sara McLaughlin. 2002. "A Kantian System? Democracy and Third-Party Conflict Resolution." *American Journal of Political Science* 46 (4): 749–59.

Mitchell, Sara McLaughlin. 2020. "Clashes at Sea: Explaining the Onset, Militarization, and Resolution of Diplomatic Maritime Claims." *Security Studies* 29 (4): 637–70.

Mitchell, Sara McLaughlin, and Paul R. Hensel. 2007. "International Institutions and Compliance with Agreements." *American Journal of Political Science* 51 (4): 721–37.

Mitchell, Sara McLaughlin, Kelly M. Kadera, and Mark J. C. Crescenzi. 2009. "Practicing Democratic Community Norms: Third Party Conflict Management and Successful Settlements." In *International Conflict Mediation: New Approaches and Findings*, edited by Jacob Bercovitch and Scott Gartner, 243–64. New York: Routledge.

Mitchell, Sara McLaughlin, and Emilia Justyna Powell. 2011. *Domestic Law Goes Global: Legal Traditions and International Courts*. Cambridge: Cambridge University Press.

Miyoshi, Mahahiro. 1996. "The State's Propensity for Control over the Settlement of Disputes." *Journal of International Affairs* 104: 43–55.

Mondre, Aletta. 2015. *Forum Shopping in International Disputes*. Basingstoke, UK: Palgrave Macmillan.

Murphy, Alexander. 2002. "National Claims to Territory in the Modern State System: Geographical Considerations." *Geopolitics* 7 (2): 193–214.

Nemeth, Stephen C., Sara McLaughlin Mitchell, Elizabeth A. Nyman, and Paul R. Hensel. 2014. "Ruling the Sea: Managing Maritime Conflicts through UNCLOS and Exclusive Economic Zones." *International Interactions* 40 (5): 711–36.

Nollkaemper, André. 2011. *National Courts and the International Rule of Law*. Oxford: Oxford University Press.

Nollkaemper, André. 2014. "The Duality of Direct Effect of International Law." *European Journal of International Law* 25 (1): 105–25.

Okafor-Yarwood, Ifesinachi. 2015. "The Guinea-Bissau–Senegal Maritime Boundary Dispute." *Marine Policy* 61: 284–90.

Opolot, James. 1980. *An Analysis of World Legal Traditions*. Jonesboro, TN: Pilgrimage.

Othman, Aida. 2007. "'And Amicable Settlement Is Best': Sulh and Dispute Resolution in Islamic Law." *Arab Law Quarterly* 21 (1): 64–90.

Otto, Jan Michiel, ed. 2010. *Sharia Incorporated: A Comparative Overview of the Legal Systems of Twelve Muslim Countries in Past and Present*. Leiden: Leiden University Press.

Oude Elferink, Alex. 2018. "Maritime Delimitation." Presentation at the Rhodes Academy of Maritime Law & Policy, Rhodes, Greece, July 10.

Owsiak, Andrew P. 2013. "Democratization and International Border Agreements." *Journal of Politics* 75 (3): 717–29.

Owsiak, Andrew P., and Derrick V. Frazier. 2014. "The Conflict Management Efforts of Allies in Interstate Disputes." *Foreign Policy Analysis* 10 (3): 243–64.

Owsiak, Andrew P., and Sara McLaughlin Mitchell. 2019. "Conflict Management in Land, River, and Maritime Claims." *Political Science Research and Methods* 7 (1): 43–61.

Owsiak, Andrew P., and John Vasquez. 2019. "The Cart and the Horse Redux: The Timing of Border Settlement and Joint Democracy." *British Journal of Political Science* 49 (1): 339–54.

Palmer, Glenn, Vito D'Orazio, Michael R. Kenwick, and Roseanne W. McManus. 2020. "Updating the Militarized Interstate Dispute Data: A Response to Gibler, Miller, and Little." *International Studies Quarterly* 64 (2); 469–75.

Park, Johann, and Patrick James. 2015. "Democracy, Territory, and Armed Conflict, 1919–1995." *Foreign Policy Analysis* 11 (1): 85–107.

Paulson, Coulter. 2004. "Compliance with Final Judgments of the International Court of Justice since 1987." *American Journal of International Law* 98 (3): 434–61.

Petrossian, Emil. 2007. "In Pursuit of the Perfect Forum: Transnational Forum Shopping in the United States and England." *Loyola of Los Angeles Law Review* 40 (4): 1257–336.

Petsche, Markus. 2011. "What's Wrong with Forum Shopping? An Attempt to Identify and Assess the Real Issues of a Controversial Practice." *International Lawyer* 45 (4): 1005–28.

Posner, Eric, and John C. Yoo. 2005. "Judicial Independence in International Tribunals." *California Law Review* 93 (1): 1–74.

Powell, Emilia Justyna. 2013. "Two Courts—Two Roads? Domestic Rule of Law and Legitimacy of International Courts." *Foreign Policy Analysis* 9 (4): 349–68.

Powell, Emilia Justyna. 2015. "Islamic Law States and Peaceful Resolution of Territorial Disputes." *International Organization* 69 (4): 777–807.

Powell, Emilia Justyna. 2016. "Islamic Law States and the Authority of the International Court of Justice: Territorial Sovereignty and Diplomatic Immunity." *Law and Contemporary Problems* 79 (1): 209–36.

Powell, Emilia Justyna. 2020. *Islamic Law and International Law: Peaceful Resolution of Disputes*. New York: Oxford University Press.

Powell, Emilia Justyna. 2021. "Comparative International Law and the Social Science Approach." *Chicago Journal of International Law* 22 (1): 147–55.

Powell, Emilia Justyna. 2022. "Complexity and Dissonance: Islamic Law States and the International Order." *International Studies Review* 24 (1). https://doi.org/10.1093/isr/viac001.

Powell, Emilia Justyna, Moritz Graefrath, and Benedikt Graf. 2022. "A Tale of Two Pressures: Islamic Law States and the Timing of Litigation." Working Paper.

Powell, Emilia Justyna, Steven Christian McDowell, Robert O'Brien, and Julia Oksasoglu. 2020. "Islam-Based Legal Language and State Governance: Democracy, Strength of the Judiciary and Human Rights." *Constitutional Political Economy* 32: 376–412. https://doi.org/10.1007/s10602-019-09298-y.

Powell, Emilia Justyna, and Sara McLaughlin Mitchell. 2007. "The International Court of Justice and the World's Three Legal Systems." *Journal of Politics* 69 (2): 397–415.

Powell, Emilia Justyna, and Sara McLaughlin Mitchell. 2022. "Forum Shopping for the Best Adjudicator: Conflict Management and the International Tribunal for the Law of the Sea (ITLOS)." *Journal of Territorial and Maritime Studies* 9 (1): 7–33.

Powell, Emilia Justyna, and Krista E. Wiegand. 2010. "Legal Systems and Peaceful Attempts to Resolve Territorial Disputes." *Conflict Management and Peace Science* 27 (2): 129–51.

Powell, Emilia Justyna, and Krista E. Wiegand. 2014. "Strategic Selection: Political and Legal Mechanisms of Territorial Dispute Resolution." *Journal of Peace Research* 51 (3): 361–74.

Powell, Emilia Justyna, and Krista E. Wiegand. 2021. "Peaceful Resolution of Territorial and Maritime Disputes." In *What Do We Know about War?*, edited by Sara McLaughlin Mitchell and John Vasquez, 191–205. Lanham, MD: Rowman and Littlefield.

Putnam, Robert D. 1988. "Diplomacy and Domestic Politics: The Logic of Two-Level Games." *International Organization* 42 (3): 427–60.

Rao, P. Chandrasekhara. 2002. "ITLOS: The First Six Years." In *Max Planck Yearbook of United Nations Law*, vol. 6, edited by J. A. Frowein and R. Wolfrum, 183–300. The Hague: Kluwer Law International.

Ratner, Steven R. 2006. "Land Feuds and Their Solutions: Finding International Law beyond the Tribunal Chamber." *American Journal of International Law* 100 (4): 808–29.

Ratner, Steven R. 2015. *The Thin Justice of International Law: A Moral Reckoning of the Law of Nations.* Oxford: Oxford University Press.

Raymond, Gregory A. 1994. "Democracies, Disputes, and Third-Party Intermediaries." *Journal of Conflict Resolution* 38 (1): 24–42.

Reed, Lucy. 2013. "Observations on the Relationship between Diplomatic and Judicial Means of Dispute Settlement." In *Diplomatic and Judicial Means of Dispute Settlement*, edited by Laurence Boisson de Chazournes, Marcelo G. Kohen, and Jorge E. Viñuales, 291–305. Leiden: Martinus Nijhoff.

Regan, Patrick M., and Aysegul Aydin. 2006. "Diplomacy and Other Forms of Intervention in Civil Wars." *Journal of Conflict Resolution* 50 (5): 736–56.

Regan, Patrick M., Richard W. Frank, and Aysegul Aydin. 2009. "Diplomatic Interventions and Civil War: A New Dataset." *Journal of Peace Research* 46 (1): 135–46.

Roach, Ashley J. 2018. "Offshore Archipelagos Enclosed by Straight Baselines: An Excessive Claim?" *Ocean Development and International Law* 49 (2): 176–202.

Roberts, Anthea. 2017. *Is International Law International?* New York: Oxford University Press.

Roberts, Anthea, Paul B. Stephan, Pierre-Hugues Verdier, and Mila Versteeg. 2015. "Comparative International Law: Framing the Field." *American Journal of International Law* 109 (3): 467–74.

Roberts, Anthea, Paul B. Stephan, Pierre-Hugues Verdier, and Mila Versteeg, eds. 2018. *Comparative International Law*. Oxford: Oxford University Press.

Robinson, Davis R., David A. Colson, and Bruce C. Rashkow. 1985. "Some Perspectives on Adjudicating before the World Court: The Gulf of Maine Case." *American Journal of International Law* 79 (3): 578–97.

Rogers, Tim. 2012. "Caribbean Crisis: Can Nicaragua Navigate Waters It Won from Colombia?" *Time*, November 28. https://world.time.com/2012/11/28/caribbean-cri sis-can-nicaragua-navigate-waters-it-won-from-colombia/#ixzz2LSHClKwb.

Romano, Cesare P. R. 2002. "International Justice and Developing Countries: A Qualitative Analysis." *Law and Practice of International Courts and Tribunals* 1 (3): 539–611.

Rosen, Lawrence. 2000. *The Justice of Islam*. Oxford: Oxford University Press.

Rosen, Mark E., and Douglas J. Jackson. 2017. "Bangladesh v. India: A Positive Step Forward in Public Order of the Seas." *CNA Analysis and Solutions*, Occasional Paper, September 1. https://www.cna.org/cna_files/pdf/DOP-2017-U-016081-Final.pdf.

Rosenne, Shabtai. 2003. *Rosenne's The World Court: What It Is and How It Works*. Edited by Terry Gill. The Hague: Martinus Nijhoff.

Savun, Burcu. 2008. "Information, Bias, and Mediation Success." *International Studies Quarterly* 52 (1): 25–47.

Scalera, Jamie, and Krista E. Wiegand. 2018. "The Motivation of European Union Mediation in Civil Conflicts." *European Security* 27 (4): 434–52.

Schofield, Clive. 2016. "A Landmark Decision in the South China Sea: The Scope and Implications of the Arbitral Tribunal's Award." *Contemporary Southeast Asia* 38 (3): 339–48.

Schulte, Constanze. 2004. *Compliance with Decisions of the International Court of Justice*. Oxford: Oxford University Press.

Schultz, Kenneth, and Henk Goemans. 2019. "Aims, Claims, and the Bargaining Model of War." *International Theory* 11 (3): 344–74.

Schultz, Thomas. 2015. "Editorial: The Evolution of International Arbitration as an Academic Field." *Journal of International Dispute Settlement* 6 (2): 229–30.

Scott, Shirley V. 2014. "Litigation versus Dispute Resolution through Political Processes." In *Litigating International Law Disputes: Weighing the Options*, edited by Natalie Klein, 21–41. Cambridge: Cambridge University Press.

Senese, Paul D., and John A. Vasquez. 2003. "A Unified Explanation of Territorial Conflict: Testing the Impact of Sampling Bias, 1919–1992." *International Studies Quarterly* 47 (2): 275–98.

Senese, Paul D., and John A. Vasquez. 2008. *The Steps to War: An Empirical Study*. Princeton: Princeton University Press.

Sepúlveda Amor, Bernardo. 2013. "Opening Remarks." In *Diplomatic and Judicial Means of Dispute Settlement*, edited by Laurence Boisson de Chazournes, Marcelo G. Kohen, and Jorge E. Viñuales, 7–10. Leiden: Martinus Nijhoff.

Shaffer, Gregory C., and Tom Ginsburg. 2012. "The Empirical Turn in International Legal Scholarship." *American Journal of International Law* 106 (1): 1–46.

Shannon, Megan. 2009. "Preventing War and Providing the Peace? International Organizations and the Management of Territorial Disputes." *Conflict Management and Peace Science* 26 (2): 144–63.

Shany, Yuval. 2003. *The Competing Jurisdictions of International Courts and Tribunals*. Oxford: Oxford University Press.

Shapiro, Martin. 1981. *Courts: A Comparative and Political Analysis*. Chicago: University of Chicago Press.

Shapiro, Martin, and Alec Stone Sweet. 2002. *On Law, Politics and Judicialization*. Oxford: Oxford University Press.

Shaw, Malcolm N. 2007. "Title, Control, and Closure? The Experience of the Eritrea–Ethiopia Boundary Commission." *International & Comparative Law Quarterly* 56 (4): 755–96.

Shaw, Malcolm N. 2017. *International Law*. 8th ed. Cambridge: Cambridge University Press.

Shelton, Dinah. 2011. *International Law and Domestic Legal Systems: Incorporation, Transformation and Persuasion*. New York: Oxford University Press.

Siems, Mathias. 2014. *Comparative Law*. Cambridge: Cambridge University Press.

Simmons, Beth A. 1999. "See You in 'Court'? The Appeal to Quasi-Judicial Legal Processes in the Settlement of Territorial Disputes." In *A Road Map to War: Territorial Dimensions of International Conflict*, edited by Paul F. Diehl, 205–37. Nashville: Vanderbilt University Press.

Simmons, Beth A. 2002. "Capacity, Commitment, and Compliance: International Institutions and Territorial Disputes." *Journal of Conflict Resolution* 46 (6):829–56.

Simmons, Beth A. 2005. "Rules over Real Estate: Trade, Territorial Conflict, and International Borders as Institutions." *Journal of Conflict Resolution* 49 (5): 823–48.

Simmons, Beth A. 2009. *Mobilizing for Human Rights: International Law in Domestic Politics*. New York: Cambridge University Press.

Singer, J. David, Stuart Bremer, and John Stuckey. 1972. "Capability Distribution, Uncertainty, and Major Power War, 1820–1965." In *Peace, War, and Numbers*, edited by Bruce Russett, 19–48. Beverly Hills: Sage.

Slantchev, Branislav L. 2003. "The Principle of Convergence in Wartime Negotiations." *American Political Science Review* 97 (4): 621–32.

Sloss, David. 2009. *The Role of Domestic Courts in Treaty Enforcement: A Comparative Study*. Cambridge: Cambridge University Press.

Smit Duijzentkunst, Bart L., and Sophia Dawkins. 2015. "Arbitrary Peace? Consent Management in International Arbitration." *European Journal of International Law* 26 (1): 139–68.

Sotomayor, Arturo C. 2015. "Legalizing and Judicializing Territorial and Maritime Border Disputes in Latin America: Causes and Unintended Consequences." In *American Crossings: Border Politics in the Western Hemisphere*, edited by Maiah Jaskoski, Arturo C. Sotomayor, and Harold A. Trinkunas, 38–65. Baltimore: Johns Hopkins University Press.

Spain, Anna. 2010. "Integration Matters: Rethinking the Architecture of International Dispute Resolution." *University of Pennsylvania Journal of International Law* 32 (1): 1–55.

Spelliscy, Shane. 2001. "The Proliferation of International Tribunals: A Chink in the Armor." *Columbia Journal of Transnational Law* 40 (1): 143–75.

Spiermann, Ole. 2005. *International Legal Argument in the Permanent Court of International Justice: The Rise of the International Judiciary*. Cambridge: Cambridge University Press.

Staton, Jeffrey K., Christopher Reenock, Jordan Holsinger, and Staffan Lindberg. 2019. "Can Courts Be Bulwarks of Democracy?" The Varieties of Democracy Institute working paper, University of Gothenburg.

Sticher, Valerie. 2021. "Negotiating Peace with Your Enemy: The Problem of Costly Concessions." *Journal of Global Security Studies* 6 (4): 1–20.

Strachan, Anna Louise. 2009. "Resolving Southeast Asian Territorial Dispute: A Role for the ICJ." Institute of Peace and Conflict Studies (IPCS) Issue Brief 133: 1–4.

Stuyt, Alexander M. 1990. *Survey of International Arbitrations, 1794–1989*. 3rd ed. Dordrecht: Martinus Nijhoff.

Svensson, Isak, and Mathilda Lundgren. 2013. "Peace from the Inside: Exploring the Role of the Insider-Partial Mediator." *International Interactions* 39 (5): 698–722.

Swearingen, Will D. 1988. "Geopolitical Origins of the Iran-Iraq War." *Geographical Review* 78 (4): 405–16.

Sykes, Alan O. 2008. "Transnational Forum Shopping as a Trade and Investment Issue." *Journal of Legal Studies* 37 (2): 339–78.

Talmon, Stefan, and Bing Bing Jia. 2014. *The South China Sea Arbitration: A Chinese Perspective*. Portland, OR: Hart.

Terres, Nora T. 1985. "The United States/Canada Gulf of Mexico Maritime Delimitation." *Maryland Journal of International Law* 9 (1): 135–80.

Thomas, William. 2015. "Case Management." Presentation at the Preparing for Third Party Settlement of Boundary & Territorial Disputes Workshop, International Boundaries Research Unit Workshop, The Hague, Netherlands, May 4–6.

Tir, Jaroslav. 2003. "Never-Ending Conflicts? Territorial Changes as Potential Solutions for Territorial Disputes." *Conflict Management and Peace Science* 20 (2): 59–84.

Tir, Jaroslav, and John Vasquez. 2012. "Territory and Geography." In *Guide to the Scientific Study of International Processes*, edited by Sara McLaughlin Mitchell, Paul F. Diehl, and James D. Morrow, 115–34. West Sussex: Wiley-Blackwell.

US Department of State Bulletin. 1985. "United States: Department of State Letter and Statement Concerning Termination of Acceptance of I.C.J. Compulsory Jurisdiction." *International Legal Materials* 24 (6): 1742–45. Accessed August 9, 2020. www.jstor.org/stable/20692919.

Untawale, Mukund G. 1974. "The Kutch-Sind Dispute: A Case Study in International Arbitration." *International and Comparative Law Quarterly* 23 (4): 818–39.

Urlacher, Brian. R. 2015. *International Relations as Negotiation*. New York: Taylor & Francis.

Urpelainen, Johannes. 2009. *A Theory of Interstate Arbitration*. Manuscript, University of Michigan.

Vabulas, Felicity, and Duncan Snidal. 2013. "Organization without Delegation: Informal Intergovernmental Organizations (IIGOs) and the Spectrum of Intergovernmental Arrangements." *Review of International Organizations* 8: 193–220.

Vabulas, Felicity, and Duncan Snidal. 2020. "Informal IGOs as Mediators of Power Shifts." *Global Policy* 11: 40–50.

Vasquez, John A. 1993. *The War Puzzle*. Cambridge: Cambridge University Press.

Vasquez, John A. 2009. *The War Puzzle Revisited*. Cambridge: Cambridge University Press.

Vasquez, John A., and Marie T. Henehan. 2001. "Territorial Disputes and the Probability of War, 1816–1992." *Journal of Peace Research* 38 (2): 123–38.

Vasquez, John A., and Marie T. Henehan. 2011. *Territory, War, and Peace*. London: Routledge, 2011.

Väyrynen, Raimo. 1984. "Regional Conflict Formations: An Intractable Problem of International Relations." *Journal of Peace Research* 21 (4): 337–59.

Verdier, Pierre-Hugues, and Mila Versteeg. 2015. "International Law in National Legal Systems: An Empirical Investigation." *American Journal of International Law* 109 (3): 514–33.

Vikør, Knut S. 2005. *Between God and the Sultan: A History of Islamic Law*. Oxford: Oxford University Press.

Wallensteen, Peter. 1984. "Incompatibility, Confrontation, and War: Four Models and Three Historical Systems, 1816–1976." *Journal of Peace Research* 18 (91): 57–90.

Walter, Barbara F. 2002. *Committing to Peace: The Successful Settlement of Civil Wars*. Princeton: Princeton University Press.

Wang, Chao. 2014. "International Arbitration of Maritime Delimitation: An Alternative for East Asia?" *Journal of East Asia and International Law* 7 (2): 427–41.

Wanis St. John, Anthony. 1997. "Third Party Mediation over Kashmir: A Modest Proposal." *International Peacekeeping* 4 (4): 1–30.

Watson, Sarah. 2015. "The Bangladesh/Myanmar Maritime Dispute: Lessons for Peaceful Resolution." The Asia Maritime Transparency Initiative, Center for Strategic and International Studies, October 19. https://amti.csis.org/the-bangladeshmyanmar-maritime-dispute-lessons-for-peaceful-resolution/.

Weintraub, Russell J. 2002. "Introduction to Symposium on International Forum Shopping." Texas International Law Journal 37 (3): 463–66.

Weiss, Bernard G. 2006. The Spirit of Islamic Law. Athens: University of Georgia Press.

Wetter, J Gillis. 1971. "The Rann of Kutch Arbitration." American Journal of International Law 65 (2): 346–57.

Whytock, Christopher. 2011. "The Evolving Forum Shopping System." Cornell Law Review 96 (3): 481–534.

Wiegand, Krista E. 2011. Enduring Territorial Disputes: Strategies of Bargaining, Coercive Diplomacy, and Settlement. Athens: University of Georgia Press.

Wiegand, Krista E. 2012. "Bahrain, Qatar, and the Hawar Islands: Resolution of a Gulf Territorial Dispute." Middle East Journal 66 (1): 79–96.

Wiegand, Krista E. 2014. "Mediation in Territorial, Maritime, and River Disputes." International Negotiation 19 (2): 343–70.

Wiegand, Krista E., and Emilia Justyna Powell. 2011a. "Past Experience, Quest for the Best Forum, and Peaceful Attempts to Resolve Territorial Disputes." Journal of Conflict Resolution 55 (1): 33–59.

Wiegand, Krista E., and Emilia Justyna Powell. 2011b. "Unexpected Companions: Bilateral Cooperation between States Involved in Territorial Disputes." Conflict Management and Peace Science 28 (3): 209–29.

Wiegand, Krista E., Emilia Justyna Powell, and Steven McDowell. 2020. "The Peaceful Resolution of Territorial Disputes Dataset, 1945–2015." Journal of Peace Research 58 (2): 304-314, https://journals.sagepub.com/doi/10.1177/0022343319895560.

Wiegand, Krista E., Eric Keels, and Erin Rowland. 2021. "Third-party Knowledge and Success in Civil War Mediation." British Journal of Politics and International Relations 23 (1): 3–21.

Wild, Patricia Berko. 1966. "The Organization of African Unity and the Algerian-Moroccan Border Conflict: A Study of New Machinery for Peacekeeping and for the Peaceful Settlement of Disputes among African States." International Organization 20 (1): 18–36.

Wilkenfeld, Jonathan, Kathleen Young, Victor Asal, and David Quinn. 2003. "Mediating International Crises: Cross National and Experimental Perspectives." Journal of Conflict Resolution 47 (3): 279–301.

Willard, Rainbow. 2009. "How to Get Less Than You Bargain For: Adjudicating the Guatemala-Belize Territorial Dispute at the I.C.J." Emory International Law Review 23: 739–82.

Wolfrum, Rüdiger. 2006. Statement by Mr. Rüdiger Wolfrum, President of the International Tribunal for the Law of the Sea on Agenda Item 71 (a) at the Plenary of the Sixty-First Session of the United Nations General Assembly. December 8. https://www.itlos.org/fileadmin/itlos/documents/statements_of_president/wolfrum/ga_081206_eng.pdf.

Wolfrum, Rüdiger. 2018a. "International Litigation—Why, When, under Which Limitations?" Presentation at the Rhodes Academy of Maritime Law and Policy, Rhodes, Greece, July 16.

Wolfrum, Rüdiger. 2018b. Comments on "Litigation and Arbitration of Disputes under UNCLOS," by Larry Martin. Rhodes Academy of Maritime Law and Policy, Rhodes, Greece, July 16.

Wolfrum, Rüdiger. 2018c. "Conciliation: An Alternative Means for the Settlement of Legal Disputes." Presentation at the Rhodes Academy of Maritime Law and Policy, Rhodes, Greece, July 19.

Wolfrum, Rüdiger. 2018d. "Intractable Conflicts: The Effectiveness of International Dispute Resolution Mechanisms." *Proceedings of the ASIL Annual Meeting* 112: 172–74.

Wotipka, Christine Min, and Francisco O. Ramirez. 2008. "World Society and Human Rights: An Event History Analysis of the Convention on the Elimination of All Forms of Discrimination against Women." In *The Global Diffusion of Markets and Democracy*, edited by Beth Simmons, Frank Dobbin, and Geoffrey Garrett, 303–43. Cambridge: Cambridge University Press.

Zacher, Mark W. 2001. "The Territorial Integrity Norm: International Boundaries and the Use of Force." *International Organization* 55 (2): 215–50.

Zartman, William. 1974. "The Political Analysis of Negotiation: How Who Gets What and When." *World Politics* 26 (3): 385–99.

Zartman, William I., and Saadia Touval. 1985. "International Mediation: Conflict Resolution and Power Politics." *Journal of Social Issues* 41: 27–45. https://spssi.online library.wiley.com/doi/abs/10.1111/j.1540-4560.1985.tb00853.x.

Zartner, Dana. 2014. *Courts, Codes, and Custom: Legal Tradition and State Policy Toward International Human Rights and Environmental Law*. Oxford: Oxford University Press.

Zou, Keyuan, and Xinchang Liu. 2015. "The Legal Status of the U-Shaped Line in the South China Sea and Its Legal Implications for Sovereignty, Sovereign Rights, and Maritime Jurisdiction." *Chinese Journal of International Law* 14: 57–77.

Index

For the benefit of digital users, indexed terms that span two pages (e.g., 52–53) may, on occasion, appear on only one of those pages.